Aristotle's Nicomachean Ethics

By the same author
Aristotle's Metaphysics (1966)
Aristotle's Physics (1969)
Aristotle's Categories and Propositions (1980)
Aristotle's Posterior Analytics (1981)
Aristotle's On the Soul (1982)
Aristotle: Selected Works—with Lloyd P. Gerson (1983)
Aristotle's Politics—with Lloyd P. Gerson (1986)

ARISTOTLE'S NICOMACHEAN ETHICS

*Translation with Commentaries
and Glossary by*
HIPPOCRATES G. APOSTLE

THE PERIPATETIC PRESS
Grinnell, Iowa

to Grace Reed Dennis

TABLE OF CONTENTS

PREFACE

The principles used in the translation of the *Ethics* are the same as those in the translations of the *Physics* and the *Metaphysics*, and their main function is to help the reader get Aristotle's meaning as accurately as possible. Briefly, they are principles of terminology and of thought, some of which will be repeated here.

English terms common to all three translations have the same meanings, with a few exceptions, and many terms proper to ethics are added. Many of the terms in the Glossary are defined or are made known dialectically or in some other way. For the term προαίρεσις the term 'intention' or the expression 'deliberate choice' will be used instead of the term '*choice*', but the definition will be the same as that given in the *Physics* and the *Metaphysics*. Difficulties arise from some allied terms or terms close in meaning, e.g., the terms φαῦλος, κακός, μοχθηρός, and πονηρός, for the exact differences of their meanings are not ascertainable from the extant works. Each of these terms, however, seems to be used consistently, and we shall assume such consistency. The choice of the corresponding English terms can only be suggested by the usage of the Greek terms and by induction. A Greek term, in some cases, has no English equivalent, and in such a case it is advisable to choose an English term whose ordinary meaning is closest to the meaning of the Greek term and to indicate the meaning given to that term.

To distinguish in printed form an expression, whether vocal or written, or a thought from what it signifies, we enclose it within quotation marks. For example, 'bravery' is a term or a concept and is not a virtue, but that which it signifies is bravery, which is a virtue. Expressions in Greek are not enclosed by quotation marks, for this is not necessary.

Terms in italics with initial capital letters signify principles posited by philosophers other than Aristotle. For example, the *One* and the *Good* are principles posited by Plato, and Anaximenes posits *Air* as the principle of simple bodies. Terms in italics without initial capital letters are used (a) sometimes for emphasis, and (b) sometimes with meanings which are somewhat different from – usually narrower than – those of the same terms without italics. For example, the terms 'desire' and '*desire*' differ in meaning, and the second is a species of the first; the meanings of such terms are given in the Glossary. Expressions appearing in brackets are added for the sake of the reader and are not translations from the Greek.

In the margins of the translation we have inserted the pages and lines of the Bekker text, which are standard. The various works of Aristotle and the Bekker pages containing each of them are listed at the beginning of the Commentaries.

The form of government which Aristotle calls δημοκρατία is a deviation or perversion of what he calls τιμοκρατία or πολιτεία, for (a) it aims not at the common good but at that of the majority or of those without property, (b) it is based not on merit but on indiscriminate freedom and equality, and (c) it differs from what Aristotle calls πολιτεία by tending to be a government by vote rather than by law. It is usually translated as 'democracy', but this is misleading; for (a), (b), and (c) are not attributes of what we mean by 'democracy'. English terms whose meanings come close to this form of government are 'ochlocracy', 'people's rule', 'people's state', and even 'people's dictatorship'. The terms τιμοκρατία and πολιτεία will be translated as 'timocracy' and 'democracy', respectively.

Students who wish to acquire the thought of Aristotle accurately should make full use of the Glossary, for if one does not grasp the meanings of the terms, one may be faced with apparent inconsistencies and falsities, which lead to unfair criticism. For example, the expressions 'to *act* justly', 'to do what is just', 'to *act* from justice', and 'to be just' have been given different meanings, and the use of four different allied expressions in English is necessary if we are to translate accurately the four corresponding Greek expressions to which Aristotle assigns different meanings.

I am grateful to the National Endowment for the Humanities for providing me with freedom from academic duties during the academic year 1968–9 when the translations of the *Ethics* and the *Posterior Analytics* were started; to Professor John M. Crossett, who read the entire manuscript and made numerous corrections and suggestions; to Professor Evangelos P. Papanoutsos, who clarified a number of passages in the *Ethics*; to Professor Norman Kretzmann, for suggesting certain key

terms in the translation; and to Mr. and Mrs. Harry Fulton, Mr. Lloyd
Gerson, Miss Janet E. Smith, Miss Susan J. Ashbrook, and Miss Ellen F.
Pill, for their secretarial and other assistance.

Grinnell College   H.G.A.

SUMMARY OF THE ETHICS

Book A

1. All human activities aim at some good. There is an ordering of goods, some of which are ends in themselves but others are means to ends; and there is a highest good for man. Ethics is a part of politics, and its subject is not so accurate as, say, that of mathematics. 1094a1–5a13.

2. Happiness is the highest good for man, but men disagree as to what happiness is, whether pleasure or honor or health or wealth or knowledge or something else. 1095a14–b13.

3. There are three main doctrines: (a) happiness is pleasure; (b) happiness is honor; (c) happiness is theoretical activity. Some difficulties faced by the first two doctrines. 1095b14–6a10.

4. Plato posits the universal good. Difficulties in such a doctrine. 1096a11–7a14.

5. Man's good is an end in itself, perfect, and self-sufficient; and these are marks of happiness. 1097a15–b21.

6. Man's good is man's function, and this is the activity in accordance with his proper nature, which is thought. So happiness is activity of the soul in accordance with complete virtue throughout life. 1097b22–8a20.

7. Happiness, then, is the first principle, and in seeking to know what it is in detail one should demand no more precision than the subject allows. 1098a21–b8.

8. The definition of happiness should be considered not only through its consequences and the dialectical arguments which support it, but also from what people say about it. 1098b9–22.

9. The definition of happiness seems to be in accord with general opinions, and it is reasonable that it should be the activity in accordance with virtue rather than the possession of virtue, for pleasure at its highest exists in activity rather than in possession. 1098b22–9b8.

10. Happiness is not endowed by nature, nor bestowed by divine providence, nor yet attained by mere learning, and it is not a matter of luck. It requires learning and also habit and diligence. 1099b9–1100a9.

11. Though bad luck may lessen the pleasure of virtuous activity and misfortune may

even mar or prevent happiness, still virtue is something stable, and a virtuous man will be happier than one without virtue under a given set of circumstances. Usually, then, a virtuous man lives happily; occassionally, misfortune may prevent happiness. 1100a10–1b9.

12. Happiness is an object of honor and not of praise; for we praise something when we relate it to something better but we honor it for its own sake, and happiness is an end in itself and not a means to an end. 1101b10–2a4.

13. Since happiness is virtuous activity, virtue should be considered. Since the parts of the soul which partake of reason are thought and desire, virtue with respect to each should be discussed. Ethical virtue is concerned with desire, intellectual virtue with thought. Ethical virtue will be considered first. 1102a5–3a10.

Book B

1. A habit of *acting* in a certain way is acquired by a repetition of *acting* in that way. Hence ethical virtue, which is a habit, is acquired by *acting* rightly, i.e., as reason dictates. 1103a14–b25.

2. *Acting* rightly is *acting* neither excessively nor deficiently but in moderation. 1103b26–5a16.

3. In *acting* rightly, a man must be disposed in a certain way; he must know what he is doing, he must deliberately choose to do this and do it for its own sake, and he must *act* with certainty and firmness. 1105a17–b18.

4. The genus of virtue is neither passion nor natural ability but acquired habit. 1105b19–6a13.

5. The differentia of virtue is moderation or the mean, and this lies between two extremes, excess and deficiency. 1106a14–b35.

6. Virtue, then, is a habit chosen deliberately, and it is a mean relative to us and disposes us to *act* by reason in the manner as defined by a prudent man. 1106b36–7a27.

7. Examples of virtue are bravery, temperance, generosity, high-mindedness, and good temper; and the corresponding vices are rashness and cowardice, intemperance and insensibility, wastefulness and stinginess, vanity and low-mindedness, and irascibility and inirascibility. 1107a28–8b10.

8. With respect to nature, it is the contrary vices that are opposed to each other, e.g., rashness is opposed to cowardice; but with respect to goodness or excellence, the two contrary vices taken together are opposed to the corresponding virtue. 1108b11–9a19.

9. Perfect ethical virtue is difficult to acquire, for many particulars enter into the corresponding *action*. It is advisable, then, to pull ourselves away from that extreme

which is more opposed to the mean, and away from our natural inclination if this tends to one of the extremes, like intemperance in the case of the young. 1109a20–b26.

Book Γ

1. The nature of voluntary and involuntary *actions*, and of those which are voluntary in a qualified way. 1109b30–10b17.

2. Difference between *actions* performed because of ignorance and those performed in ignorance. 1110b18–1a21.

3. Some misconceptions about voluntary and involuntary *actions*. 1111a22–b3.

4. Some facts about intention. It is a species of deliberation; hence the nature of deliberation should be considered first. 1111b4–2a17.

5. With the nature of deliberation settled, the definition of intention becomes clear. 1112a18–3a14.

6. The object of wish is the end, and this is the good or the apparent good. To the virtuous, the end is good; to the vicious, it is the apparent good, which is sometimes good and sometimes bad. 1113a15–b2.

7. Since virtues and vices are formed through wish and intention, which are chosen and hence are voluntary, and since *actions* are performed according to virtues and vices, we are responsible for those *actions*. 1113b3–5a3.

8. Discussion of the various virtues. The nature of bravery, rashness, and cowardice. Bravery, rashness, and cowardice in a qualified sense. 1115a4–7b22.

9. The nature of temperance, intemperance, and insensibility. 1117b24–9a20.

10. Intemperance is more voluntary than cowardice; hence it deserves more reproach. 1119a21–b18.

Book Δ

1. Generosity is a virtue with regard to giving and taking property. The vice in excess is wastefulness, that in deficiency is stinginess. 1119b22–22a17.

2. Munificence is generosity in which large sums are involved. The corresponding vice in excess takes the form of extravagance or of conspicuous consumption, and that in deficiency is meanness. 1122a18–3a33.

3. High-mindedness is a virtue with regard to high honor, and a high-minded person rightly regards himself as worthy of high honor and *acts* according to his merit. The vice in excess is vanity, and that in deficiency is low-mindedness. 1123a34–5a35.

4. With regard to moderate or small honor, the vice in excess is ambition, that in deficiency is unambition, but the virtue has no name. 1125b1–25.

5. Good temper is a virtue with regard to anger. The vice in excess is irascibility, that in deficiency is inirascibility. 1125b26–6b10.

6. In social relations, those who are moderate in aiming to please are friendly (there is no name in Greek), those with the vice in excess are complaisant, and those with the vice in deficiency are hard to get along with or are quarrelsome. Further, those who speak truly about themselves are truthful; but those who speak falsely, if their pretensions are in the direction of excess, they are boastful, but if their pretensions are in the direction of deficiency, they are ironic or self-depreciatory. 1126b11–7b32.

7. In times of relaxation, those who are humorous as they should be are witty; but those who are humorous in excess (i.e., beyond propriety) are buffoons or vulgar, and those who are deficient in humor are boorish or obtuse. 1127b33–8b10.

8. Shamefulness is not quite a virtue but is mixed, for no virtuous man should be shameful, except when he does something which is not virtuous. But it is better than shamelessness, which is bad. 1128b10–35.

Book E

1. Justice and injustice are habits which dispose us to do what is just and unjust, respectively. Hence the just and the unjust should be considered first. 1129a3–26.

2. Justice has two senses, and so does injustice. An unjust man is (a) one who does things contrary to law or (b) one who is grasping in his relation to others; a just man is contrary to an unjust man in each of the above senses. 1129a26–b11.

3. Legal justice is a disposition affecting others, and so is legal injustice. But this sense of justice is general, for a just man in this manner has all the virtues which affect others rightly. What we seek is justice in a narrower sense, and likewise for injustice. 1129b11–30a13.

4. In the narrower sense, an unjust man is a grasping man, one who gains by someone's loss, whether honor or property or safety or some other such thing. 1130a14–b5.

5. The just in the narrower sense may be (a) distributive or (b) corrective, as in unjust exchanges. If distributive, then what is just is (a) analogous (b) between persons (c) according to their merits. If A merits twice as much as B and receives twice as much of a good as B, then the distribution is just, otherwise it is unjust. 1130b6–1b24.

6. In exchanges, what is just is that the things exchanged should be equal; and if they are not, the exchange is unjust. So if an unjust exchange becomes equalized, then it becomes just; and justice here is a disposition to make just exchanges or to equalize unjust exchanges. 1131b25–2b20.

7. What is just is not the kind of reciprocity advocated by the Pythagoreans, i.e., an exchange of the same things; for a shoemaker does not wish to exchange shoes for shoes but shoes for something else. Exchanges of different things require a common measure if they are to be equal and therefore just. 1132b21–3b28.

8. Definitions of just *action, acting* justly, being treated unjustly, justice, injustice, just effect, unjust effect, doing what is just, doing what is unjust, restitution, verdict. Difference between what is just between citizens and what is just between a master and a slave or a father and his children or a husband and his wife, and also between what is naturally just and what is legally just. 1133b29–6a9.

9. Whether it is possible to be willingly treated unjustly. 1136a10–b14.

10. Whether the one who *acts* unjustly is the agent who gives less of a good or the receiver who has or gets more of a good. 1136b15–7a4.

11. Whether *acting* unjustly is just a matter of ability or includes something else also (a disposition). 1137a4–30.

12. The nature of equity, and the difference between equity and justice. 1137a31–8a3.

13. Whether it is possible for one to *act* unjustly towards himself. 1138a4–b14.

Book Z

1. Ethical virtues are ethical habits according to right reason; hence right reason should be considered, and this is intellectual virtue. 1138b18–34.

2. The parts of the soul which are concerned with reason are the estimative and the scientific, the first being concerned with what may or may not be or come to be, the second with what exists or comes to be of necessity; and the first part is concerned with judgment, the second with *knowledge* (i.e., scientific knowledge). 1138b35–9b13.

3. Science is demonstrated knowledge of that which exists of necessity and is therefore eternal. 1139b14–36.

4. Art is concerned with that which is produced and so which may or may not come to be; so art is defined as a disposition, with true reason, which can make a product, e.g., a house or a chair or steel. Bad art is the contrary of art, and it makes a product with false reason. 1140a1–23.

5. Prudence is a virtue; it is a practical disposition, with true reason, capable of taking the means necessary for man's good ends, ultimately for happiness. The contrary disposition is imprudence. 1140a24–b30.

6. Intuition (or intellect) is that part of the soul which grasps principles, e.g., the principles of mathematics or of philosophy. 1140b31–1a8.

7. Wisdom is intuition and scientific knowledge concerning the most honorable things. In a qualified sense, one may say that there is wisdom in each science or art. 1141a9–b8.

8. Some remarks concerning prudence. 1141b8–2a30.

9. Deliberation is a species of inquiry; it is judgment concerning matters of expediency relative to a given end. Good deliberation, then, is deliberation with right reason. 1142a31–b33.

10. Intelligence is a virtue which makes good judgments about things with which prudence is concerned. So while prudence takes the right steps, intelligence judges them well. 1142b34–3a18.

11. *Judgment* is right judgment by an equitable man. 1143a19–24.

12. *Judgment* and intelligence and prudence and intuition (a part of it) are somehow related to each other; and they are all concerned with individuals in practical matters. 1143a25–b17.

13. The manner in which prudence and wisdom contribute to man's ultimate good. 1143b18–5a11.

Book H

1. With respect to character, the three kinds of things to be avoided are vice, incontinence, and brutality; their contraries are virtue, continence, and what we might call 'divine virtue', for lack of a name. Virtue and vice have been discussed. Continence and incontinence will be discussed now. 1145a15–b7.

2. Some facts about continence and incontinence; but difficulties arise with respect to continence and incontinence, and there is disagreement among thinkers. 1145b8–6b5.

3. Both the continent and the incontinent man have good wishes but bad *desires*, but they differ in the manner in which their *desires* are related to their wishes and their knowledge when the objects of their *desires* are before them. 1146b6–7b19.

4. The term 'incontinence' (and also 'continence') has many senses. In the primary sense, incontinence is concerned with the objects with which intemperance is concerned; in a secondary sense and by similarity or analogy, it is concerned with anger, gain, victory, and even with brutal or morbid things. 1147b20–9a20.

5. Incontinence with respect to anger is less disgraceful than incontinence in the primary sense. 1149a21–50a8.

6. While continence and incontinence are concerned with pleasures, endurance and softness are concerned with pains; and continence is preferable to endurance. 1150a9–b28.

7. Intemperance is worse than incontinence; for the intemperate man is not aware of his vice and his reason is false, whereas the incontinent man is aware of his vice because his reason is right. 1150b29–1a28.

8. A continent man abides by right opinion, but an obstinate man abides by a chance opinion; and an obstinate man may be opinionated or ignorant or boorish. 1151a29–b22.

9. Similarity and difference between a continent and a temperate man, an incontinent and an intemperate man. An incontinent man may be shrewd but he cannot be prudent. 1151b23–2a36.

10. Some think that no pleasure is good, whether in itself or indirectly; others think that some pleasures are good but that most of them are bad; others think that the highest good is not pleasure, even if all pleasures are good. Reasons are given. 1152b1–24.

11. Examination of the doctrine that no pleasure is good. 1152b25–3a35.

12. Examination of the doctrine that the highest good is not pleasure. This doctrine contradicts the view that happiness is pleasant. Thus some pleasures are good, though others are bad. 1153b1–4a21.

13. Reasons why most men pursue bodily pleasures, even if they are bad. But bodily pleasures are not the only kind of pleasures. God alone enjoys a pleasure which is simple and perfect. 1154a22–b34.

Book Θ

1. Friendship is necessary for a good life; and it is noble in its perfect sense. 1155a3–31.

2. Problems raised concerning friendship. 1155a32–b16.

3. The things we like are three in kind, and so are the friendships which we use to attain those things. 1155b17–6b6.

4. Perfect friendship requires virtue; the other two kinds are imperfect, for virtue in them, too, is imperfect. 1156b7–8a10.

5. It is difficult to have many friends in the perfect sense, but easy in the imperfect sense. 1158a10–36.

6. There is an equality of give and take in friendships, except in cases in which friends cannot be equal or cannot reciprocate equally, as in the friendship between father and son, master and slave, mother and child. 1158b1–9a33.

7. Perfect friendship is the most abiding. 1159a33–b24.

8. Friendships tend to be just, for they exist when give and take are equal. 1159b25–60a30.

9. The various forms of government, good and bad, and their relation to friendship. 1160a31–1b10.

10. Kinds of friendships between relatives, who may be equal or unequal. 1161b11–2a33.

11. Reasons why perfect friendships are harmonious whereas the other two kinds are not. 1162a34–3a23.

12. Reasons why friendships between unequals lead to complaints and quarrels. 1163a24–b28.

Book I

1. Friendship between unequals is preserved by a give and take which is analogous. 1163b32–4a22.

2. Should the value of what is given to a friend be measured by the giver or by the one who receives? 1164a22–b21.

3. Whether a son should always obey his father; whether one should help a friend rather than a virtuous man; whether one should repay a debt or use the money to help a friend; other similar problems. 1164b22–5a35.

4. On keeping and breaking off friendships. 1165a36–b36.

5. Friendship arises from love of oneself; and since the virtues are in harmony with themselves and the most virtuous man loves his own virtues and *actions*, which are good to him, he would be a friend to the most virtuous most of all. 1166a1–b29.

6. The difference between friendship and good will. 1166b30–7a21.

7. Concord is sameness of thought about practical and expedient matters of considerable importance. 1167a22–b16.

8. The reason why the benefactors love those they have benefited more than the benefited love their benefactors. 1167b17–8a27.

9. Should a man love himself most or someone else? He loves himself most, if he is virtuous and loves virtuous *actions*, and such love is in harmony with loving others, for he is virtuous. But he is selfish if what he loves is the useful and the pleasurable, for loving these does not include loving others for their own sake. 1168a28–9b2.

10. Does a happy man need friends? Certainly, for virtuous activity (at least ethical activity) requires the presence of others, of friends most of all. 1169b3–70b19.

11. Should one have as many friends as possible? A virtuous man should not have too many; few are enough for a pleasant life. 1170b20–1a20.

12. Are friends needed in good fortune or in misfortune? They are needed on both occasions, but for different reasons. 1171a21–b28.

13. Just as virtue is for the sake of virtuous activity, so friendship is pursued for the sake of the activity of living together with others; and such activity is enhanced in the case of virtuous friends. 1171b29–2a15.

Book K

1. Concerning pleasure, some say that the good is pleasure, others that pleasure is bad. Arguments are brought forward for these doctrines, and these arguments are scrutinized. 1172a19–4a12.

2. The nature of pleasure. It is not a motion, which is incomplete activity and proceeds to its completion; it is complete activity, and so is every part of it during the corresponding part of its duration. Different activities are accompanied and perfected by different pleasures. 1174a13–6a29.

3. Concerning happiness, it is not amusement; for amusement is a relaxation and should be pursued for the sake of happiness. 1176a30–7a11.

4. Since happiness is an activity of man, it would be the best kind of activity, and this is the activity of the best part of man, i.e., of the part which thinks. The life of contemplation would be such activity, for it is most continuous and most self-sufficient, and self-sufficiency belongs to happiness. Such activity, then, is most divine, and the more we partake of it, the closer we come to the divine. 1177a12–8a8.

5. The activity according to ethical virtue, too, is pleasant, but in a secondary sense; yet it is needed, for a man must live with others, and so he must *act*. And he needs material means for ethical virtue, and, to a lesser extent, for contemplation also. 1178a9–9a32.

6. Since the study of happiness is for the sake of *action* and not just for knowledge, the conditions favorable to the formation of virtue and virtuous activity cannot be neglected. Thus forms of government and laws which promote and maintain the right education, virtue, and other requirements for happiness should be examined. This leads to politics. 1179a33–81b23.

INTRODUCTION

Unity in Aristotle's Nicomachean Ethics

I

According to Aristotle, a science has unity if its objects come under one genus or are referred to one aim. In the first case, the objects are demonstrated from principles required by that genus; in the second, the objects are demonstrated as being necessary if the aim posited is to be achieved. In plane geometry, for example, if a triangle is defined as a three-sided plane figure, the three altitudes can be demonstrated to be concurrent; in strategy, if victory is to be achieved, certain things must be available or be done.

Politics is a science of the second kind, for its objects are referred to one aim, the good of man, and this good is usually called "happiness"; and if this aim is to be achieved, certain things must exist or come to be. But is not happiness the aim of ethics also? In a way, yes, but there is a difference. Ethics is concerned mainly with the nature and definition of happiness. Politics, on the other hand, is concerned with the forms of government in a state under which men will achieve happiness as far as possible. It follows, then, that politics includes the knowledge of happiness and hence is related to ethics as a whole to a part.

Since happiness is the concern of ethics, the definition of happiness is the first principle of ethics. But happiness is not like a triangle whose conception hardly varies and whose definition is generally agreed upon by geometricians; for men's ways of life vary, and so do their opinions of what pleases them most. Besides, men's abilities to think and *act* differ also, at least in degree if not in kind, and this fact adds to the diversity of opinions as to what is best for man. Evidently, the subject of ethics does not possess the accuracy which is found in mathematics or physics, and a preliminary discussion is advisable before a definition of happiness is to be laid down.

II

In Book A of the *Nicomachean Ethics,* Aristotle examines dialectically and critically the various definitions of happiness given by eminent thinkers, discards what is badly stated and accepts what is well stated, adds his own contribution, and finally arrives at the following definition of the first principle of ethics:

> *Happiness is the activity of the soul according to virtue throughout life.*

The key terms in this definition are "activity", "soul", and "virtue", and a scientific knowledge of happiness requires a scientific knowledge of these terms and of those of their elements which are definable. Now the nature and definition of the soul are considered in the treatise *On the Soul* and are presupposed here; and activity, universally taken, is indefinable but is discussed in the *Metaphysics* and is likewise presupposed. It appears, then, that the term "virtue" in the definition of happiness is the most proper to this treatise, and the main part of the rest of the *Nicomachean Ethics* is concerned with virtue and whatever is closely related to it.

Book B discusses the definition of virtue and some of its properties, such as its origin, generation, and stability; and it does likewise with vice, for vice is contrary to virtue, and contraries as well as their intermediates (if there are any) come under the same science.

Virtues and vices are either ethical or intellectual. Those which are ethical include as elements in their definitions volition, deliberation, and intention; and a detailed discussion of these becomes the main part of Book Γ. The remainder of this Book gives some examples of virtues and vices and indicates how these examples come under the definitions of virtue and vice.

Ethical virtues and vices have species, and these are defined and discussed in detail in Books Δ and E. Book Δ discusses generosity, high-mindedness, good temper, friendliness, truthfulness, wit, and others, and also their contraries. Book E discusses justice, equity, their contraries, and their properties.

Since ethical virtue is a disposition according to right reason, and since the possession of right reason is the possession of intellectual virtue, the intellectual virtues, along with their vices, should be considered; and they are discussed in Book Z. These virtues are science, art, intuition, wisdom, and prudence. Intuition is thought directed to principles, science is thought directed to necessary truth, art is thought and skill directed to production, wisdom is thought which includes intuition and demonstrated knowledge of the most honorable things, and prudence is thought directed to the proper means concerning one's general good or the general good of a group, e.g., of a family or a state. These five virtues, taken together, are concerned with what exists of necessity and what may or may not be or come to be.

Between some contraries there are intermediates, e.g., between high and low notes there are intermediate notes. Between some virtues and vices, too, there are intermediates. Continence and incontinence are habits which lie between virtue and vice; for they are mixtures of virtue and vice, and this is because man's soul has both reason and desire. The continent man has the right reason but the wrong *desire*, and reason overpowers *desire*; the incontinent man, too, has the right reason and the wrong *desire,* but *desire* overpowers reason. These habits are discussed in Book H.

Now many ethical and intellectual virtues are directed towards others or are encouraged by others, and such virtues are stabilized and produce happiness more if they are shared with others—especially with friends—than if they are not so shared. As it is said, a friend is another self. Hence friendship among virtuous men enhances virtue and so contributes to happiness. There are several kinds of friends, and they are discussed in Books Θ and I.

Since happiness and unhappiness are activities, which are either pleasant or painful, pleasure and pain should be discussed; and they are discussed in Book K.

III

There seems to be a problem, however, which some modern philosophers might raise; for Aristotle regards ethics as a science, and a science according to him is concerned with factual judgments, that is, with statements of what is the case, whereas some regard ethics as being a normative science, that is, as a science of what ought to be the case and not of what is the case. Aristotle makes no explicit mention of what we regard to be a normative science, except perhaps in a somewhat indirect way when he uses expressions such as "one should do this" and "one ought not to do this" in his writings.

But there is a prior problem. If the expression "one should be just" is an example of a normative judgment, one may ask "Why should one be just?". If no reason is given, one may be somewhat in the dark, and if the answer is "because it is right to be just", one may still not be convinced; but if the answer is "because justice contributes to happiness", the reason is explicit and belief is more probable, and this answer is a factual and not a normative judgment. Thus the normative judgment without the factual reason is rather empty and not convincing, whereas the factual reason without the normative judgment is more likely to convince men to act justly.

One may add, Aristotle was quite aware of and enumerated the various forms of linguistic expression: factual, normative, poetic, and the rest; and he often used such forms as "one should do this" and "men ought to do this" as linguistic alternatives when the reason was stated or implied. Expressions such as "you ought to do this", "you must not do this", and "do this" are very often found in situations in which religion, the law, admonition, command and the like are involved, but they are not substitutes for true reasons in leading men to perform good *actions*.

THE NICOMACHEAN ETHICS

BOOK A

1

Every art and every *inquiry*,[1] and similarly, every *action* and every   1094*a*
intention is thought[2] to aim at some good; hence men[3] have expressed
themselves well in declaring the good to be that at which all things
aim[4]. But there appears to be a difference among the ends; for some are
activities, others are products apart from the [activities which produce   5
them]. Whenever there are ends apart from the *actions*[5] [which produce
them], the products are by nature better than the corresponding
activities.[6]

  Since there are many kinds of *actions* and arts and sciences[7], the corresponding ends are many also; for the end of the medical [science][8] is
health, that of shipbuilding is a ship, that of strategy is victory, and that of
economics is wealth. Whenever a number of such [sciences] come under   10
a single faculty[9] (as bridle-making and all other arts concerned with the
equipment of horses come under horsemanship, and as this [science] and
every military *action* comes under strategy, and similarly in the case of
other [sciences] which come under another [science]), in every case the
end of the architectonic [science] is preferable to the ends of the sub-   15
ordinate [sciences], for the latter ends are pursued for the sake of the
former end. It makes no difference whether the ends of the *actions* are
the activities themselves or something other than those activities, as in
the case of the sciences just mentioned.

  Now if of things we do there is an end which we wish for its own sake
whereas the other things we wish for the sake of this end, and if we do   20
not choose everything for the sake of something else (for in this manner
the process will go on to infinity and our desire will be empty and vain[10]),
then clearly this end would be the good and the highest good.[11] Will not
the knowledge of it, then, have a great influence on our way of life, and

would we not [as a consequence] be more likely to attain the desired end,
25   like archers who have a mark to aim at?[12] If so, then we should try to
grasp, in outline at least,[13] what that end is and to which of the sciences
or faculties it belongs. It would seem to belong to the one which is most
authoritative and most architectonic.[14] Now politics appears to be such;
1094b   for it is this which regulates what sciences are needed in a state and what
kind of sciences should be learned by each [kind of individuals] and to
what extent. The most honored faculties, too, e.g., strategy and economics
and rhetoric, are observed to come under this [faculty].[15] And since this
5   faculty uses the rest of the practical sciences and also legislates what men
should do and what they should abstain from doing, its end would include the ends of the other faculties; hence this is the end which would
be the good for mankind. For even if this end be the same for an individual as for the state, nevertheless the end of the state appears to be greater
and more complete[16] to attain and to preserve; for though this end is
10   dear also to a single individual, it appears to be more noble and more
divine[17] to a race of men[18] or to a state.

    Our *inquiry*, then, has as its aim these ends,[19] and it is a political
inquiry; and it would be adequately discussed if it is presented as clearly
as is proper to its subject-matter; for, as in hand-made articles, precision
should not be sought for alike in all discussions. Noble and just things,
15   with which politics is concerned, have so many differences and fluctuations that they are thought to exist only by custom and not by nature.[20]
Good things,[21] too, have such fluctuations because harm has come from
them to many individuals; for some men even perished because of wealth,
20   others because of bravery. So in discussing such matters and in using
[premises] concerning them, we should be content to indicate the truth
roughly and in outline, and when we deal with things which occur for the
most part and use similar [premises] for them, [we should be content to
draw] conclusions of a similar nature. The listener, too, should accept
each of these statements in the same manner;[22] for it is the mark of an
25   educated man[23] to seek as much precision in things of a given genus as
their nature allows, for to accept persuasive arguments from a mathematician appears to be [as improper as] to demand demonstrations from
a rhetorician.

    Now a man judges well the things he knows [well], and it is of these
1095a   that he is a good judge; so a good judge in a subject is one who is educated

in that subject, and a good judge without qualification is one who is educated in every subject. In view of this, a young man is not a proper student of [lectures on] politics; for he is inexperienced in *actions* concerned with human life, and discussions proceed from [premises concerning those *actions*] and deal with [those *actions*].[24] Moreover, being disposed to follow his passions, he will listen in vain and without benefit, since the   5 end of such discussions is not knowledge but *action*.[25] (And it makes no difference whether he is young in age or youthful in character, for his deficiency arises not from lack of time but because he lives and pursues things according to passion). For knowledge about such matters in such a man, as in those who are incontinent, becomes unprofitable; but in those   10 who form their desires and *act* according to [right] reason,[26] it becomes very beneficial.

Let so much, then, be taken as a preface concerning (a) the kind of student, (b) the manner in which the discussion of the subject should be accepted, and (c) the subject of the *inquiry* which is before us.

2

To resume, since all knowledge and every intention desire some good, let   15 us discuss what is that which is aimed at by politics and what is the highest of all goods achievable by *action*. Most people are almost agreed as to its name; for both ordinary and cultivated people call it "happiness", and both regard living well and *acting* well as being the same as being happy. But there is disagreement as to what happiness is, and   20 the account of it given by ordinary people is not similar to that given by the wise. For some regard it as something obvious or apparent, such as pleasure or wealth or honor, while others regard it as something else; and often the same man changes his mind about it, for when suffering from disease he regards it as being health, when poor as being wealth,   25 and when he becomes conscious of his ignorance he admires those who discuss something great and beyond his comprehension. Again, some [the Platonists] held that besides these particular goods there exists something by itself [*Goodness*, as an Idea], and that it is this [Idea] which causes these particulars to be good.[1]

To examine all the doctrines would perhaps be rather fruitless, but it is sufficient to examine only those which are most prevalent or are thought   30 to be based on some reason. Let us also not forget that arguments from principles differ from those which lead to principles. Plato, too, was right when he raised this problem and inquired whether the right way to proceed is from the principles or towards the principles, e.g., whether in a stadium the right procedure is from the judges to the goal or vice versa.[2] One should begin, of course, from what is familiar; but things are familiar in two ways, for some are familiar relative to us while others are familiar without qualification.[3] Probably we should begin from things which are familiar relative to us. Accordingly, he who is to listen effectively to lectures concerning noble and just things and, in general, to subjects dealt with by politics should be brought up well in ethical habits;[4] for the beginning [here] is the fact, and if this fact should appear to be adequate, there will be no further need of the why of it. Such a man either has or can easily get principles.[5] As for him who lacks both, let him listen to the words of Hesiod:

1095b is placed at left of line 4.

5 marks line 11.

That man's completely best who of himself
Thinks of all things, ... and he is also good
Who trusts a good advisor; but the man
Who neither for himself can think nor, listening,
Takes what he hears to heart, this man is useless.[6]

10 marks the verse block.

3

Let us continue the discussion from the point at which we digressed. It is not unreasonable that what men regard the good or happiness to be seems to come from their ways of living. Thus ordinary people or those who are most vulgar regard it as being pleasure,[1] and in view of this they like a life of sensual pleasure. Now there are thee kinds of life which stand out most; the one just mentioned, the political, and thirdly the contemplative. Ordinary people appear to be quite slavish in choosing deliberately a life of beastly pleasures, but their view has support because many men of means share the tastes of Sardanapalus.[2] Men of culture and *action* seek a life of honor; for the end of political life is almost this. But this good appears rather superficial to be what is sought; for it is thought to depend on those who bestow rather than on those who receive honor, whereas we have a strong inner sense that the good is something which belongs to the man who possesses it and cannot be taken away from him

15, 20, 25 mark lines in the left margin.

easily. Further, men seem to pursue honor in order to assure themselves that they are good;[3] at least, they seek to be honored (a) by men of prudence, and (b) among those who know them, and (c) on the basis of their virtue. Clearly, then, virtue, according to these, is superior to the other goods. And perhaps one might even regard this more than any other good to be the end of political life. But this[4] too appears to be rather incomplete, for it seems that a man may have virtue even when he is asleep, or when he goes through life without *acting*, or, besides these, when one meets with the greatest sufferings and misfortunes; but no one would regard a man living in this manner as being happy, unless he wishes to uphold a paradox. But enough of this subject, for it has been sufficiently treated in periodicals also.[5] The third kind of life is the theoretical, which we shall examine later.[6]

As for the life of a money-maker, it is one of tension; and clearly the good sought is not wealth, for wealth is instrumental and is sought for the sake of something else. So one might rather regard as ends those mentioned above,[7] for they are liked for their own sake. Yet they, too, do not appear to be the highest good, although many arguments have been used to support them. So let the discussion of these be left aside.

30

1096a

5

10

4

As for the universal *Good*, perhaps it is better to examine it and go over the difficulties arising from the way it is stated, although such an inquiry is made with reluctance because those who introduced the Forms are friends.[1] Yet it would perhaps be thought better, and also our duty, to forsake even what is close to us in order to preserve the truth, especially as we are philosophers; for while both are dear, it is sacred to honor truth above friendship.[2]

Now those who introduced this doctrine did not posit Ideas in which they assigned greater or less priority, and just for this reason neither did they set up an Idea of numbers.[3] But what is called 'good' may be in the whatness [of a thing, i.e., in a substance], and also in a quality, and in a relation [etc.], and that which exists by itself and is a substance is prior by nature to a relation [and to the rest], for a relation is like an offshoot and an accident of being; so there could be no common idea for [all] these.[4]

Further, since the term 'good' has as many senses as the term 'being'[5]

15

20

25   (for it is predicated of whatness,[6] as in the case of God and of the intellect,[7] and of a quality, as in the case of the virtues, and of a quantity, as in the case of the right amount, and of a relation, as in the case of the useful, and of time, as in the case of right time, and of place, as in the case of the right location, and similarly with the other categories), clearly it cannot be a universal which is common and one, for it would not have been used in all the categories but only in one.[8]

30   Again, since of things coming under one idea there is a single science, of all the goods, too, there would have to be a single science. But as it is, there are many sciences even of goods which come under one category. Under right time, for example, in war the science is strategy, but in disease it is medical science; and under the right amount, in nourishment it is medical science, but in exercise it is the science of gymnastics.

35   One might also raise this question: What in the world do they mean by
1096b the term 'Thing Itself' if, for example, the definition of a man is one and the same whether applied to Man Himself or to an individual man? For insofar as they are just men, they will not differ at all; and if so, neither will *Good Itself* and a particular good differ insofar as each is good.[9]

Further, if indeed a white thing which exists for a long time is not [necessarily] whiter than a white thing which exists for a day, neither will *Good Itself* by being eternal be more good than a particular good.

5   The Pythagoreans seem to have spoken more persuasively about the good when they placed the *One* in the column of goods; and Speusippus too seems to have followed closely their line of thought.[10] The discussion of these things, however, belongs elsewhere.[11]

An objection to what has been said [by us] appears to arise because the
10   arguments [of the Platonists] do not include all [kinds of] goods. Now one kind of things called 'good 'are those which are pursued and are liked for their own sake; but there are also things which somehow produce or preserve or prevent the contraries of the former kind, and these are called 'good' because the former are called 'good', but they are so called in another sense of the term. Clearly, then, things are called 'good' in two senses, some for their own sake,[12] others for the sake of these. So let us
15   separate those which are good for their own sake from those which are beneficial to other goods and consider whether the former are called 'good' according to one idea. What kind of things would one posit as being good for their own sake?[12] Are they not those which are pursued even just for

themselves, such as thinking wisely, seeing, certain pleasures, and honors? For even if we pursue these for the sake of something else, still one would posit them as being goods for their own sake.[12] But is it only the Idea 20 [i.e., *Good Itself*, which is good in this sense] and none of the other things? If so, then the species [of goods] will exist in vain. And if these too are goods for their own sake,[12] the same definition [of good] should appear in all of them, like the definition of whiteness when whiteness is present in snow and in white lead.[13] But the definitions of honor and of thinking wisely and of pleasure are distinct, and the things defined differ insofar as 25 they are good. The good, then, cannot be something common in virtue of one idea.[14] But then, in what manner are these things called 'good'? They do not seem to be like those which have the same name by chance. Are they called 'good' by coming from one thing, or by contributing to one end, or rather by analogy?[15] By 'analogy' I mean, e.g., as vision is in the body, so is the intellect in the soul, and another thing in something else.

But perhaps we should leave these aside at present, for an accurate 30 discussion concerning them belongs more properly to another philosophy; and similarly with regard to the Idea [i.e., the *Good*].[16] For even if there is some one good which is commonly predicated [of certain things] or which is separate by itself, clearly it cannot be the object of *action* or of possession by a man; but it is such an object that we are seeking now.[17] 35

Perhaps one might think that the knowledge of that separate good would be better for those goods which are objects of possession or of *action*, for 1097a by using it like a model we shall also know more the things which are good for us, and if we know them [more], we shall succeed [more] in attaining them. This argument is indeed somewhat persuasive, but it seems to clash with the sciences. For all of them aim at some good and 5 seek what is lacking, and yet they leave out the knowledge of it; and it is unreasonable that all the artists should be ignorant of so great an aid and make no attempt at all to seek it out. Furthermore, one does not see how a weaver or a carpenter will benefit in the practice of his art by knowing *Good Itself*, or how one will be a better doctor or a better general by 10 having contemplated that Idea [the *Good*]; for it appears that what a doctor examines is not health in this manner at all, but the health of man, or perhaps rather the health of an individual man, since what he cures is an individual [and not man in general].[18] So much, then, for the discussion of these.

5

15   Let us return to the good which we are seeking and inquire what it might be. It appears to be different in different *actions* or arts; for in medical art it is different from that in strategy and similarly from that in any of the rest of the arts. What then is the good in each? Is it not that for the sake of which the rest are done? This is health in the medical art, victory in

20   strategy, a house in architecture, something else in another art, and in every *action* or intention it is the end; for it is for the sake of this that the rest are done by all men.[1] So if there is some one end of all the things that are done, this would be the good achievable by *action*, but if there are many ends, these would be the corresponding goods. Thus by taking a

25   different course the argument arrives at the same thing. But we must try to state this more clearly.

    Since the ends appear to be many, and since we choose some of them (e.g., wealth, flutes, and instruments in general) for the sake of others, it is clear that not all ends are complete; but the highest good appears to be something which is complete. So if there is only one end which is complete,

30   this will be the good we are seeking, but if there are many, the most complete of these will be that good. Now what we maintain is this: that which is pursued for its own sake is more complete than that which is pursued for the sake of something else, and that which is chosen but never chosen for the sake of something else is more complete than other things which, though chosen for their own sake, are also chosen for the sake of this; and that which is complete without any qualification is that which is chosen always for its own sake and never for the sake of something else.

1097*b*   Now happiness is thought to be such an end most of all, for it is this that we choose always for its own sake and never for the sake of something else; and as for honor and pleasure and intellect and every virtue, we choose them for their own sake (for we might choose each of them when nothing else resulted from them), but we also choose them for the sake of happiness,

5   believing that through these we shall be happy. But no one chooses happiness for the sake of these, nor, in general, for the sake of some other thing.[2]

    The result appears to be still the same if we proceed from self-sufficiency, for the perfect good is thought to be self-sufficient. By 'self-sufficient' we do not mean an individual who leads just a solitary life, but one with

10   parents and children and a wife and, in general, with friends and fellow-

citizens as well, since man is by nature political.³ Some limit, however, should be set to these, for if we extend them to include one's ancestors, descendants, and friends of friends, these will proceed to infinity; but we shall examine this later.⁴ Now we posit the self-sufficient to be that which taken by itself makes one's way of life worthy of choice and lacking in   15 nothing; and such we consider happiness to be. Moreover, we posit happiness to be of all things the most worthy of choice and not capable of being increased by the addition of some other good, since if it were capable of being increased by the addition even of the least of the goods, the result would clearly be more worthy of choice; for the result would exceed [the original, i.e., happiness], and the greater of two goods is always more worthy of choice. It appears, then, that happiness is something perfect   20 and self-sufficient, and it is the end of things we do.

6

Perhaps to say that happiness is the highest good is something which appears to be agreed upon;¹ what we miss, however, is a more explicit statement as to what it is. Perhaps this might be given if the function of man is taken into consideration. For just as in a flute-player or a statue-   25 maker or any artist or, in general, in anyone who has a function or an *action* to perform the goodness or excellence lies in that function, so it would seem to be the case in a man, if indeed he has a function. But should we hold that, while a carpenter and a shoemaker have certain functions or *actions* to perform, a man has none at all but is by nature without a   30 function? Is it not more reasonable to posit that, just as an eye and a hand and a foot and any part of the body in general appear to have certain functions, so a man has some function other than these? What then would this function be?²

Now living appears to be common to plants as well as to men; but what we seek is proper to men alone. So let us leave aside the life of nutrition   1098*a* and of growth. Next there would be the life of sensation; but this, too, appears to be common also to a horse and an ox and all animals. There remains, then, the life of *action* of a being who has reason. Of that which has reason, (a) one part has reason in the sense that it may obey reason,³ (b) the other part has it in the sense that it possesses reason or in the sense   5 that it is *thinking*.⁴ Since we speak of part (b), too, in two senses, let us confine ourselves to the life with reason in activity [i.e., to the process of *thinking*], for it is this sense which is thought to be more important.[5] Accordingly, if the function of a man is an activity of the soul according to reason or not without reason,[6] and if the function of a man is generically the same as that of a good man, like that of a lyre-player and a good lyre-

10 player, and of all others without qualification, when excellence with respect to virtue is added to that function (for the function of a lyre-player is to play the lyre while that of a good lyre-player is to play it well, and if so, then we posit the function of a man to be a certain kind of life, namely, activity or *actions* of the soul with reason, and of a virtuous man we posit

15 these to be well and nobly done; so since each thing is performed well according to its proper virtue), then the good for a man turns out to be an activity of the soul according to virtue, and if the virtues are many, then according to the best and most complete virtue.[7] And we should add 'in a complete life', for one swallow does not make a spring, nor does one day;

20 and so too one day or a short time does not make a man blessed or happy.

7

Let this, then, be the outline of the good [for a man], for perhaps we should first make a sketch and later fill in the details. When a good outline has been made, it would seem that anyone could go forward and articulate the parts, for time is a good discoverer and helper in such matters. It is in

25 this way that the arts advanced, for anyone can add what is lacking. We should also recall what has been stated previously: precision should not be sought alike in all cases, but in each case only as much as the subject-matter allows and as much as is proper to the *inquiry*. Thus a carpenter and

30 a geometer make inquiries concerning the right angle in different ways; for the first does it as much as is useful for his work, while the second inquires what it is or what kind of thing it is, since his aim is to contemplate the truth.[1] We should proceed likewise in other situations and not allow side lines to dominate the main task. Again, we should not demand the

1098*b* cause in all things alike, but in some cases it is sufficient to indicate the fact well, as is also the case with principles; and the fact is first and is a principle.[2] Now some principles are perceived by induction,[3] others are observed by sensation,[4] others are acquired by some kind of habituation,[5]

5 and others in some other way.[6] So we should try to present each according

to its nature and should make a serious effort to describe them well, for they have a great influence on what follows; for a principle is thought to be more than half of the whole, and through it many of the things sought become apparent also.

8

We should consider this principle[1] not only from the conclusion and from premises leading to its definition, but also from what men say about it; for all things which belong to it are in harmony with a true [definition of it], but truth is soon bound to clash with a false [definition of it].[2] Now goods have been divided into three kinds: those which are called 'external', those of the soul, and those of the body; and we maintain that those of the soul are the most important and are goods in the highest sense, and *actions* and mental activities are activities of the soul.[3] So our account must have been stated well, at least according to this doctrine, which is an old one and agreed upon by philosophers.[4] It is also rightly said that the end is certain *actions* or activities;[5] for it is in such a manner that the goods of the soul arise, and not from the external goods. The statement that the happy man lives well and *acts* well, too, is in harmony with the definition of happiness; for we have almost said that happiness is living well or *acting* well.[6]

9

Again, all the things which men look for in happiness appear to belong to the definition given. For happiness is thought to be virtue by some, prudence by others, a sort of wisdom by others, or all of these or some of them, together with pleasure or not without pleasure by still others; and there are those who include also material prosperity. Of these opinions, some are held by ordinary men and by men of old, while others by the few and by men held in esteem; and it is reasonable that none of them should be altogether mistaken but should be right at least in one and even in most respects.

Our definition is in harmony with those who say that happiness is virtue or some sort of virtue; for the activity according to virtue is an activity of a virtue.[1] It makes perhaps no small difference, however, whether we regard the highest good to be in possession or in use, or to exist as a disposition or as an activity according to that disposition. For a dis-

1099*a*   position may be present without producing any good at all, as in a man
who is asleep or inactive for some reason or other; but with the activity
this cannot be the case, for one will of necessity be *acting*, and *acting* well.
And as at the Olympic Games it is not the most beautiful or the strongest

5   who are crowned but those who compete (for it is some of these who
become victors), so in life it is those who *act* rightly who become the
winners of good and noble things. Moreover, these men lead the kind of
life which is by its nature pleasant.² For to be pleased is something which
belongs to the soul,³ and the thing that pleases a man is that to which he
takes a liking, e.g., a horse pleases a man who likes horses, and a spectacle

10   pleases a man who likes spectacles, and similarly that which is just pleases
a man who likes what is just, and in general, virtuous things please a man
who likes things done according to virtue. Now things which give pleasure
to most men are in conflict with each other because they are not by nature
such.⁴ But things which give pleasure to those who like noble things are by
nature pleasant; and such are the *actions* according to virtue, and these are

15   both pleasant to such men and pleasant in virtue of their nature. Thus the
life of these men has no further need of pleasure as a sort of charm, to be
attached like an appendage, but has its pleasure in itself; for, besides what
we have said, no man is good who does not enjoy noble *actions*, nor would
anyone call a man 'just' who does not enjoy *acting* justly, or call a man

20   'generous' who does not enjoy generous *actions*, and similarly in all the
other cases. If this is so, then it is by their nature that *actions* according to
virtue would be pleasant. Moreover, they are also good or noble, and in
the highest degree so, if indeed a virtuous man judges them well; and he
judges them as we have stated. Happiness, then, is the highest good, and

25   the most noble, and the most pleasant, and these [three attributes] are not
separate,⁵ as the inscription at Delos claims:

That which is most just most noble is;
Health is best; by nature to obtain
What one desires is the pleasantest.⁶

30   For all of these belong to the best activities; and these activities, or one of
them⁷ – the very best – we maintain to be happiness.
But happiness appears also to require external goods, as we have mentioned;⁸ for it is impossible or not easy to *act* nobly if one is not furnished

1099*b*   with external goods. For many *actions* are done through friends or wealth

or political power, as if by means of instruments; but the lack of some
things, such as high lineage, good children, and beauty,[9] mars blessedness;
for one who is utterly ugly, or of low lineage, or lonesome and without
children is not altogether happy, and perhaps even less so if he were to   5
have very bad children or friends, or if these were good but perished. As
we have said, then, a man seems to need also such favorable conditions;
and in view of this, some [go as far as to] identify happiness with good
fortune, but others with virtue.

10

It is in view of these opinions that the problem also arises whether happiness
is acquired by learning or by habit or by some other form of training, or   10
whether it comes to us by some divine providence or even by luck.[1] Now
if there are any other gifts at all which men receive from gods, it is reasonable that happiness, too, should be god-given, especially as it is the best of
goods for men. But perhaps this problem would be more proper to another inquiry;[2] anyway, even if happiness is not god-sent but comes to us   15
through virtue or some sort of learning or training, it appears to be the
most divine[3] [of goods for men], for the prize and the end of virtue appears
to be the highest good and something godlike and blessed. It might also
be shared by many men; for it can belong, through some kind of learning
and diligence, to all those who have not been incapacitated for virtue.
So if it is better that we should be living happily in this manner rather than   20
by luck, then it is reasonable that such be the case, if indeed things which
exist by nature attain their noblest state in accordance with their nature.
The situation is similar also with things which exist or are produced according to art or any cause, especially the best.[4] But to entrust the greatest and
noblest [of human goods] to luck would be very incongruous indeed.   25
   The answer to this inquiry becomes apparent also from the definition,
for we have stated[5] that happiness is a certain kind of activity of the soul
according to virtue. As for the remaining goods, some of them exist as
necessities,[6] the others are by their nature helpful and useful as instruments
to happiness. These statements are in agreement also with what we said in
the beginning;[7] for we posited the end of politics to be the highest good,   30
and politics takes the greatest care in making the citizens of a certain
quality, i.e., good and disposed to noble *actions*. Accordingly, it is reason-

able that neither an ox nor a horse nor any other animal should be called
1100a   'happy', for none of them can partake of such activity. For the same *reason*,
too, a child cannot be happy, for it is not yet capable of such *actions* because of its age; but some of them are called 'blessed' because they are
expected to be happy in the future. For happiness requires, as we have
5   stated, both complete virtue and a complete life, since many changes and
all sorts of events caused by chance occur in a lifetime; and it is possible
for the most prosperous man to suffer great calamities in his old age, as is
told of Priam in the Trojan stories, and a man who has met such fortunes
and has come to a wretched end would not be considered happy by anyone.

11

10   Should we consider no one happy, then, while he is living but wait, as
Solon said, to see the end of his life? And if we posit also such a requirement, will it not be the case, too, that a man is happy when he is dead?
But is not this entirely absurd, especially since we have maintained that
15   happiness is some sort of an activity? Now if we do not mean to say that a
dead man is happy and if Solon did not intend to say this, but instead that
one might safely consider a man blessed only when that man is already
beyond the reach of evils and misfortunes, this too would be subject to
dispute; for it seems that something good as well as something bad may
20   come to a dead man, if indeed it does also to a living man when he is not
conscious, e.g., honors and dishonors, and also good *actions* and misfortunes of children and of descendants in general. But this too presents a
problem; for if a man has lived according to reason a blessed life till old
age and died as befitted him, many changes might occur in his descendants,
25   for some of them might turn out to be good and to attain the life they are
worthy of, while with others the contrary might be the case. It is clear, too,
that the distance in the relationship between these descendants and the man
might vary in all sorts of ways. It would thus be absurd if also the dead
men were to change along with his descendants and become at one time
happy and at another wretched; but it would be also absurd if the lives of
30   descendants contributed nothing at all, nor for some time, to the happiness
or unhappiness of their ancestors.[1]
But let us return to the first problem,[2] for perhaps from its consideration we might be able to perceive the latter problem also. Now if we are to

look to the end and only then consider a man as blessed, not as being then
blessed but as having led a blessed life earlier, is it not absurd to say that
when the man is happy it would not be true to regard him as happy, giving   35
as the *reason* the fact that we do not wish to call a man happy because of   1100*b*
(1) the possible future changes and (2) our belief (a) that happiness is
something enduring and by no means easily changed but (b) that the
fortunes of a man often take many turns? For it is clear that if we were to
go along with one's fortunes, we would have to call the same man at one   5
time 'happy' and at another 'wretched', representing a happy man as a sort
of chameleon and with an unsound foundation. It would not be right at
all, then, to base happiness on a man's fortunes.[3] For goodness or badness
in a man does not depend on these, although, as we have stated, human
life needs them, too; but it is the activities in accordance with virtue which   10
play the dominant role in happiness, while the contrary activities are
dominant in the contrary of happiness.[4]

 This statement is confirmed also by the difficulty we have just discussed.
For in none of man's actions is there so much certainty as in his virtuous
activities (which are more enduring than even scientific knowledge[5]),
and the most honorable of these are the most enduring because those who   15
are blessed live according to them most of all and most continuously; for
this seems to be the *reason* why we do not forget them.[6] The attribute
[i.e., permanence] in question, then, will belong to a happy man, and he
will be such a man throughout his life; for he will be engaged always or
most of all in *actions* and studies of things done according to virtue, and   20
he will bear the fortunes of life most nobly and with propriety in every
way like a man who is truly good and 'foursquare beyond reproach'.[7]
Now there are many events which happen by chance, some of great but
others of small weight; and it is clear that [for a virtuous man] those which
are of small weight, whether bringing good luck or its opposite, do not   25
have [much] influence on life, while those which are great and numerous
make life more blessed if they turn out well (for these, too, by their nature
add to the order and beauty of life, and the use of them becomes noble
and good), but they restrict or ruin the blessedness of a man if they turn
out to be the opposite, for they bring along pain and impede many activities.   30
Yet nobility shines out even here, when a man bears many and great
misfortunes with calm and ease, not through insensibility to pain, but
through nobility of character and highmindedness.

Thus if it is the activities that play a dominant role in life, as we have
35   said, no blessed man can become wretched; for he will never do what is
1101a   hateful or bad. For we hold that a truly good and sensible man will bear
all fortunes of life with propriety and will always *act* most nobly under
whatever the given circumstances may be, like a good general, who uses a
5   given army most effectively, or a good shoemaker, who makes the best
shoes out of a given leather, and likewise with any artist. If so, no happy
man will ever become wretched; nor of course blessed, were he to meet
with fortunes such as those of Priam. Nor again will he be subject to
variations or easily changeable; for he will not be moved from his happi-
10   ness easily, nor by any chance mishaps but by those which are great and
numerous; and in the latter case he will not again become happy in a short
time, but, if at all, in a long and complete time, during which he will
attain great and noble things.

What should prevent us, then, from saying that a man is happy when he
15   acts in accordance with complete virtue and is sufficiently furnished with
external goods, not for some chance period but during his entire life?
Should we not also add "and who will continue to live in this manner and
die as befits him", since the future is not manifest to us and since we posit
happiness to be an end and perfect in every way? If such be the case, we
20   may call 'blessed' those among the living who possess and will possess the
things already mentioned, but [we shall call them] 'blessed' [in the manner
which befits them as] men.[8] Let so much, then, be the limit of what we have
to say about these problems.

As for the fortunes that may befall a man's descendants and all his friends,
to regard them as not contributing anything at all appears very unwelcome
and contrary to the opinions of men. On the other hand, since they are
25   many and differ in various ways, some of them coming more close to him
while others less so, to discuss each of them individually appears to be a
long and endless task, but to speak of them taken as a whole and sketchily
may perhaps be sufficient. Now just as some of a man's mishaps have
some weight or influence on his life, while others seem to be rather light,
30   so the things that happen to all of a man's friends are similarly related. So
since the sufferings which affect the living differ from those which affect
the dead much more than the unlawful and terrible deeds which are acted
on the stage differ from those which are presupposed in a tragedy, this
35   difference too must be taken into acount,[9] and perhaps more so in dis-

cussing the problem whether the dead share in any good or its opposite. 1101*b*
For, even if any good or its opposite penetrates to them, this seems, from
the remarks just made, to be weak or small, either without qualification or
to them, or else to be at least so much and of such a kind as not to make
happy those who are unhappy nor to deprive happy men of their blessed- 5
ness. Good *actions* of friends, then, and bad *actions* similarly, appear to
contribute something to the dead, but they do so to such a degree and
extent as not to change happy into unhappy men or to make some other
such change.[10]

12

Having settled these problems, let us examine next whether happiness is 10
among the things which are praised or, rather, among those which are
honored; for it is at least clear that it is not one of the powers.[1] Now it
appears that whatever is praiseworthy is praised by being a certain quality
or by being somehow related to something else; for we praise a just man
and a brave man and, in general, a good man and virtue because of the 15
actions or the things which are done,[2] and we praise a [naturally] strong
man and a [natural] runner[3] and each of the others in view of the fact
that each of them has by nature a certain quality and is disposed in a
certain way towards something good or virtuous. This is clear also whenever the gods are praised, for they appear ridiculous when they are referred
to us, and this happens because praises are referred to something else, as 20
we said. So if praise is such a thing, it is clear that, of a thing which is a
highest good, there can be no praise except something greater or better;[4]
and this appears to be the case, for what we say of gods is that they are
blessed or happy, and we call the most godlike of men 'blessed'. So, too, 25
with the goods; for no man praises happiness as he does that which is
just,[5] but he calls it 'blessed', since it is something more godlike or better.
It seems that Eudoxus, too, was right in advocating pleasure in his
speeches concerning the things to be prized; for he thought that the fact
that pleasure, which is a good, is not praised indicates that it is superior to 30
the things which are praised,[6] and that such are God and the good, for all
the others are referred to these. For praise belongs to virtue, since by
means of virtue one is disposed to perform noble *actions*, while encomia
belong to activities of the body[7] and those of the soul in a similar manner.
Perhaps precision in these matters is more proper to treatises concerned 35

1102*a*   with encomia, but to us it is clear from what has been said that happiness
is among those things which are honored and are perfect. And such seems
to be the case also because happiness is a principle, for it is for the sake of
this that all *actions* are done by everyone; and our position is that the principle and the cause of good things is something worthy of honor and is
divine.[8]

13

5   Since happiness is an activity of the soul in accordance with complete
virtue, we should examine virtue; for perhaps our investigation of happiness, too, would be better if it is pursued in this manner.[1] The true statesman, too, is thought to have made the greatest effort in studying virtue,
10   for his wish is to make the citizens good and obedient to the laws. As
examples of this we have the lawgivers of the Cretans and of the Spartans,
and also some others who became such lawgivers.[2] And if this concern[3]
belongs to politics, clearly our inquiry into virtue would be in accordance
with our original intention.[4] Clearly, it is human virtue that we should be
15   examining, for what we were seeking, too, was the good and happiness for
man; and by 'human virtue' we mean not that of the body but that of the
soul, for it is of the soul, too, that happiness is stated by us to be an
activity.[5] If such be the case, it is clear that a statesman should understand
in some way the attributes of the soul, like the doctor who attends to
20   the eyes or the whole body, and to the degree that politics is more honorable and better than medical science. Now the cultivated among the
doctors take the trouble to learn many things about the body. So the
statesman, too, should be investigating attributes of the soul, both for the
25   sake of these[6] and as much as is adequate to what is sought, for greater
precision is perhaps rather burdensome in view of what he is aiming at.[7]
Some things about the soul have been sufficiently stated also in public
writings,[8] and they should be used; e.g., one part of the soul is nonrational,
the other has reason. It makes no difference for the present whether these
30   two parts are separable, like the parts of a body and of any other divisible
whole, or just distinguishable in definition but inseparable by nature, like
the convex and the concave in the circumference of a circle.[9] Of the nonrational, one part is like that which is common and vegetative, i.e., that
which is the cause of nutrition and of growth. For one would posit such
1102*b*   a power of the soul in all things which take in nutriment and in embryos;

and he would posit the same [kind of power] also in complete beings, since it is more reasonable to posit this than to posit some other kind of power.[10] Now the virtue of this power appears to be common to all things having this power and not just human, for this part of the soul or this power seems to function most in sleep, and good and evil men are least distinguishable [as being such] during sleep; and from this arises the saying that happy and wretched men do not differ during half their lives. This, of course, occurs with good reason; for sleep is an inactivity of the soul insofar as the soul is said to be good or bad, except when some motions somehow make their way to the soul a little, in which case the dreams of *good* men turn out to be better than those of ordinary men. But enough of this; and let us leave aside the nutritive part of the soul, since by its nature it does not partake of human virtue.

There seems to be also another nature of the soul which is nonrational but which participates in some way[11] in reason. For we praise reason or that part of the soul which has reason in the continent and the incontinent man, since it urges them rightly to do what is best; but it appears that these men have also another part which by its nature violates reason, and this part fights against or resists reason. For just as the paralyzed parts of the body when directed to move to the right [often] move contrariwise to the left, so it is with the soul; for incontinent men have an impulse to move in the contrary direction. But while in the body we observe this motion in the contrary direction, in the soul we do not. Perhaps in the soul, too, we should grant no less the existence of something which violates reason, i.e., a part which goes contrary to it or resists it. How this part is distinct from the part with reason does not concern us here.[12] Now this part too appears to share in reason, as we said; for at least in the continent man it obeys reason, while in the temperate or brave man, perhaps it is even more disposed to listen to reason, for it agrees with reason on all matters.[13] So the term 'nonrational', too, appears to have two meanings. For the vegetative part in no way communicates with reason, while the appetitive part and, in general, the part which desires[14] shares [in reason] in some way, namely, insofar as it listens to or obeys it; and this is the manner in which a man has reason when we speak of him as listening to or obeying his father or his friends, and not in the manner in which he has reason in mathematics.[15] That the nonrational part is in some way persuaded by reason is indicated also by advice or by any censure or urging. And if one

5

10

15

20

25

30

1103a

should say that this part, too, has reason, then also the expression 'that which has reason' would have two senses: (a) that which has reason in itself, this being the principal sense, and (b) that which listens to reason, like a child listening to a father.[16]

Virtues too are distinguished according to this difference, for we call some of them 'intellectual', e.g., wisdom and intelligence and prudence,[17] but others 'ethical', e.g., generosity and temperance. Thus, when we speak of the character of a man, we say that he is good-tempered or temperate,[18] not wise or intelligent, but we praise also the wise man in virtue of his disposition;[19] and we call "virtues" those dispositions which are praiseworthy.[20]

BOOK B

1

Since virtues are of two kinds, intellectual and ethical, an intellectual virtue   1103*a*/14
originates and grows mostly by teaching,[1] and in view of this it requires
experience and time, whereas an ethical virtue is acquired by habituation
(ethos), as is indicated by the name 'ethical', which varies slightly from
the name 'ethos'.[2] From this fact it is also clear that none of the ethical
virtues arises in us by nature [at birth], for no thing which exists by nature   20
can be changed into something else by habituation; e.g., no stone, which
moves downwards by nature, can be changed by being habituated to move
upwards, even if one were to keep on throwing it up countless of times,
nor can fire be similarly made to move downwards, nor can anything else
with some other attribute existing by nature be made to change that attribute by habituation. Hence virtues arise in us neither by nature nor contrary to nature; but by our nature we can receive them and perfect them   25
by habituation.[3]

Again, of things which come to us by nature, we first bring along the
powers and later exhibit the corresponding activities. This indeed is clear
in the case of sensations; for it is not by seeing often or hearing often that
we acquired the corresponding power of sensation, but conversely: we   30
used the power after we possessed it, we did not come to possess it after
using it. In the case of the virtues, on the other hand, we acquire them as a
result of prior activities; and this is like the case of the arts, for that which
we are to perform by art after learning, we first learn by performing,[4]
e.g., we become builders by building and lyre-players by playing the lyre.   1103*b*
Similarly, we become just by doing what is just, temperate by doing what
is temperate, and brave by doing brave deeds.[5] This is confirmed also by
what happens in states. For it is by making citizens acquire certain habits
that legislators make them good, and this is what every legislator wishes,   5
but legislators who do not do this well are making a mistake; and good
government differs from bad government in this respect.[6]

Again, it is from the same *actions* and because of the same *actions* that every virtue comes into being or is destroyed, and similarly with every art; for it is by playing the lyre well or badly that men become good or bad lyre
10   players, respectively. In the case of architects and[7] all the rest, too, the situation is analogous; for men become good architects by building houses well, and bad architects by building houses badly. For if such were not the case, there would have been no need for a teacher, but all would have become good or bad artists.[8]

Such indeed is the case with virtues also; for it is by our *actions* with
15   other men in transactions that we are in the process of becoming just or unjust, and it is by our *actions* in dangerous situations in which we are in the process of acquiring the habit of being courageous or afraid that we become brave or cowardly, respectively. It is likewise with *desires* and with anger; for, by behaving in one way or in the contrary way in corresponding situations, some men become temperate or intemperate,
20   good-tempered or irascible. In short, it is by similar activities that habits are developed in men; and in view of this, the activities in which men are engaged should be of [the right] quality, for the kinds of habits which develop follow the corresponding differences in those activities.[9] So in acquiring a habit it makes no small difference whether we are *acting* in
25   one way or in the contrary way right from our early youth; it makes a great difference, or rather all the difference.

2

Since our present study is not for the sake of contemplation, like the other theoretical inquiries – for we are inquiring what virtue is, not in order [just] to know it, but in order to become good, since otherwise there would be no benefit[1] from that inquiry – we should examine certain things
30   about *actions*, namely, how they should be done, for these are the principal [causes] also of the formation of the kinds of habits, as we have already stated.[2] Now to *act* according to right reason is commonly accepted, and let it be assumed here; later there will be a discussion concerning right reason, both as to what it is and how it is related to the other virtues.[3] But
1104a   first, let us agree on that other matter, namely, that all statements concerning matters of *action* should be made sketchily and not with precision,[4] for, as we said at first, our demands of statements should be in accordance

with the subject-matter of those statements; in matters concerning *action*
and expediency, as in those of health, there is no uniformity. And if such   5
is the universal statement, a statement concerning particulars will be even
less precise; for these do not come under any art or precept, but those who
are to *act* must always consider what is proper to the occasion, as in
medical art and in navigation.[5] Yet even though our present statement is   10
of such a nature, we should try to be of some help.

First, then, let us perceive this, that it is the nature of such things
[ethical virtues] to be destroyed by deficiency as well as by excess,[6] as we
observe in the case of strength and of health (for we should use as evidence
what is apparent for the sake of what is obscure),[7] for both excess and   15
deficiency in exercise destroy strength; and similarly, when too much or
too little drink or food is taken, it destroys health, but when the amount is
proportionate, it produces or increases or preserves health. Such is the
case also with temperance and bravery and the other [ethical] virtues; for   20
a man who flees from and fears everything and never stands his ground becomes a coward, but he who fears nothing at all but proceeds against all
dangers becomes rash, and, similarly, a man who indulges in all [bodily]
pleasures and abstains from none becomes intemperate, but he who avoids
them all, like a boor, becomes a sort of insensible man; for temperance   25
and bravery are destroyed by excess as well as by deficiency, but they are
preserved by moderation (or the mean).[8]

Furthermore, not only is each virtue generated, or grows, or is destroyed
from the same and by the same [kind of *actions*], but also the activities
[according to each virtue] will depend[9] on that same [virtue], for such is
the case with other things which are more apparent, as with strength; for   30
not only does strength come into being by taking much nourishment and
undergoing many exertions, but it is also the strong man who is most able
to do such things. Such too is the case with the virtues; for by abstaining
from [excessive bodily] pleasures we become temperate, and, in turn, when   35
we have become temperate we are most able to abstain from such pleasures.
And similarly with bravery; for by becoming habituated to show contempt   1104*b*
for and endure what is fearful we become brave, and when we have become
brave we are most able to endure what is fearful.

As a sign of what habits are we may consider the pleasures and pains
which accompany our actions; for a man who abstains from [excessive]   5
bodily pleasures and enjoys doing so is temperate, but a man who is

oppressed by so doing is intemperate, and he who faces danger and enjoys it or at least is not pained by so doing is brave, but he who is pained by so doing is a coward. Thus ethical virtue is concerned with pleasures and
10   pains; for we do what is bad for the sake of pleasure, and we abstain from doing what is noble because of[10] pain. In view of this, we should be brought up from our early youth in such a way as to enjoy and be pained by the things we should, as Plato says, for this is the right education.

Again, since virtues are concerned with *actions* and passions, and since
15   every *action* and every passion is accompanied by pleasure or pain, then for this *reason*, too, virtues would be concerned with pleasures and pains. This is indicated also by punishment, which is inflicted by means of pains; for punishment is a sort of cure, and cures by their nature are effected by means of contraries.[11] Again, as we said before,[12] every habit of the soul
20   has a nature which is related to and is concerned with those things by which it becomes by nature worse or better; but a habit becomes bad because of pleasures and pains, that is, by pursuing or avoiding pleasures or pains either when one should not, or at a time when he should not, or in the manner in which he should not, or in some other way contrary to that specified by [right] reason. It is in view of this that some thinkers[13]
25   even define the virtues as being certain states without feeling or as states of rest; but they do not define them well, for they define them in an unqualified way and do not specify them by adding "in the manner in which they should or should not, or at the time when they should" or whatever other qualifications are needed. We assume, then, that such[14] virtue is concerned with pleasures and pains and disposes us to do what is best, while vice disposes us to do the contrary.

That virtues and vices are concerned with the same things [pleasures and
30   pains] may become apparent to us also from the following. There are three objects which we choose, the noble, the expedient, and the pleasant, and there are three contrary objects which we avoid, the disgraceful, the harmful, and the painful; and a good man is apt to *succeed* in all of these, while a bad man is apt to be mistaken, especially about pleasure, for
35   pleasure is common to animals also and accompanies all objects of choice,
1105a   for also the noble and the expedient appear to be pleasant. Again, pleasure has been from infancy with us all; so it is difficult to rub off this feeling, ingrained as it is in our life. We also regulate our *actions*, some of
5   us more and others less, by pleasure and pain. Because of this, then, it is

necessary for our whole study to be concerned with pleasures and pains; for to enjoy or be pained rightly or wrongly has no small effect on our *actions*. Again, as Heraclitus says, it is more difficult to fight against pleasure than to fight against temper, and of that which is more difficult one can always acquire an art or a virtue; for excellence, too, is better in   10 that which is more difficult to achieve.[15] So because of this, too, the whole study of virtue or of politics is concerned with pleasures and pains; for he who uses these well will become good, but he who uses them badly will become bad.

Let it be affirmed, then, that virtue is concerned with pleasures and pains, that it grows by those *actions* by which it is in the process of coming into being but is destroyed if those *actions* are not done in this manner, and   15 that its activity is concerned with the same *actions* as those from which it came to be.

3

One might raise this question: How can we say that men should do what is just in order to become just, and *act* temperately in order to become temperate? For if they do what is just or temperate, they are already just   20 or temperate, just as if they do what is grammatical or musical, they are already grammarians or musicians, respectively.

But this is not the case even with the arts. For it is possible for one to write something which is grammatical by luck also or when someone else suggests it.[1] Accordingly, a man is a grammarian precisely when he does something grammatical and does it in a grammatical manner, that is, in   25 accordance with the grammatical knowledge which he possesses. Furthermore, the case of the virtues is not even similar to that of the arts.[2] For the things produced by the arts have their excellence in themselves, so it is enough that, when produced, they should be of a certain kind; things done according to virtue, on the other hand, are done justly or temperately not   30 [only] if (1) they themselves are of a certain kind, but also if (2) the agent who *acts* is of a certain disposition, namely, (a) when he knows what he does, (b) when he intends to do what he does and intends to do it for its own sake, and (c) when he *acts* with certainty and firmness.[3] Now with the exception of (a) knowledge, these [(b) and (c)] are not taken into account   1105b as requirements in the possession of the various arts;[4] but in the possession of the virtues, knowledge has little or no weight,[5] while the others [(b) and

(c)] count for not a little but for everything, for it is indeed by doing many
5   times what is just and temperate that we acquire justice and temperance.
Thus while things are just or temperate if they are such as a just or
temperate man would do,[6] a just or temperate man is not one who [just]
does these, but one who also does them as a just or a temperate man
10   would.[7] So it is well said that it is by doing what is just or temperate
that a man becomes just or temperate,[8] respectively; and no one who is
to become good will become good unless he does good things. Yet most
men do not do these; instead, they resort to merely talking about them
and think that they are philosophizing and that by so doing they will be-
15   come virtuous, thus behaving somewhat like patients who listen to their
doctors attentively but do none of the things they are ordered to do.
And just as these patients will not cure their body by behaving in this
way, so those who philosophize in such a manner will not better their soul.

4

20   Next we must inquire what virtue is.[1] Since there are three things in the
soul, and these are feelings [or passions], powers, and habits, virtue
would be one of these. By 'feelings' I mean , for example, *desire*, anger, fear,
envy, courage, gladness, friendly feeling, hatred, longing, emulation,
pity, and, in general, whatever is accompanied by pleasure or pain;[2] by
'powers' I mean those qualities in virtue of which we are disposed to be
25   affected by the above feelings, for example, those in virtue of which we are
capable of being angry or pained or feeling pity;[3] and by 'habits' I mean
those qualities in virtue of which we are well or badly disposed with
reference to the corresponding feelings, e.g., with reference to being angry
we are badly disposed if we are angry too violently or too weakly but well
disposed if we are angry moderately, and similarly with the others.
30   Now neither the virtues nor the vices are feelings; for we are said to be
good or bad not with respect to feelings but with respect to virtues or
vices, and we are praised or blamed not for our feelings (for he who is
1106a   simply afraid or angry is not praised, nor is he who is simply angry the one
who is blamed but he who is angry in a certain manner) but for our virtues
and vices. Furthermore, we are angry or afraid without deliberate choice,
while virtues are intentions of some kind or [are acquired] not without
5   deliberate choice.[4] Finally, with respect to our feelings we are said to be

moved, while with respect to virtues and vices we are said not to be moved but to be disposed in a certain manner.[5]

For the above *reasons* neither the virtues nor the vices are powers; for by being simply capable of feeling we are not said to be either good or bad, nor are we praised or blamed. And besides, it is by nature that we possess powers, but it is not by nature that we become good or bad; and we spoke   10 of this previously.[6]

So if the virtues are neither feelings nor powers, what remains is that they are habits. We have discussed, then, what virtue is as far as its genus goes.[7]

5

Concerning virtue we should state not only this, that it is a habit, but also the kind[1] of habit it is. It should be noted that every virtue (a) makes that   15 of which it is the virtue be well disposed and (b) makes it perform its function well;[2] e.g., the virtue of an eye both makes the eye a good eye and makes it perform its function well, for it is by the virtue of the eye that we see well. Similarly, the virtue of a horse makes (a) the horse a good horse   20 and also (b) good at running and carrying its rider and facing the enemy. So if such is the case in every instance, the virtue of a man, too, would be the habit from which he becomes good[3] and performs his function well. How this can be done has already been stated,[4] but it may become evident   25 also if we view the kind of nature[5] possessed by virtue. Now in everything which is continuous and divisible it is possible to take an amount which is greater than or less than or equal to the amount required, and the amounts taken may be so related either with respect to the thing itself or in relation to us; and the equal is a mean between excess and deficiency. By 'the mean', in the case of the thing itself, I mean that which lies at equal intervals from   30 the extremes, and this mean is just one thing and is the same for everyone;[6] but, when related to us, it neither exceeds nor falls short [of what is proper to each of us], and this is neither just one thing nor the same for everyone.[7] For example, if ten is many and two is few, then six is taken as the mean with respect to the thing itself, for six exceeds two and is exceeded   35 by ten by equal amounts; and this is the mean according to an arithmetic proportion.[8] But the mean relative to us should not be taken in this manner; for if ten pounds are too much and two pounds are too little for   1106*b* someone to eat, the trainer will not [necessarily] order six pounds, since

this is perhaps too much or too little for the one who is to take it; for Milo[9] it is too little, but for a beginner in athletics it is too much. It is
5   likewise in running and wrestling. And this is the way in which every scientist[10] avoids excess and deficiency but seeks and chooses the mean, not the mean with respect to the thing itself but the one in relation to a given person.

If, then, this is the manner in which every science[10] performs its function well, namely, by keeping an eye on the mean and working towards it
10   (whence arises the usual remark concerning excellent works, that nothing can be subtracted from or added to them, since both excess and deficiency destroy the excellence in them while the mean preserves it), and if, as is our manner of saying, it is with an eye on this that good artists do their work,
15   and if virtue, like nature, is more precise and better than any art,[11] then virtue would be aiming at the mean. I am speaking here of ethical virtue, for it is this which is concerned with feelings and *actions*, in which there is excess, deficiency, and moderation. For example, we may have the feelings
20   of fear, courage, *desire*, anger, pity, and any pleasure or pain in general either more or less than we should, and in both cases this is not a good thing; but to have these feelings at the right times and for the right things and towards the right men and for the right purpose and in the right manner, this is the mean and the best, and it is precisely this which belongs to virtue. In *actions*, too, there is excess, deficiency, and moderation in a similar manner. Now an [ethical] virtue is concerned with feelings and
25   *actions*, in which excess and deficiency are errors and[12] are blamed, while moderation is a *success* and is praised; and both *success* and praise belong to virtue. Virtue, then, is a kind of moderation, at least having the mean as its aim.[13] Also, a man may make an error in many ways (for evil, as the
30   Pythagoreans conjectured, belongs to the infinite, while goodness belongs to the finite),[14] but he may *succeed* in one way only; and in view of this, one of them is easy but the other hard. It is easy to miss the mark but hard to hit it. So it is because of these, too, that excess and deficiency belong to vice, but moderation to virtue.
35   For men are good in one way, bad in many.[15]

6

[Ethical] virtue, then, is a habit, disposed toward *action* by deliberate

choice, being at the mean relative to us, and defined by reason and as a   1107a
prudent man would define it. It is a mean between two vices, one by excess
and the other by deficiency; and while some of the vices exceed while the
others are deficient in what is right in feelings and *actions*, virtue finds and
chooses the mean.[1] Thus, according to its *substance* or the definition   5
stating its essence,[2] virtue is a mean [of a certain kind], but with respect
to the highest good and to excellence, it is an extreme.[3]

Not every *action* nor every feeling, however, admits of the mean, for some
of them have names which directly include badness, e.g., such feelings as   10
malicious gladness, shamelessness, and envy, and, in the case of *actions*,
adultery, theft, and murder; for all of these and others like them are blamed for being bad, not [just] their excesses or deficiencies. Accordingly, one
is never right in performing these but is always mistaken; and there is no   15
problem of whether it is good or not to do them, e.g., whether to commit
adultery with the right woman, at the right time, in the right manner, etc.,
for to perform any of these is without qualification to be mistaken. If this
were not so, we would be maintaining that in *acting* unjustly or in a cowardly way or intemperately, too, there is moderation and excess and de-   20
ficiency; for according to such a view there would be also a moderation of
excess and of deficiency, an excess of excess, and a deficiency of deficiency.
But just as there is no excess or deficiency of temperance or of bravery, because the mean is in a certain way an extreme,[4] so, too, there is no
moderation or excess or deficiency in the vices mentioned above but only a
mistake, regardless of the manner in which one *acts*; for, universally,   25
there is no moderation of excess or of deficiency, nor an excess or a
deficiency of moderation.[5]

7

We must not only state this universally, however, but also apply it to
particular cases; for, among statements about *actions*, those which are   30
[more] universal[1] are rather empty while those which are [more] particular
tend to be more true;[2] for *actions* deal with particulars, and it is with
these that our statements should be in harmony. So let us consider each
of these virtues and vices from our table.[3]

With regard to fear and courage, the mean is bravery. He who exceeds   1107b
in not fearing[4] has no name (many virtues and vices have no names),

but he who exceeds in courage is rash; and he who exceeds in fear and is deficient in courage is a coward.

5   With regard to pleasures and pains – not all of them [but mainly of the bodily senses], and less with regard to pains than with regard to pleasures – the mean is temperance while the excess is intemperance. Men deficient with regard to pleasures hardly exist, and for this reason such men happen to have no name; but let them be called 'insensible'.

With regard to giving and taking property, the mean is generosity, 10   while the excess and deficiency are, respectively, wastefulness and stinginess. Excess and deficiency in these two vices are present in contrary ways; for the wasteful man exceeds in giving away and is deficient in taking, while the stingy man exceeds in taking but is deficient in giving away. 15   (At present we are giving a sketchy and summary account of these, and this is sufficient; later[5] we shall specify them more precisely). With regard to property there are also certain other dispositions. The mean is munificence, for a munificent man differs from a generous man in that he deals with large amounts, while a generous man deals with small amounts [also].[6] The excess in large donations is extravagance or conspicuous consump- 20   tion, and the deficiency is meanness; but these vices differ from the vices opposed to generosity, and the manner in which they differ will be stated later.[7]

With regard to honor and dishonor, the mean is high-mindedness, the excess is said to be a sort of vanity, and the deficiency is low-mindedness. 25   And just as generosity was said to be related to munificence by being concerned with smaller amounts, so too there is a virtue which is concerned with smaller honors and is similarly related to high-mindedness, which is concerned with great honors; for it is possible to desire honor as one should, or more than one should, or less than one should. Now he who exceeds in his desires is called 'ambitious', he who is deficient is called 30   'unambitious', but he who desires honor in moderation has no name.[8] The dispositions too are nameless, except for that of the ambitious man, which is called 'ambition'. It is in view of this lack of name that those who are at the extremes claim to be in the middle position; and we, too, sometimes call the moderate man 'ambitious' but sometimes 'unambitious', 1108a   and sometimes we praise the ambitious man but sometimes the unambitious. The *reason* why we do this will be stated later;[9] for the present, let us continue with the other habits in the manner already proposed.[10]

With regard to anger, too, there is excess, deficiency, and moderation.   5
These habits are almost nameless, but since we say that the moderate man
is good-tempered, let us call the mean 'good temper'. As for the extremes,
let the man who exceeds be called 'irascible' and the corresponding vice
'irascibility', and let the man who is deficient be called 'inirascible' and
the corresponding deficiency 'inirascibility'.[11]

There are three other moderations which have some likeness towards   10
each other yet differ from each other; for all of them are concerned with
associations among men as they speak or *act* but differ in that one is
concerned with truth about oneself while the other two are concerned with
what is pleasurable, and of these two, one is exhibited in amusement
while the other in all situations of life. So we should consider these, too,
in order to observe better that moderation is praiseworthy in all cases   15
while the extremes are neither right nor praiseworthy but worthy of blame.
Now most of these habits, too, have no names, but we should try, as in the
other cases, to introduce names ourselves in order to make our point
clear and easy to follow.

With regard to truth, then, the moderate man is a sort of truthful man   20
and the mean may be called 'truthfulness'; but pretense which exaggerates
is boastfulness and the possessor of it is boastful, while pretense which
understates is self-depreciation and the possessor of it is self-depreciatory.

With regard to what is pleasant in amusing others, the moderate man
is witty and the corresponding disposition is wit, but the disposition which
tends to exceed is buffoonery and the possessor of it is a buffoon, while he   25
he who is deficient is a sort of boor and the corresponding habit is boorishness.

With regard to what is pleasant in the other manner, the one found in
[all] situations of life, the man who is pleasant as he should be is friendly
and the mean is friendliness; but he who behaves excessively is complaisant, if he does this not for the sake of anything else, but is a flatterer, if he
does it for his personal benefit, while he who is deficient and is unpleasant   30
in all situations is a quarrelsome sort of man or a man hard to get along
with.

There are moderations in feelings, too, and in what concerns feelings.
Thus a sense of shame is not a virtue, but a man with a sense of shame is
praised also; for here, too, one man is said to be moderate, i.e., he who
has a sense of shame, another behaves excessively, like the abashed man

35   who is ashamed of everything, and a third is deficient or is not ashamed at
all, and he is called 'shameless'.

1108b   As for righteous indignation, it is a mean between envy and malicious
gladness. These dispositions are concerned with pain and pleasure felt at
the fortunes of others; for a man with righteous indignation is pained by
the undeserved good fortune of others, an envious man, who exceeds, is
5   pained by the good fortune of all others, and a man who is maliciously glad
is so deficient in being pained as to be even joyful at the good fortunes of
others. These will be discussed elsewhere at the proper time.[12]

As for justice, since the term 'justice' does not have only one meaning,
we shall, after discussing the other habits, distinguish those meanings and
state the manner in which each of them is a mean; and in a similar manner
10   we shall discuss also the rational virtues.[13]

8

Since the kinds of habits are three, and since two of them are vices, one
with respect to excess but the other with respect to deficiency, while the
third is a virtue, which is a mean, each of them is opposed to each of the
others in some manner; for the extremes [the vices] are contrary both to
15   the mean and to each other, while the mean is contrary to the extremes;[1]
for just as the equal is greater when related to the less but less when related
to the greater, so in both feelings and *actions* the middle habits [the
moderations] exceed when related to the deficiencies but are deficient
when related to the excesses. For the brave man appears rash to the coward
20   but a coward to the rash man. Similarly, the temperate man appears
intemperate to the insensible man but insensible to the intemperate; and a
generous man appears wasteful to a stingy man but stingy to the wasteful.
Hence each man at each extreme regards the one at the middle as being
25   near the other extreme, and the coward calls the brave man 'rash' while
the rash man calls him 'a coward'; and the case with the others is analogous.

Since the three kinds of habits are opposed to one another in such a
manner, the contrariety of the extremes to each other is greater than that
to the mean, for they are further from each other than from the middle
30   just as the great is further from the small and the small from the great
than each of them is from the equal.[2] Again, in some cases one of the
extremes appears to be similar to the mean, like rashness in relation to

bravery and wastefulness in relation to generosity; but it is the extremes
which are most dissimilar to each other. Now contraries are defined as
things which are furthest from each other; so it is things which are further   35
apart which are more contrary to each other.[3]

In some cases the mean is opposed by the deficiency more than by the   1109a
excess, in others it is opposed by the excess more than by the deficiency.
For example, it is not rashness, which is an excess, but cowardice, which is
a deficiency, that is more opposed to bravery; on the other hand, it is not
insensibility, which is a deficiency, but intemperance, which is an excess,   5
that is more opposed to temperance. This happens to be the case for two
reasons. One of them comes from the thing itself. For since it is one of the
extremes that is nearer to and more like the mean, it is not this but the
other extreme that we oppose to the mean. For example, since it is rashness rather than cowardice that is thought to be more like and nearer to   10
bravery, it is cowardice rather than rashness that is more opposed to
bravery; for it is the thing which is further from the middle that is thought
to be more contrary to the middle. So this is one *reason*, and it arises from
the thing itself. The other *reason* arises from ourselves; for the vice to
which we are in some way naturally more drawn appears to be more contrary to the mean. For example, we are naturally drawn to [bodily]   15
pleasures more than to insensibility, and so we are more easily drawn to
intemperance than to propriety.[4] Thus we say that the vice to which we
yield more readily is more contrary to the mean than the contrary vice is;
and for this *reason* it is intemperance, which is an excess, and not insensibility that is more contrary to temperance.

9

We have sufficiently discussed the following: that ethical virtue is a mean;   20
the manner in which it is a mean; that it is a mean between two vices, one
with respect to excess and the other with respect to deficiency; and that it
is such a mean because it aims at what is moderate in feelings and *actions*.

In view of what has been said, it is a difficult task to become a virtuous
man, for in each case it is a difficult task to attain the mean; for example,   25
not everyone can find the mean [the center] of a circle but only he who
knows geometry. So, too, anyone can get angry or give money or spend it,
and it is easy. But to give to the right person, the right amount, at the

right time, for the right purpose, and in the right manner, this is not something that anyone can do nor is it easy to do; and it is in view of this that
30   excellence is rare and praiseworthy and noble. Accordingly, he who aims at
the mean should first keep himself away from that vice which is more contrary to the mean, as Calypso recommends also: "keep the ship away from
the surf and spray"; for one of the two extremes is more subject to mistake,
while the other is less so. So since it is difficult to attain the mean exactly,
35   we should choose as a second best, as the saying goes, that which has the
1109b   least of what is bad; and this will most likely be effected in the manner stated.

We should take into consideration also the vices to which we are easily
drawn, for some of us are by nature inclined towards some of them, others
towards others; and we come to know these by our pains and pleasures.
We should then drag ourselves towards the contrary extreme, for by
5   drawing ourselves well away from our disposition to error, we shall be
more likely to arrive at the mean, like those who straighten warped sticks
by bending them in the contrary direction.

On every occasion, what we should guard against most is the pleasurable
or pleasure,[1] for we do not judge pleasure impartially. Thus towards
pleasure we should feel just as the elders of the people felt towards Helen,
10   and we should repeat their saying on every occasion; for by getting rid of
pleasure in this manner we are less likely to be mistaken. To sum up, then,
if we do all these things, we shall best be able to attain the mean.

Perhaps all this is difficult, and especially in individual cases, for it is
15   not easy to specify, for example, how and with whom and on what kinds of
provocations and how long a man should be angry; for we do sometimes
praise those who are deficient and call them 'good-tempered' but at other
times speak of those who are harsh as being manly. Nevertheless, the man
who is blamed is not he who deviates from goodness only a little, whether
towards excess or deficiency, but he who deviates much, for the latter does
20   not escape our notice. Nor is it easy to specify by a formula the limits beyond
which one becomes blameworthy and the extent to which one should be
blamed, for this is not easy for any sensible object; such specifications
depend on individual situations, and judgement depends on the sensation
of these.[2] So much, then, is clear, that the intermediate habit is in all cases
praiseworthy, and that we should lean sometimes in the direction of excess
25   and sometimes in the direction of deficiency, for by so doing we shall most
easily attain the mean and goodness.

BOOK Γ

1

Since virtue[1] is concerned with feelings and *actions*, and since feelings and   **30**
actions which are voluntary are praised or blamed, while those which are
involuntary are pardoned and sometimes even pitied, it is (a) likewise
necessary for those who examine virtue to specify what is voluntary and
what is involuntary,[2] and also (b) useful for legislators in bestowing   **35**
honors and inflicting punishments.

   It is thought that involuntary things are those which are done by force   **1110a**
or through ignorance; and that is said to be done by force whose [moving]
principle is external and is such that the agent who *acts* or the patient who
is *acted* upon contributes nothing, as in the case of a strong wind which
carries a ship off course or the case of men who have us in their power. As
for *actions* done through fear of greater evils or for the sake of some noble   **5**
deed (e.g., a tyrant who has a man's parents and children in his power may
order him to do something disgraceful, threatening to kill them if the man
does not obey but to spare them if he obeys), there is disagreement as to
whether they are involuntary or voluntary. Something of this sort happens
also when goods are thrown overboard during a storm; for no one would
voluntarily just throw goods away,[3] but for one's safety and that of the   **10**
passengers every sane person would.

   Such *actions*, then, are mixed,[4] but they are more like voluntary than like
involuntary; for at the time they are done they are subject to choice, and
the end of the *action* depends on the right moment.[5] So when a man *acts*,
both what is voluntary and what is involuntary should be mentioned. Now   **15**
in such *actions* he *acts* voluntarily, for the [moving] principle of setting the
parts of his body in motion is also in him; and if that principle is in him,
it is up to him to *act* or not to *act*. Such *actions*, then, are voluntary, but if
they are regarded without any qualification, they are perhaps involuntary;
for no one would choose any of them taken by itself.[6] Sometimes men are   **20**
even praised for such *actions*, whenever they endure something disgraceful or painful in return for something great or noble;[7] but they are blamed

whenever they take the contrary course, for to endure what is most disgraceful for what is not noble or for mediocre ends is the mark of a bad man.[8] On some occasions a man is not praised but pardoned, whenever he
25   does things he should not do for *reasons* which are too strong for human nature and which no one would endure. Perhaps there are some things which one cannot be forced to do but would rather die than suffer the most terrible things; and as for the things which compelled Euripides' Alcmaeon to slay his mother, they appear ridiculous.[9] Sometimes, however, it is
30   difficult for one to decide which of two alternatives he should choose and which he should endure, and it is even more difficult to abide by his decision; for the most part, what men anticipate is painful but what they are compelled to do is disgraceful, and in virtue of these [i.e., the painful
1110*b*   or disgraceful] they are praised or blamed according as they are compelled to do something or not.

What sort of *actions*, then, should we say are done by force? Are they not those whose [moving] cause is without qualification external and the agent contributes nothing? But concerning those which taken by themselves are involuntary but which, when qualified, are chosen in the face of the alternative consequences, if the principle of such choice is in the agent,
5   they are involuntary when taken by themselves but, when qualified, are voluntary in the face of the alternative consequences. And in the latter case they are more like the voluntary than the involuntary; for *actions* depend on particular situations, and in such cases they are voluntary. It is not easy, however, to state definitely which of the alternatives should be chosen, for many differences arise in individual cases.

Now if one were to say that things which are pleasant and noble are
10   done by force – for, being external, they compel us – then in this way all things would be done by force[10], for it is for the sake of these [pleasant or noble] things that all men do whatever they do; but those who *act* by force or unwillingly do so painfully, while those who *act* because of pleasure or what is noble do so with pleasure.[11] So it is ridiculous for a man (a) to assign the [moving] cause to external things and not accept the responsibility himself for being easily caught by such things but (b) to
15   regard himself responsible for what is noble while making the pleasant [which is external] responsible for what is disgraceful. It seems, then, that what forces a man is that whose [moving] principle is external,[12] without the man who is forced contributing anything.

2

Everything done through ignorance is not voluntary, but if it causes pain and regret, it is involuntary; for he who through ignorance did something,   20
whatever this may be, but is not displeased at all by that *action*, though he did not *act* voluntarily, as he did not know what he was doing, neither did he *act* involuntarily if he is not pained. So of a thing done through ignorance, if the agent regrets it, he is thought to have *acted* involuntarily, but if he does not regret it, since he is different, let him be called 'nonvoluntary'; for since he differs, it is better for him to have a special name.[1]

Again, *acting* through ignorance seems to be different from acting in   25
ignorance; for he who is drunk or angry is not thought to be *acting* through ignorance but through one of the causes stated,[2] not knowing his *act* but in ignorance of it. Thus every evil man is in ignorance of what he should do and what he should abstain from doing, and it is through such error that men become unjust and in general bad.   30

Now the term 'involuntary' tends to be used not whenever a man is ignorant of what is expedient, for ignorance in intention of what should be done is a cause not of what is involuntary but of evil; and [involuntariness] is not universal ignorance (for through universal ignorance men are blamed),[3] but ignorance with respect to particulars in which *action* exists and with   1111*a*
which *action* is concerned. For it is on these particulars that both pity and pardon depend, since a man who is ignorant of some of these *acts* involuntarily.

It is perhaps better, then, to specify what these particulars are and how many there are, that is, who the agent is, what he does, on what occasion or on what object he *acts*, and sometimes with what (e.g., with an instru-   5
ment), and for the sake of what (e.g., for safety) or how he *acts* (e.g., gently or violently). Now no one would be ignorant of all of these, unless he were mad, and clearly he would not be ignorant of the agent; for indeed how can one be ignorant of himself? But one may be ignorant of what he is doing, e.g., as when one says that a word came out without realizing it, or that he did not know it was secret, as Aeschylus said after revealing the Mysteries,[4]   10
or that he only wished to show how it worked but discharged it, e.g., the catapult. One might also mistake his son for an enemy, as Merope did,[5] or a pointed spear as having a button on it, or some other kind of stone for a pumice stone; and one might strike something to save a man but

15   kill him instead,[6] or one might wish to tap a man but might knock him out,
      as in boxing.[7] Since there may be ignorance of any one of these things in
      which *action* is involved, he who was ignorant of some of them, especially
      of the most important, is thought to have *acted* involuntarily; and by
      'most important' we mean those things in which *action* is involved or on
      which the outcome depends. In addition, an *action* done involuntarily in
20   virtue of such ignorance should be followed by pain and regret.

                                        3

      Since that which is involuntary is done by force or through ignorance, the
      voluntary would seem to be that whose [moving] principle is the agent
      who knows the particulars on which the *action* depends. For surely it is
25   not well to say, as some do, that whatever is done through temper or
      desire is involuntary.[1] For first, none of the other animals would then do
      anything voluntarily, not even children.[2] Then again, do we perform no
      action through *desire* or temper voluntarily, or do we perform noble *actions*
      voluntarily but disgraceful *actions* involuntarily? But is not the latter
      alternative ridiculous, when the cause is [only] one person?[3] It would be
30   equally absurd to say that things which we should desire are involuntary.
      On the contrary, we should be angry with certain people and we should
      desire certain things, such as health and learning;[4] and involuntary *actions*
      are thought to be painful, while those according to *desire* are thought to
      be pleasant.[5] Furthermore, what is the difference, in being involuntary,
      between errors with respect to judgement and those with respect to temper?
1111*b* For both should be avoided; and it seems that passions, which are non-
      rational, are not less human, and so are those *actions* which proceed from
      temper and *desire*. It would be absurd, then, to posit them as being
      involuntary.[6]

                                        4

5   Having specified what is voluntary and what is involuntary, we shall next
      discuss intention (or deliberate choice); for intention is thought to be most
      proper to virtue and to reveal character more than *actions* do.[1]
          Now intention appears to be volition but is not the same as volition,
      since the latter is wider;[2] for children and other animals share in volition,
10   too, but not in intention, and things done on the spur of the moment are

said to be voluntary but not according to intention.[3] Those who say that intention is *desire* or temper or wish[4] or opinion of some sort do not speak rightly. For intention does not belong to non-rational beings as well, but *desire* and temper do;[5] and the incontinent man *acts* by *desire* and not by intention, while the continent man on the contrary *acts* by intention and not by *desire*.[6] Again, *desire* may be contrary to intention but not to *desire*.[7] Moreover, *desire* is of the pleasant or of the painful, but intention is neither of the painful nor of the pleasant.[8] Also, intention is temper even less than it is *desire*; for it is thought that things done through temper are least done according to intention.[9] Again, intention is not even a wish, though it appears to be close to it. For there can be no intention of what is impossible, and if one were to say that he intends to do something impossible he would be thought to be a fool; but there can be a wish of what is impossible, e.g., of immortality. Further, a wish can be also of things which might be done not by the man who wishes them, like the wish that a certain actor or athlete be the victor; but no one intends things such as these, except those which he thinks he can bring about by his own efforts. Also, a wish is of the end rather than of the means, while intention is of the means relative to the end; e.g., we wish to be healthy but we choose after deliberation the means through which we may become healthy, and we wish to be happy and speak of this, but it does not befit us to say that we choose after deliberation to be happy, and, in general, intention seems to be concerned with things which can be brought about by us.

Again, intention could not be opinion. For opinion can be of everything, of eternal and impossible things no less than of those which are up to us to do;[10] and it is subdivided by being false or true and not by being bad or good, while intention is subdivided rather by these, i.e., by being bad or good. In general, then, perhaps no one would say that intention is the same as opinion, not even the same as some opinions; for we are of a certain kind of character by having good or bad intentions and not by having opinions. And what we intend is to attain or to avoid something or to do some such thing, but what we have an opinion of is, what a thing is, or to whom it is expedient, or how it is expedient, but not at all of attaining or of avoiding something.[11] And intention is praised for being concerned with a right[12] end rather than for being right [about any given end], while opinion is praised by being true. And we deliberately choose what we most know to be good, but we may have opinion of what we do not quite

15

20

25

30

1112*a*

5

know. And we think that those who have the best intentions and those
10 who form the best opinions are not the same,[13] but that some persons
form rather good opinions, and yet, because of their vice, choose not what
they should. Whether opinion precedes or follows intention makes no
difference; for what we are considering is not this but whether or not some
opinions are the same [in nature] as intentions.

What, then, or what kind of thing is intention,[14] if indeed it is none of the
things mentioned? It appears that the object of intention is voluntary, but
15 not all voluntary things are objects of intention.[15] Is it not something
which has already been deliberated upon? For intention [is formed] with
reason or *thought*, and the name [προαιρετόν] itself seems to suggest that
it is something chosen before other things.[16]

5

Do we deliberate about everything, and are all things objects of deliberation, or is deliberation impossible about some objects? Perhaps we should
20 call 'an object of deliberation' not that which a fool or a madman might
deliberate about, but that which a sane man would.[1]

Now no one deliberates (a) about eternal things, e.g., about the universe[2]
or the fact that the diagonal of a square is incommensurable with the side,
or (b) about moving things which occur always in the same way, whether
25 necessarily or by nature or through some other cause,[3] e.g., about the sol-
stices and the daily sunrise, or (c) about things which [fairly regularly] occur now in one way and now in another, e.g., about droughts and rains,[4]
or (d) about things occurring by luck, e.g., about the finding of a treasure.[5]
Nor do we deliberate about all human affairs, e.g., no Spartan deliberates
30 about how the Scythians would best govern themselves, for things such as
this cannot occur through us.

We deliberate, then, about things which can be done by us, and these are
the things which are left; for [moving] causes are thought to be nature,
necessity, luck, and also intellect and every other cause through man.
Now each man deliberates about the things which he can do by himself.
1112b And about sciences which are accurate and self-sufficient there is no
deliberation, e.g., about the writing of the letters of the alphabet (for we
do not hesitate as to how we should write them); but we do deliberate about
things which can occur through us though not always in the same manner,[6]

e.g., about things which can occur according to medical science or the
science of money-making, and about navigation more than about gym-   5
nastics, to the extent that navigation is less precise, and also about the
rest in a similar manner, and about the arts more than about the sciences
since we are more uncertain about the arts. Thus we deliberate about things
(a) which are possible or occur for the most part, (b) whose outcome is not
clear, and (c) in which there is something indeterminate; and we call in   10
advisers on matters of importance when we are not convinced that we are
adequately informed to make a good diagnosis.

Now we deliberate not about ends but about the means to ends. For
neither does a doctor deliberate whether he should make people healthy,
nor an orator whether he should persuade, nor a statesman whether he
should enact good laws and enforce them, nor anyone else about whatever the end may be, but positing an end, each of them considers how and   15
by what means that end can be brought about; and if it appears that the
end can be brought about by a number of means, he examines further which
of these is the easiest and best, but if by one means only, he examines how
the end can be achieved by this means, and this by what further means,
and so on, until he arrives at the first cause, which is the last element in
the order of discovery.[7] For the man who deliberates resembles the man   20
who inquires and analyzes, in the manner stated, as in the case of a geometrical diagram.

It appears, however, that not all inquiry is a process of deliberation,
e.g., mathematical inquiry is not a process of deliberation;[8] but every
process of deliberation is inquiry, and the last step in the analysis is the
first step in the coming to be of an end.[9] And if after a process of deliberation we arrive at something which is impossible, we give up our inquiry,   25
e.g., if money is required but this cannot be supplied; but if we arrive at
what appears possible, we undertake to *act*. By 'possible' we mean what
may be brought about by us; for what may be brought about by our
friends is in a way what may be brought about by us, since the [moving]
principle in this case is in us.[10] Sometimes what we seek may be instru-   30
ments, at other times the use of instruments; and similarly in the other
cases, it may be the means through which, or the manner in which, or the
agent through whom the end may be brought about.

As already stated, then, it seems that man is the [moving] principle of
actions; and deliberation is about things to be *acted* upon by the man who

deliberates, and those *actions* are for the sake of other things. The object
of deliberation, then, is not an end but the means to an end; nor is it an
1113a   existing particular, such as whether this is bread or whether it has been
baked as it should, for these are objects of sensation.[11] Finally, if one were
to be always deliberating, he would keep on doing so to infinity.[12]

The object of deliberation is [generically] the same as that of intention;[13]
but the object of intention is distinguished from the other objects of
deliberation by being judged, after deliberation, to be the one to *act* on.
5   For every one ceases to inquire how he shall *act* when he brings the
[moving] principle back to himself and to the ruling part of himself;[14] for
the object to be *acted* on is the object of his intention. This is clear also
from the ancient constitutions portrayed by Homer; for under them the
kings announced to the people the things they had deliberately chosen to do.
10   Since the object of intention is the object which is deliberately desired
and which is in our power to attain, intention too would be a deliberate
desire of things which are in our power to bring about;[15] for having decided
on an alternative after deliberation, we desire that alternative in accordance
with that deliberation.

Sketchily, then, let this be our statement concerning intention, both as to
the kind of things it is concerned with and the fact that these are means
relative to ends.

6

15   We have already stated that a wish is for an end; but for some thinkers[1] a
wish is thought to be for a good, while for others[2] it is thought to be for
an apparent good. Now those who say that the object of wish is a good
are faced with the consequence that the object wished by a man who does
not choose rightly is not an object of wish (for if it were an object of wish,
20   it would also be good, but, as stated, it turns out to be bad).[3] Again, those
who say that the object of wish is the apparent good are faced with the
consequence that there can be nothing which by its nature is an object of
wish but only what seems to each man to be good; and since things
appear different to different people, the objects of wish may also turn out
to be contrary.[4] If these consequences are not satisfactory, should we
then not say that the object of wish, taken without qualification and
according to truth, is the good, while to each person it is the apparent
25   good?[5] If so, then to a virtuous man the object of wish is the truly good,

while to a bad man it is any chance thing; and such is the case with human bodies, for if they are in a good physical condition, what is healthy for them is what is truly healthy, but if they are sickly, different things are healthy for them, and similarly for what is bitter or sweet or hot or heavy, and so on. For a virtuous man judges things rightly, and in each case what appears to him to be the case is what is truly the case; for there are noble and pleasant things which are proper to each disposition, and perhaps a virtuous man differs from others most by perceiving the truth in each case, being like a standard or a measure of them. For the majority of people, on the other hand, deception seems to arise because of pleasure;[6] for pleasure appears to be a good but is not. Accordingly, they choose what is pleasant[6] as being good and avoid pain as being bad.[7]

30

1113b

7

Since the object of wish is an end while the objects of deliberation and of intention are the means to an end, *actions* concerning the means would be in accordance with intention and voluntary. But the activities of virtues are concerned with these. So virtue, too, is in our power, and also vice for a similar reason. For where it is in our power to *act*, it is also in our power not to *act*, and where it is in our power not to *act*, it is also in our power to *act*; so if to *act*, when it is noble, is in our power, then also not to *act*, which would then be disgraceful, would be in our power, and if not to *act*, when it is noble, is in our power, then also to *act*, which would then be disgraceful, would be in our power. If it is in our power, then, to do what is noble or disgraceful, and likewise not to do what is noble or disgraceful, and to *act* or not to *act* nobly or disgracefully, as stated earlier[1], is to be good or bad, then it is in our power to be *good* or bad men. The saying "No one is willingly wicked nor unwillingly blessed"[2] seems to be partly false and partly true. For none is unwillingly blessed, but evil is voluntary; or else, we should dispute the statements[3] just made and say that a man is not the [moving] principle or originator of his *actions* as he is of his children.[4] But if those statements are evident and we have no [moving] principles, other than those which exist in us, to which to refer our *actions*, then *actions* whose [moving] principles exist in us are also in our power to perform and are voluntary.

These statements seem to be confirmed by individuals in private life as

5

10

15

20

well as by legislators; for they punish or take vengeance on those who commit evil *acts* (unless these are done by force or through ignorance
25   caused not by the doers themselves), but honor those who perform noble *actions*, and they do this in order to exhort the latter but deter the former. But no one exhorts us to do whatever is neither in our power nor voluntary, as it would be useless for one to try to persuade us, for example, not to be feverish or pained or hungry or affected in any other such manner,
30   for we will be affected by these none the less. Even a man who is responsible for his ignorance is punished, if he is thought to be the cause of his ignorance, as in the case of a drunkard on whom a double penalty is imposed;[5] for the [moving] principle exists in him, since he has the power of avoiding drunkenness, which is the cause of his ignorance while drunk. Men are punished also for being ignorant of certain legal matters which
1114a   are not difficult to learn and should be known; and likewise whenever they are thought to be ignorant through negligence since it is up to them not to be ignorant, for they have the power of exercizing care. But perhaps they are of such a kind as not to exercise care. Still it is they themselves who,
5   by living without restraint, are responsible for having become men of such a kind, e.g., unjust or intemperate, whether by being malevolent or by spending their time in drinking bouts and the like; for it is particular activities [of a certain sort] which produce men of a certain kind. This is clear in the case of those who train themselves for any contest or *action*;
10   for they are constantly active. So to be ignorant of the fact that habits are acquired by the corresponding activities is the mark of an utterly insensible man.

Moreover, it is unreasonable to think that he who *acts* unjustly does not wish to be unjust or that he who lives intemperately does not wish to be intemperate. So if a man without being ignorant does things from which he will become unjust, he will be voluntarily unjust; but by mere wishing
15   he will not stop being unjust and become just, for neither will a sick man become healthy by merely wishing to become healthy. And if it happens that he became sick in this manner [i.e., not unknowingly], by leading a life of incontinence and disobeying his doctors, then he is voluntarily sick. Earlier it was certainly up to him not to become sick, but now when his condition is far gone it is no longer up to him; and this is like a man who cannot recall a stone he has already thrown off, though it was in his power earlier not to have let it fall or to have thrown

it because the moving principle existed in him. Likewise, in the case
of an unjust and an intemperate man, it was up to them at first not   20
to become such, and so they are voluntarily such; but having become
such, it is no longer up to them not to be such now.[6]

Not only are the vices of the soul voluntary, but for some men, whom
we censure, those of the body also; for no one censures those who are
ugly because of their nature, but we do censure those who are ugly because of lack of exercise or because of negligence. So too in the case of   25
physical weakness or injury; for one would never reproach a man who is
blind from birth or by disease or from a blow, but he would rather pity
him; but everyone would censure a man for being blind from habitual
drunkenness or from some other kind of intemperance. Of the bodily
defects, then, those which are in our power to induce are censured, but
those which are not in our power to induce are not censured. If so, then the   30
other vices [i.e., of the soul] which are censured are in our power to form also.

One might say that all men aim at the apparent good but cannot control
what appears to them to be good, and that the end appears to each man to   1114b
be of such a kind as to correspond to the kind of man he is. Now if each
man is in some way the [moving] cause of his own habit, he is also in some
way the cause of what appears to him. But if not, then no one is the cause
of his doing what is bad but each man does these through ignorance of the
end, thinking that by doing them he will attain the highest good for him-   5
self, and the aiming at an end is not self-chosen but one must be born with
a power, as he is with vision, by which he will judge well and will choose
what is truly good; and so a man is gifted if he is from birth well endowed
with this power, for that which is greatest is also noblest, and that which
can neither be received nor learned from another but is disposed to func-   10
tion in the manner which corresponds to its quality from birth, if it be well
and nobly endowed, will be by nature a perfect and true gift.

If these remarks are true, then, why should virtue rather than vice be
voluntary?[7] For, to both good and bad men alike, the end will be apparent
and fixed by nature or in whatever way it may be, and it is by reference to   15
this end that they will do all the rest, whatever their *actions* be. So whether
it is not by its nature that the end appears to each man such as it does but
depends on him somewhat, or whether the end is natural but virtue is
voluntary by the fact that a good man does all else voluntarily, vice too
would nonetheless be voluntary; for in the case of a bad man, too, his   20

actions will likewise be caused by him even if the end is not. If, then, as it is said, the virtues are voluntary (for we ourselves are somehow partly responsible for our habits,[8] and it is by being persons of a certain kind that we posit the end as being of a certain kind), the vices too will be voluntary for a similar reason.

25

8

We have now discussed in general the genus of virtues sketchily, stating that they are moderations, that they are habits, how they are formed, that they are disposed by their nature to *actions* by which they are formed, that they are caused by us and are voluntary, and that they are done in a manner as directed by right reason. *Actions* and habits, however, are not voluntary in a similar way. For in the case of *actions* we are masters from the beginning till the end, since we know the particulars in them; in the case of habits, on the other hand, we are masters of and know only the beginning, but what is added at each step is not known, as in the case of a bad state of health, yet the fact that it was up to us to *act* or not to *act* in a certain manner from the start is the *reason* why habits are voluntary[1].

30

1115*a*

9

Let us now take up each of the virtues and discuss what it is, what kinds of things it is concerned with, and how it is concerned with them. At the same time it will be also clear how many virtues there are.

We will begin with bravery. It was already stated earlier[1] that it is a mean with regard to fear and courage, and it is clear that the things which we fear are the fearful[2] and that these are, speaking without qualification, bad. It is in view of this that people even define fear as the anticipation of something bad. Now we fear all bad things, e.g., a bad reputation, poverty, disease, friendlessness, death, etc., but a brave man is not thought to be concerned with all of them. For there are some things which one should fear, and it is noble to do so, while not to fear them is disgraceful, e.g., a bad reputation; for he who fears this is a *good* man and has a sense of shame, while he who does not is shameless. And it is only metaphorically that a shameless person is called 'brave' by some men, since he has something which is similar to a brave man; for a brave man is fearless also. Perhaps a man should not fear poverty or disease or whatever arises not

5

10

15

from vice or is caused not by himself. Still a brave man is not a man who is fearless of these things, and he who is fearless in this way is called 'brave' in virtue of a similarity; for some men who are cowards in the dangers of war are generous and behave courageously when faced with loss of property. Nor is a man a coward if he fears insult to his wife or children, or if he fears envy or something of this sort; nor is he brave if he shows courage when he is about to be flogged.

With what kind of fearful things, then, is a brave man concerned? Is it not with the greatest? For no one else can endure terrible things more than such a man. Now the most fearful thing is death; for it is the end of one's life, and for the dead nothing is thought to be either good or bad. But it would seem that a brave man is not concerned with death on all occasions, e.g., not with death at sea or by disease. On what occasions, then? The noblest indeed; and such are those in war, for the perils here are the greatest and noblest.[3] The honors bestowed by states and monarchs to those who die in war, too, are in accord with this. So a man would be called 'brave', in the main sense of the term, if he is fearless in facing a noble death or in facing emergencies in which death is close at hand; and occasions in war are such emergencies in the highest sense. Now a brave man will be fearless also at sea and in disease, but not in the same way as seamen, for he has given up hope of safety and is distressed by a death such as this, while they are hopeful because of their experience; and, we may add, brave men behave in a manly fashion where there is room for prowess and where death is noble, but none of these belong to deaths such as those at sea.

20

25

30

35

1115b

5

10

What is fearful is not the same for all men, but we speak also of some fearful things which are beyond the endurance of man. These, then, are fearful to every sane man, while things which are not beyond the endurance of man differ in magnitude and in degree, and so do those which inspire courage. Now a brave man is undaunted as a man may be. So he will fear even such terrible things,[1] but as he should and as reason allows, for the sake of what is noble; for this is the end of virtue. It is possible, however, to fear these more than one should or less than one should, and also to fear things which are not fearful as if they were fearful. Thus one may err in fearing what he should not, or not in the manner he should, or not when

10

15

he should, and so on; and similarly with respect to things which inspire courage. So he who faces and fears those fearful things which he should, and for the right cause and in the right manner and at the right time, and who shows courage in a similar manner, is a brave man; for a brave man feels and *acts* according to the merits of the case and as reason would 20 dictate. Now the end of every activity is in conformity with the corresponding habit,[2] and bravery to a brave man is noble; and such indeed is the corresponding end, for each habit is defined by its end.[3] It is for the sake of what is noble, then, that a brave man endures and performs *actions* in accordance with bravery.

25   Of those who are in excess, he who exceeds in not fearing has no name (we have stated earlier [4] that many habits have no names), but he would be a sort of madman or insensible to pain if he feared nothing, neither earthquakes nor storms at sea, as it is said of the Celts;[5] but he who exceeds in courage in the face of fearful things is called 'rash'. A rash man is 30 thought to be also boastful and a pretender to bravery. Thus as a brave man is disposed to fearful things, so a rash man wishes to appear to be so disposed, and so the latter imitates the former in situations in which it is possible to do so; and in view of this, many such rash men are boasting cowards, for they display rashness in such situations but do not stand their ground against what is really fearful.

A man who exceeds in fear, on the other hand, is called a 'coward'; for 35 he fears the things he should not, and in the manner he should not, and all 1116a other such qualifications belong to him. And he is also deficient in courage; but he is more conspicuous for his excessive fear of painful situations than in deficiency of courage. Thus a coward is a despairing sort of man, for he is afraid of everything; but the contrary is the case with a brave man, for courage is a mark of a hopeful man. A coward, a rash man, and a brave 5 man, then, are all concerned with the same things,[6] but they are differently disposed towards them; for the first two exceed and are deficient, while the third is moderately and rightly disposed; and rash men are precipitate and eager before danger arrives but withdraw when it arrives, while brave men are ardent when facing danger but calm before danger arrives.

11

10 As we have said,[1] then, bravery is a mean with regard to things which in-

spire courage or are fearful in the situations we have stated; and it chooses and faces danger, as indicated, since it is noble to do so or disgraceful not to do so. But to die in order to avoid poverty or [the pain of rejected] love or anything which is painful is a mark not of a brave man but rather of a coward; for it is softness to avoid painful effort, and a coward faces death   15 not as something which is noble but in order to avoid what is bad.

Bravery, then, is something of this sort, but the term 'bravery' is applied to other habits also, and in five different ways.

(a) There is political bravery, which resembles bravery as defined most; for citizens seem to face dangers in order to avoid legal penalties and reproaches and for the sake of honor. And it is because of this that the   20 bravest people are thought to be those among whom cowards are regarded as worthy of dishonor but brave men as worthy or honor.[2] Homer, too, considers brave men to be such, like Diomedes and Hector. Thus Hector says,

Polydamas first will lay reproach on me,[3]

and Diomedes,

Hector shall one day say to all Trojans   25
"Tydeides was afraid, and fled from me."[4]

It is this kind of bravery which most resembles the one described earlier, since it functions because of virtue; for it functions because of a sense of shame or because of the desire of what is noble (i.e., of honor) and the avoidance of reproach, which is disgraceful. Among brave men of this kind one might include also those who are forced by their rulers to *act*   30 like this; but these are inferior, to the extent that they do so not because of a sense of shame but because of fear, avoiding not what is disgraceful but what is painful.[5] For rulers use force as Hector did, who said,

And if I find a man who shrinks from battle,
No hope is left him to escape the dogs.[6]   35

And commanders do the same when they station their troops but beat those who retreat, or when they draw them up with trenches or such   1116*b* things behind them; for in all these cases force is used. But one should be brave not because of necessity, but in view of the fact that it is noble to be brave.

(b) Experience with regard to particulars, too, is thought to be bravery
of a sort; and it is in view of this that Socrates considered bravery to
be a species of *knowledge*.[7] Such men differ by having experience in
different fields, and professional soldiers are such men in matters of war;
for in war there are many alarms which are false and which have been
seen through by these soldiers most of all. So these soldiers appear to be
brave, while others do not know the nature of those alarms. Moreover,
from their experience these soldiers are most effective in attack and in
defense, as they are able to use arms most ably and possess such as are the
best both for attack and for defense. So they fight like armed men against
unarmed men, or like trained athletes against untrained men; for in such
contests, too, it is not the bravest that fight best but those who are strongest and whose bodies are in the best condition. But when danger becomes
excessive and they are inferior in numbers and in equipment, professional
soldiers turn cowards, for they are the first to run away, while citizen
forces die at their posts; and this is what happened at the temple of
Hermes.[8] For flight from battle to the citizens was disgraceful and they
chose death instead of such safety, while the professional soldiers at first
faced danger since they believed that they were stronger, but when they
discovered their inferiority in numbers and equipment, they took to
flight in fear of death more than of disgrace; but brave men [in the main
sense] are not of such a nature.

(c) Spirit, too, is taken for bravery, for spirited men are also thought to
be brave and to face danger like wild beasts rushing at those who wounded
them; and, of course, it is a fact that brave men are spirited. For spirit (or
temper) above all things disposes one to rush against danger, whence come
Homer's remarks: "He put strength into his spirit"[9] and "He roused their
might and spirit"[10] and "Fierce might breathed through his nostrils",[11]
and also "His blood boiled;"[12] for all such expressions seem to indicate
the rousing and onset of spirit.

Now brave men *act* for the sake of what is noble, and their spirit only
helps them along; but wild beasts act because of pain, for they attack
because they have been struck or are afraid, since if they are in a forest
or a marsh they do not approach us. So when beasts, driven by pain and
temper, rush upon danger without foresight of peril, they are not brave
because of this; for if they were, hungry asses would be brave also, for
blows do not drive them away from food,[13] and so would adulterers,

who do many daring deeds because of their *desire*. Now the most natural [courage] seems to be that which comes through spirit, and it is when 5 right intention and right purpose are added to it that it becomes bravery. And so men, too, are pained when they are angry and are pleased when they take revenge; but if these are the *reasons* for which they fight, they are good fighters but not brave men, for they fight not for the sake of what is noble nor as reason dictates but because of their feelings, although they resemble the brave somewhat.

(d) Men who are hopeful, too, are not brave, for they show courage in 10 the face of danger because they were victorious often and against many enemies; and they resemble brave men because both show courage. But brave men are courageous because of the *reasons* stated,[14] while hopeful men are courageous because they think they are stronger and will not suffer anything. (Drunkards, we may add, behave in such a manner also; for they become hopeful when intoxicated). And when situations do not 15 turn out to be as expected, such men turn to flight. But it is the mark of a brave man, as already stated, to face things which are fearful to man, be they real or apparent, because it is noble to do so and disgraceful not to do so. And it is in view of this that it seems to be the mark of a braver man to be unafraid and unperturbed in alarms which are sudden rather than foreknown, for his lack of fear and his coolness result more from habit 20 than from thought, or they do so less from preparation; for one might also deliberately choose things that are foreseen by judgment or by reason, while it is by habit that one *acts* bravely when he faces sudden danger.

(e) Men who are ignorant of danger, too, appear to be brave and are not far removed from hopeful men, but they are inferior to these insofar as they have no worthy cause at all, while the latter do. Hence the latter hold their ground for a while, but those who have been deceived turn to flight 25 when they learn or suspect that the facts are contrary to what they thought; and this is what happened to the Argives when they fell in with the Spartans but took them to be Sicyonians.[15]

We have discussed, then, what kind of men are the brave and also those who only seem to be brave.

12

Though bravery is concerned with both courage and fear, it is not concerned with them alike but more with the fearful; for he who is unperturbed by 30 fearful things and rightly disposed towards them is more brave than he who is concerned with things which inspire courage. Thus it is by facing what is painful, as stated before, that men are called 'brave'. Hence bravery tends to be also painful, and it is justly praised; for it is more difficult

35   to endure what is painful than to abstain from what is pleasant.

1117b   It would seem, however, that although the end[1] according to bravery is pleasant, it is done away with by the things [pains, etc.] that go with it, as happens also in athletic contests; for the end at which boxers aim is pleasant, this being the purpose, i.e., the crown and the honors, but the

5   blows, if indeed taken on the flesh, are painful and distressing, and so is every physical exertion, and because these are numerous, the purpose, being small, appears to have nothing pleasant in it. So if such is the case with bravery also, death and wounds will be painful to a brave man or to a man who does not want them; but he faces them, since it is noble to do so

10   or disgraceful not to do so. And the more he has virtue in its entirety and the happier he is, the more he will be pained at the prospect of death; for to such a man life is most worthy and he is knowingly depriving himself of the greatest goods, and this is painful. Yet he is not less brave, but perhaps even more so, since he chooses what is noble in war [i.e., brave

15   action] instead of those goods.

Not every activity according to virtue, then, is pleasant, except insofar as it attains its end.[2] And perhaps the best soldiers may be not men who are such, [i.e., those having virtue in its entirety] but those who are less brave but have no other goodness [i.e., virtue]; for these are ready to face danger

20   and would risk their lives for a small profit.[3]

Let so much, then, be said concerning bravery, and from this discussion it is not difficult to grasp its nature sketchily.

13

Next we shall discuss temperance; for these [bravery and temperance] are thought to be virtues of the nonrational parts of the soul.[1] We have al-

25   ready stated that temperance is a mean with regard to pleasures, for it is less concerned with pains and not in the same way; and intemperance, too, appears to be concerned with the same things. So let us specify the kinds of pleasures with which temperance and intemperance are concerned.

Let the bodily pleasures be distinguished from those which are mental,

e.g., from ambition or love of learning, for when the lover of each of these   30
is pleased with that which he is disposed to love, it is not the body that
is affected but rather *thought*; and those who are concerned with such
pleasures are called neither 'temperate' nor 'intemperate'. Similarly, those
concerned with the other pleasures which are not bodily are not called
'temperate' or 'intemperate'; for those who love to tell tales and stories
and waste their days talking about trivial matters are called not 'intemper-   35
ate' but 'garrulous', nor are those who are pained over money or friends   1118*a*
called 'temperate' or 'intemperate'.

Temperance, then, would be concerned with bodily pleasures, but not
with all of them; for those who enjoy sensing objects by vision, e.g., colors
and shapes and paintings, are not called 'temperate' or 'intemperate',
although in these, too, there might seem to be such things as being pleased
as one should, or in excess, or deficiently. So too with the objects of hear-   5
ing; for no one calls 'intemperate' those who enjoy music or acting
excessively, nor does he call 'temperate' those who enjoy them as they
should. Nor again with regard to odors do we use the term 'temperate'
or 'intemperate', except in an indirect manner; for we call 'intemperate'   10
not those who enjoy odors of apples or of roses or of incense excessively,
but rather those who thus enjoy odors of perfumes or of dainty dishes,
since those who enjoy these are reminded of the objects of their *desire*.[2]
One might observe this also in others[3] who, when hungry, enjoy the smell   15
of food; so to enjoy excessively such things is a mark of an intemperate
man, for it is he who so *desires* them. In other animals, too, there is no
pleasure with respect to these sensations, except in an indirect manner.
For dogs enjoy not the odor of a hare's flesh but eating that flesh; but
what brought this about is the odor. And a lion enjoys not the lowing of   20
an ox but eating the ox, but it appears to enjoy the lowing because through
it it senses the nearness of the ox; and similarly it enjoys not seeing or
finding a stag or a wild goat but the anticipation of eating it.

Temperance and intemperance, then, are concerned with such pleasures
as the other animals share also, and it is from this fact that those pleasures   25
appear to be slavish and brutal; and those pleasures are of touch and of
taste. Even of taste, however, men appear to make little or no use; for
what we judge by taste are flavors, and this is done by those who test wine
and season dishes, but it is hardly in this that people, or at least the intemperate, derive enjoyment but in the indulgence which in all cases comes   30

through touch, whether in food or drink or sexual relations. And it is in view of this that a certain gourmand[4] prayed that his throat grow longer than that of a crane, thinking that by extended contact he would be pleased. So it is with respect to that sense which is most common to animals that intemperance arises; and it would seem that intemperance is justly reproached, as it belongs to us not as men but as animals. So to enjoy such things and to love them most of all would seem brutal. For even the most liberal of the pleasures by touch, such as those produced by rubbing and heating in gymnasiums, have been eliminated [by some authorities]; for the touch to which an intemperate man yields is not of all but only of some of the parts of the body.

Of *desires*, some are thought to be common to all men, others are peculiar to individuals and are acquired. For example, the *desire* for nourishment is natural, for everyone who is in need *desires* food or drink' and sometimes both, and also a woman's love, if he is young and in his prime, as Homer says.[5] But not everyone *desires* this kind or that kind of food or drink or woman, nor do all *desire* the same things; and it is in view of this that *desire* appears to be an individual peculiarity. Yet there is something natural about all this; for [though] different things are pleasant to different people, still there are certain things which are more pleasant to all than other things are.

Now of natural *desires* only few are in error, and in one direction only, that of excess; for to eat or drink any chance thing till one is surfeited is to exceed the natural amount, since natural *desire* should only replenish what is needed. Hence these men are called 'gluttons', since they fill their belly beyond its need.[6] Those who become such men are very slavish. As to pleasures which are peculiar to individuals, many people err and do so in many ways. For while those who are called 'fond of such-and-such' err by enjoying the things that they should not, or doing so more than most people do, or not as they should, intemperate men exceed in all respects; for they enjoy some things that they should not – for such things are hateful – and they enjoy things more than they should, and they enjoy things more than ordinary people do.

Clearly, then, excess with regard to pleasures is intemperance and is blameworthy; but with regard to pains a man is not, as in the case of bravery, called 'temperate' by facing them and 'intemperate' by not facing them, but he is called 'intemperate' by being more pained than he should when he does not get pleasurable things (and it is [the absence of] pleasure which causes him to be pained) and 'temperate' by not being pained when pleasurable things are absent or when he abstains from getting them.

14

The intemperate man, then, *desires* all pleasurable things or the most plea-   1119*a*
surable, and he is led by his *desire* to choose these instead of others;
hence he is pained when he fails to get them and *desires* them (for *desire* is
accompanied by pain, though it seems absurd to be pained because of   5
pleasure).[1]

Men who are deficient with regard to pleasures and enjoy them less than
they should scarcely exist, for such insensibility is not human; for even
the other animals distinguish kinds of food, enjoying some but not others,
so if there be someone who finds nothing pleasurable and no difference
between one kind of food and another kind, he would be far from being a   10
man.[2] Such a man has no name because he scarcely exists.

A temperate man is moderately disposed with regard to pleasures and
pains. For he is neither pleased by the things which please the intemperate
most – but is rather displeased by them – nor pleased at all by those he
should not; nor is he pleased to excess with such [i.e., by those he should
be pleased], nor pained at or *desirous* of these when they are absent – or
else he is moderately pained or *desirous* of them – nor is he pleased more   15
than he should, or when he should not, or etc. And as for the pleasurable
things which are suitable to health or to good physical condition, he will
desire them moderately and as he should, and likewise for other pleasurable things which do not impede health or good physical condition or are
not contrary to what is noble or are not beyond his means. For he who is
not disposed in this manner loves such pleasures more than they are worth,   20
while the temperate man is not of this sort but loves such pleasures as
right reason dictates.

15

Intemperance seems to be more voluntary than cowardice is. For the
former arises because of pleasure while the latter because of pain, and we
are disposed to choose pleasure but to avoid pain. And pain tends to upset
or destroy the nature of the subject which has pain, whereas pleasure does

25 no such thing but is rather voluntary; hence intemperance is more subject to reproach than cowardice. For it is easier to be habituated to pleasurable things as there are many such in life, and no danger arises by becoming habituated to them, whereas with fearful things the reverse is the case.[1] Cowardice would seem to·be voluntary not like the particular [*acts* in which it is shown], for cowardice itself is painless, but because of pain we

30 are so upset by these *acts* that we throw away our arms and commit other unseemly *acts*;[2] and in view of this, they are even thought to be done under compulsion.[3] For the intemperate man, on the other hand, particular *acts* are voluntary, for he *desires* them and wishes them, but the whole is less voluntary, for no one *desires* to be intemperate.[4]

We apply the name 'intemperance' to errors committed by children as

1119*b* well as to those committed by adults, for there is some resemblance in the two cases.[5] Which is named after which, however, makes no difference in this discussion (but clearly what came later is named after what came earlier). But the transference of the name does not seem to be bad; for that which desires disgraceful things and is increasing in desire should be pun-

5 ished, and such is *desire* or a child most of all, since children too live according to *desire* and their desire for pleasure exists in these [disgraceful things] most of all. So if their *desire* is not obedient and under the ruling principle [i.e., right reason], it will go too far; for in a senseless individual the desire for pleasure is insatiable and is sought from all sources, and the

10 exercise of *desire* increases what is natural to it, and if *desires* are great and strong, they even drive out judgement. Hence *desires* should be moderate and few and should not go contrary to [right] reason; and we call such a part of the soul [i.e., such *desire*] obedient and tempered, for just as a child should live according to the direction of his tutor, so the *desiring* part of

15 the soul should *act* according to reason. Thus the *desiring* part of the soul should be in harmony with reason; for the aim of both is something noble, and a temperate man *desires* the things he should and as he should and when he should [etc.], and this is the manner in which reason directs also.

Let this be our account concerning temperance.

BOOK Δ

1

Next we shall discuss generosity, which is thought to be a mean with regard to property; for a generous man is praised not for his *actions* in war, nor for those of a temperate man, nor yet for his judgments,[1] but for his actions with regard to giving and taking[2] property, and more so with regard to giving. By 'property' we mean all substances whose worth is measured by money.[3] Wastefulness and stinginess, too, are concerned with property, and the former is an excess but the latter a deficiency; and while we attribute stinginess always to those who care for property more than they should, we sometimes apply the term 'wastefulness' to a combination of vices, for we call 'wasteful' also the incontinent and those who spend money for their intemperance. Thus the latter are also thought to be the worst, for they have many vices at the same time. But the term 'wasteful' is not properly applied to them, for it is intended to be limited to a man who has only one vice, that of wasting his substance;[4] for a wasteful man causes his own ruin, and the wasting of his substance too is thought to be a sort of ruining himself, as if life were maintained through one's substance. It is in this limited sense, then, that we shall accept the term 'wastefulness'.

Things which are objects of need may be used well or badly, and wealth is such a useful object; and every object is used best by the man who has the virtue for the use of it, so wealth will be used best by the man who has the virtue for the use of property.[5] This is the generous man. Now the use of property is thought to be spending it or giving it away, and taking or preserving it is thought to be rather the possession of it. Hence it belongs to the generous man to give to whom he should rather than (a) to take from the sources he should or (b) not to take from the sources he should not, for to virtue belongs treating others well rather than being treated well[6] and *acting* nobly rather than not *acting* disgracefully; and it is clear that in giving as a man should he treats others well or does what is noble,

15   but in taking as he should he is treated well or does not *act* disgracefully. Gratitude too is shown to the giver and not to the receiver, and praise is bestowed to the giver more than to the receiver. Also, it is easier not to take than to give, for men should rather not give away what is theirs than not receive even more of what belongs to others.[7] Again, it is those who

20   give who are called 'generous'; but those who do not take are not praised for generosity (though they are not less praised for their justice), and those who take are not praised at all. Finally, of virtuous men the generous are almost the best liked; for they benefit others, and they do this by giving.

2

25   Now *actions* according to virtue are noble and are done for the sake of what is noble. Accordingly, a generous man too will give for the sake of what is noble and will do so rightly, for he will give to the right persons the right amounts at the right times (and to this may be added the other ·qualifications which accompany right giving); and he will do these with pleasure or without pain, for an *action* according to virtue is pleasant or painless, or else the least painful of all.[1] But he who gives to those he should not, or gives not for the sake of what is noble but for some other *reason*,[2] is not generous but may be given another name. Nor is he

30   generous if he gives painfully; for such a man would rather choose property than a noble *action*, and this is not a mark of a generous man. Nor will a generous man take from the wrong sources, for such taking is not a mark of a man who places no high value on property. Nor will a generous man be disposed to ask for money or property; for it is not a mark of a man who does good to others to receive beneficence readily. But he will take

1120b   from the right sources, e.g., from his own possessions, not as if this were something noble but as something necessary, so that he may have something to give to others. Nor will he neglect his own possessions, since it is by means of these that he wishes to supply the needs of others. Nor will he give to any chance person, so that he may have something to give to the right persons and at the right time and for a noble cause. It is also a

5   high mark of a generous man to exceed in giving, so as to leave less for himself; for it is a mark of a generous man not to attend to what is useful to himself.

Generosity is attributed to a man by taking into account the extent of his substance; for generosity depends not on the quantity of what is given but on the habit of the giver, and, in giving, this habit takes into account the extent of the substance available. Accordingly, nothing prevents a   10 man who gives less from being more generous, if he has less to give. Those who have inherited their substance are thought to be more generous than those who have earned it themselves, for they have not experienced the need of it, and all men love their own works more than those of others, like parents and poets. It is not easy for a generous man to be wealthy,   15 since he is disposed neither to receive nor to save but to give his property away and to value it not for its own sake but for the sake of giving it to others. Hence comes the charge brought against fortune, that those who are most worthy are least wealthy. But this happens not without reason; for, as with other things, one cannot possess [much] property when he makes no effort to do so. But a generous man will not give to the wrong   20 persons, or at the wrong time, and so on with other such qualifications; for otherwise he would not be *acting* in accordance with generosity, and by using up his property on those occasions he would have nothing left to use for what is right. For, as already stated, a generous man is one who spends according to the extent of his substance and for what is right to do so; but he who spends in excess is wasteful. Hence we do not call tyrants   25 'wasteful', for it is thought that their gifts and expenses cannot easily exceed the quantity of their possessions.[3]

Since generosity is a mean with regard to giving and taking property, the generous man will both donate and spend the right amounts and for the sake of what is right, alike in small and in great matters, and he will do   30 these with pleasure; and he will take from the right sources and the right amounts. For since this virtue is a mean with respect to both giving and taking, he will do both of these in the right way; for *good* taking follows *good* giving, but a taking or giving which is not *good* is contrary. Accordingly, the giving and taking which follow each other are present in the same person, but the contraries of these clearly are not.[4] But if a generous   1121a man happens to use up property in a way contrary to what is right or what is noble,[5] he will be pained, but moderately and as he should; for it is a mark of a man of virtue to be pleased or pained by the things he should and in the manner he should.

Again, the generous man is easy to deal with in matters of property, for he may be treated unjustly, at least since he does not value property   5

[much]. And he is more oppressed for not having used up money when he should have done so than pained for having used it up when he should not have done so; and he is not content with the saying of Simonides.[6]

3

The wasteful man, on the other hand, errs in these respects also; for he is neither pleased nor pained by what he should or in the manner he should, and this will become more evident as we proceed. Now we have stated that wastefulness and stinginess are excess and deficiency, and in two things, in giving and in taking;[1] for we posit spending too as coming under giving. Thus wastefulness exceeds in giving and in not taking but is deficient in taking, while stinginess is deficient in giving but exceeds in taking, except in small matters. Accordingly, the attributes of wastefulness [i.e., giving and not taking] hardly go together, for it is not easy to give to all without taking from any source; for a private individual[2] soon exhausts his substance by always giving, and it is just this individual who is regarded as being wasteful, inasmuch as it is such a man who is regarded as being to no small degree better than a stingy man.[3] For such a man may easily be cured both by age[4] and by lack of resources and may move towards the intermediate state, since he has something which belongs to a generous man, i.e., he both gives and does not take, though he does these neither as he should nor well. So if he were to get the habit of giving and taking as he should or somehow change in some other way, he might become generous; for he would then give only to those he should and would not take from the wrong sources.

It is in view of this that a wasteful man is not considered as being bad in character, for excess in giving and in not taking is a mark not of an evil or a lowly man, but of a foolish one. Such a wasteful man is thought to be much better than a stingy man, both for the *reasons* stated and also by the fact that the former benefits many while the latter benefits none, not even himself. But most wasteful men, as already stated, also take from the wrong sources and are stingy[5] by so doing. They become disposed to take because they wish to use up property but are unable to do so readily, for what is available is soon exhausted; and so they force themselves to get it from outside sources. At the same time, because they care nothing about what is noble, they take recklessly and from all sources; for they *desire* to

give, but it makes no difference to them how or from what sources they do
it. Hence their gifts are not really generous, for they are neither noble, nor
for the sake of what is noble, nor given in the right manner; but sometimes   5
such men enrich those who should be poor and give nothing to men of
virtuous character but much to those who flatter or give them pleasure in
some other way. Hence many of them are also intemperate; for they use
up their property by squandering it readily and intemperately and sink
into a life of [sensuous] pleasure because they do not live with a view to   10
what is noble. A wasteful man, then, turns to these things if left without
guidance, but with diligence he might arrive at the mean and the right
habit.[6]

Stinginess, on the other hand, is incurable, for old age and every sort of
weakness are thought to make men stingy. And it is more innate in men
than wastefulness, for most men love acquiring property more than giv-   15
ing it away. And it is widespread and of many kinds, for it seems
that there are many ways in which it is exhibited.[7] For since it consists of
two things, deficiency of giving as well as excess of taking, it does not come
to all men as a whole but sometimes in parts; and some men exceed in   20
taking [only] while others show deficiency in giving [only].

Those who are called by such names as 'misers', 'close', and 'niggards'
are all deficient in giving but neither aim at taking nor wish to take what
belongs to others, and for some of them this is because of some sort of
goodness[8] and in order to avoid what is disgraceful. For some of them   25
are thought to *act* thus, or at least they say that they do so, in order to
guard against being compelled to do something disgraceful; and among
these may be included also cheeseparers and all other such, who are so
named from their excess in not giving to anybody. Others again avoid
taking from others because they fear that it is not easy to take from others   30
without giving in return; and so they are content neither to take nor to give.

Again, some exceed with respect to taking by taking anything and from
any source, like those engaged in degraded occupations, e.g., pimps and the
like and money-lenders who lend money for a short time and at high rates.
For all these take from wrong sources and more than they should. What   1122a
is common to these appears to be disgraceful gain, for all of them put up
with a bad name for the sake of gain, even a small one; for we call those
who take property of high value which they should not or from wrong
sources, like tyrants who sack cities and strip temples, not 'stingy' but   5

rather 'wicked' or 'impious' or 'unjust'. Dice-players and also robbers and bandits, on the other hand, are stingy, since they make gain by disgraceful means; for it is for the sake of gain that both[9] busy themselves and put up with a bad name; and the latter face the greatest dangers for the sake of unjust gain, while the former make gain from their friends to whom they should be giving. So both make gain by disgraceful means, since they wish to gain from wrong sources, and all such acquisitions are due to stinginess.

There is good reason in saying that it is stinginess which is the contrary of generosity, for it is a greater vice than wastefulness, and men err more by it than by the wastefulness we described.[10]

So much, then, concerning generosity and the opposed vices.

4

Next, it would seem that we should discuss also munificence, for this too is thought to be a virtue concerned with property. Unlike generosity, however, it does not extend to all *actions* involving property but only to those requiring large expenditure, and in these it exceeds generosity in magnitude; for as the name itself suggests, munificence (μεγαλοπρέπεια)[1] is great expenditure which befits a great occasion. Now that which is great is relative to the occasion; for he who equips a trireme does not spend the same amount as he who heads a sacred legation.[2] What is fitting, then, is relative to the position of a man and to the circumstances and to the objects. The man who is called 'munificent' is not he who spends on matters of small or moderate value, as in the poet's saying "oft to a wanderer gave I,"[3] but he who spends what befits occasions requiring great expenditure; for a munificent man is generous, but a generous man is not necessarily munificent. The deficiency corresponding to such a habit is called 'meanness', while the excess is called 'conspicuous consumption' or 'extravagance' or the like, and these excesses in magnitude are not for the right occasion but are ostentatious expenses for wrong occasions and are displayed in the wrong manner. But we shall speak of these later.[4]

The munificent man is like a scientist;[5] for he has the power of perceiving what is fitting and of spending large sums with good taste. For, as we said at the beginning, a habit is defined in terms of the corresponding activity and of its objects.[6] The expenditure of a munificent man, then, is

great and fitting to the occasion; so the work or function too is of this kind, for it is in this way that the expenditure will be great and fitting to the work or function. Consequently, the work or function should be worthy   5
of the expenditure and the expenditure should be worthy of the work or function, or even exceed it. Now the munificent man will incur such expenditure for the sake of what is noble, for to do so is common to the virtues; and further, he will do so with pleasure and profusely, for over-accuracy in such matters is a mark of meanness. And he will consider how the work can be made most beautiful and most becoming rather than what the expense will be or how cheaply it can be made. So a munificent man   10
will of necessity be also generous, for a generous man too will spend the right amount and in the right manner.[7] But although generosity is concerned with the same things, in these matters it is greatness, as something grand, that is the mark of a munificent man; and with the same expense he will make the work more magnificent. For the virtue of a possession   15
is not the same as that of a work, since a possession which is worth most is that which has the highest value, like gold, but a work which is worth most is that which has greatness and is noble; for it is the contemplation of a work such as this that is admirable, and what is magnificent is admirable, and munificence is a virtue concerning a work of great magnitude.

5

Of expenditures there are such which we call 'honorable', like those connected with gods, e.g., votive offerings and stately buildings and   20
sacrifices, and similarly anything related to whatever is divine, and also those which are for the public good and issue from a desire for public honor, as when people think they should equip a chorus or a trireme or entertain a city in splendor. Now in all these, as already stated, there is also a reference to the donor, who he is and what are his means; for the   25
expenditure should be worthy of these and should befit not only the work done but also the donor. Hence a poor man could not be munificent, since he has not the means to spend as becomes the occasion; and he who tries is a fool, for his means are not worthy of the required expenditure nor do they befit the occasion, and what is done according to virtue should be right. Magnificent expenditure becomes those who have the means,   30
whether they acquired it themselves or inherited it from their ancestors

or connections and also those of high lineage or reputation or other such qualities, for all of these confer greatness and dignity. Such a man, then, would be munificent most of all, and it is in such expenditures that munific-
35   ence is shown, as was stated, for these are the greatest and most worthy of honor.

Of expenditures for private occasions, munificence becomes those which
1123a   occur just once, e.g., a wedding or the like, and anything which is of interest to the whole state or to those in high position,[1] and receptions and departures of foreign guests, and gifts as well as gifts in return, for a
5   munificent man spends not on himself but on what is of public interest, and gifts bear some resemblance to votive offerings. It is also a mark of a munificent man to build and furnish a house as becomes his wealth (for this too is a befitting ornament), and to spend rather on works which are lasting (for these are the most noble) and on what becomes every occasion
10   (for the same things do not befit both gods and men, or both a temple and a tomb), making an expenditure which is great in each genus of things, the most magnificent on a grand occasion, and a great one on any other occasion. But there is a difference between what is great in a work or function and what is great in expenditure; for the most beautiful ball or
15   bottle has the magnificence as a gift to a child, but the value of it is small and not generous. Because of this, it is a mark of a munificent man to act in a magnificent manner, whatever be the genus in which he acts; for such an action cannot be easily surpassed and has the worth which befits the expenditure. Such, then, is the munificent man.

6

The man who is in excess and is marked by conspicuous consumption,
20   on the other hand, exceeds by using up more than is right, as has been stated. For he uses up much on small matters and exhibits ostentation in bad taste, as when he gives a club dinner as if it were a wedding feast, or as when he introduces a comic chorus on the stage in purple dresses, as
25   the Megarians do. And he does all such things not for the sake of what is noble but to show off his wealth, thinking that he will be admired through these *actions*; and he spends little where he should spend much, but much where he should spend little.

As for the mean man, he is deficient in all things; and after spending a great deal on a given occasion he ruins what is noble about it for a trifle, hesitating about everything he is to do and considering how to spend the   30 least amount and, at the same time, bewailing these things and thinking that he is spending more than what is required.

Now these habits are vices, but they do not carry reproach with them because they are neither harmful to others nor very unseemly.

7

High-mindedness, as its name also seems to indicate,[1] is concerned with   35 great things, and our first task is to find out the kinds of things it is concerned with. It makes no difference whether we examine the habit itself   1123b or the man who *acts* according to that habit.

A high-minded man is thought to be one who, being worthy of great things, requires of himself that he be worthy of them; for he who does so without being worthy of them is foolish, and no virtuous man is foolish or senseless.[2] A high-minded man, then, is the man we have described. For he who is worthy of small things and requires of himself that he be   5 worthy of them is unassuming and not high-minded; for high-mindedness exists in what is great, just as also beauty exists in a body of good size, and men with small bodies may be elegant and well-proportioned but are not beautiful.[3] On the other hand, the man who requires of himself that he be worthy of great things when he is not worthy of them is called 'vain', but not every one who requires of himself that he be worthy of greater things than he is worthy of is vain.[4] As for the man who thinks himself worthy of smaller things than he is worthy of, he is called 'low-minded',   10 whether he is worthy (a) of things which are great or moderate in greatness or (b) of small things but thinks himself worthy of even smaller things. And the man who is worthy of great things but thinks himself worthy of small things is thought to be low-minded in the highest degree; for what would he have done if he were not worthy of so great things?[5]

A high-minded man is at the highest point with respect to greatness, but he is at the mean with respect to rightness, for he thinks himself worthy of what he is actually worth; the others, however, exceed or are deficient in   15 their thinking. So if a man both is and thinks himself worthy of great things, and especially of the greatest, he would be concerned with one thing most of all. Now the term 'worth' is used for external goods; and we would

posit the greatest of these to be that which we render to the gods, or that
which men in high position mostly aim at, or that which is the prize
20   awarded to the most noble. Such a thing is honor; for this is indeed the
greatest of external goods. So a high-minded man is concerned with honors
and dishonors as he should be. And, apart from the argument, high-minded men do appear to be concerned with honor; for it is great men who
think themselves worthy of honor most of all, and they do this in virtue of
their worth.[6]

25   A low-minded man is deficient in relation both to himself and to the
claims of a high-minded man. A vain man exceeds in relation to himself,
but he does not exceed the claims of the high-minded man. A high-minded
man, being indeed worthy of the greatest things, would be the best; for a
better man is always worthy of greater things and the best is worthy of the
greatest. Thus a man who is truly high-minded should be a good [i.e.,
30   virtuous] man; and greatness in every virtue would seem to be a mark of
a high-minded man.[7] And it would not be at all becoming for a high-
minded man to flee from danger, swinging his arms by his sides, or to
treat others unjustly; for why would a man, to whom nothing is great,
do what is disgraceful? If we examine the various habits one at a time,
it would appear utterly ridiculous for a high-minded man not to be good.
35   If he were bad, he would not be even worthy of honor; for honor is the
1124a   prize of virtue, and it is bestowed only on good men.

It would seem, then, that high-mindedness is a sort of ornament of the
virtues; for it makes them greater, and it cannot exist without them.[8] For
this *reason*, to be truly high-minded is difficult, for high-mindedness
without both nobility and goodness is impossible. A high-minded man,
5   then, is concerned with honors and dishonors most of all, and he will be
moderately pleased by great honors bestowed on him by virtuous men, as
if he were receiving what belongs to him or even less; for no honor could
equal the worth of his complete virtue. Yet he will of course accept it, since
virtuous men can have nothing greater to bestow on him. As for honor paid
10   to him by ordinary people and for *actions* of little worth, he will regard it
as entirely unworthy, for he will consider himself not worthy of those
actions; and likewise for dishonor, for dishonor does not apply to him
justly.

As it was stated, then, a high-minded man is concerned with honors
most of all, but with regard to wealth or political power or any good or

bad luck, too, he will be moderately disposed, however these may turn out   15
to be, and he will neither be overjoyed by good luck nor overpained by
bad luck, for neither is he so disposed as to regard honor as the greatest
thing. For political power and wealth are chosen for the sake of honor; at
any rate, those who have these wish to be honored through them. Thus
if honor, too, is of little worth to a man, the others [i.e., wealth, political
power, good luck] will be of little worth to him also.[9] It is in view of this   20
that high-minded men seem to be disdainful.

8

Good luck, too, is thought to contribute to high-mindedness. For men of
high lineage or political power or wealth consider themselves worthy of
honor; for they are superior, and that which exceeds in what is good is
thought to be more worthy of honor. Hence such things, too, are thought
to make men more high-minded,[1] for through them they are honored by
some people.

Only a good man, however, should be truly honored, although he who   25
has both virtue and these things is considered as more worthy of honor;
but those who without virtue have such goods [i.e., good birth, political
power, wealth, good luck] neither have a just claim to great things nor
are rightly called 'high-minded', for these [i.e., true claims to greatness
and high-mindedness] are not possible without complete virtue, and those
who have such goods become disdainful and insulting. For, without vir-   30
tue, it is not easy for them to bear the fruits of good luck with propriety;
and, being unable to bear them with propriety and thinking themselves   1124b
superior to others, they show contempt for others and do whatever chances
to please them. For they imitate the high-minded man without being like
him, and they do this in the manner in which they can; and so they do not
act according to virtue but show contempt for others. The high-minded   5
man shows contempt justly (for his opinion is true), while ordinary men
do so at random.[2]

Again, the high-minded man neither exposes himself to danger for
trifles nor likes danger because he values only few things, but he faces
danger for a great cause. and when he does so he is unsparing of his life,
since he considers life as not worthy under certain circumstances.

And he is the kind of man who does service to others but is ashamed to   10 receive service from them; for doing a service is a mark of a superior man, but receiving it is a mark of an inferior man. And he is disposed to do a greater service in return; for thus the man who did a service first will be still indebted and will have been treated well. And he seems to call to mind those whom he has done good to, not those from whom he has received a good; for he who received a good is inferior to the man who

15   conferred it, and a high-minded man wishes to be superior. And he hears of the former [i.e., conferring benefits] with pleasure, but of the latter, [i.e., receiving benefits] with displeasure; and it is in view of this that Thetis did not speak to Zeus of the services she had done him,[3] nor did the Lacedaimonians of the services they had done to the Athenians but only those they had received from them.[4] It is a mark of a high-minded man, too, never, or hardly ever, to ask for help but to be of help to others readily, and to be dignified with men of high position or of good fortune

20   but unassuming with those of middle class, for it is difficult and impressive to be superior to the former but easy to be so to the latter; and whereas being impressive to the former is not a mark of a lowly man, being so to the humble is crude – it is like using physical force against the physically weak.

Again, it is a mark of a high-minded man to avoid going after things held in honor or things in which others excel, and to be slow or hesitant

25   except where the honor of the deed to be done is great, and then only on few occasions but those which are great and notable. He will also be outspoken concerning his hatreds and friendships, for secrecy is a mark of fear; and he will care for truth more than for reputation; and he will speak and *act* openly, because he has contempt for fear and secrecy and

30   falsity. And hence he will be truthful, except when he is ironical, and if ironical, it will be only towards the many.

Again, a high-minded man will not submit to a life which pleases an-

1125a   other person (unless this be a friend), for this is slavish; and it is in view of such submission that all flatterers are servile and all those who have no self-respect are flatterers. Nor will he be given to admiration, for nothing is great to him. Nor will he bear grudges; for it is a mark of a high-minded

5   man not to bring up the past, especially what was bad, but rather to overlook this. Nor will he indulge in personal conversation; for he will talk neither about himself nor about others, as he cares neither to be praised by others nor to blame others, and he is not given to praising others. Hence

he will speak no evil, not even of his enemies, except when insulted.[5]

Again, he is least disposed to lament over or ask for necessities or   10
small matters, for to do so about these matters is a mark of a man who is
serious about them. And he is the kind of a man who will try to possess
things which are noble and bear no further fruit rather than those which
bear fruit and are beneficial to something else;[6] for it is a mark of a self-
sufficient man to possess the former rather than the latter. And the movements of a high-minded man are thought to be slow, and his voice deep,
and his speech steady; for he who is serious about few things is not disposed to hurry and he who regards nothing great will not raise his voice,   15
but high-pitched voices and rapid movements are caused by [those who
regard small things as great and who are serious about many things].

9

Such being the high-minded man, then, the one who is deficient is low-
minded and the one who exceeds is vain. Now these two are not thought
to be bad, for they do not cause evil [to others]; they are just mistaken.
For the low-minded man, though being worthy of good things, deprives   20
himself of the things of which he is worthy; and he seems to have something bad in view of the fact that he does not consider himself worthy of
good things and does not know himself, for otherwise he would have
desired the things he was worthy of, at least if these were good. Nevertheless,
such a man is thought to be not foolish but rather timid. Such an opinion
of himself seems to make him also worse;[1] for each man aims at that of   25
which [he thinks] he is worthy, and a low-minded man abstains from (a)
noble *actions* and pursuits, as he thinks himself not capable of achieving
them, and also from (b) acquiring external goods for similar reasons.
Vain people, on the other hand, are fools and ignorant of themselves, and
conspicuously so; for thinking themselves capable of honorable under-
takings, they make the attempt, and then they are exposed. And they   30
adorn themselves in dress and pose for effect and do other such things,
and they wish to have their good fortunes be made public and speak
about them, thinking that through these they will be honored.

Low-mindedness is opposed to high-mindedness more than vanity is;
for it is more common and also worse.

High-mindedness, then, is concerned with great honor, as stated above.   35

10

1125b   Concerning honor there seems to be another virtue also, as we stated at the
start,[1] which might be thought to be related to high-mindedness as generosity
is related to munificence; for neither this virtue nor generosity is concerned
5   with great things but both of them dispose us to *act* as we should concerning things which are moderate or small. Now just as in taking and giving
property there is a mean and an excess and a deficiency, so in the case of
honor one may desire more than is right or less than is right, or he may
desire from the right sources and in the right manner [etc.]. For we blame
10   the ambitious man for aiming at more honor than he should and from the
sources he should not, and the unambitious man for not intending to be
honored even for his noble deeds. But sometimes we praise the ambitious
man as being manly and a lover of what is noble, and at other times we
praise the unambitious man as being moderate and unassuming, as we
said at the beginning.[2] It is clear, then, that since the expression 'lover-of-
15   such-and-such' has many meanings, we do not apply the expression 'lover
of honor' [='ambitious'] always to the same thing, but when praising we
apply it to those who love honor more than ordinary people do, and when
blaming we apply it to those who love honor more than they should.
Since there is no name for the mean, the extreme dispositions seem to
struggle for its place as for something vacant; but where there is an excess
and a deficiency, there should be also a mean. Now men may desire honor
20   more than they should or less than they should; but there are also times
when they desire as they should and in the manner they should, and it is
just at those times that the habit is [truly] praised, being a mean concerning
honor but without a name. And relative to ambition, this disposition appears to be unambition, relative to unambition, it appears to be ambition,
but relative to both, it appears to be somehow both;[3] and this seems to be
25   the case with the other virtues also. And the opposition here appears to
be only between the extreme dispositions because the mean has no name.[4]

11

Good temper is a mean with respect to anger, but since there is no name
for the moderate man and hardly any for those at the extremes, we shall
make use of the term 'good temper' in applying it to the moderate man,

though this term tends to be used for the deficiency, which itself has no name.[1] The excess might be called 'irascibility'; for the feeling is anger, 30 but the things which cause anger are many and different. Accordingly, the man who is angry on the right occasions and with those he should and also in the right manner and at the right time and for the right length of time is praised; so it is this man who would be good-tempered, if good temper is truly praised. For a good-tempered man tends to be unperturbed and not to be led by his feeling but to be angered in the manner and on the occasions 35 and for the length of time [etc.] as dictated by reason. He seems to err 1126a rather in the direction of deficiency, for a good-tempered man is not disposed to take vengeance but rather to pardon.

The deficiency, whether an inirascibility[2] of a sort or whatever its name might be, is blamed. For those who do not get angry on the occasions they 5 should, and in the manner they should, and when they should, and with those they should, are thought to be fools; for they are thought to be insensitive and without pain, and since they do not get angry, they are thought not to be disposed to defend themselves. But it is slavish for a man to submit to be besmirched or to allow it against those who are close to him.

The excess may occur with respect to any of the qualifications stated, for a man may be angry with the wrong persons, or on the wrong occasions, 10 or more than he should, or too soon, or for a longer time; but not all these errors belong to the same person, since this is not possible, for badness destroys even itself, and if present in its entirety, it becomes unbearable. Now irascible men get angry quickly, and with the wrong persons, and on the wrong occasions, and more than they should; but they cease 15 being angry soon, which is the best part of it. This happens to them in view of the fact that they do not hold back their anger but retaliate openly because of the sharpness of their temper, and then their anger subsides. Hot-tempered people are excessively sharp and are disposed to be angry with anything and on every occasion; hence their name (ἀκρόχολοι).[3] Bitter people, on the other hand, are haid to appease and keep their anger 20 for a long time; for they hold back their temper. But they cease being angry when they retaliate, for vengeance brings an end to anger by producing pleasure instead of pain. But if this does not occur, they retain their grief; for no one can talk them out of it because their anger is not apparent, and it takes much time for them to digest their anger. Such people are most 25 troublesome to themselves and to their best friends. We call those harsh who show bad temper on the wrong occasions, and more than they should, and for a longer time than they should, and who are not reconciled without vengeance or punishment.

30   To good temper we oppose the excess more than the deficiency, for it is more common, since vengeance is more characteristic of men than for-giveness, and harsh people are worse to live with [than inirascible people].

What we have said earlier is also clear from what we are saying here; that is, it is not easy to specify the manner in which, or the persons with whom, or the occasions on which, or the length of time during which one should be angry, and also the limits within which one acts rightly or errs.

35   A man who deviates a little from the mean, whether in the direction of
1126b   excess or of deficiency, is not blamed; for sometimes we praise those who are deficient and call them 'good-tempered', and sometimes we call harsh men 'manly', regarding them as able to rule others. So it is not easy to state by a formula how much or in what manner a man must deviate in order to be blamed; for judgment in these matters depends on each
5   particular case and on sensation. At least so much is clear, however, that the moderate habit, according to which we are angry with the right people and on the right occasions and in the right manner and so on with the other qualifications, is worthy of praise; the excesses or deficiencies, on the other hand, should be blamed, and slightly so if they are weak, more so if they occur to a higher degree, and very much if they occur to a very high degree. So it is clear that we should keep close to the moderate habit.

10   Let this be our account, then, of the habits which have to do with anger.

12

In social relations, both those in which men live with others and those in which they communicate with others by discourse or *actions*, some men are thought to be complaisant, i.e., those who try to please others by praising everything and never going against anything said or done, think-
15   ing they should cause no pain to those they meet. Contrary to these are those who go against everything said or done and show no concern at all about causing pain to others, and they are called 'hard to get along with' and 'quarrelsome'. Clearly, then, the habits named are blameworthy; but the mean between them is praiseworthy and is the one according to

which a man will accept the right statements or *actions* in the right manner, etc., but will be displeased by the wrong ones in a similar way.[1] No name has been given to this habit but it resembles friendship most of all; for if   20 we add affection to a man with such an intermediate habit, we shall have what we mean by 'a *good* friend.'[2] But this habit differs from friendship by being without feeling or affection for those with whom one associates, for it is not with love or enmity that a person with this habit accepts [or avoids statements or *actions*] as he should, but by being a man of such-and-such a character;[3] for he will act alike towards those he does not know and   25 those he is familiar with, towards intimates and those who are not so, but in each case as is fitting, for one should not show the same concern for intimates and strangers nor cause them pain alike.[4]

Universally, then, we have stated that a man with the moderate habit will associate with people as he should, but it is by reference to what is noble or expedient that he will aim to avoid causing pain or to contribute   30 to pleasure. For this habit seems to be concerned with pleasures and pains in social relations; so if it were harmful or not noble for such a man to contribute to pleasure, he would be displeased in doing so but would deliberately choose to cause pain, and if an action were to cause harm or no small impropriety to the agent, whereas the contrary action were to   35 cause small pain, he would not accept the former action but would show his displeasure.[5] In such associations, his behaviour with men in high position would be different from that with ordinary men, that with men he is   1127*a* quite familiar with would be different from that with those he hardly knows, and similarly with respect to the other differences; and he would render to each man what befits him, choosing to give pleasure for its own sake and guarding against causing pain for its own sake, but also attending to consequences, i.e., to what is noble or expedient, if these be greater.[6]   5 And for the sake of a great future pleasure he will cause but little pain. Such is the moderate man, then, but he has received no name.

Of those who [always] try to contribute to another's pleasure, he who aims at being pleasant but not for the sake of something else is called 'complaisant', but he whose aim is personal benefit in the form of property or whatever is attainable by means of property is called 'a flatterer';[7] and,   10 as already stated, he who displeases everyone is called 'hard to get along with' or 'quarrelsome'. And it is the extreme dispositions that appear to be opposed to each other here because the mean disposition has no name.[8]

13

The mean between boastfulness [and self-depreciation] has as its objects almost the same things;[1] and this too has no name. But it is no less well to
15   go over habits such as these also, for we would know more about character if we discuss each case, and we would be more convinced that virtues are moderations if we perceive that this is so in all cases.

In living with others, those whose association aims at giving pleasure or pain have been discussed.[2] Let us now discuss in a similar manner those
20   who behave truly or falsely by way of speech or *action* or claim. Now a boastful man is thought to be one who claims reputation for things he does not possess or for things greater than he possesses, whereas a self-depreciatory man is thought to disclaim what he possesses or to belittle it; but the moderate man, viewing the situation as it is, is thought to be truth-
25   ful in his way of life and in his speech, stating that he possesses just what he has, neither more nor less. Now each of these men may act as he does either for the sake of something else or not;[3] and if his *action* is not for the sake of something else, then the kind of things he says and does and the way he lives correspond to the kind of man he is. Falsity in itself[4] is bad
30   and blameworthy, while truth [in itself] is noble and praiseworthy. So, too, a truthful person, being moderate, is praiseworthy; but he who is untruthful in either of the two forms is blameworthy, and the boastful man is more so.

Let us discuss each of them, starting with the truthful man. Now we are speaking of the man who is truthful not in the agreements he has made or
1127b   in those matters which point to injustice or justice (for these are objects of another virtue), but in those in which no such difference arises and in which he is truthful in speech and in his way of life by being a man with such a habit. Such a man would seem to be *good*. For a man who loves
5   truth and is truthful where nothing else matters will be even more truthful where something else does matter, for he will avoid falsity as something disgraceful, a thing which he avoids even for its own sake;[5] and such a man is praiseworthy. And he is inclined to understate the truth,[6] for this appears to be in better taste because excesses are wearisome.
10   A man who claims greater things than he has and for no other *reason* resembles a bad man (for otherwise he would not have enjoyed falsehood), but he appears ineffectual rather than bad. When he does this for a *reason*,

however, if it is for the sake of reputation or honor he is, like a boastful man, not much blameworthy, but if it is for the sake of money or whatever brings in money, he is rather unseemly. What makes a man boastful is not his power but his intention; for he is boastful in virtue of a habit and   15
by being a man of a certain quality, just like a liar, whether one who enjoys lying just for its own sake or one who desires reputation or gain. Thus men who boast for the sake of reputation make claims which win praise or congratulations; but those who boast for the sake of gain claim things which delight others and whose nonexistence may escape discovery, like   20
the power of a soothsayer or of a wise man or of a doctor. It is because of this that most people claim and boast about such things, for they possess the above-mentioned qualities.

Self-depreciators, by understating their virtues or *actions*, appear to be more cultivated in character, for they speak in this manner not for the sake of gain but to avoid pomposity; and, in addition, it is reputation   25
that they disclaim most of all, as Socrates used to do also. But those who disclaim also virtues or *actions* which are trivial or obvious are called 'petty dissemblers' and are contemptible; and sometimes this appears to be boastfulness, as in the case of the Spartan dress, for both excess and too much deficiency are indicative of boastfulness. But those who use self-   30
depreciation in moderation and are self-depreciatory about things which do not stare us in the eyes or are not apparent appear to be cultivated.

It is the boastful man who appears to be more opposed to the truthful man; for he is worse than the self-depreciatory man.

14

Since relaxation is a part of life also, and in relaxation one may pass the time with amusement, it seems that here too there may be a social relation   1128*a*
with propriety in which one says the right things and in the right manner, and similarly when one listens to them. There will also be a difference with respect to the kind of people one is speaking or listening to. So it is clear that concerning these, too, there is an excess and also a deficiency beyond the mean. Thus those who are beyond propriety in matters of humor are thought to be buffoons or vulgar, eager to be humorous by any   5
means and aiming at causing laughter rather than saying what is proper or causing no pain to the one laughed at; others, having nothing humorous

to say and being displeased with those who do, are thought to be boorish
10   or obtuse. Those who amuse others in a proper manner, on the other hand,
are given the name 'witty' [=εὐτράπελοι], a name suggesting men who
make good turns in one direction or another, for such motions are thought
to be marks of character; and just as men's bodies are judged by their
motions, so is character. Since humor is not hard to find and most people
15   enjoy amusement and mockery more than they should, also buffoons are
called 'witty' as if they were cultivated; but that they differ from witty
persons, and in no small way, is clear from what has been said.

To the moderate habit belongs also tact, and it is a mark of a tactful
man to say and listen to such things which befit a *good* and free man; for
20   there are some things which become such a man to say and listen to as a
part of amusement, and the amusement of a free man differs from that of a
slavish person, and so does that of an educated man from that of one who
is uneducated. One might perceive this difference in old and recent come-
dies also; for in the former humor took the form of obscene language,
25   in the latter it is rather innuendo, and these differ not a little with respect
to propriety. Should we then define a man who uses mockery well as
(a) a man who uses language becoming to a free man or as (b) a man who
does not cause pain to the listener and even gives him delight? But is not
a definition such as (b) indefinite? For different things are hateful or
pleasant to different people. But such are the things he will listen to; for
the kinds of things he will allow himself to listen to are thought to be those
30   he will make also. So he will not resort to every kind of humor; for
mockery is a species of revilement, and legislators prohibit certain kinds
of revilement, and perhaps they should have prohibited certain kinds of
mockery also.[1]

A cultivated and free man, then, will be such as to be like a law unto
himself. Accordingly, such is the moderate man, whether he be called
'tactful' or 'witty'. A buffoon, on the other hand, is a slave to humor,
35   sparing neither himself nor others if he can make people laugh, and using
1128b   such language which a cultivated man will never use and some of which
he will not even listen to. And as for a boor, he is worthless in such social
relations; for he contributes nothing and is displeased by everything.

Relaxation and amusement are thought to be indispensable to life.
5   In life, then, the moderate habits already discussed are three, and all are
concerned with discourse or *actions* in associations. They differ, however,

in that one of them is concerned with truth while the other two with what is pleasurable; and of social relations concerned with pleasure, one finds its expression in amusement while the other in the other kind of living.[2]

15

Shame should not be spoken of as being a virtue, for it resembles a feeling   10
rather than a disposition. At any rate, it is defined as a sort of fear of a bad
reputation and amounts to something which is parallel to fear of danger;
for those who are ashamed blush, whereas those who fear death turn pale.
So both appear to be in some way affections of the body, and it is in view   15
of this that shame is thought to be a feeling rather than a disposition.

Now this feeling is not becoming to every age but only to youth, for we
think that it is the young who should have a sense of shame because they
err frequently by living with their passions but are prevented from so err-
ing by a sense of shame; and we praise those among the young who have
a sense of shame, but no one would praise an older person for being   20
disposed to be ashamed since we think that he should not do anything
shameful. Surely shame should not be a mark of a *good* man, if indeed it is
a mark of a bad man, for shameful *actions* should not be performed by
anyone; and it makes no difference whether some *actions* are truly disgraceful while others are generally thought to be disgraceful (for none of
them should be performed, and so one should not be disposed to be   25
ashamed), and to be such a man as to do something disgraceful is a mark
of a bad man. And it is absurd to think that, because a man feels ashamed
whenever he does such a disgraceful thing, he is *good*; for one is ashamed
only for what he does voluntarily, but a *good* man will never willingly
do what is bad.[1] Shame might, however, be *good* hypothetically, for if a   30
good man were to *act* disgracefully, he would then feel ashamed; but
this does not apply to the virtues. [2] And if shamelessness or not having a
sense of shame when one does disgraceful things is bad, no more is it *good*
to feel ashamed at doing such things.[3] Continence, too, is not a virtue
but a mixture of a sort;[4] but this will be shown later.[5]   35

Let us now discuss justice.

BOOK E

1

1129*a*3 With regard to justice and injustice, we should consider (1) what kind of
5 *actions* they are concerned with, (2) what kind of a mean justice is, and
(3) between what extremes the just[1] is a mean. We shall examine these
according to the same method as that used in the discussions which
preceded.[2]

We observe that all men, when speaking of justice, have in mind that
kind of disposition by which one is disposed to do what is just and from
10 which one *acts* justly and wishes what is just[3]; and similarly with injustice, they have in mind that kind of disposition from which one *acts*
unjustly and wishes what is unjust. So let us, too, first make these sketchy
assumptions; for the manner of dealing with sciences and faculties is not the
same as that with dispositions. For it is the same faculty or the same
science which is thought to deal with contraries, but a disposition which
is one of two contraries does not tend to *actions* which are contraries[4];
15 e.g., from health only healthy things are done and not both contraries
[health and disease], for we say that a man walks in a healthy manner
when he walks as a healthy man would.

At times a disposition comes to be known from its contrary disposition,
but at times dispositions come to be known from the subjects to which
they are referred[5]; for (a) if good physical condition is evident, bad
20 physical condition becomes evident also, and (b) good physical condition
comes to be known from things which are related to good physical condition, and those things come to be known from good physical condition.
For if good physical condition is firmness of flesh, it is necessary both for
bad physical condition to be flabbiness of flesh and for a wholesome
object[6] to cause firmness of flesh. For the most part, if one contrary
25 term has many meanings, the other contrary has many meanings also;
e.g., if 'the just' has many meanings, 'the unjust' has many meanings
also.

2

Now it seems that 'justice' (and also 'injustice') has many meanings, but because of the closeness of these meanings the equivocation of the term escapes notice and is not so clear as it is in cases in which the meanings are far apart, e.g., as in the equivocal term κλείς, which means the collar-bone of an animal but also an instrument with which one locks the door, for the observed difference here is great. Let us then consider the various meanings of 'an unjust man'[1]. The unjust man is thought to be (a) the lawbreaker, but he is also thought to be (b) the grasping or unfair man; so clearly the just man will be the law-abiding man or the fair man.[2] Hence 'the just' means that which is lawful or that which is fair, while 'the unjust' means that which is unlawful or that which is unfair.[3]

    Since the unjust man may also be the grasping man, he would as such be concerned with goods, not all goods, but those which may come by good or bad luck[4] and which are always good if taken without qualification but not always good for a particular person. Now men pray for and pursue these goods, but they should not; what they should pray for is that the unqualified goods be goods for themselves also, but they should choose those which are good for themselves[5]. The unjust man does not always choose what is greater, but also what is less, as in the case of unqualified bad things; but since what is less bad, too, is thought to be a good in some sense[6], and since grasping is of that which is a good, for these *reasons* he is thought to be grasping. Of course, he is unfair; for unfairness is inclusive and is common to both.[7]

30

1129*b*

5

10

3

As stated before, since the lawbreaker too is unjust whereas the law-abiding man is just, it is clear that all lawful things are in some sense just; for the things specified by the legislative art are lawful, and we say that each of them is just. Now the laws deal with all matters which aim at what is commonly expedient, either to all or to the best or to those in authority, whether with respect to virtue or with respect to some other such thing [e.g., honor]; so in one way we call 'just' those things which produce or preserve happiness or its parts in a political community. Thus the law orders us to perform the *actions* of a brave man (e.g., not to desert our

15

20

post, nor take to flight, nor throw away our arms), and those of a temperate man (e.g., not to commit adultery, nor abuse anyone), and those of a good-tempered man (e.g., not to strike, nor to speak abusively), and similarly with respect to the other virtues and evil habits, commanding us

25   to do certain things and forbidding us to do others; and it does so rightly if it is rightly framed, but less well if hastily framed.[1]

This kind of justice, then, is complete virtue, but in relation to another person and not in an unqualified way.[2] And, because of this, justice is often thought to be the best of the virtues, and "neither evening nor

30   morning star"[3] is so wonderful; and, to use a proverb, "in justice is included every virtue".[4] And it is a virtue in the most complete sense, since the use of it is that of complete virtue; and it is complete, since he who possesses it can use it also towards another and not only for himself[5], for many men can use virtues whose effect applies only to their own house-

1130a hold but cannot use those virtues which affect others.[6] And it is because of this that the saying of Bias[7] is thought to be well put: "the way a man rules will show him up"; for a ruler affects others and he is a ruler in a community.[8] And for the same *reason* justice alone of the virtues, by

5   affecting others, is thought to be another's good[9]; for the just man *acts* for what is expedient for someone else, whether for a ruler or a member of the community. The worst man, then, is the one whose evil habit affects both himself and his friends,[10] while the best man is one whose virtue is directed not to himself[11] but to others, for this is a difficult task. Accordingly, this kind of justice is not a part of virtue but the whole virtue,

10   and injustice, which is its contrary, is not a part of vice but the whole vice.

What the difference is between virtue and this kind of justice, then, is clear from what we said; for [numerically] they are the same, but their essences are not the same.[12] Insofar as the disposition is defined in relation to something else, it is justice, but insofar as it is such-and-such[13] a disposition, it is a virtue without qualification.

4

But we are inquiring about that kind of justice which is a part of virtue,
15   for there exists such a kind of justice, as we said; and similarly with regard to injustice as a part of [vice]. A sign of the existence of these

kinds is the fact that a man who *acts* according to the other evil habits does so unjustly but is not grasping at all (e.g., like the man who throws away his shield through cowardice or uses abusive language because of his harsh temper or fails to help another with money because of stingi-ness), while a man who *acts* graspingly often does so neither according to   20 any of these evil habits nor according to any other form but according to some sort of wickedness[1] (for we blame him) and injustice. So there is another kind of injustice, which is a part of injustice taken as a whole vice, and also a kind of unjust thing as a part of what is unjust as a whole and in violation of the law. Again, if one commits adultery for gain and receives money for it, while another does it through *desire* but pays for it   25 and loses money[2], the latter would be regarded as intemperate rather than as grasping, whereas the former would be regarded as unjust and not as intemperate and so clearly as *acting* for the sake of gain. Again, each of the other forms of an unjust effect is always attributed to some form of evil habit, e.g., to intemperance if one commits adultery, to cowardice if   30 one deserts his comrade in battle, and to anger if one strikes; but if a man makes [undeserved] gain, this is attributed to injustice but to no [other] evil habit. So it is evident that, besides injustice taken as a whole, there is another kind of injustice which is specific, and it has the same name, for its definition falls within the same genus[3]; for both have the force [of   1130b being defined] in relation to some other person, but the narrow one is con-cerned with honor or property or safety or something (if we had a single name) which includes all these and has as its aim the pleasure which comes from gain, while the other [the wide one] is concerned with all the things with which a virtuous man is concerned.[4]   5

5

It is clear, then, that there are many kinds of justice, and that, besides the one which is the whole of virtue, there is also another. So let us find out what it is and what kind of thing it is.

The unjust has been distinguished into the unlawful and the unfair, and the just into the lawful and the fair. Now injustice with respect to what is   10 unlawful is the one we considered earlier. But since the unfair and the un-lawful are not the same but different and are related as a part to a whole (for whatever is unfair is unlawful but not everything unlawful is unfair), the unjust and injustice in the narrow sense likewise are not the same but different from those in the wide sense and are related to them as parts to wholes; for injustice as unfair is a part of injustice as a whole, and justice as a part is similarly related to justice as a whole. So we should also discuss justice and injustice as parts, and, in a similar manner, also that which is just and that which is unjust.

We may leave aside the discussion of justice and injustice with respect to the whole of virtue, the first [i.e., justice] being used as the whole of virtue in relation to another person and the second [i.e., injustice] as the corresponding whole of vice. It is also evident how the just and the unjust which exist or are done[1] according to these [justice and injustice] will be defined; for perhaps most lawful things are those done[2] by the whole of virtue, since the law orders us to live in accordance with each of the virtues and prohibits us from living according to each of the evil habits. Other lawful things are those which have been enacted and produce the whole of virtue, and they are concerned with education for the common good. As for each individual's education, in virtue of which a man becomes good without qualification[3], we must determine later whether it belongs to politics or to another inquiry[4]; for perhaps to be a good man is not the same as to be a good citizen in every case[5].

One kind of justice in the narrow sense, and of what is just according to this justice, concerns itself with the distributions of honor or property or the other things which are to be shared by the members of the state[6] (for it is these who may be so related that some possess a fair share and others an unfair share). Another kind is that whose aim is to correct the wrongs done in exchanges, and it has two parts; for of exchanges some are voluntary but others are involuntary. Voluntary exchanges are such things as sale, purchase, loan, security, use of property loaned, deposit, and hiring; and they are said to be voluntary, since they are initiated voluntarily. Of involuntary exchanges, (a) some are clandestine, such as theft, adultery, poisoning, procuring, enticing slaves away from their masters, assassination, and false witness, but (b) others are violent, such as assault, imprisonment, murder, seizure, injury, defamation, and besmirching.

6

Since an unjust man is unfair and whatever is unjust is unfair, it is clear

that there is also a mean between two unfair extremes, and this is the fair; for in any kind of *action* in which there is the greater and the less, there is also the equal[1]. So if the unjust is unfair, the just must be fair; and this indeed is thought to be the case by all, even apart from argument. So since the fair is a mean, the just would be a mean of some sort. Now the fair depends on[2] at least two things.[3] Accordingly, the just must be a   15
mean, and fair, and in relation to something,[4] and for certain persons. As a mean, it lies between certain things (and these are the greater and the less)[5]; as fair, it is in respect of two things;[6] and as just, it is in relation to certain persons. The just, then, must depend on at least four things;[7] for the persons to which it happens to be just are [at least] two, and the things   20
are distributed into [at least] two parts. And it is the same equality which exists with respect to the persons and with respect to the things, for as the latter are related, so are the former, for if the former are not equal[8], they will not have equal parts.[9] Quarrels and accusations arise, then, when those who are equal possess or are given unequal parts or when those who are unequal possess or are given equal parts.[10] Again, this is clear from what happens with respect to merit. All men agree that what is just in   25
distribution should be according to merit of some sort, but not all men agree as to what that merit should be; those who advocate mob rule assert that this is freedom,[11] oligarchs that it is wealth, others that it is high lineage, and aristocrats[12] that it is virtue.

What is just, then, is something in a proportion of some kind, for a   30
proportion is a property not merely of numbers with units as elements, but of all kinds of numbers; for it is an equality of ratios, and it exists in at least four terms.[13] Clearly, then, a discrete[14] proportion exists in four terms. But a continuous proportion[15] too exists in four terms; for it uses one term as two and mentions it twice. For example, the term B in $A:B::B:C$ is   1131b
mentioned twice; so if B is posited twice, the terms of the proportion will be four.

That which is just, too, exists in at least four terms, and the two pairs have the same ratio; for they are divided in a similar manner, as persons   5
and as things.[16] Accordingly, as the term A is to the term B, so will the term C be to the term D;[17] and by alternation, $A:C::B:D$.[18] Hence the whole $(A+C)$, too, will be similarly related to the whole $(B+D)$, and this indeed is what the distribution combines;[19] and if the combination is effected in this manner, the distribution is done justly.

7

10 The conjunction of A and C and of B and D is, then, what is just in a distribution, and what is just in the proportion here is a mean; for the proportion is a mean, and what is just is this proportion. Mathematicians call such a proportion geometrical; for in a geometrical proportion it also follows that the whole is to the whole as each term is to the corresponding

15 term. But this kind of proportion is not continuous; for in it no one term which is numerically one can be both the person[1] to whom the portion is given and that portion.[2]

That which is just, then, is that which is proportional as stated, and that which is unjust is that which violates that which is proportional in this manner. Thus one ratio may become greater but the other less. And this indeed is what actually happens; for he who *acts* unjustly gets the greater

20 portion of a good, while he who is treated unjustly gets the smaller portion.[3] It is the reverse in the case of what is bad, since that which is less bad relative to that which is greater comes under the definition of a good;[4] for what is less bad is preferable to what is greater, that which is chosen is a good, and that which is preferable [i.e., chosen more than another] is a greater good. This, then, is one kind of what is just, namely, the proportional as stated.

25 The remaining kind of what is just is the corrective, and it occurs in exchanges, both voluntary and involuntary. This form of the just is different from the previous form. For what is distributively just in things which are common exists always in accordance with the proportion stated above

30 (for even if the distribution is made from common earnings, it will be made according to the same ratio as that of the funds put into the business by the partners);[5] and the unjust which is opposed to the distributively just is in violation of this proportion. But in exchanges, though that which is

1132a just is something which is fair (and the unjust is unfair), it exists not according to that [i.e., the geometrical] proportion but according to an arithmetical proportion. For it makes no difference, here, whether it is a *good* man who deprived a bad man of something or the reverse, nor whether it is a *good* or a bad man who committed adultery; if one man

5 *acts* unjustly while the other is treated unjustly, or if one man does harm while the other is harmed, the law attends only to the amount of harm and treats both parties as equals.[6] So it is this sort of what is unjust which,

being unfair, the judge tries to equalize; for when one man receives and the other inflicts a wound, or when one man kills and the other is killed, the suffering and the *action* are distinguished as unequals, but the judge tries to equalize the two by means of a penalty which removes the gain of the 10 assailant. Of course, the terms 'gain' and 'loss' as applied to the assailant and the victim, respectively, are used here in an unqualified sort of way, even if they are not appropriate in some cases; but when a measured value is assigned to the suffering, the terms 'gain' and 'loss' are appropriately used.[7] Thus the fair is the mean between the greater and the less, and the 15 gain and the loss are, respectively, the greater and the less in contrary ways, the gain being the greater good or the lesser of what is bad while the loss is the contrary; and the mean between these two was stated to be fair, which we call 'just'. That which is correctively just, then, would be the mean between the loss and the gain. It is in view of this that those who dispute bring the matter before a judge; and to go to a judge is to go to 20 what is just, for a judge tends to be something which is just and has a soul. And they look for a judge as an intermediate, and they call judges 'mediators', thus thinking that if they get what is intermediate they will get what is just. What is just, then, is a kind of a mean, if indeed a judge too is a sort of a mean.

Now the judge restores equality to unequals; and just as, in the case of a 25 line which has been divided into two unequal segments, a geometer takes from the greater segment its excess over half the line and adds it to the smaller part to restore equality, so here. It is when the whole is divided into equal parts and each recipient receives an equal part that each of them is said to receive what belongs to him. Thus the equal [or fair] is the mean between the greater and the less according to an arithmetical proportion. 30 And it is because of this that it is called 'just', for it is a division into halves, as if one were to call it 'divided into halves' and to call a judge 'a divider into halves.'[8] For if a part is subtracted from one of two equal lines and is added to the other, the latter will exceed the former by two such parts (for if the subtracted part were not added to the latter line, this line 1132*b* would exceed the former line only by one such part). Accordingly, the latter line will exceed the intermediate [or equal line] by one such part, and the intermediate line will exceed the diminished line also by one such part. It is by this part, then, that we shall know what to subtract from the greater line and what to add to the smaller line; for the part by which the

5　intermediate [or equal] line exceeds the smaller line must be added to the
latter, and the part by which the intermediate [or equal line] is exceeded
by the greater line must be subtracted from the greater line. Thus let AX,
BY, and CZ be equal to one another; and let AE be removed from AX
and be placed next to CZ

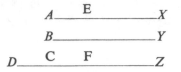

as DC. Then the whole line DCZ exceeds EX by $DC + CF$ [where CF
$= AE$], and hence it exceeds BY by DC.[9]

10　　The terms 'loss' and 'gain' here have come from voluntary exchange,[10]
where to have more than one's own is called 'to gain' but to have less than
15　the original amount is called 'to lose', as in buying and selling and in all
other exchanges which the law has allowed. But when two parties have
neither more nor less but just what they start out with, then they are said
to have what belongs to each of them and neither lose nor gain. So the
just is a mean between a gain and a loss in exchanges which violate what
20　is voluntary, and it is the possession of equal amounts before and after the
exchange.

8

Some think that what is just without qualification is reciprocity, as the
Pythagoreans said[1]; for they were defining the unqualified just as reciprocal treatment by another. But reciprocity does not fit either what is
25　distributively just or what is correctively just, yet this is the kind of
just which was meant by Rhadamanthus in:

For when the doer suffers what he's done,
At once there's justice.[2]

For in many cases this opinion conflicts with what is commonly believed.[3]
To take an example, if a magistrate strikes another, he should not be
struck in return, but if someone strikes a magistrate, he should not only be
30　struck in return but also be punished.[4] Furthermore, there is a great difference between what is done voluntarily and what is done involuntarily.[5]

　　Moreover, in associations for exchange, the kind of what is reciprocally just which holds men together is not the one based on equality but the one based on proportion; for it is by an action which is reciprocally proportional that a state continues to hold together. For what men seek is either to return something bad – otherwise they consider their position as one of slavery – or a good, failing of which there can be no give-and-take; and it is by give-and-take that men hold together.[6] And it is in view of this[7] that men give a prominent place to the Temple of the Graces, so that men may return a service, for a proper mark of grace is this: to return a service to one who has shown grace, and later to take the initiative in showing grace.[8]

1133a

5

Now a proportionate exchange is produced when the diagonal terms are combined.[9] For example, let A be an architect, B a shoemaker, C a house, and D a shoe. Then the architect must receive from the shoemaker the latter's work and must himself

give him in return his own work. First, then, if the proportion is an equality[10] and reciprocity takes place, what will be done is what we have called 'just'. If not, reciprocal give-and-take will not be equal and what is done will not be just; for nothing prevents the product of one artist from being better than that of another, and these should be equalized. This is the case with the other arts also, for they would be destroyed if what is given as a combination of quality and quantity[11] is not what is received as a combination of quantity and quality. For an association for exchange is not formed by two doctors but by a doctor and a farmer, and, in general, by artists who are different and unequal and who require equal exchanges.[12]

10

15

It is in view of this that things which are to be exchanged should in some way be comparable.[13] To effect this comparison, a coin came into existence, and this somehow functions as an intermediate or a mean; for it measures all goods exchanged and hence both excess and deficiency (e.g., it measures the number of shoes required to equal a house or a given amount of food). Accordingly, as an architect is to a shoemaker, so should the number of shoes be to one house; for if this were not so, there would be neither exchange nor association. But this proportion would be impossible if the goods exchanged were not somehow equal. All goods

20

25

to be exchanged, then, should be measurable by some standard coin or measure, as stated before. In reality, this measure is the need[14] which holds all things together; for if man had no needs at all or no needs of a similar nature, there would be no exchange or not this kind of exchange. So a coin is a sort of substitute (or representative) for need and came into 30 being by convention; and it is because of this that its name is 'coin' (=νόμισμα), for it exists by regulation (=νόμῳ) and not by nature, and it is up to us to change a given coin or make it useless.

There will be a reciprocity, then, when the equalization in the exchange becomes such that a farmer is to a shoemaker as the product of the shoe-1133b maker is to that of the farmer.[15] We should use this form of proportion, however, not after the exchange (otherwise, one of the upper terms will have both excesses)[16] but when both parties have their own products and are thus equal and capable of association and can then effect this equality [i.e., the exchange according to proportion]. Thus let A be a farmer, C be 5 food, B be a shoemaker, and D be his product, which has been equalized to C. If reciprocity could not be made in this manner, there would be no association of the parties.

That need holds these together as a single thing is clear from the fact that if the two parties, whether both or only one, do not need each other, they do not make the exchange, whereas if what each has the other needs, 10 there may be exchange, as in the exportation of corn for wine, which should then be equalized. If one does not now need something but might need it later, then money serves as a security to make a future exchange; for by bringing money later he should get what he needs.

Now this money, too, is subject to the same fluctuation in need, for its worth does not always remain the same, but it has a greater tendency to 15 remain the same. In view of this, all things should have a price on them; for in this way an exchange is always possible, and if so, also an associa-tion of men. A coin, then, like a measure, by making goods measurable by the same unit, makes their equalization possible; for neither would an association of men be possible without exchange, nor exchange without equalization, nor equalization without measurement by the same unit. It is true that goods whose difference is great cannot be measured by the 20 same unit, but when referred to the needs of men they become sufficiently measurable. There must, then, be some one unit which men posit as a standard measure; and in view of this, it is called 'a coin', for this makes

all goods comparable since all of them are then measured by that coin.
Let A be a house, B ten minae,[17] and C a bed. If the house is worth five
minae or equal to it, then A is worth or equal to half of B; and let the bed
C be one-tenth part of B. It is clear, then, how many beds are equal to one   25
house, namely, five. Clearly, then, it is in this manner that exchange took
place before money came to existence; for it makes no difference whether
a house is exchanged for five beds or for the value in coin of five beds.

9

We have stated, then, what the unjust and the just are. These having been   30
specified, it is clear that a just *action* is a mean between *acting* unjustly and
being treated unjustly; for to *act* unjustly is to get more than what one
deserves while to be treated unjustly is to get less than what one deserves.
Thus justice is a mean not in the same manner as the virtues already considered, but by being of an intermediate[1]; and injustice is of the extremes.[2]   1134a
And justice is a disposition in virtue of which the just man is said to be
disposed by intention to do what is just and to make a distribution, either
between himself and another or between others, not so as to get more of
what is choiceworthy for himself and to give less of it to another, nor to   5
take less of what is harmful and to give more of it to another (and similarly if the distribution is between others), but in such a way that the parties
receive what is proportionally equal. As for injustice, which is the contrary of justice, it is of what is unjust;[3] and this, which is in violation of
what is proportional, is an excess or deficiency of what is beneficial or
harmful, respectively. In view of this, injustice is excess and deficiency,
since it is of that which is in excess and of that which is deficient; for one-   10
self, it is an excess of what is beneficial without qualification or a deficiency
of what is harmful, while towards others, it is (a) the whole [i.e., deficiency
of what is beneficial or excess of what is harmful] in a similar manner and
(b) a violation of the proportionally equal [if the distribution is between
others], regardless of which [party gets the excess of what is beneficial or
the deficiency of what is harmful]. In an unjust effect, to receive less of
a good is to be treated unjustly, and to get more of a good is to *act* unjustly.[4]

Let such be our discussion of justice and injustice, and similarly of what   15
is just and what is unjust in general.

10

Since it is possible to *act* unjustly and still not be unjust,[1] what kind of unjust effects must one bring about to be unjust with respect to each kind of injustice, e.g., must one be a thief, or an adulterer, or a bandit? Is it not the case that the question, raised in this manner, does not show the differ-
20   ence? For a man may commit adultery with a woman whom he knows, but he may do so because of passion and not because of intention.[2] Accordingly, he *acts* unjustly but he is not unjust. And just as a man stole without being a thief, so he committed adultery without being an adulterer, and similarly in the other cases.

We have stated previously how reciprocity is related to what is just;[3]
25   but we must not forget that what we are seeking is what is just without qualification as well as politically[4]. This exists among men who share their life for the sake of self-sufficiency and who are free and equal, whether proportionately or numerically. So what applies to those who do not possess these attributes is not what is politically just but only what is just in
30   a qualified way or in virtue of some likeness;[5] for what is just [without qualification] belongs to those who come under the law also, and the law applies to situations where there may be injustice, for a verdict is a judgement of what is just or unjust [in this sense].

Now where there is injustice, there one finds unjust *actions* also, but injustice does not exist in every unjust *action*; and unjust *actions* occur when one takes for himself not the equal but the greater share of un-
35   qualified goods or the lesser share of what is unqualifiedly bad. It is in view of this that we do not allow a man to rule but a written document,[6]
1134*b*   since a man tends to do this [i.e., to take more] for himself or to become a tyrant. The ruler [by law], on the other hand, is a guardian of what is just, and, if so, then he is also a preserver of what is fair. And since he is not thought to have more for himself (for he does not take for himself more of the unqualified goods,[7] unless these are proportionally [equal, even if
5   numerically greater], and in view of this he is regarded as acting for others; and it is because of this that justice is said to be another's good, as stated previously),[8] if indeed he is just, some reward should be given to him, such as honor or privilege. Those who regard such rewards insufficient, on the other hand, become tyrants.

What is just for a master or a father, on the other hand, is not the same

as what is just for citizens but is similar to it; for there can be no unquali-   10
fied injustice towards what belongs to oneself since a man's possession or
child (till it reaches the age when it becomes separate) is like a part of
himself, and no one intends to harm himself. In view of this, there can be
no injustice towards oneself.[9] Hence what is just or unjust for a master or
a father is not political; for the politically just or unjust was stated to be
according to law[10] and to exist among those who by nature live according
to law, and these were stated to be equal in ruling and in being ruled.[11]   15
Hence what is just applies to one's wife more than to one's children or
possessions,[12] for this is what is just in a household; but this, too, is
distinct from what is politically just.

   That which is politically just may be natural or legal. It is natural if it
has the same power everywhere[13] and is not subject to what one thinks   20
of it or not; it is legal if originally it makes no difference whether it takes
one form or another but, after a form is posited, it does make a difference,
e.g., the specification that a prisoner's ransom shall be one mina, or that
a goat shall be sacrificed and not two sheep, and in addition, all laws
passed for individual cases, like that concerning a sacrifice in honor of
Brasydas [a Spartan general] or any particular decree.

   There are some who think that all kinds of justice are such as these [i.e.,   25
legal], in view of the fact that what exists by nature is unchangeable and
has the same power everywhere, like fire, which burns here as well as in
Persia, but that things which are just are observed to be subject to change.
Such is not the case, however, although there is a sense in which this is
true. Perhaps among the gods, at least, this is not the case at all,[14] but
among us there is something which is just by nature, even if all of what is
just is subject to change. Nevertheless, some of what is just exists by   30
nature and some not by nature.[15] Now of things which can be otherwise,
what kind exist by nature also and what kind exist not by nature but by
law or convention, if indeed they are alike in being both subject to change,
is clear from the examples which follow; and the same distinction applies
to the other cases. The right hand is by nature stronger, although it is possible for some men to become ambidextrous.[16] As for the things which are   35
just by convention or expediency, they are like standard measures; for   1035*a*
measures of wine or of corn are not everywhere equal but larger in whole-
sale and smaller in retail markets. Similarly, what is just according to men
and not by nature is not the same everywhere, since forms of government,

5   too, are not all the same; nevertheless, there is only one form of government which is by nature the best everywhere.[17]

Of that which is just and according to law [universally taken], each is
related to the individuals under it in a universal manner; for the things
which are done are [numerically] many, while each of the former, being a
universal, is one.[18] There is also a difference between an unjust effect and
what is unjust, and between a restitution and what is just; for that which
10 is unjust exists by nature or by enactment,[19] but when that thing is done,[20]
it is an unjust effect, whereas prior to being done it is not yet so but is
unjust.[21] So, too, with a restitution; but the common term is rather 'a just
effect', while the correction of an unjust effect is called 'a restitution'.[22]
Each of these should be examined later[23] with respect to the nature and
15 number of the species under it and the kind of things each species is concerned with.

Just and unjust things being those which we have stated, a man *acts* unjustly or justly when he does these things voluntarily; but when he does
them involuntarily, he *acts* neither unjustly nor justly, except by accident,[24]
for it is by accident that what he does is unjust or just. Thus an unjust and
20 a just effect are distinguished by being voluntary and [not] involuntary;
for when that which is unjust is done voluntarily, the man is blamed, and
at the same time the thing done is an unjust effect. Hence there are some
unjust things which are not yet unjust effects, namely, when voluntariness
is not present in them. By 'voluntary', as stated earlier,[25] I mean that
which, being in a man's power to do, he does knowingly and not in ig-
25 norance of the person *acted* upon or of the means used or of the purpose
of his action, e.g., not in ignorance of whom he strikes and with what and
why, if he does each of these [striking a man, using an instrument, having
a purpose] not by accident nor by force (as when A uses by force B's hand
to strike C, in which case B's act is not voluntary since it was not in his
power to act so). Thus the man struck may be the striker's father, but the
30 striker may know that he is striking a man or one of those present and
still not know that it is his father; and a similar distinction may be made
with regard to the purpose and the whole *action*. That which is done
through ignorance, then, or is done not through ignorance but either (a)
when it is not in the power of the doer to *act* or not *act* or (b) when it is
done under compulsion, is involuntary; for even of things existing by
1135b nature there are many which we know and do or which affect us, but

which are neither voluntary nor involuntary, e.g., getting old or dying.[26] What is done by accident, too, applies alike to what is unjust and to what is just. For a man might return a deposit unwillingly and because he is   5 afraid, in which case we should not say that he does what is just or that he *acts* justly, unless it be by accident; and, in a similar way, a man who is forced unwillingly not to return a deposit should not be considered as *acting* unjustly or as doing what is unjust, except by accident.[27]

Of voluntary *actions*, some we perform by intention, others not by intention; we perform by intention those about which we have previously   10 deliberated, and we perform not by intention those about which we have not previously deliberated. Thus there are three kinds of harm which arise in associations among men. Those ones done with ignorance result from error, and they are done when the person *acted* upon or the instrument used or the outcome of the *action* is not what the agent supposed it to be; for he may have thought that he was not striking, or not with this instrument, or not this man, or not for the sake of this [i.e., what actually occurred], but what happened is not what he thought would happen   15 (e.g., he struck not to wound the man but to urge him on, or he struck but not him, or he struck but not in the way he thought). Accordingly, (1) when the harm done is contrary to calculation, it is a mishap; (2) when it is not contrary to calculation yet without vice, it results from error, for one is mistaken when the source which causes the harm is in him, but he meets with a mishap when the source is outside of him; (3) when a man   20 *acts* knowingly but (a) without previous deliberation, the harm is an unjust effect (e.g., like those through anger or other passions which are compelling or natural to men), for although men *act* unjustly when they cause harm and are mistaken, and the effect is unjust, still they are not yet unjust or wicked because of these *actions*, since the harm done results not through an evil habit; but (b) when a man acts by intention, he is unjust   25 and evil. Hence *actions* proceeding from anger are rightly judged as done not by forethought; for it is not the man in anger who first starts to act but the man who provokes him to anger. Moreover, the dispute here is not whether the angry man *acted* or not but whether his *action* was just or not; for anger is caused by what appears to be an *act* of injustice. For the dispute is not about the occurrence of the act (as it is in exchanges in which   30 one of the parties is of necessity evil, if the dispute is not caused by forgetfulness);[28] both parties agree as to what has occurred but disagree as to

whether it was just (whereas in exchanges, the man who plots against a
second man is not ignorant of it), so while one of them, the second, thinks
1136a   he is being treated unjustly, the first does not so think. So if a man causes
harm by intention, he *acts* unjustly;[29] and it is precisely in virtue of such
unjust effects,[30] which are in violation of what is proportional or fair, that
the man who *acts* unjustly is unjust. Similarly, a man is just when he *acts*
5   justly by intention; and he *acts* justly if he *acts* only voluntarily.[31]

Of involuntary *acts*, some are pardonable but others not; for the errors
which men make not merely in ignorance but because of ignorance are
pardonable,[32] while those which are made not because of ignorance, but
in ignorance and yet because of a passion which is neither physical nor
such that men are likely to do,[33] are not pardonable.

11

10   One may wonder whether to be treated unjustly and to *act* unjustly have
been adequately specified.[1] (1) If it is possible to say truly, as Euripides
expressed it in a strange manner,

"I killed my mother, the tale is briefly told."
"Were you both willing, or unwilling both?",[2]

15   is it truly possible for a man to be willingly treated unjustly, or is a man
always unwilling to be treated unjustly, just as *acting* unjustly is always
voluntary? Is a man, then, treated unjustly always in this manner [in-
voluntarily], or always in that manner [voluntarily], as in the case of
acting unjustly, or sometimes voluntarily and sometimes involuntarily?
And (2) similarly, when one is treated justly; for it is always voluntarily
20   that one *acts* justly, so it is reasonable that there should be a similar
opposition in being treated unjustly and in being treated justly and that
each of these should be either [always] voluntary or [always] involuntary.[3]
But it would also seem strange if being treated justly, too, were posited as
being always voluntary; for some people are treated justly but unwillingly.[4]

One might raise also a second problem, whether everyone who suffers
what is unjust is treated unjustly, or is the case of suffering what is unjust
25   like that of doing what is unjust?[5] For in both cases it is possible to partake of what is just by accident, and clearly the situation is similar in

partaking of what is unjust; for to do what is unjust is not the same as to *act* unjustly, and to suffer what is unjust is not the same as to be treated unjustly. It is likewise with *acting* justly and being treated justly; for it is impossible for a man to be treated unjustly if another man does not *act* unjustly, or for a man to be treated justly if another man does not *act*   30 justly.[6] But if to *act* unjustly without qualification is to harm someone voluntarily, and if 'voluntarily' means knowing the thing one does and also the person *acted* upon and the instrument used and the manner in which he *acts*, and if the incontinent man voluntarily harms himself, then he would voluntarily be treated unjustly, and so it would be possible for one to *act* unjustly towards himself. But this, too, is one of the problems,   1136*b* namely, whether it is possible for a man to *act* unjustly towards himself.[7] In addition, a man, because of his incontinence, might voluntarily be harmed by another man who *acts* voluntarily, and so it would [seem to] be possible for a man to be voluntarily treated unjustly.[8]

But is our specification right? If not, we should add to "harming another with knowledge of the man harmed and of the instrument used and of the manner" the expression "against his wish". Accordingly, a man   5 may voluntarily be harmed or suffer what is unjust, but no one is voluntarily treated unjustly, for no one wishes to be treated unjustly, not even the incontinent man, although the latter may do something which is against his own wish; for no one wishes what he considers not to be good, and it is the incontinent man himself who does what he thinks he should not do.[9] As for the man who gives what is his own, as Homer tells of Glaucon's   10 having given Diomedes

Armour of gold for brazen, worth the price of
A hundred beeves for nine,[10]

he is not unjustly treated; for it is up to him to give, while it is not up to him to be treated unjustly since this would require another man to *act* unjustly.[11] With regard to being treated unjustly, then, it is clear that it is not voluntary.

12

Of the problems which we intended to discuss, there still remain two: the   15 third is, whether the man who *acts* unjustly is (a) the distributor who assigns to another more than the latter deserves or (b) the latter who receives more than he deserves, and the fourth is, whether it is possible for a man to *act* unjustly towards himself or not.[1]

Now if, in the third problem, alternative (a) is possible and it is the giver who *acts* unjustly and not he who receives more, then he who
20 knowingly and voluntarily gives another more than he gives himself *acts* unjustly towards himself.[2] This indeed is what moderate[3] men are thought to do; for a *good* man tends to take less than he deserves. But is not this an unqualified statement? For a *good* man gets more than his share of some other good, e.g., more reputation or, simply stated, more of what is noble.[4] Moreover, the problem is also solved in view of the definition of *acting* unjustly; for one does not suffer contrary to his own wish, and so
25 he is not being treated unjustly through his *act* of giving another more, but, if at all, he is only harmed.[5] It is also evident that it is the distributor who *acts* unjustly, but not always he who ends up having more;[6] for he who *acts* unjustly is not he who ends up having what is unjust,[7] but he who voluntarily does this, and that which acts here is the source which begins the *action*, and this is in the person who makes the distribution and
30 not in the person who receives. Again, since 'to act' has many senses, and since there is a sense in which that which kills may be something lifeless, or a hand, or a servant who is ordered to do so, these do not *act* unjustly, although what they do is unjust. Again, if one gave a judgement in ignorance [of all the relevant particulars], neither does he *act* unjustly according to what is legally just nor is his judgement unjust, except in a certain sense; for what is legally just is distinct from the first kind of what
1137a is just.[8] But if it is with knowledge that he gives a judgement which is unjust, then he too gets more, whether this be a favor or vengeance. Accordingly, as in the case of a man who takes for himself the greater part of an unjust effect, so here a man who judges unjustly because of any of these [favor or revenge] gets more; for if, for example, the unjust gain which results from his judgement is a plot of land, he still gets money from the gainer if not a share of the land.

13

5   Men think that it is in their power to *act* unjustly, and hence that it is easy to be just also. But such is not the case; for to commit adultery or strike a neighbor or deliver a bribe is easy and in our power, but to do these by

being disposed in a certain way is neither easy nor in our power.[1] Likewise, men think that one needs no wisdom to know what is just and what   10
is unjust, since it is not hard to understand what the laws state. It is not
these [to have the power and to understand the laws], however, that are
just, except indirectly, but the manner in which just things are done or
distributed,[2] and to do just things in a certain manner is a greater task
than to know what produces health (though even here it is easy to know
that honey and wine and hellebore and cautery and surgery produce   15
health, but to know how to use these, and for whom, and when, etc., in
bringing about health, is such a task that only a doctor can succeed).[3]

For this very *reason*, too, men think that it is in the power of the just
man to *act* unjustly no less than in the power of the unjust man, since the
just man is not less but even more able to do each of these unjust things;
for he is able to commit adultery or to strike a neighbor, and a brave man   20
can throw away his shield and turn to flight in this or that direction. Yet
to *act* in a cowardly way or unjustly is not simply to do these things, except
accidentally,[4] but to do so by being disposed in a certain manner, just as
to practice medicine or to heal is not just to use or not to use a knife, nor   25
just to give or not to give medicine, but to do so in such-and-such a
manner.[5]

What is just exists among those who participate in unqualified goods[6]
and who may have them in excess or in deficiency. For some beings (e.g.,
perhaps the gods) can have no excess of these goods;[7] others (the incurably
bad) get no benefit from any part of them but always harm, still others   30
are benefited up to a point. For this *reason*, justice and injustice belong
only to men.

14

Next we shall consider equity and the equitable (or *good*) and discuss how equity is related to justice, and how the equitable is related to
what is just, for upon examination they appear to be neither the same in
an unqualified way[1] nor different in genus; and while sometimes we   35
praise what is equitable and the equitable man (and in such a way that
even in other instances of praise we use the term 'equitable' instead of the   1137*b*
term 'good', and by 'a more equitable thing' we mean a thing which is
better), at other times it appears absurd, if we are to follow reason, that
what is equitable, though in violation of what is just, is nevertheless

praiseworthy. For either (a) what is just is not good, or (b) what is equi-
5   table is not just, if what is equitable is different from what is just,[2] or else
(c) they are the same if both of them are good.

The problem regarding what is equitable, then, arises mainly because
of the above arguments, all of which are in some sense right and in no way
contrary to each other; for the equitable is just although it is better than
one kind of what is just, and it is better than that kind of what is just not
10   by coming under another genus.[3] So the just[4] and the equitable are the
same [generically], and though both of them are good, the equitable is
superior.

What causes the problem is the fact that the equitable is just not according to law but as something which is a correction of what is legally
just. The *reason* for being better than, or a correction of, the legally just
is the fact that all laws are universal in statement but about some things it
is not possible for a universal statement to be right.[5] So in certain cases,
15   in which a universal statement is necessary but no universal statement can
be [completely] right, the law accepts what is mostly or in the majority
of cases right without being ignorant that there is error in so doing. And in
doing this, it is nonetheless right, for the error lies neither in the statement
of the law nor in the lawgiver, but in the nature of the subject; for from
the start the subject matter of *actions* which are done is of such a nature.
20   So when the law makes a universal statement about a subject but an instance of that subject is not rightly covered by that statement, then it is
right to correct the omission made by the legislator when he left some error in his unqualified [i.e., universal] statement; for the legislator himself
would have made that correction had he been present, or he would have
legislated accordingly if he had known.[6]

Thus the equitable is just; and it is better than a certain kind of what is
25   just, not the unqualified just[7] but that which has error because it is stated
in an unqualified manner [i.e., universally]. And this is the nature of the
equitable, namely, a correction[8] of the law insofar as the law errs because
it is or must be stated universally. And the *reason* why not all things come
under the law is this, that it is impossible to lay down the law for some
things, and so a decree[9] is needed. For of that which is indefinite, the rule
30   too is indefinite, like the leaden rule used in Lesbian construction;[10] for
the rule here is not rigid but adapts itself to the shape of the stone, and so
does the decree when applied to its [variable] subject matter.

It is clear, then, what the equitable is: it is what is just, and it is better than one kind of what is just. It is also evident from this who the equitable man is; for he who is disposed and intends to do equitable things and is not overly just in insisting that his neighbor get less but is content to take less, although he has the law on his side, is an equitable man, and the corresponding disposition is equity, which is one kind of justice and not a disposition of a different genus.

35

1138a

15

Whether a man can *act* unjustly towards himself or not is evident from what has been said. Now (1) just things of one kind are those done with respect to every virtue laid down by the law, e.g., the law commands us not to commit suicide, and it forbids us to do what it commands us not to do. Furthermore, when a man voluntarily harms another not in retaliation but in violation of the law, he *acts* unjustly, and in doing so voluntarily he knows the person harmed and the instrument used, etc. But the man who ·voluntarily kills himself through anger does so in violation of right reason, and the law does not permit this; so he *acts* unjustly. But towards whom? Surely towards the state and not towards himself;[1] for he suffers voluntarily, but no one is voluntarily treated unjustly. And it is in view of this that the state imposes a penalty by attaching a certain dishonor to those who kill themselves and who thus *act* unjustly towards the state.[2]

5

10

Again, a man who is unjust by only *acting* unjustly and is not wholly bad[3] cannot *act* unjustly towards himself (for this *action* is different from the other;[4] for there is a sense in which an unjust man is wicked like a coward and not in the sense of being wholly wicked,[5] and so he does not *act* unjustly in virtue of this [whole wickedness]); for otherwise (a) he would be subtracting and adding the same thing to the same person at the same time, and this is impossible, since what is just or unjust requires more than one person.[6] Besides, (b) to *act* unjustly is voluntary or by intention and is prior in time; for he who, because he has suffered, performs the same *act* in return is not thought to be *acting* unjustly, while he who *acts* on himself would be suffering and acting the same thing at the same time.[7] Again, (c) in *acting* unjustly towards himself he would be treated unjustly but voluntarily.[8]

15

20

Finally, no one *acts* unjustly without doing some specific thing which

25

is an unjust effect; but no one commits adultery with his own wife or breaks into his own house or steals his own property.[9]

In general, the problem of whether it is possible for one to *act* unjustly towards himself or not is solved by the specification we made with regard to whether it is possible for one to voluntarily be treated unjustly.[10]

It is also evident that both are bad, i.e., to be treated unjustly and to *act*
30   unjustly; for the one is to have less and the other is to have more than the mean, which is like that which is healthy in medical science or that which causes a good physical condition in gymnastics. To *act* unjustly, however, is worse; for *acting* unjustly is done with vice and is blameworthy, and this vice is either complete or unqualified or close to it (for not all voluntary *acts* are done with injustice),[11] while he who is treated unjustly does not
35   [in being so treated] have vice or injustice.[12] In itself, then, being treated
1138*b*   unjustly is less bad than *acting* unjustly, but nothing prevents it from being by accident a greater evil. Art, of course, is not concerned with accidents, and it states, for example, that pleurisy is a greater disease than a hurt caused by a stumble;[13] but the reverse might happen by accident, e.g., if a
5   soldier, by stumbling, happens to get caught by the enemy and be put to death.[14]

Metaphorically or by similarity (a) what is just may arise between the parts of a man but not between the man [as a whole] and himself, and (b) between a master and a slave or between members of a household not every kind of what is just may arise;[15] for in such discussions[16] the rational part of the soul is distinguished from the nonrational part. It is indeed by
10   attending to these parts that people also think that a man may be unjust to himself, for these parts may suffer something contrary to their desires; so what is just between these, too, is like what is just between a man who rules and a man who is ruled.[17]

Concerning justice and the other ethical virtues, then, let this be our account.

BOOK Z

1

Since we have stated earlier that one should choose the mean and not   18 1138*b*
excess or deficiency,[1] and since the mean is such as right reason[2] declares   20
it to be, let us go over this next. Now in each of the habits we have mentioned,[3] as in all the other cases also [art, inquiry, *action*, intention],[4] there
is an aim in view towards which a man who has reason intensifies or slows
down [his feelings or *actions*], and there is a definition of the mean which,
we maintain, lies between excess and deficiency and exists in accordance   25
with right reason. Such a statement is indeed true, but not at all clear;[5] for
in other endeavors, too, of which there is a science, it is true to say that
we should exert ourselves or slacken neither more nor less but in moderation and as right reason states, but with this alone a man would not know   30
any more, e.g., [he would not know] what kind of medicine to apply to the
body if some one were to say "whatever medical science prescribes and as
the doctor orders". So with regards to the dispositions of the soul, too, one
should not only state this truth but also specify what right reason is and
what its definition is.

2

In distinguishing the virtues of the soul we stated[1] that some are ethical   35
and the others intellectual. We have already discussed the ethical virtues;   1139*a*
as for the others, we shall proceed as follows, after some preliminary
remarks about the soul.

We have stated previously that there are two parts of the soul, the one
which has reason and the other which is nonrational.[2] As we must now sub-   5
divide the part which has reason in the same manner, let it be assumed that
there are two parts which have reason: (a) that by which we perceive the
kinds of things whose principles cannot be other than they are [i.e., cannot
vary], and (b) that by which we investigate the kinds of things whose principles may be other than they are [i.e., can vary];[3] for corresponding to

10   distinct genera of things there are in the soul generically distinct parts, each of which is by its nature concerned with its own genus of things, if indeed it is in virtue of a certain likeness and kinship to each genus of things that the knowledge of those things belongs to each of those parts.[4] So let one part of the soul be called 'scientific'; and let the other be called 'estimative', for to deliberate and to estimate[5] are the same [generically], and no one deliberates about the things which cannot be other than they

15   are. So the estimative part is one part of the soul which has reason. We must consider, then, what is the best disposition with respect to each of these parts, for that disposition would be the virtue of each part, and each virtue is relative to its proper function.

      There are three parts of the soul which have authority over *action* or truth: sense [i.e., power of sensation], intellect (or intuition), and desire. Of these, sense is not a principle[6] of any *action*; and this is clear from the

20   fact that brutes have sense but do not participate in *action*. Now what affirmation and denial are to *thought*, pursuit and avoidance are to desire; so since ethical virtue is a habit through intention while intention is desire through deliberation, reason should, because of these, be true and

25   desire should be right, if indeed intention is to be good, and what reason asserts desire should pursue.[7] So this *thought* or truth is practical, while goodness[8] or badness in *thought* which is theoretical but neither practical nor productive is, respectively, truth or falsity; for this is the function of the *thinking* part of the soul, while the function of the part which is both

30   practical and *thinking* is truth in agreement with right desire. Now the principle of *action* is intention, but as a source of motion and not as a purpose, whereas that of intention is desire and reason for the sake of something;[9] hence intention cannot exist without intuition and *thought*,[10]

35   nor without ethical habit,[11] for goodness or its opposite in *action* cannot exist without *thought* and character.[12] It is not *thought* as such that can move anything, but *thought* which is for the sake of something and is

1139b practical, for it is this that rules productive *thought* also; for he who produces does so for the sake of something [a product], though a product is not an end without qualification but is relative to something else and is a qualified end.[13] But an object of *action* [is an end without qualification], for a good *action* is [such] an end, and this is what we desire. Hence inten-

5   tion is either a desiring intellect or a *thinking* desire, and such a principle is a man.[14]

An object of intention cannot be a past event, e.g., no one intends the destruction of Troy in the past, for no one deliberates about past events but only about future events and what may or may not turn out to be the case. Past events cannot be undone, and Agathon was right in saying,

Of this alone, you see, is God deprived,   10
To make undone whatever has been done.[15]

The function of both thinking parts of the soul, then, is truth; so the disposition according to which each part attains truth in the highest sense is the virtue of that part.

3

Let us start our discussion, then, once more from the beginning. Let [us   15
posit that] the things by which the soul possesses truth when it affirms or denies something are five in number: art, *knowledge* [or scientific knowledge], prudence, wisdom, and intuition, for one may think falsely by belief or opinion,[1] [so we leave these out].

What *knowledge* is, if we are to speak precisely and not follow meta-phorical language, is evident from the following. We all believe that the   20
thing which we *know* cannot be other than it is;[2] and as for the things which may be other than they are [i.e., may or may not be],[3] when they are outside of our observation, we are not in a position to know whether they exist or not.[4] Thus the object of *knowledge* exists of necessity, and hence it is eternal; for all things which exist of necessity without qualifica-tion are eternal,[5] and what is eternal is ungenerable and indestructible. Further, it is thought that all *knowledge* can be taught and that all objects   25
of *knowledge* can be learned. Now all teaching proceeds from what is previously known, as we have already stated in the *Analytics*; for it may proceed either by induction or by syllogism.[6] But induction is a starting point and leads to the universal,[7] while a syllogism proceeds from the universal. Hence there are principles from which a syllogism is formed   30
and of which there is no syllogism;[8] so it is by induction that principles are acquired. Thus *knowledge* is a disposition acquired by way of demon-stration,[9] and to this may be added the other specifications given in the *Analytics*;[10] for it is when one is both convinced and is familiar with the principles in a certain manner that he has *knowledge*, since he will have

35   *knowledge* only by accident if he is not convinced of the principles more
than of the conclusion.[11]

Let *knowledge*, then, be specified in this manner.

4

1140*a*   That which may or may not be can be an object produced as well as an
object of *action*.[1] Now production is distinct from *action* (and one may be
convinced of this from public writings), and so practical dispositions with
5   reason are distinct from productive dispositions with reason; and in view
of this, the two exclude each other, for no *action* is a production, and no
production is an *action*.[2] Since architecture is an art and is a species of a
disposition with reason and ability to produce something, and since there
is no art which is not a disposition with reason and ability to produce
10   something and no disposition such as this which is not an art, art would
be the same [in essence or definition] as a disposition with true[3] reason
and with ability to produce something. Every art is concerned with
bringing something into existence, and to think by art is to investigate how
to generate something which may or may not exist and of which the
[moving] principle is in the producer and not in the thing produced; for
art is not concerned with things which exist or come to be of necessity, nor
15   with things which do so according to their nature, for these have the
[moving] principle in themselves.[4] So since production and *action* are different, art must be concerned with production and not with *action*. And
in some sense both luck and art are concerned with the same things;[5] as
20   Agathon says, "art is fond of luck, and luck of art."[6]

As we have stated, then, art is a disposition tending to produce with
true reason something which may or may not be, while bad art, which is
its contrary, is a disposition tending to produce with false reason something which may or may not be.

5

25   Concerning prudence, we might arrive at its nature by examining the
nature of those whom we call 'prudent'. A prudent man is thought to be
one who is able to deliberate well concerning what is good and expedient
for himself, not with respect to a part, e.g., not the kinds of things which

are good and useful for health or strength, but the kinds of things which are good and expedient for living well [in general].[1] A sign of this is the fact that even in some particular respect we call 'prudent' those who make good judgments about things for a particular good end of which there is 30 no art.[2] So a man who deliberates [well] might be prudent in a general way also.[3]

Now no one deliberates about things which cannot vary, nor about those which he cannot himself do. Hence since scientific knowledge is acquired by means of demonstration, and since there can be no demonstration of things whose principles may vary (for all these things may 35 vary, and it is not possible to deliberate about necessary things), prudence 1140b cannot be scientific knowledge or art;[4] it cannot be scientific knowledge since the object of *action* may vary, and it cannot be art since the genus of *action* is different from that of production. What remains, then, is this: prudence is a disposition with true reason and ability for *actions* con- 5 cerning what is good or bad for man; for the end of production is some other thing [i.e., a product], but in the case of *action* there is no other end (for a good *action* is itself the end). It is because of this that we consider Pericles and others like him to be prudent, for they are able to perceive what is good for themselves as well as for other men; and we regard also 10 financial administrators and statesmen to be such.[5] And it is from this disposition that the term 'temperance' (=σωφροσύνη) is named after the term 'prudence' (=φρόνησις), as if indicating something which preserves prudence (=σώζουσα τὴν φρόνησιν). And temperance does preserve such a belief [i.e., prudence];[6] for it is not every kind of belief that the pleasant and the painful corrupt or pervert, like the belief that the 15 triangle has or has not its angles equal to two right angles, but only those concerned with objects of *action*.[7] For the starting-point[8] of an *action* is the purpose of that *action*. But to him who is corrupted because of pleasure or pain the starting-point[8] is not apparent, nor is it apparent that he should choose and do everything for the sake of this and because of this starting-point; for vice is destructive of the starting-point.[8] 20

Prudence, then, must be a disposition with true reason and ability for *actions* concerning human goods. Further, while there is virtue with respect to art, there is no virtue with respect to prudence;[9] and while in art he who errs willingly is preferable, in the case of prudence he who does so is the reverse, as in the case of virtues.[10] So it is clear that prudence is a

25   virtue and not an art. And as there are in the soul two parts which have
     reason, prudence would be a virtue in one of them, that which can form
     opinions; for both opinion and prudence are about things which may or
     may not be. Finally, prudence is not just a disposition with reason; and a
     sign of this is the fact that a disposition with reason may be forgotten,[11]
30   but prudence cannot.

6

     Since scientific knowledge is belief of universal and necessary things, and
     since there are principles of whatever is demonstrable and of all scientific
     knowledge (for scientific knowledge is knowledge with the aid of reason),
     a principle of what is scientifically known cannot be scientific knowledge
35   or art or prudence; for what is scientifically known is demonstrable, while
1141a art and prudence are about things which may or may not be. Nor is
     wisdom of [just] these principles; for it is possible for a wise man to give
     some demonstrations. So if the [dispositions or principles] by which we
     think truly and never think falsely concerning things which cannot vary
5   (or even those which can vary)[1] may be scientific knowledge, prudence,
     wisdom, and intuition, since they [the dispositions or principles] cannot
     be three of them (prudence, scientific knowledge, wisdom), we are left
     with intuition [as the disposition] of those principles.

7

10   In the arts, we attribute wisdom to men who are most accurate in their
     field, e.g., we say that Phidias the sculptor is wise and Polyclitus the statue-
     maker is wise, and by 'wisdom' here we mean nothing but the virtue of
     an art. But we regard some men as being wise in general and not in a
     particular field or in some other qualified way, as Homer says in *Margites*,

15   The Gods, then, did not make him wise at digging
     Nor plowing nor at any other thing.[1]

     So clearly wisdom would be the most accurate of the sciences. Thus the
     wise man must not only know what follows from the principles, but also
     possess truth about the principles.[2]
          Wisdom, then, would be intuition[3] and scientific knowledge of the most
20   honorable objects, as if it were scientific knowledge with its own leader;[4]

for it would be absurd to regard politics or prudence as the best [disposi-tion], if man is not the best of beings in the universe.[5] If indeed what is healthy or what is good is different for men and for fishes, while what is white or what is straight is always the same, everyone would say that what is wise is always the same while what is prudent may be different; for they 25 would say that a prudent creature is one which perceives well matters which are for its own good and they would entrust those matters to that creature[6]. It is in view of this that people say that some brutes too are prudent, namely, those which appear to have the power of foresight with regard to their own way of life. It is also evident that wisdom and politics are not the same. For if by 'wisdom' one were to mean the disposition 30 which is concerned with things which are to one's benefit, there would be many kinds of wisdom; for there would be not one kind of wisdom con-cerned with the good of all kinds of animals but a different kind for each species of animals, unless one were to go as far as to say that there is one medical art for all the kinds of things also. And if one were to say that man is the best of the animals, this too would make no difference; for there are also other things much more divine in their nature than man, 1141*b* like the most visible objects of which the universe is composed.[7]

From what has been said, then, it is clear that wisdom is scientific knowledge and intuition of the objects which are most honorable by their nature. It is in view of this that Anaxagoras and Thales and others like them, who are seen to ignore what is expedient to themselves, are called 5 'wise' but not 'prudent'; and they are said to have understanding of things which are great and admirable and difficult to know and divine but which are not instrumental for other things,[8] for they do not seek human goods.

8

Prudence, on the other hand, is concerned with things which are human and objects of deliberation; for we maintain that the function of a prudent man is especially this, to deliberate well, and no one deliberates about in- 10 variable things or about things not having an end which is a good attain-able by *action*; and a man who deliberates well without qualification is one who, by judgment, can aim well at the things which are attainable by *action* and are best for man.

Now prudence is not limited to what is universal but must know also 15 the particulars; for it is practical, and *action* is concerned with particulars.[1] And it is in view of this that some men, without universal knowledge but with experience in other things, are more practical than those who have universal knowledge only; for if a man knew universally that light meats are digestible and healthy but did not know what kinds of meats 20 are light, he would not produce health, but a man who knows that chicken is light and healthy is more likely to produce health. Now prudence is concerned with *actions*; so we should have both kinds of knowledge, or else the latter rather than the former, which is universal.[2] Nevertheless, in this case too there should be one kind of knowledge which is architectonic.[3]

Both politics and prudence are the same disposition, but in essence they 25 are not the same.[4] Of prudence concerned with the state, the one which is architectonic is legislative, while the other which is concerned with particulars has the common name 'political prudence'; and the latter is concerned with particular *actions* and deliberations, for a particular measure voted on is like an individual thing to be *acted* upon. In view of this, only those engaged in such *actions* are called 'public servants', for only these *act* like manual laborers.[5]

30 Prudence is thought to be concerned most of all with matters relating to the person in whom it exists and with him only; and this disposition has the common name 'prudence'. Of the other kinds, one is financial management, another is law-giving, and a third is political, of which one part is deliberative and the other judicial.

9

One kind of prudence,[1] then, would be knowing what is good for oneself, 1142*a* and this differs much from the others; and a man who knows and is engaged in matters which concern himself is thought to be prudent, while public servants are thought to busy themselves with other people's business. For this reason Euripides says,[2]

But how might I be wise, who could, unbusied,
Listed as one among the army's mass,
Have had an equal share? ....
5 For those who do too much and are excessive ....

For these[3] seek what is good for themselves and think that this is what they should be doing. And from this opinion arose the belief that only these are prudent, although perhaps one's own good cannot exist without financial management nor without some form of government.[4] Moreover, 10 how one should manage his own household is not clear and needs consideration. A sign of what has been said[5] is also the *reason* why young men become geometricians and mathematicians and wise[6] in such [fields] but do not seem to become prudent. That *reason* is the fact that prudence is concerned with particulars, which become familiar from experience; but 15 a young man is not experienced, for experience requires much time.[7] And if one were to inquire why it is possible for a boy to become a mathematician but not wise or a physicist, the answer is this: the objects of mathematics exist by abstraction while the principles of philosophy and of physics are acquired from experience;[8] and young men have no conviction of their principles but only use words, while the nature of the objects 20 of physics and of wisdom is not unclear to physicists and wise men. Further, error in deliberation may be either about the universal or about the particular; for we may err either concerning the fact that all heavy water is bad or concerning the fact that this sample of water is heavy.[9]

It is evident, then, that prudence is not scientific knowledge; for it is concerned with the ultimate particular, as we said, and such is the object 25 of *action*. It is thus opposed to intuition; for intuition is of definitions, for which there is no reasoning,[10] while prudence is of the ultimate particular, which is an object not of science but of sensation, not the sensation of proper sensibles, but like that by which we sense that the ultimate particular in mathematics is a triangle (for even in mathematics there is a stop in the direction of the particular).[11] But this kind of sensation is closer to sensation [in the main sense] than to prudence, while the sensa- 30 tion of the other [i.e., by prudence] is of another kind.[12]

10

Inquiry differs from deliberation; for deliberation is a species of inquiry.[1] We should also grasp the nature of good deliberation,[2] whether it is scientific knowledge of some kind or opinion or discernment or a thing in some other genus. Now it is not scientific knowledge; for scientists do not inquire about the things they know, while good deliberation is a kind 1142*b* of deliberation, and he who deliberates inquires and makes estimates. Again, it is not discernment, for discernment acts without the use of

reason and quickly, while those who deliberate take much time, and
5   people say that we should *act* quickly on the conclusions of deliberation
but we should deliberate slowly. Finally, acuteness is distinct from good
deliberation; for acuteness is a species of discernment. Nor is good de-
10   liberation a kind of opinion. But since he who deliberates badly is in error
while he who deliberates well is right, it is clear that good deliberation is
a kind of rightness, but neither of scientific knowledge nor of opinion. For
there can be no rightness (nor error) of scientific knowledge,[3] and rightness of opinion is its truth;[4] and the objects of opinion have already been
specified.[5] Yet good deliberation does not exist without the use of reason.
It remains, then, that it is [rightness] of *thinking*, for this [i.e., *thinking*] is
not yet assertion; for opinion too is not inquiry but is already an asser-
15   tion, while he who deliberates, whether well or badly, is in the process of
inquiring and estimating. But good deliberation is a kind of rightness of
deliberation;[6] so first, we should inquire what deliberation is and of what
object.

Since "rightness" has many senses, clearly good deliberation is not
rightness in every sense; for the incontinent or the bad man will, from
his judgment, [usually] attain that which he sets out to do, and so he will
20   have deliberated rightly, but what he has chosen is a great evil. Now to
deliberate well is thought to be a kind of good; for good deliberation is
rightness of such deliberation which brings about a good. But it is possible
to attain a good even by a false syllogism, i.e., to attain what needs be
done by a false middle term and not through the true term;[7] so this, too,
25   is not yet good deliberation, for it is deliberation in virtue of which one
attains what he should but not through the middle term he should. Again,
one man may attain an object after a long deliberation while another may
attain it quickly. Still a good deliberation is not quite attained in this
manner; for it is rightness with respect to that which is beneficial as well as
with respect to the proper object and the proper manner and the proper
time [etc.][8]. Finally, one may deliberate well either in an unqualified way
30   or relative to a qualified end.[9] Thus an unqualified good deliberation
succeeds with reference to an unqualified end while a qualified good
deliberation *succeeds* with reference to a qualified end. Accordingly, if to
deliberate well is a mark of a prudent man, good deliberation would be
rightness with respect to what is expedient in relation to an end[10] whose
prudence is true belief.

11

Intelligence or good intelligence, in virtue of which men are said to be in-   1143*a*
telligent or of good intelligence, is neither altogether the same as scientific
knowledge or as opinion (for all men would have been intelligent), nor is
it the same as any scientific knowledge in particular, like medical knowledge, which is concerned with health, or like geometry, which is concerned with magnitudes; for intelligence is concerned neither with eternal
or immovable objects[1] nor with any kind of things which are in the process   5
of becoming but with things about which one might raise questions and
deliberate.[2] Thus intelligence is concerned [generically] with the same
kind of objects as prudence, but intelligence is not the same [in definition]
as prudence. Prudence gives orders, for its end is what should or should
not be done, while intelligence only judges, for intelligence and good   10
intelligence are the same,[3] and so are men of intelligence and of good
intelligence. Now intelligence is neither the possession nor the acquiring
of prudence. But just as a learner is said to be intelligent when he uses
scientific knowledge, so a man is said to be intelligent when he uses opinion in judging objects of prudence, when someone else speaks about
them, and does so excellently;[4] for 'well' and 'excellently' are the same.[5]   15
And it is from this source that the name 'intelligence', according to which
men are said to be of good intelligence, came into use, namely, from its
use in learning; for 'learning' is often used to mean being intelligent.[6]

What we call '*judgment*', in virtue of which we say that a man is a good
judge or has *judgment*, is right judgment of an equitable man. A sign of   20
this is the fact that we speak of the equitable man as being the most
likely to forgive and of equity as showing forgiveness in certain cases.[7]
As for forgiveness, it is a species of right *judgment* of an equitable man;
and it is right by being of that which is true.[8]

12

Now all these dispositions are directed to the same things, and with good   25
reason. For when we speak of *judgment* and intelligence and prudence and
intuition, we regard the same men as having *judgment*, having intuition,
being prudent, and being intelligent, since all these are faculties dealing
with ultimates and particulars; and in having judgment about things with   30

which a prudent man is concerned, one is intelligent and has good *judgment* or is disposed to forgive, for equitable things are common to all good men in their relation to other men. Now all objects of *action* are particulars and ultimates; for both a prudent man should know them, and also
35   intelligence and *judgment* are concerned with them, and these objects are
1143*b*   ultimates.[1] And intuition, too, is of ultimates, and in both directions, for of both the primary terms[2] and the ultimate particulars there is intuition and not reasoning; and intuition with respect to demonstrations is of immovable terms and of that which is primary,[3] whereas in *practical* [reasonings intuition] is of the ultimate and variable objects and of the other [i.e., minor] premises, since these are principles of final cause;[4] for
5   it is from particulars that we come to universals.[5] Accordingly, we should have sensation[6] of these particulars, and this is intuition. And in view of this, it is thought that these [powers] are natural and that, while no one is by nature wise, one [by nature] has *judgment* and intelligence and intuition. A sign of this is the fact that these [powers] are thought to follow certain stages of our life, e.g., that such-and-such an age possesses intui-
10   tion or *judgment,* as if nature were the cause of it. Hence intuition is both a beginning and an end; for demonstrations come from these and are about these.[7] Consequently, one should pay attention to the undemonstrated assertions and opinions of experienced and older and prudent men no less than to demonstrations; for they observe rightly because they gained an eye from experience.[8]
15   We have stated, then, what prudence and wisdom are, and with what objects each is concerned, and that each of them is a virtue of a different part of the soul.

13

One might raise certain problems concerning these virtues:[1] Of what use are they? Wisdom investigates none of the things which make a man
20   happy, for it is not concerned with any generation of objects;[2] and though prudence does this, for what purpose is it needed, if indeed prudence is concerned with things which are just and noble and good for a man but which will be done by a good man anyway,[3] and if by merely knowing
25   them we are no more able to *act*, since the [ethical] virtues are habits,[4] just as we are no more able to perform, by knowing things which are healthy or in good physical condition, those things which do not them-

selves produce but come to be from the corresponding habits (for we are no more able to *act* in a healthy or well-conditioned manner by having medical science or the science of gymnastics)?[5] If, on the other hand, we are to posit a prudent man to be not for the sake of these but for the sake of coming to be virtuous, prudence would be of no use to those who are already virtuous, nor to those who do not possess virtue, for it would   30 make no difference whether they possess prudence themselves or obey those who possess it; and it would be enough for us if, in the case of prudence, we use the same argument as we did in the case of health, for although we wish to be healthy, still we do not learn medical science. Again, it would seem strange that prudence, which is inferior to wisdom, should be more authoritative than wisdom; for prudence, whose role is to   35 act, has a ruling and ordering function with respect to its objects.[6] These problems, then, should be discussed, for at present we have only raised them.

First, we maintain that these [wisdom and prudence] must be worthy of   1144*a* choice for their own sake, at least since each of them is a virtue of the corresponding part of the soul, even if neither of them produces anything.[7] But more than this, they do produce something, not as the medical art produces health, but as health [as a habit produces a healthy activity], and it is in this sense that wisdom produces happiness;[8] for being a part of the   5 whole of virtue, wisdom produces happiness by its possession[9] and its exercise.

Again, a man's work is completed by prudence as well as by ethical virtue; for while virtue makes the end in view right, prudence makes the means towards it right. But of the fourth part of the soul,[10] i.e., of the nutritive part, there is no such virtue; for that part cannot *act* or refrain   10 from *acting*.[11]

As for the argument that through prudence we are no more able to perform noble and just *actions*, let us begin a little way back and use the following principle. Just as we say that those who do what is just may not yet be just, as in the case of those who perform what is ordained by the   15 law but do so unwillingly or through ignorance or for some other reason but not for the sake of what is just (even if they do what they should and whatever a virtuous man ought to do),[12] so it seems that in order to be good a man must be disposed in a certain way, that is, he must *act* by intention and for the sake of the things done. Now that which makes the   20 intention right is virtue,[13] but the things which are by their nature done for the sake of [that intention] depend not on virtue but on another power.[14] Let us attend to these matters more clearly for a moment.

There is a power which is called 'shrewdness', and this is such as to 25 enable us to *act* successfully upon the means leading to an aim we set before us. If the aim is noble, that power is praiseworthy, but if the aim is bad, the power is called 'unscrupulousness'. It is in view of this that we speak even of prudent men as being shrewd or unscrupulous.[15] Now prudence is not shrewdness itself, but neither can it exist without this 30 power. And this disposition [i.e., prudence] develops by means of this eye of the soul,[16] but not without virtue,[17] as we have already stated and as is clear; for the syllogisms of things to be *acted* upon have a starting point,[18] such as this: "since such is the end, which is the best", whatever this may be; and for the sake of argument let any chance end which is the best be taken. This end is not apparent to a man who is not good, for his evil 35 habit perverts him and causes him to be mistaken about the starting-point[18] of *action*. Hence it is evident that a man cannot be prudent if he 1144*b* is not good.

Let us then examine also virtue once more; for virtue, too, has its parallel, that is, as prudence is related to shrewdness (by being similar but not the same), so natural virtue is related to virtue in the main sense.[19] For 5 all men think that each part of one's character exists in him by nature in some sense, since from the moment of birth we are in some sense just and temperate and brave and the like;[20] but we seek goodness taken in the main sense as something which is distinct from natural goodness, and we regard such [virtues as justice, temperance, and bravery] as existing in another manner. For natural dispositions exist also in children and in 10 brutes, but without intellect[21] they appear to be harmful. What seems to be observed is thus much, that just as a strong body in motion but without vision stumbles heavily because of its lack of vision, so it is in the case we are considering; so if a man acquires intellect, there will be a difference in his *action*, and it is only then that his disposition, though similar to the corresponding natural disposition, will be a virtue in the main sense. So 15 just as there are two kinds of dispositions in the part of the soul which forms opinions,[22] shrewdness and prudence, so also in the ethical part of the soul there are two dispositions, the one being natural virtue and the other being virtue in the main sense, and of these the one in the main sense cannot come into being without prudence.

In view of this, some thinkers assert that every virtue is a species of prudence; and Socrates was in one sense right in his inquiries concerning virtue but in another sense mistaken, for he was mistaken in regarding   20 every virtue to be prudence, but he spoke well in thinking that without prudence virtues cannot exist.[23] A sign of this is the following: all men who nowadays give a definition of a virtue, besides stating the objects to which the virtue is directed, add also the expression "a disposition according to right reason"; and, of course, reason is right if it is in accordance with prudence. So it seems that all men somehow have a strong inner sense that such a habit is a virtue in accordance with prudence. But   25 we must go a little further, for virtue is a habit not only according to right reason, but also with right reason;[24] and right reason about such things is prudence. Thus Socrates thought that virtues are [right] reasons (for he thought that virtue was *knowledge*), but we say that they are with reason.   30

It is clear from what has been said, then, that a man cannot be good in the main sense without prudence, nor can he be prudent without ethical virtue.[25] This fact would also refute the argument by which one might claim that the virtues are separable from each other; for [one might say that] the same man may not be most gifted by nature for all the virtues, and so he may have acquired some of them but not others. Now with   35 respect to the natural virtues, this is possible;[26] but with respect to those   1145*a* by which a man is called 'good' without qualification[27] it is not possible, for when this one [virtue] exists, i.e., prudence,[28] all the others are present also. It is also clear that, even if prudence were not practical, it would be needed because it is a virtue of a part of the soul, and that there can be no right intention without prudence or virtue; for the one[29] [i.e., virtue]   5 posits the end while the other [i.e., prudence] makes us do those things which bring about that end. Moreover, prudence does not rule wisdom or the best part of the soul, just as the medical art does not rule health; for prudence does not use wisdom but sees to it that wisdom is acquired. So prudence gives orders for the sake of wisdom but does not give orders to wisdom.[30] Further, saying that prudence rules wisdom is like saying   10 that politics rules the gods since it gives orders about all matters that belong to a state.

BOOK H

1

1145*a* 15   Next, let us make another start and list the three kinds of things which should be avoided in regard to character, namely, vice, incontinence, and brutality.[1] The contraries of two of these are clear, for the first is called 'virtue' and the second 'continence'; as for the contrary of brutality, it

20   would be most fitting to say that it is a virtue above us, one that is heroic and divine, as Homer made Priam say of Hector that he was exceptionally good,

He seemed no son of mortal man, but of God.[2]

So if, as they say, men become gods because they exceed in virtue, then
25   clearly the disposition opposed to that which is brutal would be one such as this; for just as in a brute there can be neither vice nor virtue, so in a god, but the disposition of a god would be more honorable than virtue, while that of a brute would be generically different from vice.[3]

Now as it is rarely that a divine man exists, if we are to use that expression of the Spartans whenever their admiration for a man is exceptionally high (for they call him 'a divine man'), so too a brutal man among men

30   high (for they call him 'a divine man'), so too a brutal man among men rarely exists. A brutal man is most likely to exist among barbarians, but sometimes also because of disease or injury; and we apply such bad expression also to those among men who go beyond the limits of vice. Some

35   mention concerning such a disposition will be made later,[4] and vice has already been discussed. We should now discuss incontinence, softness, and

1145*b*   effeteness, and also continence and endurance; for we should regard these habits as being neither the same as the virtues or the vices nor generically different.[5] So as in other cases we should, after laying down the facts as they appear and going over the difficulties,[6] indicate as far as possible the

5   truth of all the accepted opinions concerning these affections, or if not, the truth of most of those opinions or of the most important ones; for if the difficulties that cause concern are refuted and the accepted opinions are left standing, we shall have established our case sufficiently.

2

Now (1) both continence and endurance are thought to be among the things which are good and praiseworthy, but incontinence and softness among the things which are bad and blameworthy; and it is the same man   10
who is thought to be continent and disposed to abide by his judgement, or who is thought to be incontinent and disposed to depart from his judgement. And (2) it is thought that the incontinent man knows that to do certain things is bad but does them because of passion, and that the continent man knows that his *desires* are bad but does not follow them because of his reason. And (3) it is said that (a) a temperate man is continent and disposed to endure, and, according to some, every such man is   15
temperate, but, according to others, this is not so, and that (b) according to some, an intemperate man is incontinent and an incontinent man is intemperate indiscriminately, but, according to others, the two are different. (4) As for the prudent man, sometimes people say that he cannot be incontinent, but at other times they say that some prudent and shrewd men are incontinent. Finally, (5) men are called 'incontinent' even with respect to temper, or honor, or profit. These, then, are the things that are   20
said.[1]

3

One might raise the problem of how a man who has the right belief[1] of how to *act* can *act* incontinently.

Some say that if he has *knowledge* of how to *act* rightly, he cannot be incontinent; for, as *Socrates* thought, it would be strange for a man to   25
have *knowledge* and yet allow something else to rule him and drag him about like a slave.[2] For *Socrates* was entirely opposed to this view and held that there is no such thing as incontinence; for he thought that no one with the right belief does what is contrary to the best, but if a man does so, it is through ignorance.[3] Now this argument obviously disagrees with what appears to be the case; and if a man *acting* by passion does so through ignorance, we should look into the manner in which this ignorance arises.[4] For it is evident that an incontinent man, before getting into   30
a state of passion, does not think that he should do what he does when in passion.

There are some thinkers who partly agree with this view but partly disagree; for they admit that there is nothing stronger than *knowledge*,[5] but they do not agree with the view that no man *acts* contrary to what in his opinion is the better course, and because of this view they say that when an incontinent man is ruled by pleasures he does not have *knowledge* but opinion. But if it is opinion and not *knowledge*, and if the belief which resists the passion is not strong but weak,[6] as in men who hesitate, we should pardon those who fail to abide by that belief when they face a strong *desire*,[7] though not those who are ruled by an evil habit or any of the other blameworthy habits.

Is it then prudence which resists *desire*? For this is the strongest of the virtues. But it is absurd to think that prudence resists *desire*, for the same man would then be at the same time prudent and incontinent,[8] and no one would maintain that a prudent man would willingly perform the worst of *actions*. Moreover, it has been shown earlier that a prudent man has a disposition for [right] *action*, for he is concerned with the ultimates [i.e., particular *actions* or things] and [already] possesses the other virtues.[9]

Again, if to be continent one must have strong and bad *desires*, neither will the temperate man be continent nor will the continent man be temperate; for it is not the mark of a temperate man to have excessive or bad *desires*.[10] But the continent man must have such *desires*. For if his *desires* are for a good purpose, his disposition which prevents him from following them will be bad and so not all continence will be good;[11] but if they are weak and not bad, continence will not impress us, nor will there be anything great in continence if they are weak but bad.[12]

Again, if continence disposes a man to abide by every opinion, it may be bad, e.g., like that of a man who abides by a false opinion also; and if incontinence disposes a man to abandon every opinion, it may be good, like that of Neoptolemus in the *Philoctetes* of Sophocles, for he is to be praised for not abiding by what he was persuaded by Odysseus to do, because he is pained at telling a lie.[13]

Again, the sophistic argument, which is false, presents a problem. For, because of the wish to refute what is contrary to accepted opinion in order that one may be regarded as shrewd when he succeeds, the syllogism which is formed gives rise to a difficulty; for *thought* is tied like a knot, when it does not wish to rest because it dislikes the conclusion, and it cannot advance because it cannot refute the argument. There follows from a certain argument that imprudence, taken along with incontinence, is a

virtue; for a man does the contrary of what he believes because of
incontinence, but he believes that what is good is bad and hence that he   30
should not do it, so he will do what is good and not what is bad.[14]

Again, a man who by conviction *acts* badly or pursues pleasurable
things or deliberately chooses them would be thought to be better than a
man who does any of these not through judgement but through incontinence; for the former is more disposed to being cured because he might
be persuaded to change his mind. But the incontinent man is open to the
proverbial charge "When water chokes, what should one take to wash it   35
down with?"; for if he were persuaded of what he does, he might be   1146*b*
persuaded to change his mind and stop it, but as it is, although he is
persuaded to do what he should, he does something else nonetheless.[15]

Finally, if incontinence and continence are concerned with every kind
of object, who is incontinent in an unqualified sense? For no one has
every kind of incontinence, but we speak of some men as being incontinent in an unqualified sense.[16]   5

4

The difficulties that arise are such as the ones stated, and we should refute
some of them but allow the others to stand; for the solution of a difficulty
is the discovery of a truth.[1] We should consider, then, (a) whether incontinent men *act* knowingly or not, and, if knowingly, in what way; also (b)
the kinds of things which both continent and incontinent men are posited   10
to be concerned with, i.e., whether they are concerned with every kind of
pleasure and pain or with certain definite kinds; also (c) whether the
continent man and the man who endures are the same or different; and
similarly (d) the other problems which are closely related to this investigation.

The starting-point of our inquiry is (1) the problem of whether conti-   15
nent and incontinent men differ (a) in respect to the objects with which
they are concerned, or (b) in the manner in which they are disposed
towards the objects, that is, whether the incontinent man is incontinent
only with respect to such-and-such objects or with respect to his manner
[towards objects], or (c) with respect to both the objects and the manner.[2]
Second, there is (2) the problem of whether incontinence and continence
are concerned with all kinds of objects or not. Now the incontinent man

20   in the unqualified sense is concerned not with all kinds of objects but only
     with those with which the intemperate man is concerned,[3] and he is in-
     continent by being disposed towards the objects not in any manner what-
     soever (for then incontinence might be the same as intemperance), but in
     a specified manner.[4] For an intemperate man is led on to the objects by
     deliberate choice, thinking that he should always pursue pleasure as it
     comes, whereas an incontinent man thinks that he should not do so, and
     yet he does.[5]

                                     5

25   As to the view that it is true opinion and not *knowledge* against which a
     man *acts* incontinently,[1] this makes no difference to the argument; for
     some men who have opinions show no hesitation but think that they have
     accurate knowledge. So if one argues that it is because of the weakness of
     their convictions that those who have opinions are more likely to *act*
     against their belief than those who have *knowledge*, we answer that there
     may be no difference between [having] *knowledge* and [having] opinion;
30   for some men are no less convinced of their opinions about things than
     others of the things they *know*, as is clear in Heraclitus.[2] But since we use
     the term "to *know*" in two senses (for both the man who has *knowledge*
     but is not using it and he who is using it are said to *know*), there will be a
     difference between having without exercising one's *knowledge* as to what
35   one should do, and having but also exercising that *knowledge*; for it is the
     latter which is thought to be strange and not when one does not exercise
     that *knowledge*.[3]

1147a   Again, since there are two ways in which premises exist, nothing pre-
     vents a man from having both premises but *acting* contrary to *knowledge*,
     although he is using the universal but not the particular; for things to be
     acted upon are particulars.[4] There is also a difference in the case of the
5   universal, for it may apply to the agent or it may apply to the thing, as in
     (a) the premises "dry food benefits every man" and "X is a man", or in (b)
     "such-and-such food is dry", but as to "Y is such-and-such", either the
     agent does not possess it or he is not exercising it.[5] Thus there will be such
     a great difference between these ways of knowing, that to know in one
     way would not seem absurd but to know in the other way would seem
10   strange.[6]
          Again, the possession of *knowledge* may belong to a man in a manner

distinct from those just stated; for in having but not using that *knowledge* we observe such a difference in his disposition that in one sense he has but in another he does not have that *knowledge*, as in the case of a man who is asleep or mad or drunk. Now such is the disposition of those who are under the influence of passions; for fits of anger and sexual *desires* and   15 other such passions clearly disturb even the body, and in some men they also cause madness. So it is clear that incontinent men must be said to be disposed like these. The fact that such men make scientific statements when so disposed is no sign that they know what they are saying; for even those under the influence of passions [i.e., drunkards, madmen] recite   20 demonstrations and verses of Empedocles, and also beginners [in science] string together statements [which prove a conclusion], but they do not quite understand what they are saying,[7] for these expressions must sink in, and this requires time. So incontinent men must be regarded as using language in the way actors do on the stage.

Again, the cause may be observed also from physical considerations.[8]   25 Now one premise is a universal opinion, but the other premise is concerned with a particular, and sensation has authority over particulars. And when from these two premises a unity is formed,[9] then, in one case,[10] the soul must assert the conclusion, but where action is required, it must *act* immediately.[11] For example, if the premises are "everything sweet should be tasted" and "*X* (which is one of the particulars) is sweet", then   30 the man who is able to *act* and is not prevented from *acting* must at the same time *act* on this [i.e., on the conclusion]. Accordingly, if there is in the soul a universal belief which forbids us to taste sweets and another belief, namely, "everything sweet is pleasant", and if there is also before us a particular *X* which is sweet (and this is used) and a *desire* in us to taste what is sweet, then the former belief tells us to avoid tasting *X* but *desire* bids us to taste *X*, for each of these parts [of the soul, i.e., wish and *desire*]   35 can move us;[12] so what turns out is that we become incontinent somehow   1147*b* by argument or opinion, not one which is contrary to itself except in virtue of an accident,[13] for it is *desire* and not opinion which is contrary to right reason. For this *reason*, too, brutes are not incontinent, for they have no universal beliefs but only appearance and memory of particulars.[14]   5

As to how an incontinent man is freed from ignorance and regains *knowledge*, the argument is the same as that for a man who is drunk or asleep, and it is not peculiar to this passion, and we should learn it from

the physiologists.[15] Now since it is the last [i.e., the minor] premise which
is an opinion about a sensible object and has authority over our *actions*,
the man in passion either does not possess this *knowledge* or his possession of it, as we said, is not [actually] *knowing* but a mere verbal expression of it, like that of a drunkard who utters verses of Empedocles. And
because of the fact that the last term is not universal or scientific nor is
thought to be similar to the universal, what Socrates sought to show also
seems to follow; for it is not in the presence of what is thought to be *knowledge* in the main sense that the passion arises, nor is it *knowledge* which is
dragged about through the passion, but [only the knowledge] of sensibles.[16]

Concerning the man who does or does not know, then, and how he can
knowingly be incontinent, let this be our account.

6

We should next discuss whether there is a man who is incontinent without
qualification or whether every man is incontinent with respect to a particular thing, and, if there is, with what kinds of objects he is concerned.

It is evident that those who are continent or enduring or incontinent or
soft are concerned with pleasures and pains. Since of things which produce pleasure some are necessary while others are chosen for themselves
but admit of excess, those which are necessary are bodily (by such I mean
those concerned with food and sexual relations and other such bodily
necessities with which intemperance and temperance were posited to be
concerned), whereas those which are not necessary may be chosen for
themselves (by such I mean victory, honor, wealth, and other such good
and pleasant things). Now men who, with regard to the latter [victory,
honor, wealth, etc.], go to excess in violation of right reason, which
they possess, are called 'incontinent' not in an unqualified way but with
the qualification 'with respect to money' or 'with respect to gain' or 'with
respect to honor' or 'with respect to anger'; and they are not incontinent
in an unqualified way, since they are different from the others, but are
called 'incontinent' in virtue of a similarity,[1] like the victor in the
Olympian games whose proper name was 'Man', for the common definition of 'man' for him differed little from that of his proper name, but it
was still different.[2] A sign of this is the fact that [unqualified] incontinence is blamed not only as an error but also as a sort of vice, whether in

an unqualified way or partly,[3] whereas none of those [who are incontinent with respect to honor or wealth or etc.] is so blamed.

So of those who are concerned with bodily enjoyments, with which a   5
temperate and an intemperate man are said to be concerned, he who excessively pursues pleasurable things and avoids painful things (i.e., those of hunger, thirst, heat, cold, and [in general] all objects of touch and taste), not by deliberate choice but contrary to it or to *thought*, is called   10
'incontinent', not with the qualification 'with respect to this or that', e.g. with respect to anger, but just 'incontinent' without qualification. A sign of this is the fact that men are also called 'soft' with respect to these pleasures or pains but not with respect to any of the other pleasures or pains. And this is why we group together the incontinent and the in-   15
temperate and also the continent and the temperate man (but none of the others), because they are concerned in some way with the same kind of pleasures or pains.[4] Now though they are all concerned with the same things, they are not concerned with them in the same way, but the temperate and the intemperate *act* by deliberate choice while the conti- nent and the incontinent *act* not by deliberate choice. Hence we should rather call 'intemperate' the man[5] who with no *desire* or with weak *desire* pursues excessive pleasures and avoids moderate pains than[6] the man who does these because of strong *desires*; for what would the former do   20
if he had vigorous *desires* and were strongly pained by the lack of the necessary pleasures?

Now some *desires* and pleasures are generically noble[7] or good (for, according to our previous distinction, some pleasurable things are by nature choiceworthy, others are the contraries of these, and others are   25
intermediate)[8], e.g., wealth, gain, victory, and honor, and with regard to all such things and their intermediates men are blamed not for being affected by them or for *desiring* them or for liking them but for doing so somehow in excess. It is in view of this that [we blame] those who yield to or pursue in violation of reason something which is by nature noble or   30
good, like those who pay attention to honor or to their children or parents more than they should (for these things too are goods, and those who pay [the proper] attention to them are praised; but there is also an excess with regard to these if, like Niobe, one were to vie even with the gods,[9] or if one were to be like Satyrus,[10] who was nicknamed "father-lover", for   1148*b*
Satyrus was thought to be very foolish in his regard for his father). Now

there is no evil habit at all concerning these [honor, wealth, etc.] because of what we said, namely, that each of them is by nature choiceworthy for its own sake; but the excesses of them are bad and should be avoided.
5   Similarly, there is no incontinence concerning them either, for incontinence should be not only avoided but also blamed; but because of the similarity of the passions [when in excess], men call each of them 'incontinence', adding in each case that to which it applies, like the doctor and the actor who are called 'a bad doctor' and 'a bad actor', respectively, for one would not call each of them 'bad' in an unqualified way.[11] So just as in the latter case each qualification [i.e., "badness" in the case of medicine or
10   acting] is made not because this badness is a vice but because it is similar [to badness in an unqualified way] by analogy, so it is clear that in the other case, too, incontinence and continence should be regarded to be only those dispositions which are concerned with the same objects as temperance and intemperance are concerned, whereas the names 'continence' and 'incontinence' should be regarded as being concerned with temper [and the like only] in virtue of a similarity. This is why we add a qualification and call a man 'incontinent with respect to temper', and we do likewise with respect to honor or gain.[12]
15   Since (1) some things are by nature pleasant, and of these some are pleasant without qualification while others are pleasant to certain genera of animals or of men, but (2) others are pleasant not by nature, and of these (a) some become pleasant because of injury, (b) others through habit, and (c) still others because of evil natures, it is possible to observe corresponding dispositions in each of (2). I mean, for example, (2c) brutal
20   dispositions, like that of the woman who is said to rip open pregnant women and devour the fetus, or like that of some savage men near the Black Sea who are said to enjoy eating raw meat or human flesh or lend each other their children for personal enjoyment, or like that which is said
25   of Phalaris in the story.[13] Now these dispositions are brutal, but (2a) others are produced in some men because of a disease or madness, as in the case of the man who sacrificed and ate his mother or the slave who ate the liver of his fellow-slave, and (2b) still others are morbid by habit, like that of plucking out one's hair or biting one's nails or eating charcoal or earth,
30   or like homosexuality; for in some men these arise by nature while in others they arise from habituation, as in those who have been abused from childhood.

Now no one would call 'incontinent' those whose disposition is caused by nature, just as no one would call women 'incontinent' for playing the passive rather than the active part in intercourse;[14] and the case of those who are morbidly disposed by habituation is similar. Accordingly, each of these dispositions, like brutality, lies outside of the limits of vice; and he who masters or yields to each of them is not [continent or] incontinent in an unqualified way but only in virtue of a similarity, just as the angry man who is disposed in this manner with respect to this feeling should be called ['continent' or] 'incontinent' not in an unqualified way but in a qualified way. For every excessive disposition[15] of imprudence or cowardice or intemperance or harsh temper is either brutal or morbid. Thus a man who is by nature such as to fear everything, even the noise of a mouse, is a coward in a brutal manner, and the man who feared a weasel did so because of disease; and of imprudent people, those who are by nature irrational and lead only a life of sensation are brutal, like some races of distant barbarians, while those who are irrational because of disease are morbid, like those who are epileptic or mad. It is possible to possess one of these dispositions only at times and not yield to it, e.g., Phalaris might have restrained his *desire* to eat a child or his *desire* for unnatural sexual pleasure; but it is also possible to yield to that disposition and not only possess it. Thus just as an evil habit is called 'evil' in an unqualified sense when it is human but by addition of a qualification when it is brutal or morbid and is not called 'evil' in an unqualified way, so it is clear that of incontinence, too, one kind is brutal and another is morbid, but incontinence in a unqualified way is only that which parallels human intemperance.

1149*a*

5

10

15

20

7

It is clear, then, that continence and incontinence are concerned only with those objects with which intemperance and temperance are concerned, and that it is incontinence of another kind which is concerned with other objects, and the latter is called 'incontinence' metaphorically and not in a unqualified way. We will also show that incontinence with respect to temper is less disgraceful than incontinence with respect to *desires*. For temper[1] seems to listen to reason to some extent, but inattentively, like hasty servants who take off before having heard all that was said and then fail to carry out the right order, or like dogs who bark when they hear the

25

30   sound of a man approaching without looking to see whether he is a friend; so although temper listens, it does not, because of its excited and hasty nature, hear the order but rushes to take vengeance. For argument or appearance has indicated that an insult or slight has been inflicted, then temper, as if having concluded that it must fight against this,[2] is immedia-

35   tely provoked. *Desire*, on the other hand, if thought or sensation only

1149*b*   states that a thing is pleasant, rushes to enjoy it.[3] So while temper follows reason somehow, *desire* does not and is therefore more disgraceful; for he who is incontinent in his temper is conquered by reason in a way, while he who is incontinent in his *desire* is conquered by his *desire* but not by his reason.

Again, we are inclined to pardon desires which are natural more than
5   those which are not natural, seeing that we are more inclined to pardon even those *desires* which are common to all, and to the extent that they are common. But anger and harsh temper are more natural than *desires* which are excessive or are of things which are not necessary,[4] as in the case of the man who defended himself for beating his father by saying "He too
10   beat his father, and his father beat his", and, pointing to his child he said, "and he will beat me when he becomes a man, for it runs in the family"; another example is the man who, when being dragged out of the house by his son, ordered him to stop at the doorway, for he too dragged his own father as far as the doorway.

Again, the more men plot against others, the more unjust they are. Now a man with temper is not disposed to plot against others, and temper
15   does not lead to treachery but is open; but *desire* is called, as the poets say of Aphrodite, "the guileweaving daughter of Cyprus",[5] and Homer speaks of her embroidered girdle as being "alluring, which steals even the wits of the wise".[6] So if indeed this kind of incontinence[7] is more unjust and more disgraceful than that with respect to temper, then it is also in-
20   continence in an unqualified sense and somehow a vice.

Again, no one is pained when he insults another; but everyone who acts in anger acts with pain, while he who insults another does so with pleasure. So if the acts at which it is just to be most angered are more unjust, also incontinence through *desire* would be more unjust than that through anger; for he who insults another is not in temper.[8]

It is clear, then, in what way incontinence with respect to *desire* is more
25   disgraceful than incontinence with respect to temper, and that both con-

tinence and incontinence [in the unqualified sense] are concerned with bodily *desires* and pleasures. Let us consider the differences among these.

As we said at the start,[9] (a) some dispositions are human and natural,[10] both in genus and in magnitude,[11] (b) others are brutal, and (c) still others occur because of injuries or diseases. Temperance and intemperance are   30 concerned only with (a) the first of these; and in view of this, we do not speak of the brutes as being temperate or intemperate, except metaphorically, and whenever one genus of animals differs in general from another in wantonness or destructiveness or omnivorous greed, for animals have no power of deliberating or judging things, but their nature lies   35 outside of these, like that of madmen. Brutality is less bad than vice, but   1150a more fearful;[12] for there is no corruption of the best part of a brute, as it is in a man, since brutes do not have such a part to be corrupted. So to compare brutes with men with respect to vice would be like comparing a lifeless with a living thing; for the badness of that which has no principle   5 is always less harmful than the badness of that which has a principle, and the principle here is the intellect.[13] So it would be like comparing injustice to an unjust man;[14] for there is a sense in which each of these is worse than the other, since a man might do a great many times as much evil as a brute.[15]

8

With regard to pleasures and pains and *desires* and aversions arising through touch and taste, to which both intemperance and temperance   10 were restricted earlier, one may be so disposed as to be conquered even by those of them which most people master, another may be so disposed as to master even those by which most people are conquered; and with regard to such pleasures, the first man is incontinent while the second is continent, but with regard to such pains, the first is soft while the second is enduring. Most people are disposed to be between these two, even if   15 they tend towards the worse habits.

Now since some of those pleasures are necessary, while others are not but are necessary up to a point and their excesses or deficiencies are not necessary, and similarly with regard to *desires* and pains, the man who pursues the excesses of pleasurable things either as excesses or through   20 intention,[1] and for their own sake but not for the sake of some other result, is said to be intemperate; for such a man is not disposed to regret and is therefore incurable,[2] since he who is without regret is incurable. The man who is deficient is opposed to the intemperate,[3] and the man who is intermediate is said to be temperate. Similarly, there is a man who avoids bodily pains, not because he is conquered by them but because he chooses

25   so deliberately. Of those who do not deliberately choose to *act* so, some yield for the sake of pleasure while the others yield to avoid the pain which comes from *desire*. So these two kinds differ from each other.

Now everyone would regard a man who does something disgraceful without *desire* or with a weak *desire* to be worse than a man who so *acts* with a strong *desire*, and he would regard a man who strikes another

30   without being angry as being worse than a man who does so when angry; for what would the first man in each case have done if he were in passion [i.e., with a strong *desire*, or angry]? In view of this, the intemperate man is worse than the incontinent.[4] So of the two habits considered, one of them[5] is more of a kind of softness, whereas the man with the other kind is intemperate.

The continent man is opposed to the incontinent, while the enduring man is opposed to the soft man; for being enduring depends on with-

35   standing something, while continence depends on mastery of something, and withstanding is different from mastery, just as being unconquered is

1150b different from conquering.[6] Hence continence is preferable to endurance.[7] As for the man who is deficient in those things which most men resist and can do so successfully, he is said to be soft or effete, for effeteness too is a kind of softness, like that of the man who lets his cloak trail to avoid the

5   pain of lifting it, or that of the man who imitates the sick but does not regard himself as wretched, though he is like a wretched man.

Similar remarks apply both to continence and to incontinence.[8] It is not surprising for a man to be overcome by strong and overwhelming pleasures or pains, but pardonable, if he tries to resist, like Theodectes'

10   Philoctetes when he was bitten by a snake,[9] or Cercyon in the *Alope* of Carcinus,[10] and like those who try to hold back their laughter but burst out in a guffaw, as happened to Xenophantus;[11] but it is surprising if a man is overcome and cannot resist those pleasures or pains which most men can withstand, when he is so overcome not because of heredity or

15   disease, like the hereditary softness of the kings of the Scythians, or that which distinguishes the female from the male.[12]

A man given to amusement, too, is thought to be intemperate, but he

is soft; for amusement is a slowing down, if indeed it is relaxation,[13] and such a man is excessively disposed to amusement.

Of incontinence, one kind is impetuosity but another is weakness,[14] for some men do not abide by what they have already deliberated upon be- 20 cause of their passion, while others yield to their passion because they have not deliberated; for some men are like those who do not feel tickled after having first tickled others, and so having prior observation of and anticipating the result and having prepared themselves and their judg- ment, they are not overcome by their passion, whether the anticipated 25 result be pleasant or painful. It is sharp-tempered and irritable men who are most disposed to impetuous incontinence; for they do not abide by their reason because they are disposed to follow their imagination, the latter because of their hastiness and the former because of the intensity of their passion.

9

As we stated,[1] then, the intemperate man is not disposed to regret, for he 30 abides by his intention; but every incontinent man is disposed to regret. In view of this, the truth is not such as expressed when the difficulty was raised,[2] but the intemperate man is incurable whereas the incontinent man is curable; for an evil habit[3] is like a disease such as dropsy or consump- tion while incontinence is like epilepsy, since the first habit is continuous while the second is a wickedness which is not continuous.[4] And in general, 35 the genus of incontinence is different from that of vice,[5] for bad men are unaware of their vice, but the incontinent are not unaware of their in- continence (and of incontinent men, those who lose control of themselves 1151a are better than those who have reason but do not abide by it, for the latter are overcome by a weaker passion and are not without previous de- liberation like the former);[6] for an incontinent man is like a man who gets drunk quickly and with a little wine, which is less than what most people 5 get drunk with.[7]

It is evident, then, that incontinence is not a vice, except perhaps in a qualified way, for incontinence is contrary to one's deliberate choice while vice is in accordance with it; but with respect to the corresponding *actions* there is a similarity, as Demodocus remarked concerning the Milesians: "The Milesians are not unintelligent but *act* like unintelligent men." Also, 10 incontinent men are not unjust, though they do unjust things.

Since the incontinent man is of such a kind that he pursues bodily pleasures excessively and contrary to right reason not because he is convinced that he should, while the intemperate man is convinced that he should because he is of such a kind as to pursue them, the former can be easily persuaded to change while the latter cannot be so persuaded. For
15   virtue[8] preserves the principle but an evil habit destroys it, and that principle in *actions* is the final cause, like the hypotheses in mathematics;[9] so neither in mathematics is there an argument which can teach[10] the principles, nor is there one here in ethics but only the virtue, whether natural or acquired by habit, of right opinion concerning the principle.[11]
20   Such a man, then, is the temperate man, whereas contrary to him is the intemperate man.

But there is a kind of man who, because of his passion, loses control of himself and *acts* contrary to his right reason, and it is passion that rules him when he *acts* not according to his right reason, but passion does not rule him in such a way as to make him convinced that he should be following such pleasures without restraint. This is the incontinent man, being
25   better than the intemperate man, and being bad but in a qualified way; for the best thing in him, which is the principle,[12] is preserved. Contrary to this kind of man there is the other kind of man, who abides by his convictions and does not, because of his passion, lose control of himself.[13] It is evident from these remarks, then, that one of the habits is good but the other is bad.[14]

10

Earlier[1] we raised the problem whether the continent man is he who
30   abides by any kind of reason and any kind of intention, or he who abides by the right intention only, and whether the incontinent man is he who fails to abide by any kind of intention and any kind of reason, or he who fails to abide by a reason which is not false and by an intention which is right.[2] Is it not (a) in virtue of an accident that one man abides while another fails to abide by any kind of reason or any kind of intention but
35   (b) essentially that one abides while another fails to abide by a true reason and a right intention? For if one chooses or pursues A for the sake of B,
1151b essentially he pursues or chooses B, but indirectly he pursues or chooses A.[3] Now by 'without qualification' we mean essentially, so it is in a qualified way that one man abides by while another departs from any kind of

opinion, but it is without qualification when one abides by, whereas another departs from, a true opinion.[4]

There are also men who tend to cling to their opinions and are called   5
'obstinate', like those who are hard to convince or not easy to persuade; and these are somewhat like the continent man,[5] as the wasteful is like the generous man and the rash is like the brave man, but they differ in many ways. For the continent man will not change through passion or *desire*, though he may be easily persuaded by some other reasons; but the other   10
[i.e., the obstinate] will not be persuaded by reason, since such men may be attracted by *desires*, and many of them yield to pleasures.

Those who are obstinate may be the opinionated, or the ignorant, or the boorish. The opinionated are obstinate because of pleasure and pain, for they are pleased with their victory if they have not been persuaded   15
to change, and they are pained if their opinions, like decrees, are overthrown; so they resemble the incontinent more than the continent man.[6] There are some, however, who do not abide by their opinions, but not because of incontinence, e.g., Neoptolemus in Sophocles' *Philoctetes*. It was for the sake of pleasure that he did not abide by his opinion, but a noble pleasure; for telling the truth was noble to him, though he was con-   20
vinced by Odysseus to tell a lie.[7] For not everyone who does something for the sake of pleasure is intemperate or bad or incontinent, but only he who does it for the sake of a disgraceful pleasure.

11

Since there is also such a man who enjoys bodily things less than he should and who, being such a man, does not abide by [right] reason,[1] the one   25
between him and the incontinent would be the continent man; for the incontinent man does not abide by reason because he is disposed to enjoy bodily things more than he should, whereas the first does not abide by reason because he is less disposed to such enjoyment, but the continent man abides by reason and does not change, whether because of excess or deficiency. Now if continence is indeed a virtue,[2] both the contrary habits must be bad, and they appear to be such; but because one of the contrary   30
habits appears in few men and seldom, just as temperance is thought to be contrary only to intemperance, so is continence to incontinence.[3] And since many things are called by the same name by virtue of a similarity,

the term 'continence', too, is used for the habit of the temperate man by
35 virtue of a similarity, for both a continent man and a temperate man are
such that, for the sake of bodily pleasures, they do nothing contrary to
1152a   reason; yet the continent has, while the temperate does not have, bad
desires, and the temperate is such that he is not pleased by *acting* contrary
to reason whereas the continent is such that he would be pleased by
acting contrary to reason but does not yield to such *action*. The incontinent man and the intemperate man, too, have a similarity, though they
5 are different;⁴ for both pursue the bodily pleasures, but the intemperate
thinks that he should pursue them while the incontinent thinks that he
should not.

The same man cannot be both prudent and incontinent at the same time;
for it was shown⁵ that a prudent man is at the same time virtuous in
character. Further, a man is prudent not only by knowing what the good
is but also by being disposed to *act* accordingly, whereas the incontinent
10 man is not so disposed. Nothing prevents a shrewd man, however, from
being incontinent (and it is in view of this that sometimes certain men are
thought to be prudent but incontinent), and this is because shrewdness
differs from prudence in the manner stated at the start of this discussion;⁶
and though they are close with respect to their definition, they differ in
what they choose deliberately. Nor again is the incontinent man like the
15 man who understands and contemplates, but he is like the man who is
asleep or drunk.⁷ And he *acts* voluntarily (for in some sense he knows
both what he does and for what *reason* he is doing it),⁸ but he is not
wicked, for his intention⁹ is *good*; so he is half-wicked. And he is not unjust, for he does not plot against others;¹⁰ for one kind of an incontinent
man does not abide by what he has deliberated upon,¹¹ while the irritable
20 kind does not deliberate at all. And so the incontinent man resembles a
state which passes all the right decrees and has good laws but uses none of
them, as Anaxandrides jestingly remarked,

The state wished it, which cares nothing for laws.¹²

The wicked man, on the other hand, resembles a state which uses its laws
but uses wicked laws.¹³
25   Now incontinence and continence are concerned with that which
exceeds what most men habitually do; for the continent man abides by
his intention more whereas the incontinent man abides less than most men

can. Of the kinds of incontinence, that of irritable men is more curable than that of those who deliberate but do not abide by their intention; and that of those who acquired the disposition of incontinence is more curable than that of those who have it by nature, for it is easier to change a habit 30 than to change nature.[14] But it is difficult to change even a habit, because it resembles nature, as Evenus, too, says:

I say, my friend, that practice becomes chronic,
And ends by being nature to a man.[15]

We have discussed, then, what continence, incontinence, endurance, 35 and softness are, and how these habits are related to each other.

12

The study of pleasure and pain belongs to the political philosopher; for it 1152b is he who directs the end of man, and it is with a view to this end that we call in an unqualified way one thing 'good' and another 'bad'.[1] Further, the examination of pleasure and pain is also necessary; for we posited ethical 5 virtue and ethical vice as being concerned with pleasures and pains,[2] and most men say that happiness exists with pleasure,[3] for which reason they gave the name 'blessed' to a man who enjoys things.[4]

(1) Some men think that no pleasure is good, whether in itself or indirectly;[5] for they think that goodness and pleasure are not the same. (2) 10 Others think that some pleasures are good but that most of them are bad. (3) The third view is that even if all pleasures are good, still the highest good cannot be pleasure.

(1) According to the first view, (a) no pleasure at all is good, for every pleasure is observed to be a generation towards a nature and no generation comes under the same genus as that of ends; e.g., no process of building comes under the same genus as that of a house.[6] (b) A temperate 15 man avoids pleasures. (c) A prudent man pursues what is painless, not what is pleasurable.[7] (d) Pleasures impede wise thinking, and the more one enjoys pleasurable things, the more he is impeded in thinking, as in the case of sexual pleasures, for while these last no one can think of anything.[8] (e) There is no art concerning pleasure; but every good is the work of an art. (f) Finally, those who pursue pleasures are children and brutes.[9] 20

(2) The reasons for the doctrine that not all pleasures are good are:

(a) there are also pleasures which are disgraceful and objects of reproach, and (b) there are also harmful pleasures, for some pleasurable things lead to disease.

(3) The reason given for the doctrine that pleasure is not the highest good is that pleasure is not an end but a process.[10]

These, then, are almost all the things that are said about pleasure.

13

25 That it is not because of what has been said that pleasure is not a good or the highest good is clear from the following.

First, since 'good' has two senses (for a thing may be good without qualification or good for someone[1]), natures and dispositions, too, will follow these two senses as goods, and so will motions and generations; and of those which are thought to be bad, some are bad without qualifica-
30 tion, though not bad for a certain person but worthy of choice by him, and some are not worthy of choice even by a certain person, except sometimes or for a little while; and there are also those which appear to be but are not pleasures, those which are with pain and for the sake of cure, e.g., those of the sick.[2]

Second, since that which is good may be an activity or a disposition, processes which restore us to our natural disposition are accidentally
35 pleasant. Now the activity depending on *desire* is an activity of that part of a disposition or a nature which remains normal,[3] seeing that there are
1153a also pleasures without pain or *desire*, like theoretical activities, in which nature is not in need of anything. A sign of this is the fact that men do not enjoy the same pleasurable things when their nature is in the process of being restored as when it is in its settled state, but in a settled state they enjoy the things which are pleasurable without qualification while in the
5 process of restoration they enjoy even the contraries, e.g., acid or bitter objects, none of which is pleasurable by nature or pleasurable without qualification. So the pleasures too are not the same; for as the kinds of pleasurable things are related to each other, so are the corresponding kinds of pleasures which arise from them.[4]

Again, there is no necessity that there should be something else which is better than pleasure, like the end of a process according to some thinkers, for pleasures are not processes and not all pleasures are accom-

panied by a process but are actualities and ends,[5] and they arise not when   10
we are coming to be something but when we are using something;[6] and
not all of them are followed by an end different from themselves but only
those which lead to the completion of a nature.[7] In view of this, it is also
not right to say that pleasure is a sensible process; one should rather say
that it is an actuality of a disposition according to its nature and call it   15
'unimpeded' instead of 'sensible'.[8] Some regard it as a process by taking
it to be a good in the main sense, for they think that actuality is a process;
but these two are different.[9]

To say that pleasures are bad because some pleasurable things are unhealthy is like saying that health is bad because some healthy things are
bad for moneymaking.[10] Now both pleasant and healthy things may be
bad in the manner stated, but they are not bad in virtue of this [i.e., the
pleasure or health in them]; for study, too, is sometimes harmful to   20
health, but neither wise thinking nor any other disposition is impeded by
its own pleasure except by those from different sources, for the pleasures
of theoretical activity or of learning will make us theorize or learn even
more.[11]

There is a good reason why pleasure is not the work of an art; for there
is no art of any actuality, but there is an art of the corresponding faculty,   25
although the art of the perfumer and that of the cook are thought to be
arts of pleasure.[12]

The views that the temperate man avoids pleasure, that the prudent
man pursues a painless life, and that children and brutes pursue pleasure
are refuted by the same argument. For since we have stated[13] in what way
pleasures are good in an unqualified manner and in what way some   30
pleasures are not good, it is pleasures of the latter kind that brutes and
children pursue and it is the painlessness of avoiding such pleasures that
the prudent man pursues, and it is in virtue of the excessive pursuit of
such bodily pleasures (for these are bodily), which are accompanied by
desire and pain, that an intemperate man is intemperate. This is why the
temperate man avoids such pleasures, but he, too, has his own pleasures.[14]   35

14

Moreover, it is generally agreed that pain is bad and should be avoided;   1153*b*
for some pains are bad without qualification while the others are bad by

impeding us in a qualified way.[1] Now the contrary of that which is to be avoided, insofar as the latter is something to be avoided and is bad, is good. So pleasure is of necessity a good of some sort. But the manner in
5   which Speusippus tried to refute pleasure, [saying that pleasure is contrary to pain and to painlessness] just as the greater is contrary to the less and to the equal, does not result in a refutation; for he would not say that pleasure is a species of badness.[2]

Again, nothing prevents a certain pleasure from being the highest good if some pleasures are bad, just as nothing prevents a certain science from being the best when some sciences are bad.[3] Perhaps it is even necessary,
10   if indeed each disposition has unimpeded activities, that happiness, whether it is the unimpeded activity of all or of one of these dispositions,[4] be the most choiceworthy of all; and this activity is pleasure. Thus the highest good would be a certain pleasure, even if most of the pleasures might happen to be without qualification bad. And it is because of this
15   that all men regard a happy life as being pleasant, and so it is with good reason that they weave pleasure into happiness; for no activity is perfect if it is impeded, and happiness is perfect. This is why a happy man requires also the goods of the body and external goods and those of luck, for thus he will not be impeded by the lack of them.[5] As for those who say that the
20   man who is tortured or suffers great misfortunes is happy if he is good, they are talking nonsense, whether willingly or not.[6] And because also good luck is needed, some think that good luck is the same as happiness; but it is not, for even good luck is an impediment to happiness if it is excessive, and then perhaps it is no longer just to call it 'good luck', for its
25   limits are determined by its relation to happiness.[7] Again, the fact that all animals, both brutes and men, pursue pleasure is a sign that pleasure is in some sense the highest good;[8] for

No voice is wholly lost that is the voice of many men.[9]

30   But since it is not the same nature or disposition that is or is thought to be the highest good [for all], neither is it the same pleasure that all pursue; yet [speaking generically] all pursue pleasure. And perhaps what they pursue is not the pleasure they think or say they do, but the one which is the same for all, for all [animals] have by nature something divine in them.[10] But it is the bodily pleasures that have usurped the name 'plea-
35   sure' both because men make reference to them most often and because

everybody participates in them; so men think that only those are pleasures, because they alone are familiar.   1154*a*

It is also evident that if pleasure or the corresponding activity is not a
good, a happy man cannot live pleasantly; for why should he need
pleasure, if indeed it is not a good and if he can also live painfully? For if
indeed pleasure is not good or bad, neither would pain be good or bad.   5
But then, why should he avoid pain? Certainly the life of a virtuous man
would not be more pleasant [than that of any other man] if his activities
were not more pleasant.[11]

With regard to the bodily pleasures, we should consider those who say
that some pleasures, i.e., noble pleasures, are highly choiceworthy, but   10
not the bodily pleasures and those with which an intemperate man is concerned.[12] Then why are the pains, which are contrary [to the latter
pleasures], evil? For the contrary of bad is good.[13] Are the necessary
pleasures good in the sense that even that which is not bad is good,[14] or
are they good up to a point? For in dispositions and motions in which
there is no excess over what is better,[15] neither is there an excess of pleasure, but in those in which there is an excess over what is better, there is   15
also an excess of pleasure. Now there can be an excess of bodily goods,
and a man is bad by pursuing the excess of them and not just those which
are needed (for all men enjoy in some way food and wine and sexual
relations, but not [always] as they should). But the contrary is the case
with pain. The bad man avoids not the excess of pain, but all pain;[16] for   20
pain here is contrary not to the excess of pleasure but to the man who
pursues the excess of pleasure.

15

Since we should state not only the truth, but also the *reason* for the falsity
(since this contributes towards producing conviction, for when the *reason*
why the false appears to be true is reasonably evident, one becomes more   25
convinced of the truth), we should state the *reason* why bodily pleasures
appear more worthy of choice.[1]

First, then, it is a fact that bodily pleasures drive out pains;[2] and
because of the excesses of pain, men pursue excessive pleasures and bodily
pleasures in general as remedies for their excessive pains. Now remedies
for excessive pains are intense; so they are pursued because they appear   30

in contrast with excessive pains.[3] And indeed, as already stated, pleasures are thought not to be good for two *reasons*: (a) some pleasurable *actions* belong to beings of a bad nature, either from birth, as in the case of a brute, or through habit, like the *actions* of bad men, and (b) others are remedies of a nature in need, but to possess [a perfect nature] is better than to be in the process of getting it; but these [pleasurable remedies] occur during the process of being made perfect and are therefore indirectly *good*.[4] Second, men who cannot enjoy other pleasures pursue bodily pleasures because of their intensity, and they even create thirsts for themselves [in order to enjoy more such pleasures].[5] Now when these pleasures are harmless, they are not subject to censure, but when they are harmful, this is bad;[6] for those engaged in them have no other pleasures to enjoy, and to have no pleasures at all is painful to most men because of their nature (for an animal is always in a state of exertion,[7] as confirmed also by natural scientists,[8] who say that seeing and hearing are painful), but (as the saying goes) we are already used to this. Similarly, young men, because they are growing, are disposed like drunken men, and youth is pleasant.[9] Men of irritable nature, on the other hand, are always in need of remedy, for their body constantly irritates them because of its constitution, and they are always in a state of strong desire; but their pain is driven out by a contrary or by any chance pleasure, if that pleasure is strong, and for these *reasons* they become intemperate and bad. But pleasures without pains do not admit of excess; and these are pleasures produced by things which are pleasurable by nature and not in virtue of an accident. By 'pleasurable in virtue of an accident' here I mean those pleasurable things which cause remedy, for the fact that we are cured when the remaining healthy part of us does something is thought to be the *reason* why that which cures is pleasurable; and by 'pleasurable by nature' I mean those which cause an *action* of such [i.e., of complete or healthy] nature.[10]

The same thing is not always pleasurable to us because our nature is not simple, but there is in us also something else in virtue of which we are destructible; and so if one [part of our nature] does something, this goes against the other [part of our] nature,[11] and when there is an equilibrium,[12] what is done seems to be neither painful nor pleasant. If the nature of a being were simple, the same *action* would always be the most pleasant. This is why God always enjoys just one pleasure, which is also simple; for actuality exists not only in motion but also in [something which is] motionless, and pleasure depends on rest more than on motion.[13] And it is because of wickedness that, as the poet says, "change is the most sweet of all";[14] for just as a wicked man is of a changing disposition, so is a   30 nature which is in need of change, for that nature is neither simple nor *good.*

We have now discussed continence and incontinence, and also pleasure and pain, both what each of them is and in what way some of them are good while the others are bad. What remains to discuss next is friendship.

BOOK Θ

1

1155a 3 After what has just been said, a discussion of friendship would follow, for friendship is a virtue or something with virtue,[1] and, besides, it is most
5 necessary to life;[2] for no one would choose to live without friends, though he were to have all the other goods. Also those who possess wealth or have acquired authority or power are thought to need friends most of all; for of what benefit is the possession of such goods without the opportunity of beneficence, which is most exercised towards friends and most praised
10 when so exercised, or how can such goods be guarded and be preserved without friends? For the greater these goods, the more insecure they are. In poverty and other misfortunes, too, we regard our friends as our only refuge. Friends help the young in guarding them from error,[3] and they help the old who, because of their weakness, need attention or additional
15 support for their *actions*, and they help those in their prime of life to do noble *actions*, as in the saying: "And the two are coming together",[4] for with friends men are more able to think and to *act*.

Again, it seems that by nature parents show a friendly feeling towards their offspring, and the offspring towards their parents, and this is the case not only among men but also among birds and most animals; and the same feeling is shown among members of the same race towards one
20 another, and especially among men, in view of which we praise those who are friendly towards other men. In travels, too, one may observe how close and dear every man is to another man. Friendship seems to hold a state together, too, and lawgivers seem to pay more attention to friendship
25 than to justice; for concord seems to be somewhat akin to friendship, and this they aim at most of all and try their utmost to drive out faction, which is inimical to the state. And when men are friends, they have no need of justice at all,[5] but when they are just, they still need friendship; and a thing which is most just is thought to be done in a friendly way.[6]

Friendship is not only necessary, but also noble. For we praise those

who like their friends, and to have many friends is considered as one of the   30
noble things in life;[7] and some men regard good men and friends to be
the same.[8]

2

The disagreements concerning friendship are not few. Some posit friendship as being a likeness of some sort and friends to be men who are alike;
hence the sayings 'like as like',[1] 'birds of a feather flock together',[2] and   35
other such. Others take the contrary position and say 'two of a trade
never agree'.[3] Still others seek causes for these things which are higher and   1155b
more physical,[4] like Euripides, who says, "parched earth loves rain, and
lofty heaven filled with rain loves to fall to earth",[5] and Heraclitus, who
says "it is opposites that help each other", and "sweetest harmonies from   5
different tones arise", and "all things from *Strife* arise";[6] and contrary
to these are others and also Empedocles, who says, "like aims at like".[7]

Now problems which belong to physics[8] may be left aside (for they are
not proper to the present inquiry); so we shall examine just those which
pertain to men and are proper to character and feelings, e.g., whether   10
friendship can be formed between any two men or whether those who are
evil cannot be friends, and whether there is only one kind of friendship or
many. For those who think that there is only one, using as a reason the
fact that friendship admits of degree, have based their conviction on insufficient evidence; for things which differ in kind, too, admit of degree.[9]   15
This has already been discussed.[10]

Perhaps these matters will become evident after we come to know what
the likeable object is;[11] for it seems that not every object is liked but only
the likeable, and this is the good or the pleasant or the useful.[12] But it
would seem that the useful is that through which some good[13] or pleasure   20
is produced; so what is likeable as an end would be the good or the
pleasurable. But do men like the good [without qualification] or that
which is good for themselves? Sometimes these kinds of goods clash; and
the same applies to the pleasurable. Now it is thought that each man
likes what is good for himself, and that, although the likeable is the good
without qualification, what each man likes is what is good for himself. Yet   25
each man likes not what is good for himself but what appears to him to be
good for himself. But it makes no difference, for what is likeable will be
what appears to be so.[14]

There are three kinds of things because of which one may like something, but when one likes an inanimate object, men do not call this 'friendship'; for the object liked does not like in return, and [a man or animal] does not wish that object's good (for it would perhaps be ridiculous for a man to wish the wine's good, though he might, if at all, wish that it be preserved so as to be available to himself). In speaking of a friend, on the other hand, we say that we should wish the things that are good for his own sake. But we call 'well-disposed' those who wish in this manner someone's good, if the latter does not also return the same wish; for there is friendship when good will is reciprocal. Should we not, then, add also 'provided that good will does not escape their notice'? For many people are well-disposed towards those whom they have not seen but whom they regard as *good* or useful to others, and one of these might have the same reciprocal feeling. Two such persons, then, appear to be well-disposed towards each other; but how could one call them friends if they are unaware of each other's dispositions? To be friends, then, two men should be well-disposed towards each other and wish each other's good without being unaware of this, and for one of the *reasons*[15] already stated.

3

Now these *reasons* differ in kind; so the likings and the friendships, too, differ in kind. Hence there are three kinds of friendship, equal in number to the kinds of likeable things; for with respect to each kind there is a reciprocal liking of which both parties are not unaware. Now those who like each other wish each other's good exactly in the respect in which they like each other. So those who like each other because of their usefulness to each other do so not for the sake of the person liked but insofar as some good may be obtained from each other. It is likewise with those who like each other for the sake of pleasure; for men like the witty not for their character but for the pleasure received. Thus he who likes another for the sake of usefulness or of pleasure does so, respectively, for the sake of what is good or pleasurable for himself, and so he likes another not for what the latter is but insofar as the latter is useful or can give pleasure to him. These kinds of friendship, then, exist in virtue of an attribute,[1] for a man is liked not in virtue of what he is but insofar as he gives some good or pleasure. Accordingly, such friendships are easily dissolved, since the parties do not long continue to be similarly disposed; for if they are no longer pleasant or useful to each other, they stop liking each other.

Now the useful does not persist long but changes from time to time.[2] So when the cause of men's friendship is broken, their friendship too is dissolved, since friendship exists in relation to that cause. Such friendship is thought to occur especially between old people – for men at that age   25 tend to pursue what is beneficial and not what is pleasurable – and to occur between those who are young or in their prime of life but who tend to pursue what is expedient. Such friends do not live together much, for sometimes they are not even pleasant to each other; nor indeed do they have a need for such social relation unless they are beneficial to each other, for they are pleasant to each other only as long as they expect   30 some good from each other. Under such friendships come also those between hosts and guests.

Friendship between young men is thought to exist for the sake of receiving pleasure, for they live by their passions and pursue mostly what is pleasurable to themselves and what exists at the moment;[3] but with increasing age what is pleasant to them changes also. Hence young men become friends quickly and stop being friends quickly; for friendship   35 changes along with that which is pleasurable, and such pleasure changes   1156b quickly. Young men are also amorous, for the greater part of amorous friendship occurs by passion and for the sake of pleasure; and it is in view of this that they become friendly and soon end that friendship, and often do these the same day. But they do wish to spend their days   5 and live together, for what friendship means to them is living in this manner.

4

Perfect friendship exists between men who are good and are alike with respect to virtue;[1] for, insofar as they are good, it is in a similar manner that they wish each other's goods, and such men are good in themselves.   10 Now those who wish the good of their friends for the sake of their friends are friends in the highest degree; for they are so disposed because of what they are and not in virtue of an attribute.[2] Accordingly, their friendship lasts as long as they are good, and virtue is something stable.[3] And each friend is good without qualification and also good to his friend; for good men are good without qualification as well as beneficial to each other.[4]

15 And they are likewise pleasant, since good men are pleasant without qualification and also pleasant to each other; for a man's own *actions* and the *actions* which are similar to them are pleasant to himself, and the *actions* of good men are the same or similar.[5] And there is good reason for such a friendship to be stable, for in it all the things that should belong

20 to friends come together. For all friendship is for the sake of good or of pleasure, whether without qualification or for the one who feels friendly, and it exists in virtue of a similarity; and all the things named belong to this kind of friendship in virtue of each[6] such friend, for in that friendship the other things are similar also, and the unqualified good is pleasurable without qualification also. Now it is these[7] that are liked most, and in these both the friendly feeling and friendship exist in the highest degree

25 and are best. Such friendships are likely to be rare indeed, for few men can be such friends.[8] Further, such friendships require time and familiarity; for, as the proverb says, it is impossible for men to know each other well until 'they have consumed together much salt', nor can they accept each other and be friends till each has shown himself dear and trustworthy

30 to the other. Those who quickly show the marks of friendship towards each other wish to be friends indeed but are not, unless both are dear to each other and also have come to know this; for while a wish for friendship may arise quickly, friendship itself is not formed quickly.

5

This kind of friendship, then, is perfect both in duration and in the other

35 respects,[1] and in all respects each gets from the other the same or similar goods, those which should indeed belong to friends. As to the friendship

1157*a* for the sake of pleasure, it bears some likeness to this, for good men are also pleasant to each other; and it is likewise with the one for the sake of usefulness, for good men are also such [i.e., useful] to each other.[2] Among friendships for pleasure or the useful, too, those are most enduring in which friends continue to get the same thing from each other, e.g.,

5 pleasure, and not only thus but also in which they get pleasure of the same kind, as between two witty persons and not as between a lover and his beloved. For the latter are not pleased by the same thing, but the lover is pleased by beholding his beloved, and the beloved is pleased by receiving

attention from the lover; and when the prime of youth fades away, some-times this friendship fades away, too, for the view of the beloved is not pleasant to the lover and so the beloved gets no attention. Many of these   10 who are alike in character, on the other hand, retain their friendship, if familiarity makes them satisfied with each other's character. But those who exchange not what is pleasant but what is useful in their love-affairs are friends to a lesser extent and their friendship is less enduring. And those who are friends for the sake of usefulness stop being friends when the exchange of what is expedient terminates; for what they came to like   15 in their friendship was not each other but what was profitable. According-ly, for the sake of pleasure or of usefulness even bad men may be friends to each other, or one of them may be *good* and the other bad, or one of them may be neither good nor bad and the other may be anyone [bad or good or neither]; but it is clear that only good men can be friends for the sake of each other, for bad men do not enjoy each other's company unless   20 some benefit is exchanged.

Again, only the friendship of good men cannot be harmed by slander; for it is not easy for a good man to believe what anyone says about his good friend who has stood the test of time. And it is among good men that trust and unwillingness to *act* unjustly and whatever else belongs to true friendship are expected without question, while in the other kinds of friendship nothing prevents the contraries of these from taking   25 place.

Now since men call 'friends' also those who associate with each other for the sake of usefulness, as states do (for the alliances between states are thought to be formed for the sake of expediency), and also those who like each other for the sake of pleasure, as boys do, perhaps we too should call these 'friends' but add that there are many kinds of friendship.[3] But   30 friendship in the primary and principal sense[4] will be that between good men just because they are good, while those between the rest will be in virtue of some similarity; for men in the latter friendships will be friends insofar as they exchange only a part of what is good or is similar to it, for the pleasurable too is a part of what is good in the case of those who are friends because they like the pleasurable. These friendships, however, do not often go together, nor is it often that men become friends for the sake of both the useful and the pleasurable; for it is not often that accidents   35 are joined together.

6

1157*b* These being the kinds into which friendship is divided, bad men will be friends for the sake of pleasure or what is useful, as this is the way in which they are similar, while good men will be friends for the sake of each other, for they will be friends just because they are good. The latter, then, will be friends without qualification, while the former will be friends

5 in virtue of some attribute and by resemblance to these.[1]

Just as in the case of virtues some men are called 'good' in virtue of their habits while others in virtue of their activities, so too in the case of friendship; for some enjoy living with each other and giving goods to each other, while those who are asleep or are separated by distances, though

10 not actually present with each other, are so disposed as to *act* as friends towards each other when they meet, for distances do not break up a friendship entirely but only the exercise of it. But if friends are apart from each other for a long time, this seems to make them forget their friendship; hence the saying

Lack of discourse has broken many a friendship.[2]

15 Neither old nor sour men appear disposed to make friends, for they are disposed to give but little pleasure; and no one is inclined to spend his days with one who causes pain or gives no pleasure, for nature[3] appears to avoid pain most of all and to aim at pleasure.

Those who accept each other but are not living together appear to be well-disposed men rather than friends; for nothing stands out among

20 friends so much as living together. For while the needy desire benefits, the blessed desire to spend their days with others also, for solitude befits these least of all.[4] But it is impossible for men to pass the time together unless they are pleasant and enjoy the same things, and comrades are thought to have these attributes.

7

25 Friendship in the highest degree exists between good men, as we have often stated. For it is the good or pleasurable without qualification which is thought to be likeable and choiceworthy, while it is that which is good or pleasant to each man that is thought to be such [i.e., likeable and choiceworthy] by him; and a good man [is likeable and choiceworthy] by a good man for both these *reasons*.[1] Now liking resembles a feeling, while friend-

ship resembles a disposition. For liking is directed no less towards in- 30
animate things; but to like in return requires intention, and intention
proceeds from a disposition.[2] Again, good men wish what is good for
those whom they like for the latter's sake, not by feeling but by disposition. And in liking a friend, they like what is good for themselves; for a
good man, in becoming a friend, becomes a good thing to his friend.[3] Accordingly, each of two such friends both likes what is good for himself 35
and returns as much as he receives in [good] wishes and in pleasure;[4] for,
as is said, 'friendship is equality', and indeed these [liking and returning] 1158a
belong to good men most of all.

Among sour and older men, on the other hand, friendship is less likely
to be formed, and this to the extent that they are harder to get along with
and enjoy less being in company with others, for these things [getting
along easily and enjoying company] most of all are thought to be marks
and causes of friendship. It is in view of this that young men become 5
friends quickly; but not so in the case of old men, for these do not become
friends with those whose company they do not enjoy, and similarly with
sour people. But such men may still be well disposed towards each other;
for they want good things and meet each others's needs, but they are
hardly friends because they neither spend their days together nor enjoy
each other's company, and these things most of all are thought to be 10
marks of friendship.

It is impossible to be a friend to many men in a perfect friendship, just
as it is impossible to be in love with many persons at the same time; for
love is like an excess,[5] and such excess is by its nature felt towards one
person only, and it is not easy for many people to satisfy very much the
same person at the same time,[6] or perhaps for many persons to be good[7]
at the same time. Besides, one must also acquire experience and become 15
familiar with many persons, and this is extremely difficult. But it is possible to satisfy many persons by means of[8] what is useful or pleasurable,
for there are many such who seek the useful or the pleasurable, and the
services required take little time. Of these two friendships, the one for
the sake of what is pleasurable seems to be a friendship to a higher
degree,[9] whenever both parties receive the same things and enjoy each
other or the same things, like the friendships of the young; for in these 20
generosity is shown to a higher degree, whereas friendship for the sake of
what is useful belongs to the commercially-minded.

As for the prosperous, they have no need of the useful, but they do need what is pleasurable; for they wish to live with others, and though they can bear what is painful for a short time, no one can endure it continu-
25   ously, not even if this be the *Good Itself*,[10] if it were painful to him. So they seek friends who are pleasant; and perhaps these should be also good, and good for them too, for thus they will have all that friends should have. As for those in positions of authority, they appear to use different kinds of friends separately; for some friends are useful and others are
30   pleasant, and the same men are not frequently both useful and pleasant. For men in authority in general do not seek pleasant friends who are also virtuous, nor useful men who have noble ends; they seek witty friends if they aim at pleasure, and shrewd friends to carry out orders, and these [i.e., wit and shrewdness] are not frequently found in the same man. We have already stated that a virtuous man is at the same time pleasant and useful; but such a man does not become a friend of a superior man unless
35   he, in turn, is superior to him in virtue, otherwise there is no proportional equality when he is surpassed.[11] But such men rarely become friends.[12]

8

1158*b*   Now the friendships which have been discussed depend on equality of exchange.[1] For friends receive the same things from each other and wish the same things for each other; or else one thing is exchanged for a differ-ent thing, e.g., pleasure for benefit. But these are friendships to a lesser
5   degree and are less permanent, as already stated. And they are thought to be and not to be friendships because of likeness and unlikeness, respectively, to the same thing (e.g., pleasure, or usefulness); for, on the one hand, they appear to be friendships on account of their likeness to the friendship according to virtue (for one friend has pleasure as an end while the other has usefulness, and these ends belong to the friendship according to virtue also), but, on the other, they appear not to be friendships be-
10   cause of their unlikeness to the friendship according to virtue, for this friendship is unshaken by outside slander and is enduring, while the others are quickly dissolved and differ in many other respects.

There is another kind of friendship in which one of the parties is super-ior, e.g., that of a father to his son and, in general, of an elder to a younger person, as well as that of a husband to his wife and of every ruler to his

subject. These friendships differ also from each other; for that between   15
parents and children is not the same as that between rulers and subjects,[2]
nor is that of a father towards his son the same as that of a son towards
his father, or that of a husband towards his wife the same as that of a wife
towards her husband. For the virtue and function of a friend in each of
these friendships is different, and the *reasons* why friends like each other
in each of them are different also. Accordingly, both the affections of these
friends for each other and their friendships are different. Certainly, each   20
such friend neither receives from the other the same as he gives to the
other, nor should he seek to do so; but when children give to their
parents what they should to those who brought them into the world, and
when parents give to their children what should be given to one's offspring,
the friendship of such persons will be enduring and *good*. So, too, the
feeling of affection in all friendships which exist according to superiority
should be proportional, e.g., the better party should be liked more than   25
he likes, and so should the party which bestows greater benefits; and
similarly in each of the other cases. For whenever the feeling of affection
is shown according to merit, then in a certain sense there arises an equality,[3] which is indeed regarded as belonging to a friendship.

9

Equality in what is just does not appear to be similar to equality in friend-   30
ship; for the equal[1] in what is just is primarily according to merit but
secondarily according to quantity, while in friendship the equal according
to quantity is primary but that according to merit is secondary.[2] This becomes clear if there is a great interval between the virtues or vices or
wealth or whatever else exists in the parties to an association; for then
they are no longer friends, nor do they expect to be.[3] And this is most evi-   35
dent in the case of the gods; for their superiority in all the goods is the
greatest. This is also clear in the case of kings, for those who are far in-   1159*a*
ferior to them do not expect to be their friends; nor do those of no account
expect to be friends with the best or wisest of men. In such cases, of course,
an accurate definition cannot be given of the extent to which men can
differ and still become friends; for the differences between friends may   5
be widened but their friendship may still remain, but if the interval is
great, as between a man and God, there can be no friendship at all.

It is in view of this that the problem arises whether men wish for their friends the greatest of goods, e.g., that of being gods, for then these will be neither friends to them any longer nor goods to them; for a friend is a good to his friend. So if it was well stated that a man wishes good for his
10   friend for the latter's sake, the latter will have to remain such as he is; and the former will wish the greatest goods for the sake of the latter while the latter is still a man, though perhaps not all the greatest goods, for a man wishes the goods for himself most of all.[4]

Most people, because of their ambition, seem to wish to be liked rather than to like, and in view of this most people like flatterers; for a flatterer is a friend in an inferior position, or a man who pretends to be such a
15   friend and to like rather than to be liked. But being liked by someone is thought to be close to being honored by him, and indeed this[5] is what most people aim at. And they seem to choose honor not for its own sake but for something else; for most people enjoy being honored by men of
20   means because of expectation, since they think that they will obtain from them whatever they might need, and so they enjoy honor as a sign of future favors. As for those who desire honor from *good* men or from men of knowledge, their aim is to assure their own high opinion of themselves; and so, basing their conviction on the judgment of those men, they enjoy
25   thinking that they are good men.[6] But it is for its own sake that people enjoy being liked; so it would seem that being liked is better than being honored and that friendship is chosen for its own sake. On the other hand, friendship is thought to depend on liking more than on being liked. A sign of this is the fact that mothers enjoy loving their children more than being loved by them; for some of them who give their children to others to
30   bring them up love and know their children but do not seek to be loved in return (whenever both are not possible) but are satisfied in seeing them do well, and they love their children even if the children, because of ignorance, give back nothing that is due to their mothers.

10

Since friendship depends more on loving than on being loved, and since it
35   is those who love their friends who are praised, loving rather than being loved seems to be the virtue of a friend, and so it is those showing this
1159*b*   [feeling or disposition] according to merit who endure as friends and who

have an enduring friendship. And such is the manner in which unequals
can be friends in the highest degree, for in this way they can be equalized.[1]
But it is equality and likeness that is more conducive to friendship, and
especially likeness in virtue.[2] For the virtuous, being steadfast in themselves [in view of their virtue], remain steadfast towards each other also,   5
and they neither ask others to do what is bad nor do they themselves do
such things for others, but one might say that they even prevent such
things from being done; for good men as such neither err nor allow their
friends to fall into error. Wicked men, on the other hand, have nothing
to be certain about, for they do not even remain alike [in their feelings
and *actions*];[3] they become friends but for a short time, enjoying each   10
other's evil habits.

As for those who are useful or pleasant, they remain friends for a longer
time, that is, for as long as they give each other pleasures or benefits.
Friendship for the sake of usefulness seems to arise mostly between men
with contrary needs, e.g., between the poor and the rich or between the
ignorant and the learned, for a man aims at something which he happens
to need, offering something else in exchange; and we might bring in under   15
this the lover and his beloved and also the beautiful and the ugly. And it is
in view of this[4] that lovers sometimes appear ridiculous when they demand to be loved as they themselves love; if indeed they are just as
lovable, perhaps their claim is reasonable, but if they are not such at all,
it is ridiculous. But perhaps a contrary as such does not even aim at the   20
other contrary, except indirectly, since desire is for the intermediate; for
this is what is good, e.g., for that which is dry it is to arrive at the intermediate state and not to become wet, and similarly for that which is hot
and the others.[5] But let us leave these problems aside, for they are rather
foreign to the present inquiry.

11

As stated at the start of this discussion,[1] both friendship and what is just   25
seem to be concerned with the same things and to belong to the same
persons; for in every association there seems to be both something which
is just and also a friendship.[2] At least, men address their fellow-voyagers
and fellow-soldiers as friends also, and similarly with those in any of the
other associations. Friendship goes as far as the members associate with   30

each other; for what is just extends as far also. And it has been rightly said, "to friends all things are common"; for friendship exists in an association. Now brothers and comrades have all things in common, but other people have only certain things in common, some more, some fewer; for of friendships, too, some are to a higher degree but others to a lower degree. Just things, too, differ; for the things that are just for parents towards their children are not the same as those between brothers, nor are those between comrades the same as those between citizens, and similarly with the other kinds of friendships. Accordingly, unjust things towards men are different also; and they become more unjust by being directed towards the more friendly, e.g., it is more abominable to defraud a comrade than a citizen, or to refuse help to a brother than to a stranger, or to strike a father than any one else. What is just, too, increases by nature along with friendship, since they depend on the same kind of things and extend equally to them.

Now all other kinds of associations are like parts of the political association; for people come together for the sake of something expedient and bring along something which contributes to their life. The political association itself is thought to have originated and to continue to exist for the sake of expediency; for the lawgivers, too, are aiming at this and say that what is commonly expedient is just. Each of the other associations, then, is aiming at some part of what is expedient; e.g., sailors undertake a voyage for the sake of making money or some other such thing, fellow-soldiers go to war for the sake of spoils or victory or capturing a city, and similarly for the members of a tribe or of a town. Again, some associations seem to be formed for the sake of pleasure, e.g., religious associations and social clubs, for these are formed for the sake of sacrifice and company, respectively. All these, however, seem to come under the political association, for the aim of a political association seems not to be limited to the expediency of the moment but to extend to life as a whole; and they make sacrifices and arrange gatherings for these, pay honours to the gods, or provide pleasant relaxations for their members. For the ancient sacrifices and gatherings appear to have occurred after the harvest as a sort of first-fruits, since it is at that time that men had most leisure.

All other associations, then, appear to be parts of the political association; and the kinds of friendships will correspond to the kinds of associations.

12

There are three forms of government; and the corresponding deviations from these, being as it were corruptions, are equal in number. Two of them are kingdom and aristocracy; and the third, which it seems proper to call 'timocracy', is based on property qualification but is usually called by   35
most people 'democracy'. The best of these is kingdom, the worst is timo-   1160*b*
cracy. The deviation from kingdom is tyranny, since both are monarchies and differ most[1]; for a tyrant looks for what is expedient for himself while the king looks for what is expedient for his subjects. For a ruler is not a king unless he is self-sufficient and superior to his subjects in all good things, and if he is such, he has no need of anything; accordingly, he would   5
look not for his own benefit but for that of his subjects, for if he were not such, he would be a king by ballot.[2]

Tyranny is the contrary of kingdom, for a tyrant pursues what is good for himself.[3] And it is more evident that tyranny is the worst deviation; and the contrary of the best is the worst.

Kingdom passes over into tyranny; for tyranny is a bad monarchy and   10
an evil king[4] becomes a tyrant. Aristocracy passes over into oligarchy by the badness of the rulers, who distribute the goods of the state in violation of merit, taking most or all of the goods for themselves, keeping the positions of authority always for themselves, and paying attention to wealth   15
most of all. Accordingly, these rulers are few and evil, instead of being the most equitable. Timocracy passes over into mob rule; for these border each other, since timocracy too tends to be the rule of the many and since all those who have the property qualification in it count as equals.

Of the forms of government which deviate, that of mob rule is the least   20
evil,[5] for this kind of state deviates only to a slight extent.

It is in this manner, then, that forms of government change most frequently, for it is in this manner that the transitions are smallest and easiest.[6]

One may observe similarities and in a way examples of these forms of government in households also. The association of a father with his children has the appearance of a kingdom, for a father is concerned with   25
the care of his children. It is in view of this that Homer, too, addresses Zeus as 'father', for kingdom tends to be a paternal rule. In Persia, on the other hand, the rule of fathers is tyrannical, for they use their children as

30   slaves. The rule of a master over his slaves, too, is tyrannical; for in it
things are done for what is expedient to the master. Now this rule appears[7] to be right, but the rule of a father in Persia is in error; for the rule
over different kinds of subjects should be different. The rule of a husband
over his wife appears aristocratic, for a husband rules in virtue of merit
and is concerned with things that befit a husband; and he assigns to his
35   wife those matters which befit a wife. But if a husband rules over every-
1161a   thing, his rule becomes oligarchical; for then he does this in violation of
merit and not to the extent that he is superior. Sometimes it is the wives
who, having become heiresses, rule their husbands; and then they rule not
according to virtue but because of wealth or power, as in oligarchies. As
for the association of brothers, it resembles a timocracy, for brothers are
5   equal, except for their differences in age; hence if they differ much in age,
their friendship is no longer fraternal. Mob rule exists mostly in a communal arrangement where there is no master (for here all men are equal),
and also in a communal arrangement in which the ruler is weak and each
member has the power to do what he pleases.[8]

13

10   In each form of government friendship exists to the extent that what is just
exists. In the friendship of a king towards his subjects there is a superiority
of good services for his subjects, for a king makes his subjects good, if indeed by being good he sees to it that they *act* well, as a shepherd does for
15   his sheep; whence Homer called Agamemnon 'shepherd of people'. Such
too is the friendship of a father towards his children, although it differs
in the magnitude of good services; for he is the cause of their existence,
which is thought to be the greatest good, and also of their nurture and
education. These things apply to ancestors also, for the relation of a
father to his sons or of ancestors to descendants or of a king to his subjects
20   is by nature that of a ruler to one who is ruled. And these are friendships
by virtue of superiority; hence parents are also honored.[1] Accordingly,
also what is just in those friendships is not the same for the two parties but
is according to merit; for friendship, too, exists in this manner. The
friendship of a husband towards his wife, too, is the same as that which
depends on aristocratic superiority. For it is in accordance with virtue,[2]
and the greater good should go to the superior party, and to each party

should go what befits that party; for what is just, too, exists in this manner.   25
The friendship of brothers, however, is like that of comrades; for they
are equal and of about the same age, and such persons are for the most
part alike in feelings and in character. Like this, too, is the friendship of
the members in a timocracy, for its citizens tend to be equal and equitable;
and indeed their rule exists by turns and on the basis of equality, and so
does their friendship.   30

In forms of government which deviate, just as there is but little that is
just, so too there is little friendship, and friendship exists least in the worst
form of government; for in a tyranny there is no friendship at all or very
little of it. For in relations in which there is nothing common to the ruler
and to the ruled, there is no friendship, as there is nothing just. The relation is like that of an artist to his tool, or that of the soul to its body, or   35
that of a master to his slave, for in each of these the former is benefited by   1161*b*
using the latter;[3] and there is no friendship or anything just towards inanimate things. Nor is there friendship towards a horse or an ox or
towards a slave as a slave, for there is nothing common to the two parties;
for a slave is a living tool, and a tool is a lifeless slave. Accordingly, there   5
can be no friendship towards a slave as a slave, but there may be friendship towards him as a man; for there seems to be something just between
every man and every one who can participate in an association where
there is law or agreement, and hence in a friendship to the extent that each
of them is a man.[4] So in tyrannies, too, there are friendships and what is
just, though to a small extent; but friendships in perverted constitutions
are most likely to exist where there is mob rule, for where men are equal,   10
they have many things in common.[5]

14

As we have stated, then, every kind of friendship exists in an association;
but one might mark off from the rest the friendships of kinsmen and of
comrades. Friendships of fellow-citizens and of fellow-tribesmen and of
fellow-voyagers and other such are more like friendships by [mere] association, for they appear to be based on a sort of [mere] agreement.[1] To   15
these we may add also the friendship between host and guest.

Friendships between kinsmen, too, appear to be of many kinds, but all
depend on paternal friendship; for parents love their children as if these

were parts of themselves, and children love their parents since their being
20   comes from their parents. Parents know that their offspring come from
them, however, more than the offspring know that they come from their
parents, and parents feel close to their offspring more than the latter do
to their parents; for that which comes from a person is that person's very
own, like a tooth or a hair or any of his possessions, but this is not at all
related to that person in this way, or is less so related.² And as for the
25   length of time, parents love their children from the moment of their birth,
whereas children begin to love their parents years after birth, when they
have gained intelligence or sense. From these remarks it is also clear why
mothers love their children more than fathers do.

Parents, then, love their children as they love themselves (for what
comes from them is like other selves, being different by having been
30   separated), and children love their parents as being born of them; but
brothers love each other by having been born of the same parents, for
sameness in relation to the same parents produces sameness in relation to
each other (whence come the expressions 'the same blood' and 'the same
roots' and other such). Thus they are in a certain sense the same even if
they are separate persons. Being brought up together and being of about
the same age, too, contribute a great deal to their friendship; for, as the
35   saying goes, 'two of an age', and it is men familiar with each other who
become comrades; in view of this, the friendship of brothers, too, re-
1162a   sembles that of comrades. As for cousins and all other kinsmen, their
closeness arises from these,³ for all of them come ultimately from the
same parents; and they are more close or less close to each other by being,
respectively, nearer or farther from their first ancestor.⁴

5   The friendship of children towards parents, and of men towards gods,
is one towards something good and superior; for parents have done the
greatest of goods, since they are the causes of the existence and nurture of
their children and then of their education. And such friendship possesses
more pleasure and usefulness than that towards strangers, and to the
extent that their life has more in common. The friendship between
10   brothers has the good attributes present in that between comrades; and it
is a friendship to a higher degree for brothers who are *good*, and in
general for those who are alike, and to the extent that they are closer to
each other and are fond of each other from birth and that, born of the
same parents, they are alike in character and upbringing and have been

educated alike. And the test of time here has been the longest and most   15
certain. Friendly relations between the rest of kinsmen, too, exist but in
proportion to their closeness.

The friendship between husband and wife is thought to exist by nature;
for men by nature tend to form couples more than to be political, and they
do this to the extent that a household is prior and more necessary than a
state and that reproduction is more common to animals.[5] Accordingly,
associations in the other animals exist only to that extent, but men live   20
together not only for the sake of reproduction but for other things in life
as well;[6] for the functions among men are divided from the start, and
those of a husband are different from those of a wife, and so by contributing to the common stock whatever is proper to each they supply each
other's needs.[7] It is for these *reasons*, too, that this friendship is thought
to be both useful and pleasant; and if both are *good*, it may also be a   25
friendship through virtue, for there is a virtue for each of them, and both
would enjoy such a state of affairs.[8] As for children, they seem to keep
husband and wife together, and this is why childless marriages are more
easily dissolved; for children are a common good to both of them, and
what is common holds them together.

To ask how a husband and a wife, or any two friends in general, should   30
live together appears to be none other than to ask how it is just for them
to live; for what is just towards a friend[9] does not appear to be the same
as what is just towards a stranger, or a comrade, or a classmate.

15

Since there are three kinds of friendships, as we stated at first,[1] and since   35
in each kind one may be a friend to another by virtue of equality or by
virtue of superiority (for two men who become friends may be alike good
or one may be superior to the other in goodness, and similarly if they are   1162*b*
friends by being pleasant to each other or because they are useful to each
other, whether the benefits received are equal or different), those who are
equal should bring about equality by being equally disposed in their love
for each other and in other respects, while those who are unequal should
do so by being disposed in a manner proportionate to their superiority
or inferiority.[2]

There are good reasons why accusations and complaints occur exclu-   5

sively or most of all in friendships which are based on usefulness. For those who are friends through virtue are eager to treat each other well, since this is a mark of virtue and of friendship, and when both strive to do this, there can be neither accusations nor quarrels; for no one is dis-
10   pleased with a man who likes him and treats him well; on the contrary, if he is grateful, he requites the other by returning a good. And he who is superior in achieving what he aims at would not accuse his friend, for each of them aims at the other's good. In friendships for the sake of pleasure, too, complaints hardly arise; for both friends get what they desire,
15   if they enjoy each other's company. And a man would appear ridiculous were he to accuse his friend of not receiving delight from him, when he can part company at will. Friendships for the sake of usefulness, on the other hand, give rise to accusations. For by using each other for their own benefit, each of them always wants more than he gives and thinks that he receives less than his due, and he complains of not receiving what
20   he deserves and has asked for; and in conferring a benefit, each cannot supply as much as the other wants.

It seems that, just as there are two kinds of things which are just, one unwritten and the other according to law, so there are two kinds of friendship based on usefulness, one ethical and the other legal. Accordingly, accusations arise especially whenever exchanges are made not accord-
25   ing to the same kind of friendship and the parties break off their friendship.

Now legal friendship is formed on specified terms; and it may be purely commercial and carried out immediately, or it may be more liberal with respect to time but agreed upon as to its terms. The debt in the latter case is clear and not subject to dispute, and the postponement has an ele-
30   ment of friendship; and it is in view of this that some states allow no suits concerning those debts but think that men should accept the consequences regarding exchanges based on trust.

Ethical friendship, on the other hand, is not formed on specified terms; a gift or any other good is bestowed as to a friend. But the giver expects to receive as much, or more, as if what he gave were not a gift but something lent to be used; and if at the end of the exchange he is not as well off,
35   he accuses the receiver. This happens because all or most people, though wishing what is noble, deliberately choose what is beneficial to themselves.
1163a Now to treat others well without seeking a return is noble, but to receive

the services of another is beneficial. So if the receiver is able, he should return the equivalent of what he received and do so voluntarily;[3] for no one should be made an unwilling friend. It would really be as if one made a mistake at the start and received a good from a person from whom he should not have received it; for he received the good not from a friend, nor from one whose *action* was for its own sake.[4] Accordingly, he who 5 has so received a service should dissolve the friendship as if it were made on specified terms. And he should grant that, if he could, he would return the equivalent of the service rendered, for if he could not, neither would the giver have expected to receive it; so if he can, he should return the service.[5] But a man should first consider carefully (a) the person from whom he receives a service and (b) the terms on which he does this, so that with both these in mind he may accept or decline it.

There is disagreement as to whether a good which is to be returned 10 should be measured by the receiver's benefit or by the giver's service. For the recipients belittle the goods received by saying that such goods meant little to the benefactors and could have been received from others; the benefactors, on the other hand, claim that they have conferred the greatest 15 of goods and those which could not have been conferred by others, and that they did this at a time of risk or some other such need.[6]

Now if the friendship is one for the sake of usefulness, should not the measure be the benefit of the receiver? For it is he who wants the benefit, and the benefactor supplies this with the expectation of an equivalent return; accordingly, the assistance given is as great as the benefit which he receives, and so what he should return is as much as he has been benefited, 20 or even more, for this is more noble. But in friendships based on virtue accusations do not arise, and it is the intention of the giver which seems to be the measure; for the main principle in virtue and in character lies in intention.[7]

16

Disagreements arise also in friendships in which one party is superior to the other, for each claims to deserve more; and whenever this happens, the 25 friendship is dissolved.[1] For the better of the two parties thinks that he should by right have more, since he thinks that more should be given to a good man than to one who is less good. It is likewise with the man who is more beneficial to others, since it is said that those who are not useful to

others should not have as much as those who are useful; for it is said that the association becomes a public service and not a friendship if the actions
30   in a friendship are not measured by what they are worth. For men think that, just as in a business partnership those who contribute more money should receive more, so it should be in a friendship. But the man who is in need or is inferior takes the opposite view; for he thinks that a mark of a good friend is to assist the needy. Where is the advantage, he asks, of
35   being a friend to a virtuous or powerful man if one is to gain nothing from him?[2]

1163b   It seems that each of these is right in his claim and that each of them should get more than the other out of the friendship, not more of the same thing, however, but the superior should get more honor and the needy should get more gain; for the prize of virtue and of beneficence is honor,
5   but that which relieves a need is gain. In a state, too, this appears to be the manner in which goods are distributed, since the man who is honored is not he who contributes nothing to the common weal; for a common good is bestowed upon the man who renders service to the public, and honor is a common good. For one cannot expect to make money out of the public and be honored at the same time, since no one puts up with getting less
10   in all respects. So they pay honor to the man who takes a loss in money but give money to the man who wants money; for what effects equality and preserves a friendship is what each gets according to merit, as already stated.

Among unequals, too, this should be the manner of their association; the party who is benefited financially or towards virtue should repay in
15   honor, since this is what he can do. For friendship calls for what is possible, not something according to merit, since a return according to merit does not even exist in all friendships, as in the case of honors paid to gods or to parents; for here one could not ever return the equivalent of what he has received, but he is thought to be *good* if in return he renders as much service as he can. In view of this, it would even seem that it is not up to a
20   son to repudiate his father, although a father may disown his son; for a son should repay what he owes, and there is nothing he can do which will be the equivalent of what he has received, so he will always be in debt. But a creditor may remit a debt owed by the debtor; and so can a father. Still it seems that perhaps no one would ever disown a son who has not gone too far in his evil habits; for apart from the natural affection of a

father for his son, it is human not to reject the help of a son. An evil son,   25
on the other hand, will regard helping his father as something to be avoided or not eagerly pursued; for most people wish to be treated well but
avoid doing so to others since there is no gain in it.

Concerning friendship, then, this account may be taken as sufficient.

1

1163*b* 32   In every friendship between dissimilar parties, it is analogy that equalizes and preserves the friendship, as already stated.[1] In a political friendship, for example, a shoemaker gets for his shoes a return according to their

1164*a*   worth, and so do a weaver and the rest. Now here a common coin has been introduced as a common measure, and all articles of exchange are referred to this and are measured by this.[2] But in the friendship of love, sometimes the lover complains that his excess of love is not returned in

5   kind (though he may happen to have nothing lovable about him), while often the beloved complains that the lover promised everything before but now fails to fulfill his promises; and such things happen when the lover loves the beloved for the sake of pleasure while the beloved loves the lover for the sake of usefulness, but they do not both have what is expected of them. Now these being the *reasons* of their friendship, if they are

10   not fulfilled, the friendship is dissolved; for each loved the other not for the latter's sake but for some of his attributes, which are not permanent,[3] and so neither are such friendships permanent. A friendship based on character, on the other hand, is by its nature permanent,[4] as stated previously.

    Differences arise between friends also when what they get is not what

15   they desire; for when they do not get what they aim at, it is like getting nothing. And this is what happened to a bard who was promised a greater reward if he sang better, but when he asked the next morning for what had been promised him, he was told that he had received pleasure for pleasure.[5] Now if such were what each wished, it would have been satisfactory; but if one wished delight but the other gain, and if the former received his

20   but the latter did not, the terms of their association were not fulfilled in a satisfactory manner, for what each happens to want is what he attends to getting, and it is for the sake of this that he gives of his own.

    But who is to fix the worth of what is given or received: he who is to give or he who is to receive? He who is to give seems to leave it to the other.

And it is said that this is what Protagoras was doing; for whenever he was   25
to teach any subject whatever, he would have the learner himself set whatever value he thought the *knowledge* received was worth, and Protagoras
received that amount. In such cases some men are satisfied with the statement 'let the fee be what it is worth to the receiver'.[6] As for those who get
the money first and then fail to do what they said they would, there is good
reason for charges against them because their promises were excessive,   30
for they do not fulfill their agreements. Perhaps this is what the sophists
find necessary to do, because no one would give money for what they
actually *know*.[7] Charges against these men, then, are brought with good
reason since they do not do what they were paid for. But in friendships in
which there is no mutual agreement concerning services done, those who
give for the sake of the receiver are not subject to accusation, as we stated   35
earlier,[8] for such is the friendship according to virtue; and the return to   1164*b*
them should be made according to intention, for this is a mark of a
[perfect] friend and of virtue. So too, it seems, should be the return to a
man under whom one has studied philosophy, for the worth of philosophy
cannot be measured in money, and there is no equivalent value which can
match it; but perhaps it is enough, as is done for gods and parents, to   5
return what one can.

But if what is given is not of this sort but is given with a view to a return,[9]
perhaps the best return should be that which seems fair to both, and if this
cannot be done, it would seem not only necessary but also just that he who
first receives the service should fix the worth of the return; for the amount   10
of benefit which he receives or the amount of return he would choose to
pay for the pleasure he receives will then be whatever amount the giver
will get from the receiver as a return for the worth of what he gave. For in
sales, too, this appears to take place, and in some places there are laws
which prohibit suits arising out of voluntary contracts, on the principle
that one should settle with a person he has trusted in the same way as he   15
has negotiated with him; for it is thought more just that the man to fix
the terms should be the one who was entrusted than the one who entrusted
him. For most things are not valued equally by the possessors of them and
by those who want them, since what is owned and is offered to another
appears to be highly valued by the owner; yet the return is made on the
terms fixed by the receiver. Perhaps the value set should be not what it   20
appears to be worth to the owner but what he valued it before he owned it.

2

Problems arise also from such as the following: whether one should give preference to and obey his father in all things, or rather trust the doctor
25   when sick and vote for a man who is skilled in war as general; and likewise, whether one should render service to a friend or rather to a virtuous man, and whether one should return gratitude to a benefactor or rather give to a comrade, if both are not possible. But are not all such problems difficult to settle with accuracy? For there are all sorts of differences with
30   respect to magnitude, to what is noble, and to what is necessary.

It is clear, however, that one should not favor the same person in all things. Thus, for the most part, one should rather repay a service received than favor his comrade, and one should rather pay back (as if a loan borrowed) to a creditor than donate to a comrade. Perhaps this, too, should not always be so. For example, should a man who has been ransomed
35   from bandits ransom his ransomer (or pay him if he demands payment
1165a   even if not captured), whoever he may be, or rather ransom his father? It would seem that he should ransom his father rather than even himself.[1] As we have stated, then, in general a debt should be repaid, but if that which is to be given as a debt is outweighed by what is noble or urgent,
5   then one should turn rather to these;[2] for sometimes it is not even fair to repay a service received, as when a man does service to someone whom he knows to be virtuous and the latter considers repaying the former whom he regards as evil.[3] Thus sometimes one should not even lend money to one from whom he borrowed and returned; for A may have lent to B, who is a *good* man, with the expectation of recovering the loan,
10   while B does not expect to recover a loan he might make to A, who is wicked. Accordingly, if the truth is such as stated, A's request for a loan is not fair, and if it is not such as stated but B regards it as such, he would not be thought unreasonable in refusing a loan to A. So as we have often stated,[4] discussions concerning feelings and *actions* have as much definiteness as there is in their subject matter.
15   It is clear, then, that neither should we make the same return to all, nor give preference to a father in everything, just as one does not sacrifice everything to Zeus; but since we should return different things to parents, brothers, comrades, and benefactors, our returns to each of them should be proper and fitting. And this is what men appear to do. For to a

wedding they invite their relatives, since they all have family ties, and 20
wedding activities are concerned with these; and for the same *reason* they
think that at funerals relatives should meet before all others. And it would
seem that in the matter of nourishment we should assist our parents most
of all, as if we owe it to them, and that it is more noble to assist those who
caused our being than to assist ourselves. And we should pay honor to our
parents as we do to the gods, but not every kind of honor; for we do not 25
pay the same kind of honor to our father as to our mother, nor the same
kind to a wise man as to a general, but to our father what is due to him as
a father, and likewise to our mother. And to every older person we should
pay the honor which befits his age, e.g., by rising to greet him and finding
seats for him and the like, while with our comrades and brothers we
should be freespoken and share everything. And to our relatives and fel- 30
low-tribesman and fellow-citizens and each of the rest we should always
try to render what is proper to each, showing discrimination as to what
belongs to each of them with respect to closeness of relation and to virtue
or usefulness. Now it is easier to make judgments concerning those who
are similarly related to us but more laborious concerning those who differ;
yet we should not for that *reason* abstain but should decide each case as 35
far as we can.

3

Another problem that arises is whether we should or should not end our
friendship with those who do not remain the same [in character or 1165*b*
thought]. But is there anything absurd in ending a friendship based on
usefulness or pleasure, when such a friend no longer has usefulness or
pleasure to offer? For what such friends desired was usefulness or
pleasure, and when this ceases, it is reasonable that the friendship too
should cease. But we might complain if our friend pretended to love us 5
for our character but actually loved us for our usefulness or the pleasure
we gave him; for, as we pointed out at the outset,[1] most differences between friends arise when they are not actually friends in the manner in
which they think they are. Accordingly, when one has the mistaken belief
that his friend loves him because of his character, while his friend is doing
nothing of this sort, he has only himself to blame;[2] but when he is de- 10
ceived by the pretense of his friend, it is just that he should accuse his de-
ceiver, and more so than when one accuses those who deceive him with

counterfeit coin, inasmuch as malevolence in friendship affects something which is more honorable.[3]

Again, if one accepts another as a friend, taking him as a good man, but the latter turns out to be evil and is regarded to be such, should he still be kept as a friend? Is this not impossible, if indeed not everything should be loved but only what is good? A wicked man is not worthy of being a friend, and one should not befriend him; for one should neither love what is wicked nor be like a bad man, and we have already said[4] that a man is a friend to someone who is like him. Should the friendship, then, be broken off immediately, or not in all cases, but only when one's friend is incurable in his evil habits? If correction is possible, he should be helped in improving his character more than in improving him financially, inasmuch as character is better and more proper to friendship than financial aid. But a friend who breaks off a friendship [when his friend is beyond correction] would seem to be doing nothing absurd, for it was not to such a man that he was a friend [at first]; so if his friend changed [in character] and cannot be restored, he should break off the friendship.

But if one friend were to remain the same while the other were to become better and far superior in virtue, should the latter treat the former as a friend, or should he not? This becomes most clear when the difference [in character or thought] becomes great, as in the case of boyhood friendships; for if one of them were to remain childish in his *thinking* while the other were to rise into eminence, how could they be friends if they have no common interests and neither enjoy nor are pained by the same things? For they will not even have [the same *thoughts* or feelings] towards each other, and without these, as we saw, they cannot be friends since they cannot live together; and we have already discussed these matters.[5] Should the superior friend, then, treat the other in no other way than as if he had never been his friend? Perhaps he should keep remembrance of the earlier intimacy; and just as we think that we should favor our friends rather than strangers, so we should show some regard for those because of our earlier friendship, if the friendship did not end because of excessive evil habits.

4

1166a   Our [dispositions, feelings, and *actions*] which are directed towards our

friends and by which friendships are defined seem to have originated from those of a man in relation to himself. For some men posit a friend as being (1) a person who wishes and does what is good or appears to be good to another for the other's sake, or as being (2) a person who wishes another person to exist and live for his own [the latter's] sake; and this is   5
just how mothers feel towards their children, and of friends those who have quarreled.[1] Others posit a friend as being (3) a person who passes the time with and chooses the same things as another, or as being (4) a person who shares the sorrows and joys of another, who is called 'a friend'; and this, too, happens with mothers most of all. Friendship, too, is defined by some one of these.[2]   10

Each of the above definitions is attributed to a *good* man in relation to himself, and it is attributed to others in relation to themselves insofar as they regard themselves as being such [i.e., *good*]; for, as stated earlier,[3] virtue or a virtuous man seems to be like a measure of each man since it is a virtuous man who has harmonious thoughts[4], who desires the same   15
things with respect to every part of the soul,[5] and who wishes and does for himself what is both good and appears so (for a good man makes a serious effort to do what is good) and does so for his own sake, all these being for the sake of the *thinking* part of the soul, which is thought to be the very man himself.[6] And a virtuous man wishes himself to live and be preserved, and especially that part by which he thinks wisely, for existence is a good thing to a virtuous man. Now each man wishes what is for him-   20
self good; but no one chooses to become another man and have every-thing if it is that other man who has everything (for, as it is, God does possess the good), but he would if he were to remain just what he is.[7] And it would seem that each man is that part of himself which thinks or that part most of all. And such a man wishes to live together with himself, for he does so with pleasure; for his memories of past *actions* make life delight-   25
ful, and his expectations of the future are good, and such thoughts are plea-sant to himself. And it is by *thought* that he is well supplied with objects of contemplation. And he feels grief or pleasure with himself most of all; for it is always the same thing that is painful or pleasant, not one thing at one time and another at another time, since he has, so to say, no regrets.[8]

Since each of these attributes belongs to a *good* man in relation to him-   30
self, then, and since being disposed toward a friend is like being disposed

towards oneself (for a friend is another self), friendship too is thought to be some of these attributes, and friends to be those who have those attributes. Whether there can be friendship or not of a man towards himself
35   is a problem which may be dismissed at present; but friendship would seem to be possible insofar as there exist two or more of the attributes
1166b stated, and the excess[9] of friendship resembles the love of a man towards himself.

Now the attributes stated appear to belong also to most people, even if they are bad. Do these men, then, share in those attributes to the extent that they are satisfied with themselves and regard themselves as *good*?
5   But, at least to those who are altogether bad and perform impious *acts*, none of these attributes belongs or appears to belong. And they hardly belong to bad men; for they are in conflict with themselves, and they *desire* certain things but wish things which are different from those *desired*, like incontinent men. For they choose things which are pleasant
10   but harmful instead of those which they think to be good for themselves; others, through cowardice and laziness, avoid doing what they consider best for themselves; still others, who have committed many terrible deeds and are hated because of their evil habits, shun life or commit suicide.[10] And evil men seek companions to spend their days with and try to escape
15   from themselves; for, when by themselves, they recall many distressing things and expect others of this sort, but when they are with others they forget them. And having nothing lovable to show, they have no feeling of love for themselves. And so they feel neither joy nor sorrow with them-
20   selves, for their soul is divided against itself; and when they abstain from doing certain things,[11] one part of the soul is pained because of their evil habits while another part is pleased, the first part pulling in one direction while the second pulls in the opposite direction, as if these parts were trying to break the man apart. And if he cannot be pained and pleased at the same time but, soon after being pleased, is pained by the fact that he was pleased, he would also wish that the things which pleased him had
25   not occurred; for bad men are full of regrets.

Thus it appears that a bad man is not disposed to love himself, because he has nothing lovable in himself. So if to be in such a state is to be in a wretched state, we should make every effort to avoid evil habits and try to be *good*, for it is in this way that a man can be friendly to himself and become a friend to another man.

5

Good will resembles friendship, and yet it is not friendship; for we may   30
have good will towards strangers and those who are not aware of our good
will, but this is not so with friendship, as we pointed out earlier.[1] Nor is
it a feeling of love; for it has no intensity or desire, which accompany a
feeling of love. Again, a feeling of love is felt towards those we are
familiar with, but good will may arise also in a moment, as it does towards   35
competitors in games; for we become well-disposed towards them and   1167a
share in their wish to win, and yet we would do nothing for them, for, as
we said, we become well-disposed in a moment and we like them only
superficially.

Good will, then, is like the beginning of a friendship, just like the
pleasure of being in love with another by sight; for no one is in love if he   5
has not first been pleased by the beautiful form of the beloved, and he who
enjoys the form of a person is not by this alone in love, unless he also
longs for that person when absent and *desires* his presence. So, too, men
cannot be friends unless they have first become well-disposed towards
each other, but those who are well-disposed are not by this alone friends;
for they only wish what is good for those towards whom they are well-
disposed but would neither participate in any *actions* with them nor   10
trouble themselves for them. Thus one might say, using a metaphor, that
good will is untilled friendship; and it is when good will is prolonged and
reaches the point of familiarity that it becomes friendship, not the friendship that exists for the sake of usefulness or pleasure, for no good will
arises in these [as such, but only the friendship according to virtue]. For
the man who has received beneficence renders good will [only] in return
for what he has received, thus doing what is just; and the man who wishes   15
to do a good deed to another with the expectation of material gain through
him seems to be well-disposed not to him but rather to himself,[2] just as a
man who displays attention to another for the sake of usefulness is not a
friend[3] to him.

In general, good will in a man arises through virtue or *goodness* of
some kind,[4] when someone appears to him beautiful[5] or brave or
something of the sort, as we pointed out in the case of competitors in   20
contests.

6

Concord, too, appears to be a mark of friendliness, and for this reason it is not [the same in definition as] sameness of opinion; for the latter might belong also to those who do not know each other. Nor do we say that those who have the same thoughts on anything whatsoever have concord,

25　like those who have the same thoughts concerning heavenly objects (for to have the same thoughts concerning these is not a mark of friendship), but we say that states have concord when they have the same thoughts concerning matters of expediency and have the same intentions and do what is thought to be of common interest. So men are in concord about matters to be *acted* upon, and of these about matters which are of con-

30　siderable importance and can belong to both or to all parties,[1] as in the case of a state when all its citizens are of the opinion that the offices in it should be elective, or that they should form an alliance with the Spartans, or that Pittacus should be their ruler (when he himself was willing to rule).[2] But when each of two men wishes himself to be the leader, like the captains in the *Phoenissae*,[3] they are in a state of discord; for two parties are said to

35　have concord not if they have just the same thought, whatever this may be, but also if their thought is about the same subject, e.g., when both the com-

1167*b*　mon people and *good* men think that the best should rule, for it is in this manner that all will get what they aim at.[4]

　　Concord appears to be political friendship, as the phrase is used; for it is concerned with matters of expediency and those which affect our whole

5　life. Such concord exists in *good* men, for these have the same thoughts in themselves as well as in relation to one another,[5] having the same things in mind so to speak; for the things wished by such men are constant and do not ebb and flow like the water in the strait of Euripus,[6] and they also wish what is just and expedient, and these are the things they commonly aim at. Bad men, on the other hand, cannot have the same thoughts

10　except to a small extent, just as in the case of friendship, since in matters of benefit they aim at getting more than their share, and where exertion or public service is required they fall short, and in wishing these things, each of them criticizes his neighbor and prevents the work from being completed; for if they do not attend to the common task, it is ruined. Thus in

15　trying to make each other do the work and being themselves unwilling to do what is just, they end up in a state of discord.

7

It seems that benefactors love those they have benefited more than the latter love the former, and men raise questions about this as if it were contrary to reason. What appears to most people is that those who are benefited are   20 debtors and that the benefactors are creditors, and hence that, just as in loans, debtors wish that their creditors did not exist while creditors even care for the safety of their debtors, so the benefactors wish those they have benefited to keep on living in order to return the favor while those who   25 are benefited do not care about making the return. Now Epicharmus would perhaps think that these people say this "because they view things from the wicked side",[1] but their attitude is human, for most people are un-grateful, and they aim to receive rather than to confer benefits.

It would seem, however, that the cause is more natural and is not simi-lar to that of men who have lent money; for these have no feeling of love   30 for their debtors but wish them alive in order to receive what is owed them, while those who have conferred services feel love and affection for those they have benefited, even if the latter neither are nor would in the future be useful to them. And this is just what happens with artists, for every artist loves his own work of art more than he would be loved by it   35 if it were to become alive; and perhaps this is what happens especially   1168a with poets, for they have an excessive love for their own poems and are fond of them as if they were their own children.

Such indeed seems to be the disposition of a benefactor also; for the service received by another is the benefactor's own work, and so he loves this work more than it loves him. The cause of this is the fact that existence   5 is to all a thing they choose and love, and we exist by being in activity; for we exist by living and *acting*. Now the artist engaged in activity is in some sense his work, and so he is fond of his work because he is fond of existence also. And this is natural; for that which he is potentially is indicated by his work which exists in actuality.[2] At the same time, the result of a   10 benefactor's *action* is noble to him, and he enjoys it in the person in whom it exists,[3] but the service of the benefactor is not noble to the person who receives it but is,[4] if anything, only expedient to him, and this is less pleasant to him and less worthy of being loved.[5]

What is pleasant to a man is the activity in the present, the expectation of what is to be in the future, and the memory of what happened in the

15 past; but what is most pleasant of these is the activity in the present, and
likewise this is the most lovable.[6] Now to a man who has produced [a
good work] his work is enduring (for what is noble is lasting), but to the
man who has received the benefit the usefulness of it passes away;[7] and the
memory of what is noble is pleasant to the benefactor, but the memory of
what is useful is hardly or less pleasant to the man who has been benefited.[8]
In the case of anticipation the reverse seems to be the case.[9] Again, loving
20 resembles acting, but being loved resembles being acted upon; and to love
and to do things from love belong to those who are superior in *action*.[10]
Finally, all men are more fond of what they have acquired with than without effort, e.g., those who have made money are more fond of it than those
who have inherited it; and indeed it seems that in being well treated one
makes no effort, while in treating another well one makes an effort.[11]
25 These are the *reasons*, too, why mothers love their children more than
fathers do; for giving birth to a baby is more painful to a mother than to
a father, and a mother knows more that it is her own baby than a father
does. This,[12] too, would seem to apply to benefactors.

8

Another problem raised is whether one should love himself most or some-
30 one else. For people censure those who love themselves most and call them
'self-lovers', using the term in a disgraceful sense. And a bad man is
thought to do everything for his own sake, and the more so if he is more
evil (and people criticize him for never going out of his way to do something for others), while a *good* man is thought to *act* for the sake of what
35 is noble, more so if he is better, and for the sake of his friend, disregarding
his own good.

1168*b*   But the facts are not in harmony with these arguments, and not without
good reason. For men say one should love his best friend most, and a best
friend is one who wishes the good of another for that other's sake, even
if no one is to know this. But these attributes belong most of all to a man
5 in relation to himself, and so do all the others by which a friend is defined;
for it was stated[1] that it is from one's relation to himself that all the attributes of love have been extended to his relation to others. And all proverbs
are in agreement with this view, e.g., 'a single soul', 'to friends all goods
are common', 'equality is friendship', and 'charity begins at home';[2] for

all these belong to a man in relation to himself most of all, since he is, one   10
might say, his own best friend and hence he should love himself most of
all.[3]

It is reasonable, then, to raise the question as to which of the two views
should be followed, as there is something convincing in both. But perhaps
we should analyze such arguments and determine the extent to which and
the manner in which each of them is true. Thus if we were to grasp the
sense in which the term 'self-lover' is used in each argument, perhaps the
truth might become clear.

Those who use the term as one of reproach call 'self-lovers' men who   15
take for themselves a larger share than they should, whether of property
or of honors or of bodily pleasures;[4] for these are the things which most
men desire and work hard for as if they were the best of all, and hence
these are the objects of contention. Accordingly, those who get more than
their share of these things aim to gratify their *desires* and, in general, their   20
passions and the nonrational part of their soul. Now such are most men;
hence the name 'self-love', too, has received a meaning from what is
mostly done, i.e., something which is bad. So those who are called
'self-lovers' in this sense are justly reproached.

That most men usually call 'self-lovers' those who take such things
[property, honor, bodily pleasures] for themselves more than they should,
then, is not unclear; for if a man were always earnest to do, above all   25
things, what is just or temperate or any other thing according to virtue
and, in general, if he were always earnest to safeguard for himself what is
noble, no one would call him 'self-lover' in this sense or blame him. But
such a man would seem to be a self-lover more [than the first man, but in
a second sense];[5] at any rate, he takes for himself the goods which are
noblest and best, and he favors the supreme part[6] in himself, and all the   30
other parts of the soul obey this part. And just as a state or any other
systematic whole is thought to be that which is its supreme part most of
all, so is a man;[7] and so a self-lover in the highest sense is he who loves
and favors this part. Again, a man is called 'continent' or 'incontinent'
according as his intellect rules the other parts of the soul or not,[8] respec-   35
tively, as if he were this part; and men are thought to have *acted* on their   1169*a*
own and to have *acted* voluntarily when they have done so with reason
most of all. It is not unclear, then, that each man is his intellect or his intellect most of all, and that a *good* man cherishes this part most of all.[9] So

he would be a self-lover most of all but different in kind from the one who
5   is reproached, and he differs from the latter as much as a life according to
reason differs from one according to passion, and he desires what is noble
rather than what is thought to be expedient.[10] Accordingly, all men welcome and praise those who are exceptionally earnest in performing noble
actions; and when all men strive for what is noble and exert themselves
10   to do the noblest deeds, then all the common needs would be supplied
and each individual would attain the greatest of goods, if indeed virtue
is such a thing.[11]

A good man, then, should be a self-lover [in this second sense], for he
will both help himself to do what is noble and be beneficial to others; but
an evil man should not [be a self-lover in the first sense], for in following
15   bad passions he will harm both himself and his neighbors. What an evil
man should do, then, is not in harmony with what he does;[12] but what a
good man should do is just what he does, for intellect in every case chooses
what is best for itself,[13] and a *good* man obeys his intellect.

It is also true of a virtuous man that he will do many things for the sake
20   of his friends and his country and he will, if need be, even die for them;
for he will forgo property and honors and, in general, the goods most men
compete for and will keep for himself only what is noble, since he would
rather choose intense pleasure for a short period than weak pleasure for a
long period,[14] and he would rather live a year nobly than many years
aimlessly, and he would rather perform one great and noble *action* than
25   many small ones. Perhaps this is the case of a man who dies for another or
others; he certainly chooses for himself what is great and noble. And
such a man would give away wealth if wealth is worth more to his friends
than to himself; for while his friends benefit by wealth, he earns nobility,
and so he takes for himself a greater good.[15] With honors and offices, too,
30   the situation is similar; for he would allow his friends to have them all,
since this is noble of him to do and praiseworthy. It is with good reason,
then, that he is thought to be a virtuous man, preferring what is noble to
everything else. He may even allow his friend to perform a [noble] *action*,
since being the *reason* for his friend's performing that *action* is nobler than
35   performing it himself. So in all *actions* worthy of praise a virtuous man
appears to take for himself what is more noble.

1169*b*   As we said, then, it is in this sense that a man should be a self-lover, not
in the sense in which most people are.

9

Another problem which is raised is whether a happy man needs friends or not. What is said is this: (a) a blessed and self-sufficient man has no need of friends since he has the things that are good, and so, being self-suffi-   5
cient, he has no need of anything more; but a friend, being another self, would supply him with what he cannot by himself supply. Whence the saying,

When God does well provide, what need is there for friends?[1]

(b) On the other hand, it seems absurd to assign all the goods to a happy man but allow him no friends, who are thought to be the greatest of   10
external goods. And if it is a mark of a friend to do rather than to receive good, and a mark of a good man and of a man of virtue to do service, and nobler to do good to friends than to strangers, a virtuous man will need friends to do good to. It is in view of this that also the problem is raised whether one needs friends in times of good fortune or in times of misfortune, since both an unfortunate man needs the services of others and a   15
fortunate man needs others to be of service to. Perhaps it is absurd, too, to regard the blessed man as a solitary man; for no man with all the other goods would choose to live alone, seeing that man is a political being and is disposed by nature to live with others. So living with others, too, belongs to a happy man, for the goods he has are by nature so. And   20
clearly, it is better to pass the days with friends and *good* men than with strangers and ordinary men. A happy man, then, does need friends.[2]

What is the meaning of the first argument, then, and in what way is it true? Is it that most men regard friends to be those who are useful? Now a blessed man will have no need of such friends since he already has the   25
goods. Nor indeed will he need friends for the sake of pleasure (or he will need them but little[3]), for, as his life is pleasant, he needs no further plea-
sure coming from outside. And since he does not need such friends, he is thought not to need friends.[4]

But perhaps this is not true; for we have stated at the outset[5] that happiness is an activity of a certain kind, and clearly an activity is something in progress and not something like a possession. Now since being   30
happy depends on living and on being in activity and the activity of a good man is virtuous and pleasant by its nature, as stated at the outset,[6] and

since what is close to us is also pleasant and we are able to perceive our
35   neighbors more than ourselves and their *actions* more than our own, then
1170*a*   the *actions* of virtuous men are pleasant to those who are good and are
their friends since they possess both marks [7] which are by nature pleasant.
Hence a blessed man will need such friends, if indeed he deliberately
chooses to contemplate *actions* which are *good* and close to him; and such
are the *actions* of his friends who are good.

5   Again, men think that a blessed man should live pleasantly. A solitary
life for a man, however, is hard, for it is not easy for him to be continuously active by himself, but it is easier to be continuously active with others
and towards others. His activity with others and towards others, then, will
be more continuous and pleasant by its nature, and this is a requirement
for a blessed man; for a virtuous man as such enjoys *actions* according to
10   virtue but is displeased with *actions* issuing from vice, just as a musician
is pleased with beautiful tunes but is pained by bad ones.[8]

Again, as Theognis says, one would also get some practice in virtue by
living with good men.[9]

If we inquire more into the nature of things [10] [than dialectically or
logically], a virtuous friend seems by nature choiceworthy by a virtuous
15   man. For that which is by nature good was stated to be in virtue of its
goodness also good and pleasurable to a virtuous man. Now people define
living by a power of sensation in the case of animals, and by a power of
sensation or of thinking in the case of men; [11] but a power is referred to
the corresponding activity, and that which is important is the activity; [12]
so living seems to lie principally in sensing or thinking. But living is
20   among those things which are in themselves good and pleasant; for it has
definiteness, and that which is definite is of the nature of a good.[13] Now
that which is by nature good is also good to a *good* man; hence it seems to
be pleasant to all men. But we should not include an evil or corrupt life,
nor a life in pain, for such a life is indefinite, as are the attributes which
25   belong to it; and this will become more evident later when we discuss pain.
Now since living itself is good and pleasant (and this seems to be the case
since all men desire it, and especially those who are *good* and blessed; for
it is to these that life is most choiceworthy, and the most blessed life
belongs to them), and since he who sees is aware that he sees, he who
30   hears is aware that he hears, he who walks is aware that he walks, and
similarly in the other cases, there is something in us which is aware that

we are in activity, and so we would be aware that we are sensing and we would be thinking that we are thinking. But [to be aware] that we are sensing or [to think that] we are thinking [is to be aware] that we exist, for to exist [for men] was stated to be sensing or thinking; and being aware   1170*b* that one lives is in itself one of the things which are pleasant, for life is by nature good, and to be aware that good belongs to oneself is pleasant.[14] Now living is choiceworthy, and especially by those who are good, since existence to them is good and pleasant; for they are pleased by being   5 aware of that which is in itself good. And just as a virtuous man is disposed towards himself, so is he disposed towards his friend, for his friend is another self. So just as one's own existence is a choiceworthy object to a man, so is that of a friend, or almost so. But existence was stated to be choiceworthy to a man because he is aware of himself as being good, and such awareness is pleasant in itself. Hence he should be aware also of the   10 fact that his friend exists, and this would come about by living together with him and sharing in conversation and *thoughts*; for 'living together' in the case of men would be taken to mean a thing as this and not, as in the case of cattle, feeding in the same place. So since to a blessed man existence, which is by nature good and pleasant, is in virtue of itself a   15 choiceworthy object, and since a friend's existence, too, is almost so, then also a friend would be a choiceworthy object to him. But that which is choiceworthy to him should belong to him, or else he will feel the need of it.[15] Hence he who is to be happy will need virtuous friends.

10

Should we make, then, as many friends as possible, or, as in hospitality,   20 which is thought to be aptly described by the saying "neither a man of many guests nor a man of none",[1] so in friendship is it fitting for a man not to be friendless nor again to have an excessive number of friends?

Now to friends whose purpose is usefulness the above saying would seem to be quite suitable; for to return the services of many friends would   25 be a laborious task, and life is not long enough to do so. Hence a number of friends greater than that which is sufficient for one's life would be superfluous and would impede noble living, and so there is no need of them. In the case of friendship for the sake of pleasure, too, few friends are enough, like a small amount of seasoning in food.

30   In the case of virtuous men, should there be as many friends as possible, or is there, as in the case of a city, a proper limit of them? For neither would ten men make a city, nor will it remain a city if increased to one hundred thousand men. Perhaps a plurality has no unity unless it falls
1171a within certain limits. So in the case of friends, too, there is a limited plurality, and perhaps there is an upper limit of those with whom one could live together [nobly]; for, as we remarked, this is thought to be friendship at its best. It is clear, then, that one cannot live together with many friends and attend to all of them in turn. Further, they, too, will
5   have to be friends with each other, if all of them are to spend their days together; and this can hardly be fulfilled with a large number of them. It is difficult, too, to share the joys or sorrows in an intimate way with a great number of friends; for it is quite likely that at the same time one will be sharing pleasures with one of them but grieving with another. Surely,
10   then, it is well to seek not too many friends but as many as are enough to live together with, for it would not seem possible to be much of a friend to many persons. It is in view of this, too, that one cannot be in love with many persons, for love tends to be a sort of excess of friendship, and this can be felt towards one person only; so strong friendship, too, can exist towards few persons only.

And such seems to be actually the case; for people do not make many
15   friends as comrades, and great friendships of this sort which are mentioned in verse are between two persons only.[2] Those who have very many friends or treat everyone intimately are thought to be nobody's friend, except in a political sense, and they are called 'complaisant'. It is possible, however, to be politically a friend to many and be not complaisant but a truly *good* man; but it is impossible to be a friend to many persons through virtue
20   and for their own sake, and one should be content to find even few friends such as these.

11

Is it in times of good fortune or in times of misfortune that friends are needed more? They are sought in both; for both those who are unfortunate need assistance, and those who are fortunate need people to live with and to treat well, since they wish to *act* well. Now in times of bad fortune
25   friendship is more of a necessity, in which case what is needed here is something useful; but in times of good fortune friendship is more noble,

in which case what is sought is *good* men as friends, for what one prefers in this case is to be of service to others and to live with them.[1]

The presence itself of friends is pleasant even in times of misfortune, since those in grief are alleviated when friends share their sorrow. Hence one might even ask whether it is the sharing by friends of the pain, as if of a burden, which lessens the pain, or not that but their presence, which is pleasant, and the thought of their sympathy. At present, let us leave aside the problem of whether grief is alleviated for any of these or for some other *reason*; at any rate, what we have stated appears to take place. It seems, however, that the presence of friends is a sort of mixture of pleasure and pain. For seeing our friends is itself pleasant, especially in times of bad fortune, and this becomes a sort of remedy against pain; for a friend, if tactful, is a comfort by his presence and by his words since he knows our character and the things that please us or pain us. On the other hand, to see them pained at our bad fortunes is painful to us, for every [good man] avoids causing pain to his friends. In view of this, those of a manly nature avoid sharing their grief with their friends, and if they are not too insensible to grief, they cannot stand having their friends grieve, and, in general, they do not allow fellow-mourners because they themselves are not disposed to mourning; but women and men with a weak nature enjoy having others lament with them and love them as friends and companions in grief. It is clear, however, that in all matters we ought to imitate the better man.[2]

In times of good fortune, on the other hand, the presence of our friends makes our pastime pleasant and creates the impression upon us that they take pleasure in our own good. Hence it would seem that we should be eager to invite our friends to share our good fortune, since this is a mark of beneficence and is noble, but that we should be slow to summon them in times of bad fortune, for we should have them share as little of what is bad as possible (whence the saying 'enough is my misfortune').[3] The best time to summon them would be when at the cost of a small inconvenience they can be of great benefit to us. Conversely, perhaps it is fitting that we should be eager to go uninvited to our friends when they meet with bad fortune (for it is a mark of a good friend to do good, and especially to friends who are in need and who would regard it unworthy in calling us; for this would be nobler and more pleasant to both friends), and to assist them eagerly in their good fortunes (for friends are needed in these) but

30

35
1171*b*

5

10

15

20

25   show no eagerness to accept a return, for it is not noble to be eager in
getting a benefit. But perhaps we should be careful not to be thought unpleasant by turning down their kindness, for this happens occasionally.
    The presence of friends, then, appears to be worthy of choice in all cases.

12

In a friendship, is living together the thing that is most worthy of choice,
30   like seeing for lovers, who love this most of all and prefer this sensation to
all the rest, since it is in virtue of this sensation that love exists and comes
into being? For friendship is an association, and as a man is related to
himself, so is he related to his friend also. Now a man's awareness of him-
35   self is worthy of choice; and so is that of his friend. But the activity
1172a   in this [awareness][1] exists in living together; so it is reasonable that this is
what they aim at. And whatever each man regards existence to be or
whatever he chooses to live for, this is what he wishes to engage in with
his friends. Hence some friends drink together, others play dice together,
5   others exercise or hunt or philosophize together, and in every case friends
spend their days together in whatever they love most of life; for since they
wish to live together, they do and participate in those things in which they
think they can live together.[2] Accordingly, a friendship of bad men becomes
10   evil; for, being fickle, bad men participate in bad pursuits, and they
become evil by becoming like each other. The friendship of *good* men, on
the other hand, is *good*, and it grows as their companionship continues;
and they seem to become even better men by acting together and cor-
recting each other, for each models himself on what he approves of the
other. Whence the saying,

Good men from good things learn.[3]

15   Concerning friendship, then, let this be the extent of our discussion.
We may proceed to discuss pleasure next.

BOOK K

1

After what has been said, perhaps a discussion of pleasure comes next; for 1172a
pleasure is thought to be closely associated with human nature most of all, 20
and this is the reason why we guide the education of the young by means
of pleasure and pain. And it also seems that to enjoy the things we should
and to hate the things we should contribute most to the formation of virtuous character, for these [1] are present with us throughout our life and have
influence and power in forming virtue and making our life happy, since 25
we deliberately choose what is pleasant and avoid what is painful. And it
would seem that we should least of all omit the discussion of such matters,
especially when there is much disagreement concerning them. For some
thinkers say that the good is pleasure,[2] but others, taking the contrary
position, say that pleasure is altogether bad, and some of the latter are
perhaps convinced that such is actually the case,[3] while others think that 30
to represent pleasure as bad has a better effect on our way of life, even if
this is not so, for they think that most men are inclined towards pleasures
and are slaves of pleasures and hence should be led towards the contrary
direction, since it is in this way that they will arrive at the mean.[4]

But surely these thinkers are not stating the case well; for arguments
concerning passions and *actions* are less convincing than facts, and when 35
arguments disagree with what is observed, they fall into contempt and
discredit truth as well. For if a man speaks disapprovingly of pleasure 1172b
and is sometimes seen to aim at it, his inclination towards it is thought to
indicate that all pleasure is such that men aim at it; for most people
are not given to making distinctions.[5] So true arguments concerning
pleasure and pain seem to be most useful not only to knowledge, but to 5
our way of life as well; for, being in harmony with the facts, they impart
conviction, and hence they exhort intelligent men to live according to
them. But enough of such remarks; let us go over what is said about
pleasure.

2

10   Eudoxus thought that the good is pleasure because he observed all ani-
      mals, both rational and nonrational, aiming at it. He argued that since
      in everything the object of choice is *good* and the object mostly chosen is
      the best, and since the fact that all animals are drawn to the same thing
      indicates that this is the highest good for all of them (for each animal finds
      its own good just as it finds its own food), that which is good for all
15   animals and at which all animals aim is the good.[1]
          These arguments carried conviction more because of his virtuous
      character than because of themselves as arguments, for Eudoxus was re-
      garded as being exceptionally temperate; so men thought that he was
      saying these things not as a friend of pleasure but as if such was the truth
      of the matter. He held that his doctrine was no less evident from argu-
      ments by the use of contraries, for he regarded pain in itself as being an
20   object avoided by all and its contrary as being in a similar way an object
      chosen by all. He maintained that a choiceworthy object in the highest
      sense is one which does not exist for the sake of another nor is chosen for
      the sake of another, and that pleasure is agreed upon as being such an
      object; for no one asks for what further reason one is pleased, so pleasure
      must be chosen for its own sake. And when pleasure is added to any good
25   thing, e.g., to a just or a temperate *action*, he regarded the result as being
      more choiceworthy than that thing and so goodness itself as being in-
      creased by additional goodness.
          Now the above argument seems to show merely that pleasure is one of
      the goods, and not a higher good than another kind of good; for any kind
      of good whatever would thus be more worthy of choice when another
      good is added to it than when it is by itself.[2] It is indeed by an argument
      such as this that Plato, too, refutes the statement that the good is plea-
30   sure; for, according to him, a pleasant life is preferable with rather than
      without prudence, and if the combination of the two is better, the good
      cannot be pleasure, for the good itself[3] cannot become more choiceworthy
      by the addition of anything.[4] It is clear, then, that neither can a thing,
      other than pleasure, be the good if the addition of what is good by itself
      makes the combination more choiceworthy. What thing, then, is such
35   that we too can participate in? For it is a thing such as this that we are
      looking for.

Those who object to the view that that at which all creatures aim is good are talking nonsense. For that which is thought by all to be the case is said to be the case, and he who rejects this conviction will hardly assert anything which is more convincing; for if only senseless creatures desired certain things, there might be something in what they say, but if also prudent creatures desire them, how could there be anything in what they are saying? Perhaps even in bad creatures there is some natural good which is better than they themselves are and which aims at its proper good.[5]

Nor does the argument which concerns the contrary of pleasure seem to be stated well, for they[6] say that, if pain is bad, it does not follow that pleasure is good; for evil may be opposed to evil, and both of them may be opposed to what is neither of them, and in saying these they do not speak badly, but these statements are not true of the things [pleasure and pain] in question. For if both pleasure and pain were evil, both would have been avoided, and if neither was evil, neither would have been avoided or both would have been similarly related to us.[7] But as it is, men appear to avoid pain as an evil but to choose pleasure as a good; so this is the manner in which pleasure and pain are opposed.

Again, the fact that pleasure is not a quality is not a reason for excluding it from being a good; for neither the activities of virtue nor happiness is a quality, but they are goods.[8]

Some thinkers say that the good is definite, but that pleasure is indefinite since it admits of degree.[9] Now if they judge this from the fact that one is pleased, [for one may be pleased sometimes more and sometimes less,] the same will be the case with justice and the other virtues, according to which men are obviously said to be such-and-such and also to *act* to a higher or to a lower degree; for men may be more just or more brave, and they may *act* more justly or less justly, and more temperately or less temperately.[10] But if they think that indefiniteness is present in the pleasures themselves, perhaps they are not stating the cause, [e.g.,] whether some pleasures are unmixed but others are mixed. For what prevents pleasure from being like health, which is definite yet admits of degree? For proportion is not the same in all things which admit of it, nor does a single proportion exist in the same thing always, but it may deviate up to a point and still persist, and so it may vary in degree. So such may be the case with pleasure.[11]

1173*a*

5

10

15

20

25

Again, positing the good as being perfect but motions and genera-
30   tions as being imperfect,[12] they try to show that pleasure is a motion
or a generation. But they do not seem to speak well, nor is pleasure a
motion. For quickness and slowness are thought to be proper to every
motion, or if a motion by its nature is not [quicker or slower], as in the
case of the motion of the universe, still it is quicker or slower than other
motions; but quickness and slowness do not belong to pleasure.[13] For
1173b   though we may come to be pleased quickly as we may get angry quickly,
while we are being pleased we are not pleased quickly, not even in relation
to something else, but we can walk or grow, or the like, quickly. So
while we may change into a state of pleasure quickly or slowly, we cannot
be in activity with respect to pleasure in a quick or slow way, i.e., our
state of being pleased is not quick or slow.[14]

5   Again, how can pleasure be a generation? For a thing generated is not
thought to be generated from any chance thing, but it is generated from
that into which it may be dissolved, and of that whose generation is
pleasure the destruction would be pain.[15]

They say, too, that pain is the lack of that which exists according to
nature, but that pleasure is the replenishment of it. Now these [i.e., lack
and replenishment] are attributes of the body. So if pleasure is the re-
10   plenishment of that which exists according to nature, then also that in
which there is replenishment would be that which is pleased. Hence this
would be the body. But this is not thought to be the case; so neither can
pleasure be replenishment, but one is pleased when replenishment is
taking place, and he is pained when he is being operated on.[16]

This doctrine [that pleasure is replenishment] seems to have originated
from the fact that pains and pleasures are associated with food; for men
15   in pain because of the need of food are pleased while taking in food. But
this does not happen with regard to all kinds of pleasures; for the pleasures of learning and, with respect to sensation, those through smell and
many sounds and sights, and also those of memories and expectations
are not preceded by pain. These pleasures, then, would be the generations
20   of what objects? There has been no lack of anything of which these could
be the replenishment.[17]

Against those who bring forward the pleasures which deserve reproach
one might reply that these are not pleasant; for [he might argue that] if
they are pleasures to those who are badly disposed, one should not regard

them as pleasures except to those who are so disposed, just as we do not regard things which are wholesome or sweet or bitter to sick people as being such to healthy people, or things which appear white to those 25 suffering from a disease of the eye as being such to those with healthy eyes.[18] Or, one might reply that pleasures are worthy of choice but not those which deserve reproach, just as wealth is worthy of choice but not at the cost of betraying one's country, or as health is worthy of choice but not at the cost of eating any chance food. Or else, one might reply that pleasures differ in kind; for those which come from noble *actions* are different from those which come from disgraceful *actions*, and one cannot get the kind of pleasure of a just man without being himself just, nor the 30 pleasure of a musical man without being himself musical, and similarly with the others. The difference between a friend and a flatterer, too, seems to bring out the point that pleasure is not a good or that pleasures differ in kind; for a friend's company is regarded as being for the sake of what is good whereas that of a flatterer is for the sake of giving pleasure, and a flatterer is reproached whereas a friend is praised, and this fact indicates 1174*a* that the ends of the two associations are different. Further, no one would choose to live all his life with the *thoughts* of a child and with the greatest pleasures a child is capable of, or to enjoy doing something which is most disgraceful, even if he were to suffer no pain at all.[19] There are many things, too, we would make an effort in doing even if they were to bring 5 us no pleasure at all, such as seeing, remembering, knowing, and having virtues; and it makes no difference if pleasures follow these activities of necessity, for we would choose them even if no pleasure were to come from them.[20] It seems clear, then, that neither is pleasure the good,[21] nor is every pleasure worthy of choice, and that some pleasures are worthy of 10 choice in virtue of their nature and differ in kind or by the fact that they come from different sources.

Let the above, then, suffice as an account of the things that are said about pleasure and pain.

3

What pleasure is or what kind of thing it is might become more evident if we take up the discussion by starting from a principle.[1]

Now seeing is thought to be complete at any interval of time; for it 15 needs no thing which, when it comes into being later, will complete the form of seeing. Pleasure, too, resembles a thing such as seeing; for it is a whole, and no pleasure at an interval of time can be taken whose form will be completed by pleasure at a later interval.

20   In view of this, pleasure is not a motion, for every motion takes time and is for the sake of an end; e.g., the process of building is complete when that which is aimed at [e.g., a house] is made. So this motion is complete either in the whole interval of time or at the moment when the house is completed. But within every part of the time which is required for the whole motion, the corresponding partial motion is incomplete, and the partial motions are different from each other and from the whole motion, for the fitting of the stones is different in kind from the fluting of the columns, and these are different from the construction of the [whole]

25   temple; and the construction of the temple is complete (for nothing is missing from the end proposed), whereas the construction of the foundation or of the triglyph is incomplete (for each is a motion of a part of the temple). So they differ in kind, and it is not possible to find in any interval of time a motion which is complete in form, but, if at all, only in the whole interval of time. It is likewise with walking and the rest of the

30   motions. For since locomotion is a motion from one place to another, and of locomotion there are different species (flying, walking, jumping, and the like), differences arise not only in this manner, but also in, let us say, walking itself; for the starting point and the goal are not the same in the whole racecourse and in a part of it, nor are they the same in tra-

1174b   versing two different parts of it, (for one goes over not just a line but a line which is in place, and the place of one line is different from that of another. We have discussed motion with accuracy elsewhere).[2] So it seems that motions are not complete within every interval of time; but most[3] of them

5   are incomplete and differ in kind, if indeed their starting point and end also cause a difference in those motions.[4]

        The form of pleasure, on the other hand, is complete in every interval of time during which one is pleased. So it is clear that pleasure and motion would be [generically] different, and that pleasure would be among the things which are wholes and which are complete within any interval. This would seem to be the case also from the fact that it is not possible for a thing to move except in time, but it is possible to be pleased [not in time]; for [to be pleased] in a moment is a whole. From these remarks it is also

10   clear that those who call pleasure 'a motion' or 'a generation' do not

speak well, for these are predicated not of all things but of things which are divisible into parts and also of things which are not wholes.[5] For there is no generation of seeing or of a point or of a unit, nor is any of these a motion or a generation; and so neither is there a generation of pleasure, for this is a whole.[6]

4

Since every faculty of sensation, when active, is directed towards a sensible object, and since such a faculty when in excellent condition acts perfectly on the noblest sensible object coming under it (for perfect activity in the highest sense seems to be an activity such as this, and it makes no difference whether we regard the faculty itself as acting or the organ in which that faculty resides), it follows that the best activity of each faculty is the activity which is best disposed towards the best object coming under that faculty. This activity would be the most perfect and most pleasant; for there is pleasure with respect to every faculty of sensation, and likewise with *thought* and contemplation, and the most pleasant activity is the most perfect, and the most perfect is that of a [faculty or organ] which is excellently disposed towards the best object coming under it. Now it is pleasure that makes the activity perfect. But pleasure does not perfect the activity in the same way as the sensible object or sensation does, although both of them are *good*, just as health and the doctor are not alike causes of being healthy.[1]

It is clear that pleasure arises with respect to each faculty of sensation, for we speak of sights and of things heard as being pleasant. It is also clear that these activities are most pleasant whenever both the faculty is at its best and its activity is directed towards its best corresponding object; and if both the object sensed and he who senses it are such, there will always be pleasure provided both the agent and that which is acted upon[2] are present. But pleasure perfects the activity not as a disposition which resides in the agent[3] but as an end which supervenes like the bloom of manhood to those in their prime of life; so while the object which is being thought or sensed and that which thinks or judges it continue to be as they should, there will be pleasure in the activity, for when both the agent and the object acted upon remain in a similar condition and are related to each other in the same manner, the result produced is by nature the same.

How is it, then, that no one is continuously pleased? But do we not

15

20

25

30

1175a

5   become weary? For human activities cannot continue indefinitely; so
neither can pleasure, for it accompanies such activities. For the same
reason, some things delight us when they are new but later fail to do so
in a similar way; for at first *thought* is attracted and its activity towards
them is intense, as in the case of vision when men look intently at a thing,
10 but afterwards the activity does not have the same quality but loses its
force, and hence its pleasure too fades away.[4]

One might think that all men desire pleasure, since they all aim at
living. Now life is a kind of activity, and a man directs his activities to the
things and with the things which he loves most; for example, the musician
uses the faculty of hearing to listen to tunes, and he who loves learning
15 uses his *thought* on theoretical objects, and similarly in each case. But
pleasure perfects the activities, and also living, which men desire. It is with
good reason, then, that men desire also pleasure; for this makes living
perfect for each man, and this[5] is worthy of choice. Whether we choose
living for the sake of pleasure or pleasure for the sake of living may be
20 left aside for the present. For living and pleasure appear to go together
and not to admit separation; for there can be no pleasure without activity,
and pleasure perfects every activity.

5

It is in view of this that pleasures, too, are thought to differ in kind, for
we think that things which are different in kind are perfected by different
things.[1] For this is the way in which both natural things and those coming
under art appear to be perfected, e.g., animals and trees, and also paint-
25 ings, statues, houses, and furniture; and, in a similar way, also activities
which differ in kind appear to be perfected by things which differ in kind.
Now the activities of *thought* differ in kind from those with respect to
sensation, and those within each genus [i.e., those with respect to *thought*,
or those with respect to sensation] differ in kind within themselves; so the
corresponding pleasures which complete these activities, too, will be
different.[2] This might appear to be the case also from the fact that each of
30 the pleasures resides in the activity which is perfected by that pleasure.
For an activity is increased along with the pleasure which is proper to it;
for those who engage in activity with pleasure judge things better or *think*
them out more accurately than those who take little or no pleasure in

those activities, e.g., those who become geometricians and think out each geometrical object better are those who enjoy geometrical thinking, and, similarly, it is by enjoying their activity that those who love music or   35 constructing a building, etc., make progress in their proper field. What causes each of them to advance further in his own field is pleasure, and that which causes such advance is proper to that field; and attributes   1175b proper to subjects which are different in kind are themselves different in kind.[3]

This becomes even more apparent from the fact that activities are obstructed by the pleasures of other activities; e.g., those who love to hear flute-playing are unable to attend to an argument when they hear attentively someone playing the flute, for they enjoy listening to the flute more   5 than the activity of attending to the argument, and so the pleasure of hearing flute-playing destroys the activity connected with the argument. It is likewise in all other cases in which a man is engaged in two things at the same time; for the more pleasant activity pushes the other activity back, and if the former activity is much more pleasant, it pushes the latter activity even further back so that the man cannot even attend to the latter   10 activity. For this reason, when we enjoy anything very much we do nothing else at all; and when we lose interest in something, we do other things, e.g., those who eat sweets in theaters do so most when actors are bad.

Now since the pleasure which is proper to the activities of a given kind makes those activities more accurate, more enduring, and better, while   15 alien pleasures impair them, it is clear that proper and alien pleasures are much different; for alien pleasures have almost[4] the effect which proper pains have, since proper pains destroy those activities. For example, if writing or counting numbers is unpleasant and painful to a man, he does not write or does not count since these activities are painful. But the   20 effects of an activity arising from its proper pleasures and its proper pains are contrary – and proper pleasures and pains are said to be those which supervene on an activity in virtue of its own nature – while alien pleasures, as already stated, have an effect which is just about the same as [proper] pains have, for they too destroy that activity, though not in the same manner.

Since activities differ by being *good* or bad, and since some should be   25 chosen, others should be avoided, and others are neutral with respect to choice or avoidance, pleasures, too, differ in a similar way; for corresponding to each activity there is a proper pleasure. Accordingly, the pleasure proper to a good activity is *good*, while that proper to a bad activity is evil; for of *desires*, too, those of noble activities are praised

30   while those of disgraceful activities are blamed.[5] But the pleasures in activities are more proper to them than the corresponding desires; for the desires are distinct from the activities both in time and in nature,[6] while the proper pleasures are quite close to them and are so indistinguishable from them that men disagree as to whether activities and pleasures are the same or not. Still, pleasure does not seem to be the same as *thought* or

35   sensation, for this would be strange, but they appear to some to be the same because they are not separated. Just as activities are distinct, then,

1176a   so are the corresponding pleasures.[7] Now vision differs from touch in purity, and so do hearing and smell from taste.[8] So the corresponding pleasures, too, differ in a similar way, and those of *thought* differ from these, and within each of the two [genera, i.e., of sensation and of *thought*] there are differences.[9]

Each animal is thought to have a proper pleasure, just as it has a proper

5   function; for a given pleasure is proper to its corresponding activity. This would appear to be so if each species of animals is considered also; for the pleasures of a horse, of a dog, and of a man are different; and as Heraclitus says, "Donkeys would choose sweepings rather than gold",[10] for food is more pleasant to them than gold. So the pleasures of different animals are themselves different in kind, and it is reasonable to think that the

10   pleasures within each species do not differ. But in the case of men, at least, the pleasures vary to no small extent; for the same things delight some men but pain others, and they are painful or hateful to some but pleasant or lovable to others. This happens in the case of sweet things, too; for they do not seem the same to those who have fever and to those

15   who are healthy, nor hot both to a sickly man and to one in good physical condition, and similarly in other cases. In all such cases, then, what is thought to be the case is what appears to a virtuous man. And if this is well stated (as is thought to be) and the measure of each thing is virtue or a good man as such [i.e., as virtuous], those things, too, will be pleasures which appear to him to be pleasures and those things will be pleasur-

20   able which a good man enjoys. And if the things which distress him appear pleasant to some persons, there is nothing surprising about this (for men

are ruined or impaired in various ways), and such things are not pleasurable but only to these persons and to others who are disposed in such a manner. So it is clear that we should not speak of those pleasures which are generally regarded to be disgraceful as being really pleasures, except to those who are corrupt.[11] But of pleasures which are thought to be *good*, what kind or which should be said to belong to a man? Are they not clear   25 from [a consideration of] the corresponding activities? For it is these activities that the pleasures accompany. So whether there is one or more than one activity that belongs to a perfect and blessed man, it is the pleasures which perfect those activities that would primarily be called the 'pleasures' belonging to a man, and the others would be called 'pleasures' in a secondary sense or to a small degree, like the corresponding activities.[12]

6

After a discussion of the virtues and friendship and pleasures, what re-   30 mains is a sketchy discussion of happiness, since this is what we posited as the end of whatever is human. Our discussion will be shorter if we review what has already been stated.

We have said[1] that happiness is not a disposition; for otherwise it might belong also to a man who sleeps all his life and so lives like a plant, or to a   35 man who suffers the greatest of misfortunes. So since this is not satis-   1176b factory but happiness should be posited as being rather an activity of some sort, as we have stated earlier,[2] and since some activities are necessary and are chosen for the sake of something else while others [are chosen just] for their own sake, it is clear that happiness should be posited as chosen for its own sake and not for the sake of something else, for   5 happiness has no need of anything else but is self-sufficient.

Activities which are chosen for their own sake are those from which nothing else is sought beyond them. Now such are thought to be the *actions* in accordance with virtue, for doing what is noble or good is something chosen for its own sake. And such, too, are thought to be the amusements, which are pleasant, since they are chosen not for the sake of some-   10 thing else; for men are harmed rather than benefited by them, when they neglect their bodies and the acquisition of property.[3] Most people who are regarded as happy resort to pastimes such as these; and this is the reason why witty men are highly favored by tyrants, for they offer the   15 kind of pleasure which tyrants aim at, and tyrants need such men. So these pastimes are thought to contribute to happiness because it is in these that men in despotic positions spend their time.

But perhaps the apparent happiness of such men is no sign that they are really happy, for virtue and thought, from which good activities arise, do not depend on despotic power; and the fact that such men, who have

20   never tasted pure and liberal pleasure, resort to bodily pleasures is no *reason* for regarding these pleasures as being more choiceworthy, for children too regard the things they value as being the best. It is with good reason, then, that just as different things appear to be of value to children and to men, so different things appear to be of value to bad men and to

25   *good* men. Accordingly, as we have often stated,[4] things which are both valuable and pleasant are those which appear such to a good man. The activity most choiceworthy to each man, then, is the one in accordance with his own disposition, and so the activity most choiceworthy to a virtuous man would be the one which proceeds according to virtue. Consequently, happiness is not found in amusement, for it would be also absurd to maintain that the end of man is amusement and that men work

30   and suffer all their life for the sake of amusement. For, in short, we choose everything for the sake of something else, except happiness, since happiness is the end of a man. So to be serious and work hard for the sake of amusement appears foolish and very childish, but to amuse oneself for the sake of serious work seems, as Anarchasis[5] put it, to be right; for amusement

35   is like relaxation, and we need relaxation since we cannot keep on working

1177a   hard continuously. Thus amusement is not the end, for it is chosen for the sake of serious activity.

A happy life, on the other hand, is thought to be a life according to virtue; and it proceeds with seriousness but does not exist in amusement. And we speak of serious things as being better than those which are

5   humorous or amusing, and we speak of the activity of the better part of a man or of a better man as being always better; and the activity of what is better is superior and so makes one more happy. Any man, even one with a slavish nature, can indulge in the bodily pleasures no less than the best man, but no one would attribute happiness to a man with a slavish nature, unless he attributes to him also a way of life which is human; for happiness

10   is not found in such pastimes but in activities according to virtue, as we have already stated.[6]

7

Since happiness is an activity according to virtue, it is reasonable that it should be an activity according to the highest virtue; and this would be an activity of the best part of man. So whether this be intellect or something else which is thought to rule and guide us by its nature and to have com-   15 prehension of noble and divine objects, being itself divine or else the most divine part in us, its activity according to its proper virtue would be perfect happiness. That this activity is contemplative has already been mentioned;[1] and this would seem to be in agreement both with our previous remarks[2] and with the truth.

(1) This activity is the highest of all since the intellect (a) is the best of   20 the parts in us and (b) is concerned with the best of the known objects.

(2) It is the most continuous of our activities; for (a) we are more able to be engaged continuously in theoretical activity than to perform any *action* continuously,[3] and (b) we think that pleasure should be intermingled with happiness; and it is agreed that the most pleasant of our virtuous activities is the one in accordance with wisdom. Indeed, philosophy is re-   25 garded as possessing pleasures which are wonderful in purity as well as in certainty, and it is reasonable for men who have understanding to pass their time more pleasantly than those who [merely] inquire.[4]

(3) What goes by the name 'self-sufficiency', too, would apply to theoretical activity most of all; for although wise men and just men and all the rest have need of the necessities of life, when they are all sufficiently   30 provided with them, a just man needs others towards whom and with whom he will *act* justly, and similarly in the case of a temperate man, a brave man, and each of the others, while a wise man is able to theorize even if he were alone, and the wiser he is, the more he can do so by himself. Perhaps it is better for him to have colleagues;[5] but still, he is the   1177b most self-sufficient of all.

(4) This activity alone is thought to be loved for its own sake; for nothing results from it except contemplation itself, while from practical activities we gain for ourselves, either more or less, other things besides the *action* itself.

(5) Happiness is thought to depend on leisure; for we toil[6] for the sake   5 of leisurely activity, and we are at war for the sake of peaceful activity. Now the activities of the practical virtues are concerned with political or

military matters, and the *actions* concerning these matters are thought to be toilsome. Military *actions* are altogether toilsome; for no reasonable
10   man chooses to wage a war for its own sake or to prepare for a war for its own sake; for if a man were to make enemies of his friends for the sake of fighting or killing, he would be regarded as utterly bloodthirsty. The activity of a man in politics, too, is toilsome and aims at something other than itself, namely, power or honor or, at any rate, at one's own or the
15   citizens' happiness, which is different from the political [*action* itself] and is clearly sought as an activity which is different.

So if political and military *actions* among virtuous *actions* stand out in fineness and greatness and, being toilsome, are aimed at some other end but are not chosen for their own sake, whereas the activity of the intellect,
20   being theoretical, is thought to be superior in seriousness and to aim at no other end besides itself but to have its own pleasure which increases that activity, then also self-sufficiency and leisure and freedom from weariness (as much as are possible for man) and all the other things which are attributed to a blessed man appear to exist in this activity. This, then,
25   would be the perfect happiness for man, if extended to the full length of life, for none of the attributes of happiness is incomplete.

Such a life, of course, would be above that of a man, for a man will live in this manner not insofar as he is a man, but insofar as he has something divine in him; and the activity of this divine part of the soul is as much superior to that of the other kind of virtue as that divine part is
30   superior to the composite soul of a man.[7] So since the intellect is divine relative to a man, the life according to this intellect, too, will be divine relative to human life.[8] Thus we should not follow the recommendation of thinkers who say that those who are men should think only of human things and that mortals should think only of mortal things, but we should try as far as possible to partake of immortality and to make every effort to
1178*a*   live according to the best part of the soul in us; for even if this part be of small measure, it surpasses all the others by far in power and worth. It would seem, too, that each man is this part, if indeed this is the dominant part and is better than the other parts; so it would be strange if a man did not choose the life proper to himself but that proper to another. And what
5   was stated earlier[9] is appropriate here also: that which is by nature proper to each thing is the best and most pleasant for that thing. So for a man, too, the life according to his intellect is the best and most pleasant,

if indeed a man in the highest sense is his intellect. Hence this life, too, is the happiest.[10]

8

The life according to the other kind of virtue[1] is happy in a secondary way, since the activities according to that virtue are concerned with human   10
affairs; for it is according to the virtues which relate one man to another that we perform just and brave and other *actions* relating to contracts and needs and all other sorts, observing in each case what is fitting with regard to our passions. All these appear to be concerned with human affairs. Some of them are thought to result even from the body, and the virtue of   15
character is thought to be in many ways closely associated with the passions.

Prudence, too, is bound up with ethical virtue, and ethical virtue is bound up with prudence, if indeed the principles of prudence are in accordance with ethical virtues and the rightness of the ethical virtues is in accordance with prudence. Since these ethical virtues are connected with the passions also, they would be concerned with the composite nature of   20
man;[2] and the virtues of that composite are concerned with human affairs. So the life and happiness in accordance with these virtues, too, would be human.

The virtue of the intellect, on the other hand, is separated [from the passions]; and let this much be said about this virtue, for detailed accuracy about it would take us beyond our present purpose.[3] We might add, too, that this virtue would seem to require external resources only to a small extent, or less than ethical virtue does; for if granting that both   25
kinds of virtue require the necessities of life equally, even if a statesman's effort concerning the body and other such things is greater than that of the theoretical thinker (for there would be little difference here), still there will be much difference in what their activities require.[4] For a generous man will need property for his generous *actions*, and so will a just man   30
if he is to reciprocate for the services done to him (for wishes are not clearly seen, and even unjust men pretend that they wish to *act* justly); and a brave man will need power, if he is to perform an *action* according to virtue, while a temperate man will need the means, for how else can he manifest himself as being a temperate man rather than one of the others [i.e., stingy or wasteful]?

35   Disagreement arises as to whether the more important part of virtue[5]
is intention or the corresponding *actions*, since virtue depends on both.
1178b Clearly, perfection of virtue depends on both. As for *actions*, they require
many things, and more of these are required if the *actions* are greater and
nobler. A theoretical thinker, on the other hand, requires none of such
things, at least for his activity, and one might say that these even obstruct
5   theoretical activity;[6] but insofar as he is a man[7] and lives with many
others, he will choose to *act* according to [ethical] virtue, so he will need
such things to live as a man.[7]

That perfect happiness is contemplative activity would be evident also
from the following. We regard the gods as being most blessed and happy;
10   but what kind of *actions* must we attribute to them? Are they just *actions*?
Will they not appear ridiculous if they are regarded as making contracts
and returning deposits and all other such things? Are they brave *actions*?
Are they to be regarded as facing dangers and risking their lives for
something noble? Are they generous *actions*? But whom will they give
15   gifts to? It would be absurd, too, if they are regarded as using money or
some such thing. And what would their temperate *actions* be? Is it not
vulgar to praise them for not having bad *desires*? If we were to go through
all of these ethical virtues, all praises or honors concerning the
corresponding *actions* would appear trivial and unworthy of the gods. Yet
all believe that the gods are living and in activity, for surely we cannot
20   regard them as being asleep like Endymion. So if *action*, and production
even more so, are omitted from their lives, is not contemplation the only
activity left?[8]

The activity of a god, then, which surpasses all other activites in blessedness, would be contemplative. Consequently, of human activities, too,
that which is closest in kind to this would be the happiest. A sign of this is
25   the fact that none of the other animals share in happiness but are completely deprived of such activity; for while the entire life of the gods is
blessed, the life of men exists as a sort of likeness of such [blessed]
activity,[9] but none of the other animals is happy since none of them shares
in contemplation. So while contemplation endures, happiness does so
30   also, and those who are more contemplative are more happy also, not
in virtue of some other attribute but in virtue of contemplation, for contemplation is by its nature honorable.[10] Happiness, then, would be a kind
of contemplation.

9

Being human, however, a man will need external resources also; for his nature is not self-sufficient for contemplation but he needs a healthy body and nourishment and other services. Still, we must not think that the man who is to be happy will need many and great external goods if he cannot be blessed without them; for self-sufficiency and *action* do not depend on the excess of them, and one can do noble things even if he is not a ruler of land and sea since he can *act* according to virtue even with moderate means. This can be plainly seen from the fact that private citizens are thought to do *good* deeds no less than those in power, but even more. So it is enough if one has as much as that [i.e., moderate means], for the life of a man whose activity proceeds according to virtue will be happy.

Perhaps Solon, too, expressed it well when he spoke of happy men as being those who were moderately supplied with external means but who have performed the noblest *actions* – so he thought – and have lived a temperate life;[1] for it is possible for one to *act* as he should with moderate possessions. Anaxagoras, too, seems to have regarded the happy man to be neither wealthy nor in a position of power, when he said[2] that he would not be surprised if a happy man appeared strange to most men, for they judge a man by externals since these are the only things they perceive. The opinions of the wise, then, seem to be in harmony with our arguments. But while these opinions, too, carry some conviction, still the truth concerning practical matters is judged by what men do and how they live, for it is these that carry authority. So we should examine the statements which we have already made by referring them to the deeds and the lives of men, and we should accept them as true if they harmonize with the facts but should regard them merely as arguments if they clash with those facts.

Now he who proceeds in his activities according to his intellect and cultivates his intellect seems to be best disposed and most dear to the gods; for if the gods had any care for human matters, as they are thought to have,[3] it would be also reasonable that they should take joy in what is best and most akin to themselves (this would be man's intellect) and should reward those who love and honor this most, as if they cared for their friends and were *acting* rightly and nobly. Clearly, all these attributes belong to the wise man most of all; so it is he who would be most dear to the gods, and it is also reasonable that he would be the most happy of

35
1179*a*

5

10

15

20

25

30

men. Thus if we view the matter in this manner, it is again the wise man who would be the most happy of men.

10

If we have sufficiently discussed in a sketchy manner these matters and the virtues, and also friendship and pleasure, should we think that we achieved what we have intended to do, or, as the saying goes, is the end in practical matters not speculation and knowledge but rather *action*? With regard to virtue, to be sure, it is not enough to know what it is, but we should try to acquire and use it or try to become good in some other way.[1] Now if arguments alone were enough to make us *good*, they would with justice, according to Theognis,[2] have brought us many and great rewards, and we should have obtained these. As a matter of fact, however, while arguments appear to have an effect in exhorting and stimulating the liberally-minded among young men and might cause the character of those who come from high lineage and are truly lovers of what is noble to be possessed of virtue, they cannot exhort ordinary men to do good and noble deeds, for it is the nature of these men to obey not a sense of shame but fear, and to abstain from what is bad not because this is disgraceful but because of the penalties which they would receive, since by leading a life of passion such men pursue the corresponding pleasures and the means to them but avoid the opposite pains, having no conception of what is noble and truly pleasant as they have never tasted it. What argument, then, would reform these men? It is not possible or not easy to remove by argument the long-standing habits which are deeply rooted in one's character. So when all the means through which we can become *good* are available, perhaps we should be content if we were to get some share of virtue.

Some think that men become good by nature, others think that they do so by habituation, still others, by teaching. Now it is clear that nature's part is not in our power to do anything about but is present in those who are truly fortunate through some divine cause.[3] Perhaps argument and teaching, too, cannot reach all men, but the soul of the listener, like the earth which is to nourish the seed, should first be cultivated by habit to enjoy or hate things properly; for he who lives according to passion would neither listen to an argument which dissuades him nor understand it, and if he is disposed in this manner, how can he be persuaded to change? In general, passion seems to yield not to argument but to force. So one's character must be somehow predisposed towards virtue, liking what is noble and disliking what is disgraceful.

But it is difficult for one to be guided rightly towards virtue from an early age unless he is brought up under such [i.e., right] laws; for a life of temperance and endurance is not pleasant to most people, especially to the young. For this reason the nurture and pursuits of the young should be regulated by laws, for when they become habitual they are not painful.[4] Getting the right nurture and care while young, however, is perhaps not sufficient; but since young men should pursue and be habituated to these also when they have become adults, laws would be needed for these too, and, in general, laws would be needed for man's entire life, for most people obey necessity rather than argument, and penalties rather than what is noble. In view of this, some think that legislators (a) should urge men to pursue virtue and should exhort them to act for the sake of what is noble, expecting those who are well on their way in their habits of acting well to follow the advice, (b) should impose punishments and penalties on those who disobey and are of inferior nature,[5] and (c) should banish permanently those who are incurable; for they think that a man who is *good* and lives with a view to what is noble will obey reason, while a bad man who desires [just bodily] pleasures should be punished by pain like a beast of burden. And for this reason they also say that the pains inflicted should be those which are most contrary to the pleasures these men love. So if, as already stated, the man who is to be good should be well nurtured and acquire the proper habits so that he may live in *good* pursuits and neither willingly nor unwillingly do what is bad, these [proper habits] would be attained by those who live according to intellect and an order which is right and has effective strength. Now paternal command possesses neither strength nor necessity, nor in general does that of a single man, unless he be a king or some such person; but the law has compelling power and is an expression issuing from a sort of prudence and intellect. And while we are hostile to those who oppose our impulses, even if these men are right, we do not feel oppressed by the law when it ordains us to do what is *good*.[6]

Only in the state of Sparta and a few others does the legislator seem to pay attention to the nurture and pursuits of the citizens; in most states

30

35

1180*a*

5

10

15

20

25

such matters have been neglected, and each man lives as he wishes, 'ruling children and wife' [7] like Cyclops. Now it is best that there should be a
30   care which is both public and right about these matters, with power to administer them. But if the state has shown neglect, it would seem that each citizen should help his children and friends towards virtue, or even deliberately choose to do something about education. And, from what has been said, it would seem that he can do so[8] best by becoming a lawgiver, for
35   public cares are clearly administered by laws, and they are administered
1180b   well by good laws; and it would seem to make no difference whether these are written or unwritten, or whether they are for private or group education, as in the case of music and gymnastics and other pursuits. For just
5   as in a state it is laws and customs that prevail, so in a household it is the dictates and habits of a father that prevail, and more so in a household because of his close relation to them and the services he confers, for children by nature are predisposed to love and obey the father. Further, private education is superior to group education, as in the case of medical treatment; for though in general rest and abstinence from food are bene-
10   ficial to a man with fever, to a particular man perhaps this is not so, and perhaps a boxing instructor does not prescribe the same mode of boxing to all his students. So it would seem that greater accuracy in detail is attained if each person is attended privately, for in this way he is more likely to receive what suits him. But a physician or an athletic instructor or any expert can best attend to an individual if he knows universally, i.e.,
15   that such and such is the case for all men or for all men of a certain kind, for scientific knowledge is predicated of what is common and is universal.[9] Now perhaps nothing prevents even an unscientific man from attending well to some one thing, e.g., to a certain man, if he has accurately observed through experience what happens to him, like some people who
20   seem to be their own best doctors but are unable to help anybody else.[10] But if one wishes to become an artist or a scientist, it would seem that he should none the less proceed to the universal and know it as far as possible, for we have stated that sciences are concerned with universals. And perhaps he, too, who wishes to make men (whether many or few) better by
25   attending to them should try to become a lawgiver, if it is through laws that we can become good; for it is not a chance person who can make anyone put before us be well disposed but, if anyone at all, the man who knows, as in medical science and in all others which use diligence or prudence.

Should we not, then, inquire next from what source or how one can become a lawgiver? Is it not, as in the other cases, from statesmen, since **30** legislation, as already stated, is thought to be a part of political science? Or is there no similarity between politics and the other sciences and faculties?[11] For in the other sciences and faculties, the same persons appear both to impart those faculties to others and to practice them, as in the case of doctors and painters; but as regards politics, while the sophists **35** profess to teach it, it is not they who practice it but those engaged in **1181a** politics, who *act* by some sort of capacity or experience rather than by *thought*, for we do not observe them writing or speaking about such matters (though perhaps writing or speaking would be nobler than making speeches in courts or assemblies), nor do we observe them making **5** statesmen of their sons or of any of their friends.[12] But it would have been reasonable for them to do so, if indeed they could; for neither could they have bequeathed anything better to their states, nor would they have deliberately chosen for themselves or for those dearest to them some other thing more than this faculty. Anyway, experience seems to contribute not a little, for otherwise they would not have become statesmen with **10** political familiarity alone; hence it seems that those who aim to know politics need also experience.

As for those of the sophists who profess to know politics, they appear to be very far from teaching it; for, in general, they do not even know what kind of thing it is or what it is concerned with, otherwise they would not have posited it as being the same as rhetoric,[13] or even inferior to it, **15** nor would they have thought it easy to legislate by collecting the laws which are well thought of. Thus they say that it is possible to select the best laws, as if (a) that selection did not require intelligence and (b) right judgment in making the selection were not the greatest thing, as in the case of music; for while experienced men judge rightly the works in their **20** field and understand by what means and in what manner they are achieved, and also what combinations of them harmonize, inexperienced men should be content if they do not fail to notice whether the work is well or badly made, as in painting.

Now laws are like works of political art. But how can one proceed from **1181b** them to become a lawgiver or to judge which of them are best? For medical men too do not appear to be made just by reading medical books, though they try to state not only the treatment but, after classifying the

dispositions, also how one may be cured and how he should be taken care
5   of. Yet while these books are thought to be of benefit to those with experience, they are of no use to those without medical science. So perhaps
the collection of laws and of constitutions, too, would be of good use to
those who can theorize and judge what is well or badly stated and what
kinds of laws or constitutions are suitable to a given situation; but those
10   who go over such collection without the habit of speculation or judgment
cannot form good judgments, except by chance, although they might gain
more intelligence concerning them.

Since our predecessors left the subject of lawgiving without scrutiny,
perhaps it is better if we make a greater effort to examine it, and especially
15   the subject concerning constitutions in general, so that we may complete
as best as we can the philosophy concerning human affairs. First, then, let
us try to go over those parts which have been stated well by our predecessors, then from the constitutions we have collected let us investigate
what kinds of things tend to preserve or destroy the states or each of the
20   forms of government and why some states are well while others are badly
administered; for, after having investigated these matters, perhaps we
would also be in a better position to perceive what form of government is
best, how each form of government should be ordered, and what laws
and customs each should use. So let us start to discuss these.

COMMENTARIES

The references given in the Commentaries and in the Glossary are to the standard pages (sections) and lines according to Bekker's edition of Aristotle's works (Berlin, 1831). In particular, pages 1094a1–1181b23 cover the Nicomachean Ethics, and these pages (and lines) appear as such in the margins of the translation. The Bekker pages covering each of Aristotle's works are as follows:

Categories: 1a1–15b33.
Nature of Propositions (De Interpretatione): 16a1–24b9.
Prior Analytics: 24a10–70b38.
Posterior Analytics: 71a1–100b17.
Topics: 100a18–164b19.
Sophistical Refutations: 164a20–184b8.
Physics: 184a10–267b26.
On the Heavens: 268a1–313b23.
On Generation and Destruction: 314a1–338b19.
Meteorology: 338a20–390b22.
On the Universe, To Alexander: 391a1–401b29.
On the Soul: 402a1–435b25.
On Sensation and Sensibles: 436a1–449a31.
On Memory and Recollection: 449b1–453b11.
On Sleep and Wakefulness: 453b11–458a32.
On Dreams: 458a33–462b11.
On Divination from Dreams: 462b12–464b18.
On Longevity and Shortness of Life: 464b19–467b9.
On Youth, Old Age, Life, and Death: 467b10–470b5.
On Respiration: 470b6–480b30.
On Breath: 481a1–486b4.
A Treatise on Animals: 486a5–638b37.
On Parts of Animals: 639a1–697b30.
On Motion of Animals: 698a1–704b3.
On Locomotion of Animals: 704a4–714b23.

On Generation of Animals: 715a1–789b20.

On Colors: 791a1–799b20.

On Objects of Hearing: 800a1–804b39.

Physiognomy: 805a1–814b9.

On Plants: 815a10–830b4.

On Reported Marvels: 830a5–847b10.

Mechanics: 847a11–858b31.

Problems: 859a1–967b27.

On Indivisible Lines: 968a1–972b33.

Positions and Names of Winds: 973a1–b25.

On Xenophanes, Zeno, and Gorgias: 974a1–980b21.

Metaphysics: 980a21–1093b29.

Nicomachean Ethics: 1094a1–1181b23.

Great Ethics: 1181a24–1213b30.

Eudemean Ethics: 1214a1–1249b25.

On Virtues and Vices: 1249a26–1251b37.

Politics: 1252a1–1342b34.

Household Management: 1343a1–1353b27.

Rhetoric: 1354a1–1420b4.

Rhetoric for Alexander: 1420a5–1447b7.

Poetics: 1447a8–1462b18.

BOOK A

1

¹ Since the aim of art is to produce something, e.g., steel or houses, and that of intention is *action*, e.g., temperate or intemperate *action*, perhaps the aim of *inquiry* is just knowledge, i.e., truth. Certainly the truths in science (axioms, hypotheses, and theorems) are included, and perhaps some other intellectual virtues, but it is not clear whether '*inquiry*' applies to other kinds of truths or not. So the problem here is whether the terms '*inquiry*', 'art', '*action*', and 'intention' cover all of men's activities or just the important ones.

² The expression 'is thought' or 'seems' usually indicates a dialectical statement, i.e., one which is generally accepted as true.

³ Eudoxus, a great mathematician and astronomer and older than Aristotle, seems to have been one of them. 1172b9–15.

⁴ The expression 'all things aim' needs qualification, for inanimate things do not aim at anything, and that which is aimed at may be only an apparent good. Perhaps the expression belongs to Eudoxus, who restricted it to rational and nonrational animals and regarded pleasure as the good (1172b9–15). At this stage, of course, the expression may be regarded as dialectically true only.

⁵ If by definition an *action* has no other end but is an end in itself (1140b6–7), it appears that no product should come out of that *action*. Perhaps the reference is to activities which are usually productions but are sometimes pursued for their own sake, regardless of the product. For example, one may enjoy making chairs as an end in itself, as a hobby, and here his activity seems to be an *action*, although there is also a product besides the activity. If so, the expression 'by nature' which follows seems to fit in, for usually (or by nature) the production of a chair is for the sake of the chair and we prefer the chair to the production of it, and it is only occasionally that we prefer the act of producing and regard it as an *action*. Perhaps Aristotle uses '*action*' in a wide sense also, a sense which includes also

activities which are pursued for their own sake but result in products which are proximate and not final.

There is another alternative: '*action*' here may be used generically to apply to any human activity with a purpose, whether thinking, production, or *action* in its narrow sense. 1325b14–23.

6 We usually prefer a house to the activity of building it; and in general, a product is by nature better than the activity which produces it, for the activity is usually for the sake of that product.

7 Does the term 'sciences' apply only to theoretical sciences or to all three kinds (productive, practical, theoretical)? If to all three kinds, then 'arts' in the text is unnecessary; but if only to theoretical sciences, then truth is the end of such sciences. 993b19–23, 1025b18–28, 1064a10–9.

8 We may use 'art' instead of 'science'; Aristotle is not explicit. Perhaps both are right, depending on the point of view. When a student studies medicine, he first learns the truths related to health and disease, and in doing this he is learning a theoretical science. Later he becomes an intern and uses his knowledge to develop the skill. Finally he becomes a doctor and uses the art, which includes knowledge and skill, to heal. Thus one may say either that medical science exists for the sake of medical art and ultimately for the sake of healing, or that medical art (which presupposes medical science) exists for the sake of healing. The term 'sciences' is used at the end of the paragraph.

There is another alternative. The term 'science' seems to be used also in a wide sense to apply to theoretical, productive, and practical sciences. If so, both 'art' and 'science' would be correct, although 'art' would be more explicit than 'science'. 1025b18–24.

9 One of the meanings of 'faculty' ($=\delta\acute{\upsilon}\nu\alpha\mu\iota\varsigma$) is power to act; so perhaps the term, as used here at least, applies to a productive or a practical science but not to a theoretical science. The phrase 'sciences or faculties' in line 1094a26 seems to suggest this point also. 1046b2–4.

10 A desire is empty if it has no specified end or purpose, and it is vain if the end or purpose desired cannot be reached (197b22–32). So if one chooses A for the sake of B, B for the sake of C, and so on to infinity, either he has no final end in view, or he will never reach it if he has one. 994a1–b31.

11 That this end is the highest good follows from lines 1094a14–6.

12 This question, which indicates an affirmative answer, suggests the

necessity of studying ethics for the sake of attaining the highest good, i.e., happiness.

13 It would be useless to start by giving the student a full definition of happiness in terms of its indefinable elements without dialectical reasons which he can understand and accept, and to omit a definition of it would be to deny him an indication of the purpose or the subject of ethics. What remains, then, is a sketchy but plausible definition to function as a guideline of the rest of the course.

14 If it belongs to politics both (a) to know the highest good for its citizens and (b) to bring it about and preserve it, then politics is the most architectonic and most authoritative science since (a) the highest good includes all other goods as parts in some way or other, and since (b) it belongs to politics to order and bring about all the other goods. Here, (a) is concerned with knowledge, (b) with *action*, for politics as a practical science requires both.

15 The aim of strategy, or part of that aim, is to safeguard the state and hence the good of the state; the aim of economics is wealth, which is an instrumental good; and the aim of rhetoric is persuasion, and it is part of the aim of the state to persuade its citizens to do certain things and to abstain from doing others so that they may attain the highest good.

16 The good of the state is the good of all its citizens, not the good of just one individual; hence it is greater and more complete than the good of just one individual.

17 The term 'divine' is derived from 'divinity', which is a synonym of 'God', and the corresponding Greek terms (θεῖος, θεός) are similarly related; and since God is the highest good and eternal, that which is more divine is a higher good and closer to that which is eternal. So since a state (or a race of men) includes any one of its individuals and continues to exist even after a given individual passes away, the good of the state is more divine than that of a given individual.

18 The Macedonians would be a race of men, or the Greeks, or the Persians. An alternative to 'a race of men' would be 'a people'.

19 The two ends are the attainment and the preservation of the good of the state.

20 Noble and just things may be considered in two ways, (a) their manner of existence, and (b) our thoughts concerning them. Two instances of *actions* which one may call 'just' usually reveal more differences than two

instances of triangles, and in view of this indefiniteness the same *action* may be called 'just' in one state or by one individual and 'unjust' in another state or by another individual. Because of this, some think that nothing is by nature just but that justice exists by custom or by law or by convention.

21 These goods are not noble or just, but mainly instrumental, like wealth, or even the virtues, for in a bad state (e.g., in a dictatorship) virtuous men may suffer.

22 Since the subject of ethics is not highly precise, both the premises used and the conclusions drawn concerning it are expected to be of the same nature; and the listener, too, should not demand more than this.

23 Concerning the nature of an educated man, see 639a1–15, 1005b3–5, 1006a5–9, 1282a1–12.

24 If one has little experience in a field, he has induced only a few true premises from which to proceed to discuss and draw conclusions in that field. Politics is such a field for a young man, for he has little experience of the variety of *actions* among men and has induced only few true premises, and so he cannot be a good judge of political *actions*.

25 Concerning a thing to be done, a man may follow either his reason or his passion, and these two may conflict. So he may listen to reason and know what should be done, but, like the incontinent man, he may follow his passion or *desire*. The intemperate man is even worse, for he rejects even reason and thinks that following his *desire* is better for him. Younger men, of course, are inclined to follow their passions more than older men do. 1389a2–b12.

26 These are men whose reason rules and directs both their *desires* and their *actions*.

2

1 For Plato and his followers, the Ideas (or Forms) exist by themselves apart from the particulars and serve as models for them; they are eternal, changeless, perfect, and the causes of the existing particulars. Thus there is Triangle (or Triangle Itself), which is the Idea of a triangle, and there are likewise Justice, Man, Equality, etc., and these are the causes of the corresponding particulars. For a given genus or species of things there is only one Idea.

2 In geometry it is not difficult for the student to understand at the start

the definition of a triangle, a circle, a right angle, etc., to accept as true such axioms as 'Equals result if equals are added to equals' and 'The whole is greater than the part', and then to proceed to the theorems. But the objects of ethics, such as happiness, virtue, and pleasure, are not easy to define or to understand when defined, and the truth of the axioms and postulates concerning them, e.g., 'Happiness is the highest good for man', is not so evident or acceptable. So the teacher is faced with the problem of making all these understandable or acceptable as true, and the dialectical procedure is highly advisable. Hence he must begin with what the student already knows and accepts as true and proceed to establish those principles by the use of induction, example, analogy, and other such devices.

The example given is not spelled out. Perhaps there were two ways of running: from the judges to the finishing line, and from that line to the judges.

3 Things familiar relative to us are things as first known by us chronologically, and they are usually known through their accidents and confusedly. Thus 'mama' has not the same meaning for a child and for an adult, and the same applies to 'circle', 'number', and 'happiness'. Things familiar without qualification, on the other hand, are things which are known as they are after analysis, and such knowledge of them is scientific and is used in a science. Further, things familiar relative to us are not known in the same way, for usually different people know them through different accidents; but things familiar without qualification are known (for Aristotle) in the same way by all, for the definition of a circle is the same for all who learn geometry, and no accidents are included in that definition. 71b33–2a5, 184a16–b14.

4 If a student's ethical habits are not in accordance with ethical knowledge but are contrary to it, and habits are hard to change (8b26–35), it would be difficult for him to accept ethical knowledge and *act* according to it.

5 If a student has good habits, he also has the knowledge (potentially at least) of the fact that those habits are good, even if he is not aware of the principles (of the why or the *reasons*) from which the knowledge of that fact follows. Such a student, then, knows the fact concerning his habits, and it is a fact that he has those habits; and under these circumstances, it would not be difficult for him, assuming that he is sufficiently intelligent, to learn the corresponding ethical principles (i.e., to learn the why).

[6] Hesiod, *Works and Days* 293, 295–7. Translated by John M. Crossett.

3

[1] The bodily pleasures are meant.
[2] An Assyrian monarch, famous for leading a life of sensual pleasure.
[3] The word 'good' here means virtuous.
[4] He is referring to virtue.
[5] It is not clear whether these were for philosophers or for the general public, and whether they were writings by Aristotle or by other thinkers also.
[6] 1177a12–1179a32.
[7] Bodily pleasures and honor or virtue.

4

[1] He is referring to his teacher Plato, and to other Platonists, such as Speusippus and Xenocrates.
[2] The principle here is that one should choose the better of two good things (here, friendship and truth) which are ends in themselves. But can two good things conflict? A friend is a good thing, but if he is partly mistaken, one should reject only his mistake and not the whole friendship.
[3] For Aristotle, A is said to be prior in existence to B if A exists when B exists, but B does not necessarily exist if A exists. Thus, if knowledge of mathematics exists, a man exists, but the converse is not necessarily true; and so a man is prior in existence to mathematical knowledge. Now Plato posited the *One* and the *Dyad* (also called '*Great* and *Small*') as the two first principles, form and matter, respectively, and from these he generated first Two, then Three, then Four, and the rest of the Numbers, all of which were Ideas or Forms (987a29–8a17, 1084a2–7). And to avoid a logical difficulty, Plato did not posit Number as an Idea; for since number as a genus is prior in existence to two or to any other of its species, then, correspondingly, Number as an Idea would have to be prior in existence to Two or to Three, etc., contrary to the assumption that the *One* is first in existence and Two comes next.
[4] In the case of the *Good*, since for Plato it is an Idea and indivisible and simple and has no species under it, any two goods among the sensibles

should be alike imitations of the *Good* and participate in it in the same way, and so no one good should be prior in existence to another good. But this is not the case, for a substance is prior in existence to an attribute of it, and both may be good, e.g., both Socrates and his bravery are regarded as good, and Socrates is prior in existence to his bravery. If so, then since *Goodness* as one thing cannot be prior to itself, either it does not exist or '*Goodness*' has more than one meaning; and both these alternatives contradict Plato's theory of Ideas.

5 The term 'being' is not univocal; it is like the term 'healthy', which has many senses. 1003a33–b15.

6 The term 'whatness' here signifies a substance, like a man or a chair or a tree.

7 Is the intellect a substance? For Aristotle, perhaps the part of man's intellect which is active (not passive) and which is separable from the body is a substance. The term νοῦς (= 'intellect') means also God, who is a substance and not an attribute. 413b24–7, 1070a24–7.

8 Since the categories exclude each other (for a quality is not a quantity, e.g., redness is not a line, and similarly for the others), if 'goodness' were a predicate in one category, it would not then be a predicate in another with the same meaning. But it is a predicate within many categories; hence it cannot have only one meaning.

9 For Plato, the Ideas Man Himself, Equality Itself, Redness Itself, and the others have the general grammatical form 'Thing Itself', and perhaps Plato added the word 'Itself' to indicate the Ideas as separate, unique, and apart from the particulars. Anyway, if the definition of a man is the same for both an individual man and Man Himself, since a definition signifies the nature of a thing and neither more nor less, both an individual man and Man Himself will not differ in their nature, and Man Himself as an Idea is not needed for the study of men. If 'Itself' adds to the Idea something which cannot be in the individual, such as eternality or perfection or even separateness for the attributes which are inseparable from individual substances, then an individual man cannot participate wholly in Man Himself but only in that part of Man Himself which belongs to individual men also, but then no definition of an Idea as a whole will be applicable to an individual man. There are other philosophical difficulties.

10 Some Pythagoreans made ten pairs of contraries the principles of all

things, divided them into two columns, and regarded the principles in the first column as good, and perhaps those in the second column as bad or not good. The principles as goods were *Finite, Odd, One, Right, Male, Rest, Straightness, Light, Goodness,* and *Square*; the others were *Infinite, Even, Many, Left, Female, Motion, Curvature, Darkness, Badness,* and *Oblong.* Evidently, the things in the first column belong to more than one category, for we find there a quantity, a quality, a relation, and the like; and this seems to be somewhat in agreement with Aristotle's view when he says that the good is found in all categories. 986a22–b2.

Speusippus held that the first principles are indeterminate and imperfect and hence that the most beautiful and the highest good develops later in the generation of things, like a man from a sperm and a flower or fruit from a seed. But there are things which are good and exist in various categories and which are not principles (Aristotle's statement implies that this view was held by Speusippus); hence the good exists in many categories and 'goodness' has more than one sense. 1072b30–3a3, 1091a29–b3.

It appears, then, that some Pythagoreans and Speusippus are closer to Aristotle's view than Plato is.

11 The philosophical difficulties faced by Plato's theory of Ideas are treated by Aristotle in his *Metaphysics*, especially in 985b23–993a10 and in books M and N.

12 Alternatives to 'for their own sake' are 'in themselves' or 'in virtue of themselves'. Thus the goods in virtue of themselves have goodness in themselves and are not called 'good' by being referred to other things which have goodness.

13 If the *Good Itself* is the only thing which is pursued for its own sake, then thinking wisely and seeing and being pleased and honored are species of things which are pursued in vain, for they are not pursued for the sake of *Good Itself*. If, on the other hand, these too are pursued for their own sake, the definition of good would apply equally to these and to *Good Itself*, and so *Good Itself* would be no more of a good or no better than these kinds of goods, and hence it would be no model or cause and so of no help to a man who pursues these goods. See Comm. 1, Section 2.

14 What is more, the definitions of these species of good insofar as they are good are different; hence the term 'good' cannot have just one meaning, and, as indicated earlier, cannot be under a single category.

[15] Perhaps by 'coming from one thing' Aristotle has in mind a derivative term, like 'brave' from 'bravery', and 'healthy' from 'health'; by 'contributing to one end' perhaps he means things which are useful to one end, like medicine and surgical instruments and whatever is needed to bring about health. By 'analogy' he means sameness of relation, e.g., sight is to the eye as hearing is to the ear; and this seems to be the loosest of the senses of 'one'. 1016b31–5.

[16] The discussion of unity, analogy, and Plato's Ideas belongs to First Philosophy (i.e., to Metaphysics).

[17] Things which are good for a man are either his activities or his possessions; and his possessions, whether external (like money) or internal (like virtues), are instrumental and for the sake of his activities, so if happiness as the highest good for a man is an activity, then *Good Itself*, which is separate, cannot be the highest good for a man.

[18] One might argue that knowledge of *Good Itself* may serve as a model for attaining the good for a man. But (a) as a matter of fact, scientists do not use such knowledge, and (b) they do not need it, for *Good Itself* is too general to be of use to a particular good with which a man is concerned.

Argument (b) above presupposes Aristotle's principle that the differentia is a new principle and cannot be reduced to the genus, so that knowledge of the differentia is necessary in knowing the properties of a species. So to know and pursue the highest good for an individual man, one must know the specific differences of the various goods. 998b30–1, 1057b22–3.

5

[1] Two points are indicated here: (a) different *actions* and different arts are concerned with specific goods and not with the same general good, and (b) the goods considered are the ends of *actions* and arts and not instrumental goods. What about theoretical activities? Perhaps '*action*' here is used to include these; or, if not so used, perhaps *actions* and arts are mentioned as examples to illustrate (a) and (b).

[2] Two kinds of ends are indicated, complete and incomplete. Wealth is the end of economics, and health is the end of the medical art, but both wealth and health are also means to other ends; for health is for the sake of healthy activity, and wealth for the sake of using it for other ends. Further, one who likes teaching for its own sake also makes money and

uses it for other pleasant ends. So the problem which arises here is whether there is an end (whether one or many) which is never pursued for the sake of another end. If there is, this would be complete while the others would be incomplete. But if there are many complete ends, must there be or can there be one among them which is most complete? If so, completeness among ends would appear to admit of degree or comparison.

Now some goods are only instrumental, others are pursued for their own sake and may also be pursued for the sake of something else, and others are pursued for their own sake and never for the sake of something else; and for a given individual perhaps the last is most complete or the most complete, while the second, though complete, is not the most complete since it may be pursued also for the sake of another end. It appears, then, that if A is pursued by M for its own sake and also for the sake of B, the whole which consists of A and B is more complete than A. So if happiness applies to the whole life of M, it must be a whole with such parts that, though each part is pursued for its own sake and is complete during its interval, it is less complete than M's activity during his whole life. Further, happiness is not just a mere addition of pleasures during their corresponding intervals, for there are different kinds of pleasures, and some are necessary (those of eating, drinking, sex, etc.) while others are of a different kind (theoretical activity, musical activity, etc.). It appears, then, that the various kinds of pleasure must be proportioned in a certain manner if they are to produce happiness, for usually no man is regarded as happy if all he does is eat and play cards everyday.

[3] Man is by nature political, that is, a citizen of a state; for he has the powers (thinking, reasoning, etc.) which make this possible, and by nature these powers tend to actualize themselves.

[4] 1100a10–1b9, 1170b20–1a20.

6

[1] In calling happiness 'the highest good' one calls it, at best, by its genus and leaves out the differentia, or else he uses an attribute or a property and not its nature or part of it. The term 'good' is too wide, and the word 'highest' indicates a comparison and does not signify the nature of happiness.

[2] Aristotle's procedure through example is dialectical, i.e., from that

which is more familiar to us to that which is less so but which is the nature of the thing. The function of an eye or an ear is obvious; that of a man is less so, for, among other things, a selection and a synthesis of goods is required.

3 This is the part of the soul which *desires* and from which such virtues or vices may arise as temperance, intemperance, bravery, and the like.

4 This is the part connected with the intellectual virtues or their contraries.

5 One may have intellectual virtues and he may or may not be exercising them; but the importance lies in the exercise of them, for to have them without using them is like having life but being asleep instead of being awake. The virtues are acquired for the sake of the corresponding activities.

6 The expression 'according to reason' applies to the part of the soul which uses reason or thinks, and it is from this part alone that the intellectual virtues arise; but the expression 'not without reason' applies to the part of the soul which may obey or be persuaded by reason, and from this as a part the ethical virtues may arise.

7 The meaning of the expression 'according to the best and most complete virtue' is not spelled out. If only one virtue is indicated, let us say wisdom, a difficulty arises, for a man as a political animal requires other virtues also, but if more than one, then perhaps 'complete virtue' indicates a set of virtues properly ordered according to their need and importance. Perhaps at this stage the expression is sufficiently plausible, for the definition is given only in outline, as stated in the next paragraph.

7

1 The carpenter is an artist, and the aim of an artist is production and not truth; so if he uses the right angle correctly, this is sufficient for his purposes, and knowledge of the definition and the properties of a right angle do not increase his effectiveness as a carpenter. Perhaps the expression 'what it is' signifies the genus of the right angle while 'what kind of a thing it is' signifies the differentia.

2 Perhaps the true axioms and hypotheses are meant, for it is only such truths which can signify facts but have no reasons. Such principles, of course, cannot be demonstrated, for then they would be theorems and not principles. But it can be shown dialectically that they are true. With

the definition of happiness as given, Aristotle's concern is to show dialectically that happiness thus defined is the highest good for men.

3 These seem to be general principles of the sciences, like the principle that bodies of specific gravity greater than that of water sink in water.

4 These seem to be particular principles or premises, and they are needed, for *actions* and productions are concerned ultimately with particulars.

5 These seem to be such habits as virtues and vices and skills.

6 These may be intuitions, for what cannot be defined may be intuited after abstraction, like straightness in a straight line and quantity in a triangle.

8

1 He is referring to the definition of happiness arrived at dialectically, for this definition is the principle of ethics. See also Comm. 6.

2 Concerning a thing, one may argue its definition dialectically from certain premises; but if the definition does not indicate the attributes (either most or all) which are said to belong to the thing by the most competent men, or if it contradicts one or more of those attributes, then one may reject the definition on the principle that it does not signify the thing such men have in mind. In general, if D is a definition given of T, and if attributes A are commonly said to belong to T, then A should not be contradicted by D or its consequences but should be present in them somehow.

3 Examples of external goods are friends and wealth, examples of goods of the body are beauty and strength, and examples of goods of the soul are virtues and certain proper pleasures. Most Greek philosophers (e.g., Plato) regarded the goods of the soul to be better than those of the body, and those of the body better than external goods. External goods, of course, are instrumental and their goodness depends on the goodness of the soul; and since in the soul the virtues are for the sake of the corresponding activities, Aristotle mentions only the *actions* and the other activities of the soul.

4 The definition of happiness is in accord with the manner in which other philosophers divided the goods and regarded those of the soul as better.

5 The definition is in accord with those thinkers who regarded the end of man as being *actions* or activities of a certain kind.

6 The definition is in accord with those who said that happiness is living

well or *acting* well. But while 'living well and *acting* well' states the fact, it does not give the cause; for one lives well or *acts* well because he lives or *acts* in a certain manner, namely, virtuously.

Professor H. H. Joachim, in his *Aristotle's Nicomachean Ethics* (Oxford Press, 1955, pp. 55–6), sees two difficulties in arriving at a definition of happiness: (a) whether one has a right to apply the principles of attaining strict scientific definitions of attributes (*Posterior Analytics* 93a1–4a19) to the attainment of the definition of an attribute in the sphere of action, and (b) whether it is possible to reduce Aristotle's argument concerning happiness to syllogistic form. We may suggest an attempt.

We assume that happiness exists in the soul; so the subject to which it belongs is the soul, not to every soul but only to a certain kind of soul, namely, the one which possesses the virtues. Moreover, it exists in the virtuous soul not of necessity, but for the most part, since misfortunes or external compulsion or lack of necessities may prevent activity according to virtue. Let $A \equiv$ soul, $B \equiv$ virtuous activity, and $C \equiv$ pleasant activity (or pleasure, or living well, or *acting* well) and let us assume that C is extended throughout life. Then C belongs to B, B belongs to A, and hence C belongs to A because of B. The definition of happiness may then be: 'C in A through B', that is, 'pleasure in the soul through virtuous activity'. This compares analogously with the definition of thunder (94a3–9) which is: 'noise in the clouds because of the quenching of fire', and with the definition of the eclipse (93a29–b7) which is: 'the privation of light from the Moon caused by the interposition of the Earth'. We have then the proportion,

$$A : B : C :: \text{clouds} : \text{quenching of fire} : \text{noise,}$$

and similarly in the case of the eclipse.

Aristotle uses only 'activity' for C, but he assumes it to be by nature pleasant, at least under certain conditions, and considers it in 1099a7–25, in Book K, and elsewhere.

Perhaps Professor Joachim confuses ethical activity with ethics as a science. Activities, whether complete or incomplete, exist also in physics, but this does not prevent physics from being a science. Similarly, ethics is a science, and the fact that its subject is not so precisely treated does not disqualify it from being a science. This point is considered generically by Aristotle in his *Posterior Analytics* (75b33–6). Moreover, if the end of ethics as a practical science is *action*, such an end presupposes ethics as a science or as knowledge, and ethics as knowledge does not differ from a theoretical science except for the fact that some prudence or education is needed when one considers how precisely it should be taught or learned. The form of an ethical proposition is not necessarily '*A* should do *B*'; for though one may use this form linguistically, one may also use 'doing *B* makes *A* happy', and this is a proposition to which truth or falsity applies. Ethics is like the medical art, for here too one first learns the facts of medicine (or medical science) and then proceeds to acquire the skills in accordance with medical science in order to act on the patient.

9

1 The phrase 'activity according to virtue' is a part of Aristotle's definition, and those who identify happiness with virtue or a species of it are right at least by using the term 'virtue', whether explicitly (when they say happiness is virtue) or implicitly (e.g., when they say it is prudence, for prudence is a kind of virtue). They err, however, in omitting to say that it is the activity of virtue and not virtue itself.

2 Pleasure as an element of happiness is indicated here. Thus even the ordinary man is partly right in thinking that happiness is pleasure, especially of the senses, but he errs in limiting himself to the pleasures of the senses and in not pursuing these according to reason; for bodily pleasures not pursued according to reason are inferior to those pursued according to reason and also bring harm to the individual.

3 What is pleased is not the body but always the soul, whether by material things, like food, or by immaterial things, like beauty or mathematical knowledge.

4 For example, a man who likes having friends and also torturing them cannot get both pleasures, for these are in conflict with each other; and a man who likes getting drunk is harmed in other ways. So the pleasure of torturing people or of getting drunk is not by nature pleasure. Pleasure in accordance with the virtues, on the other hand, are in harmony with each other, and these are by nature pleasures.

5 They are distinguishable in definition, but they all belong to a happy man. In other words, just as one cannot separate in a circular line the convex side from the concave, so one cannot separate the three given attri-

butes from the happy man; but one can distinguish them just as a mathematician distinguishes convexity from concavity.

6 Translated by John M. Crossett.

7 Perhaps the problem suggested is whether happiness belongs only to one kind of the best activities, the theoretical, or to all of them, or else to a certain combination of them.

8 As mentioned in 1096a5–7 and in 1098b26, some men regard happiness as wealth. These too have a point, for wealth is needed to perform some *actions*, e.g., to be generous or use money for research; but they are mistaken in regarding wealth as an end and not only as a means.

9 Apparently, high lineage, good children, and beauty are listed here as external goods. Perhaps they are regarded as external to the soul, for one's physical form is not a part of his soul. Children, too, are external in this sense; and high lineage, too, appears to be external. See Comm. 3, Section 8.

10

1 The alternatives are: (1) happiness is acquired by one's effort, (a) by learning, as in the case of a theoretical science (Plato's position), or (b) by habit, as in the case of the ethical virtues, or (c) by training, as of an art or skill; (2) happiness comes from outside, either (a) from divine providence or the gods, or (b) by just luck or chance.

2 Perhaps first philosophy or theology.

3 Since happiness is an activity according to virtue, which cannot be acquired without the intellect, happiness as the highest human good is closest to God's good; for of all animals only men possess intellect, which is divine, and God is Intellect in the highest sense. 430a17–23, 1074b15–7, 1177a12–7, 1177b30–1.

4 If certain things can be produced by luck as well as by art, they can be best produced by art; and since art imitates nature, things by nature can attain their best according to their nature rather than by luck, especially if their nature uses intellect, which is the best that a thing by nature can have.

5 1098a15–20.

6 Perhaps these are food, drink, and the like.

7 1094a27–b7.

11

¹ The main question is: when can we safely say that a man is happy? Problems arise regardless of the position one may take. While a man is living he cannot be safely called 'happy', since happiness applies to one's whole life and one may suffer great misfortunes in his later life. When a man is dead he cannot be safely called "happy" because happiness is an activity and a dead man is not active. If we consider the whole of a man's life and say, after his death, that he has lived happily (for a dead man is beyond the reach of evils or misfortunes), another difficulty arises; for just as honors or dishonors affect a living man when living but not conscious (e.g., when he is asleep), so the *actions* and fortunes of a dead man's descendants or friends should affect him even if he is dead, and to deny that such *actions* and fortunes have any effect at all would seem unreasonable.

² This is raised in the first sentence of this Section.

³ The argument amounts to this: if happiness is to be regarded as something which is enduring and which makes it possible for us to say truly that a man who is still living is happy, then one's fortunes, which are subject to change, should not play a dominant role in his happiness.

⁴ The key to the solution is the phrase 'activities in accordance with virtue'. Virtues are hard to displace (8b27–35); hence the ethical activities of a virtuous man will tend to remain virtuous. And since activities according to virtue play the dominant role in happiness, while fortune plays a minor role, a virtuous man will tend to *act* virtuously throughout his life and so be happy, or at least not wretched.

⁵ Habits are used more frequently than scientific knowledge; hence they tend to be more enduring.

⁶ The arguments seem to indicate that a virtuous man who lives happily or blessedly is very likely to continue to live and die in this manner, and that if he meets with misfortunes, though he will not attain blessedness, still he will not become wretched. Further, under the same fortunes, a virtuous man will live better or be happier than one who is not virtuous, just as a good shoemaker will do a better job with a given workable leather than a bad shoemaker.

⁷ Simonides, Fragment 4, Diehl.

⁸ Blessedness in its highest form belongs only to the gods, and to men it belongs to such a degree as their nature allows.

⁹ The meaning is not spelled out, but we will venture an interpretation. If on the stage a murder is presupposed or even stated, it has much less effect on the audience than if it is enacted, and in both cases the effect is on those who are living. But the *actions* of a man's friends and relatives affect his happiness less than his own *actions* do, for one's own *actions* play the dominant role; hence the *actions* of his friends and relatives will affect him even less when he is dead.

¹⁰ In other words, *actions* of friends affect a dead man's happiness or unhappiness to a small degree or extent.

12

¹ Happiness is an activity, for this follows from its definition. But a faculty or power is not an activity, for one may have the power to act and still not be acting, or he may have mathematical knowledge but be sleeping. Hence happiness is not a power.

² Goods may be divided into two kinds, (a) those which are ends in themselves, like pleasure and happiness, and (b) those which are good for something else, like instruments and virtues, for virtues are for the sake of virtuous activities. We honor goods of the first kind but we praise those of the second. For example, we praise temperance, which is a virtue and a quality in a temperate man, because it is used for the sake of temperate *actions*; but we honor the gods because they are ends in themselves and not good for higher ends. We praise even human *actions*, if these are referred to similar but perfect *actions* which function as ideals or standards.

³ When we praise strength and running ability in a man, it is usually assumed he will use it for a good purpose.

⁴ Since good ends are better than the means to them, honor, which is an attribute of a good end, is better than praise, which is the corresponding attribute of the means to that end. We honor a king or a scientist, but we praise children. Concerning praise, see also 1219b8–16, 1367b21–36.

⁵ That which is just exists for the sake of happiness.

⁶ Since pleasure, according to Eudoxus, is an end in itself and the highest good for man, it is a thing to be prized, i.e., to be honored or blessed but not praised. 1172b9–28.

⁷ An alternative to 'activities' is 'functions'; and it is assumed that the

activities he is referring to, whether of the body or of the soul, are good and are ends in themselves.

[8] Happiness for a man is a cause in the sense of a final cause, for he does everything for the sake of happiness; and it is a principle, for he posits this as the first thing to guide or determine all his activities.

13

[1] This is a logical argument; for since 'virtue' is included in the definition of happiness, if a man does not know what virtue is, neither will he know what happiness is. So far, the definition of happiness has been stated in a sketchy manner; further specification is still to be supplied.

[2] The point here is not whether these lawgivers were right and adequate in their conception of what happiness is and in framing the right laws to carry out what they set out to do, but whether they included laws aimed at making the citizens virtuous and obedient to the laws. 1269a29–72b23.

[3] If a true statesman wishes to make the citizens virtuous and obedient to the laws, then, inductively, politics should include in its aim the wishes of a true statesman.

[4] Perhaps he is referring to the inquiry into the good or the highest good for man (1097a15–6, b22–4), which is the concern of politics (1094a26–b8).

[5] This sentence suggests that there are other kinds of virtue besides human virtue. For example, there are virtues of the body, such as beauty and health (1361b3–7), and also virtues of animals, as of a horse (1106a19–21). In view of this, some translators use 'excellence' instead of 'virtue' for ἀρετή.

[6] To investigate the soul for its own sake is to seek knowledge for its own sake and not for the sake of application or of something else.

[7] Since a statesman's concern is to make the citizens good and obedient to the laws, his primary concern in seeking knowledge is to apply it to this end. So if knowledge of a certain fact is necessary for this end, knowledge of the causes of that fact may not contribute more. A bank teller, for example, does not need to know the laws of algebra (commutative, associative, etc.) or the consequent demonstrations in order to add and subtract correctly, and such knowledge would be burdensome.

[8] A more literal translation would be 'outside writings', and perhaps these writings were Aristotle's and were meant for the public. I assume that the *Eudemean Ethics* was written by Aristotle. 1140a3, 1218b34.

9 One might raise the problem whether the rational and the nonrational parts of the soul are separable or not separable but just distinguishable; but for the statesman it makes no difference, for knowledge of the solution to this problem does not contribute to making the citizens more virtuous or more obedient to the laws. See Comm. 5 of Section 9.

10 Evidently, plants have this power; but so do animals, and also men. So since all of them take in nutriment and grow, it is reasonable to posit in all of them the same kind of power, i.e., a power which is defined in the same way.

11 It participates by listening to or obeying the part of the soul which has reason, not by doing any thinking; it may also refuse to listen to or obey reason. The appetitive part, which *desires*, is such.

12 Whether this part is separable or just distinguishable does not affect the present problem.

13 The existence of the part which listens to or obeys reason may be shown by an example. Both a continent and an incontinent man admit that they should not get drunk, and they admit this by the part of their soul which has reason. But the incontinent man gets drunk while the continent man does not. Why? Perhaps because there is another part of the soul, and in the incontinent man this part overrules the part which has reason but in the continent man it is overruled. Further evidence of the existence of such a part is the fact that both the continent and the incontinent man *desire* to drink and are pained if they do not drink, and since it is not the part that has reason which so *desires* and is so pained, it must be some other part, which may be called 'the appetitive part' or 'the *desiring* part'.

14 The term 'desire' is a genus, and the kinds of desire are: *desire*, wish, and temper. Perhaps the desiring parts here are *desire* and temper.

15 The part of the soul which knows mathematics is the intellectual part and not the desiring part, but the part which listens to or obeys the father is a desiring part, e.g., the *desiring* part in *actions* done through *desire*, such as *actions* involving the bodily pleasures.

16 The problem here is partly linguistic. The vegetative part of the soul neither has nor can obey or disobey reason; the rational part is that which can know and initiate reason; but the *desiring* part lies between: it cannot know or initiate reason but can only listen to and obey or disobey reason. If we call this part 'nonrational', this term will have two meanings. If we call it 'having reason', this term too will have two meanings. So it makes

no difference linguistically; and we might as well follow convention and call that part 'nonrational', as long as we know what those meanings are.

[17] These virtues are discussed in Book Z.

[18] When we speak of the character of a man we speak of his ethical virtues or vices, not his intellectual dispositions.

[19] The term 'praise' is applied to all the virtues, ethical as well as intellectual.

[20] This is to be taken not as a definition of virtue but as a statement of fact about virtue.

BOOK B

1

¹ Why 'mostly'? The intellectual virtues are demonstrated knowledge, wisdom, prudence, art, and intuition. Intuition cannot be taught; and not all demonstrated knowledge or art is learned from others, for some men discover these themselves. Prudence, too, requires ingenuity, and this comes to men by nature (1144a23–b17).

² The term ἠθικός varies slightly from the term ἔθος.

³ The ethical virtues and vices are acquired by habituation, which takes time; they are not inherited by us at birth. So men are not born virtuous or vicious. What we inherit at birth, however, is the capacity to acquire and perfect virtues or vices.

⁴ When we learn an art by performing, before having learned the art our performances are in the process of becoming artistic and are not yet artistic. This point will be further considered in 1105a17–26.

⁵ One may do something which is just and still be unjust or not just; for he may wish to deceive someone in order to gain power or for some other reason. But if he continually does what is just for its own sake, either he is already just or he is on the way of becoming just. The same applies to brave and temperate *actions*. Justice, injustice, and attributes related to them are discussed at length in Book E.

⁶ Since the wish or ultimate aim of legislators is (or should be) to promote the happiness of the citizens as far as is possible, and since happiness is achieved through virtue, they fail in their function if they do not lay down or execute laws which aim to promote virtue.

⁷ Perhaps the phrase 'from the same *actions*' indicates that one starts and uses (as materials, so to say) certain *actions* in order to acquire the corresponding virtue, while the phrase 'because of the same *actions*' indicates the form of those *actions* as a cause, namely, the repeated sequence of them, which causes a virtue, or the lack of that sequence, which destroys or blocks the formation of that virtue.

8 If repetition of certain *actions* in a certain manner did not cause a certain habit, e.g., a virtue, then one would not need the repetition to acquire or have that virtue, and a teacher who can direct that repetition would be useless. If so, then a virtue could only be inherited or bestowed by God or begotten by chance, but these alternatives have been ruled out. 1099b9–25.

9 Repeated activities of the right kind cause virtues, but of the wrong and opposite kind they cause vices.

2

1 One would get some theoretical benefit in knowing what virtue is but this would be secondary and for the sake of something else, for knowledge in a practical science is for the sake of *action*.

2 1103a31–b25.

3 Right reason comes under intellectual virtue, and this, considered at length in Book Z, is indicated later in this Book when *action* according to the mean is discussed.

4 If the subject-matter lacks definiteness, statements concerning it should be given in outline; and if it admits of variation, precise statements concerning it may be untrue or misleading. For example, the kinds of situations in which one may face danger are perhaps infinite, and many volumes would be required to consider them all; and to specify the amount a generous man should give (say, ten dollars) would make him extravagant in one case but stingy in another.

5 The more we rise to the universal, the more accurate we can make our statements. For example, if we posit only few general mathematical axioms, e.g., $a+b=b+a$, $a+0=a$, $(a+b)+c=a+(b+c)$, and include the theorems which follow from them, our science will be very accurate; but if we add many more till we reach the subject of calculus, the accuracy lessens and even disagreements arise as to the truth or falsity of some statements in the system. 87a31–7.

6 Excess and deficiency belong to the *actions* which are implied. For example, giving too much money and to everyone or meeting every kind of danger would be an *action* in excess, and similarly for an *action* in deficiency.

7 This is the dialectical method of proceeding from what is more known to what is less known to us. Strength and health are more apparent than the virtues, and, in general, the things of the body are more known than the things of the soul.

⁸ The terms 'mean' and 'moderation' will be used synonymously.

⁹ The manner of dependence is indicated by the examples which follow. In general, one who possesses a virtue will perform the activities corresponding to that virtue with ease and pleasure, but one who does not possess it will perform those same activities with difficulty and painfully.

¹⁰ The expression 'because of' has the same meaning here as the expression 'for the sake of avoiding'.

¹¹ Unless the term 'cure' has a narrow meaning, the argument appears to be dialectical.

¹² 1104a27–9.

¹³ Perhaps Speusippus and other Platonists are meant. Their argument may be that, since vice arises through passions, i.e., by pursuing pleasures and avoiding pains, virtue would arise when one has no such passions but is in a state of rest.

¹⁴ Perhaps ethical virtue is meant.

¹⁵ The argument is dialectical, for Heraclitus is a well-known philosopher. Controlling pleasures is more difficult than controlling temper; that which is more difficult requires greater effort; that which requires greater effort is better and requires a greater art; hence controlling pleasures is better than controlling temper and requires a greater art.

3

¹ *Actions* here are compared with productions. Productions are introduced since they are more familiar to us than *actions*. Now even in productions, one is not called an 'artist' unless he has learned that art, and if he produces a work of art without being an artist, he does so by luck, or he merely imitates or copies from someone else. So just as an artist must acquire the art before producing a work of art by art and not by luck, so a virtuous man must acquire the virtue before he performs an *action* virtuously.

² *Actions* here are contrasted with productions. An artist takes some material and by means of his art changes it into a work of art. His activity is a production, and his aim is a product. For example, a doctor changes a sick man into a healthy man, and a builder makes a house out of certain materials. One who *acts*, on the other hand, does not produce a work of art; his activity ends in the *action* itself, as in the case of a man who drinks

too much or one who gives generously, and the manner in which he *acts* makes a difference.

³ A just man is one who does what is just and *acts* according to the whole of (2). But a man who does what is just or performs a just *action* may *act* only according to (1) and (2a), for he may perform the *action* for appearances sake in order to gain power or to attain some other bad end. See Comm. 5 of Section 1.

⁴ A good shoemaker will produce good shoes even if he takes no pleasure in his work.

⁵ It does not take much knowledge to abstain from excessive drinking; what counts most in ethical virtues is a man's intention.

⁶ By 'such as a just or a temperate man would do' he means just or temperate things or *actions* without reference to 2 (b) and 2 (c), as explained in Comm. 3 of this section and in Comm. 5 of Section 1.

⁷ By 'does them as a just man would' he means he does them justly, as explained in Comm. 3 of this section and in Comm. 5 of Section 1.

⁸ In other words, it is by doing what is just or temperate that one acquires the virtue of *acting* justly or temperately, respectively.

4

¹ The inquiry in this Section is limited to the genus of ethical virtue and does not include the differentia of it.

² Perhaps a list of most of the feelings is better for the reader than a definition here, for, at the early stages of learning, induction and examples are better than definition. An alternative to 'friendly feeling' is 'love'.

³ The powers of the soul indicated are possessed by nature, i.e., we are born with them. 9a14–27.

⁴ We do not deliberate and choose to be angry or afraid or to have some other such feeling; for anger and fear and the others occur instantaneously. Ethical virtues, on the other hand, are acquired by intention, i.e., deliberate choice.

⁵ Feelings come and go, but vices and virtues, once acquired, persist for a long time. Thus a virtuous man possesses virtue whether awake or asleep, whether *acting* virtuously or not *acting* at all, and he possesses virtue for a long time. 8b26–35.

⁶ 1103a14–b2.

7 The ultimate genus of virtues, ethical as well as intellectual, is not 'habit' but 'quality', which is a category, and habits form one subdivision of qualities. The discussion in Book B, of course, is limited to ethical virtues.

5

1 An alternative to 'kind' is 'quality'. The quality he is referring to is the differentia of ethical virtue, for what is required is the definition of ethical virtue, and the differentia is still to be supplied. 1020a33–b1.

2 Are not (a) and (b) the same thing? Not quite. To use a more familiar example, the disposition of a good steel knife, assuming it has the proper shape, is the quality of hardness in the steel, whether it is in the process of cutting or not; its effective performance is its successful operation while in the process of cutting.

3 The term 'good' means virtuous when predicated of a man.

4 1104a11–27.

5 Perhaps he is referring to continuity, which is somehow related to virtue and virtuous activity, as indicated in the next sentence. For example, colors are qualities, and the change from white to black is continuous. This change is a motion, and though motion is not a quantity in its nature, it is continuous in a secondary sense (1020a26–32). So since the thing is never stationary during its qualitative motion, the various colors between white and black are infinite, for the motion is infinitely divisible, and corresponding to each moment of time the color during the motion is distinct in degree. Similarly, if A and C are the extreme amounts of food one may eat and B is the mean or right amount, the amounts from A to C vary continuously, and so do the corresponding habits with respect to such amounts. Hence the habits too may vary continuously, not as quantities, but as qualities which depend on quantities, and the variation is one of degree. What applies to the habit of eating applies also to the habit of giving to others and to all other ethical habits.

6 This is the arithmetic mean. For example, if 4 and 20 are the extremes, the arithmetic mean would be half the sum of 4 and 20, or 12.

7 The mean relative to us is not a geometric mean, as some commentators think, but varies from person to person; and it varies even for the same person, if the circumstances are not exactly the same. If that mean were geometric, it would be definite and not vary, and Aristotle would have

mentioned it, as he mentioned the arithmetic mean in the case of the thing itself.

⁸ Perhaps 'arithmetic proportion' is not the right English expression. Anyway, if the arithmetic proportion is given as being $A:B::B:C$, where $A > B$ and $B > C$, then $A - B = B - C$. In other words, A, B, and C form an arithmetic progression, in which B is the arithmetic average of A and C. For example, the numbers 20, 15, and 10 form the arithmetic proportion $20:15::15:10$, and 15 is the average of 20 and 10.

⁹ Milo of Crotona was famous for extraordinary bodily strength. He was six times victor in wrestling at the Olympic games, and as often at the Pythian games. He is said to have carried a heifer of four years old on his shoulders through the stadium at Olympia and afterwards to have eaten the whole of it in a single day.

¹⁰ The term 'scientist' or 'science' as used here does not apply to a theoretical scientist or science, for a theoretical science investigates truths, and a statement about a fact cannot be true for one man and false for another. It applies, then, to a scientist concerned with production or *action* in which the mean with respect to us is sought, e.g., to a trainer in gymnastics or to a man in politics.

¹¹ According to Aristotle, an ethical virtue is like a second nature, for by living according to it continuously we behave as if we inherited it, like vision and other natural powers. Also, since it is used more than art, it is more accurate than art, and since it is concerned with ends, while art is concerned with products, which are means, it is better than art. 194a21–2, 381b6, 396b11–2.

¹² Perhaps καί should be added after ἔλλειψις in line 1106b26, and we have translated accordingly.

¹³ One may *act* virtuously but fail to attain the mean; but this failure results by accident and not because of the *action*, for accidental causes are in general unknown, and in such a case no mistake has been committed. Perhaps it is in view of this that the qualification 'at least' is added; for what is important is the intended *action*, which almost always assures *success*, the exceptions occurring when an accident intervenes.

¹⁴ For most Pythagoreans (985b23–6b2), the ultimate elements of all things are the *Infinite* and the *Finite*, also called '*Even*' and '*Odd*', respectively; and these are analogous to matter and form, respectively. But form is definite, and matter is indefinite, and most ancient philosophers

attributed goodness to what is definite but badness to what is indefinite. Further, the mean is definite and unique, but the deviations from it are many or infinite; so to attain the mean is difficult, but to miss it easy. Hence a habit must be acquired to attain the mean, like the skill of hitting the target and like the mathematical knowledge to locate the mean (i.e., the center) of the circle. 1109a24–6.

15 The author is not known.

6

1 It is not clear whether the definition given here is the first sentence (while the second sentence explains it further) or includes both sentences.

Lines 1105a26–33 state that a virtuous man must be disposed in a certain manner, namely, (a) he must know what he is doing, (b) he must intend to perform the *action* and do it for its own sake, and (c) he must *act* with certainty and firmness; and lines 1099a7–21 state that virtuous activity is pleasant, except perhaps when the end sought is not attained (1117b15–6). Perhaps the pleasantness of the activity is included in the phrase 'do it for its own sake', for to do something in this manner, one must like it (1099a7–11). Again, the mean must apply not only to the *action* but also to the feeling; for not only must a generous man give the right amount (which is a mean), but his feeling about it must also be right (must be a mean), since he should neither be displeased nor be overjoyed by his *action*. The mean (or what is right) in both feeling and *action* is mentioned in the second sentence, but only the term 'mean' appears in the first sentence; so perhaps the second sentence explains further the meaning of the first.

A further difficulty arises from the expression 'defined by reason and as a prudent man would define it'. Perhaps the expression indicates the intellectual requirement for an ethical virtue; for to *act* ethically some knowledge is required. But do the expressions 'defined by reason' and 'as a prudent man would define it' mean the same thing or not? Perhaps reason would define the *action* in a general way by stating, for example, that one should seek the mean, etc., while the prudent man must also take into account all the particular facts and specify the *action* in detail, e.g., specify the *action* of a brave or a generous man in a given situation. Prudence at this stage has not been discussed, perhaps because Aristotle does not wish to discuss it at this time. It is discussed in Book Z.

² By *substance* he means the nature or essence of virtue, and that nature exists in the virtue itself; and the formula of virtue is just an expression or a definition, either written or stated or in thought, which signifies the nature, but an expression about a virtue is not the virtue itself and does not exist in that virtue.

³ In other words, given the same feelings, such as fear and courage, and the *actions* attended by them, there correspond two vices, cowardice and rashness, and also a mean, bravery; and bravery is the best habit with respect to fear and courage and the corresponding *actions*, and so it is an extreme with respect to excellence.

⁴ See previous commentary.

⁵ The impossibility of an excess of excess, of a deficiency of deficiency, and of the rest, is similar to that of a motion of motion, whose proof is given in 225b10–6a23. The interval between excess and deficiency is analogous to the line between two points; and just as a point is indivisible and does not admit of differences of degree, so is the case of excess or of deficiency or of the mean itself, for each is indivisible and analogous to a point.

7

¹ Of course, all statements in ethics, except those which mention individuals such as Socrates, are universal, although some of them are more universal than others. For example, 'virtue is good' is more universal than 'bravery is good'. So the universality meant is one of degree, and we added 'more' before 'universal' to indicate this; and we did likewise before 'particular' later in the sentence.

² As we proceed to a more universal term, we lose more specific content or meaning. For example, we know more about an individual if we call it 'a man' than if we call it 'an animal', and even more than if we call it 'a living thing' or 'a thing'; and the term 'a thing', which is most universal, has the least meaning. Hence, as we rise to the more universal, the term becomes more general or more empty in meaning. Moreover, overgeneralizing may hide exceptions, and sometimes this leads to falsity.

³ Apparently, a list of virtues and vices existed in Aristotle's school. There is a list in the Eudemian Ethics (1220b38–1a12), perhaps an earlier work of Aristotle.

⁴ He who exceeds in not fearing is not necessarily either brave or rash, for

he may also lack courage. He is like a man who is excessively unaware of danger.

5 1119b22–1122a17.

6 Lines 1107b17–19, 1122a28–9, and 1122b10–1 indicate that 'generosity' is used in two senses: as a species, which excludes donations of large amounts, and as a genus, which includes such amounts also. Whenever a Greek term is lacking in cases such as this, Aristotle often uses this device.

7 1122a18–3a33.

8 The analysis of habits in terms of excess, deficiency, and the mean sometimes leads to possible habits which seldom exist and have no name. Aristotle is usually content to indicate their existence without coining a name for them.

9 1108b11–9a19, 1125b11–8.

10 By 'the manner proposed' he means sketchily and summarily (1107b14).

11 The words 'inirascible' and 'inirascibility' are not in the English language; Ross used them for convenience, and we shall do likewise.

12 Books Γ, Δ, and E, 1115a4–1138b14.

13 What does 'rational' mean here? The term λογικός is derived from λόγος, and here it may refer to the intellectual virtues discussed in Book Z, or to those concerned with relations among men by way of speech (1108a11), these being truthfulness, wit, friendship, and their corresponding vices, and these are discussed in Book Δ, 1126b11–8b9; friendship is further discussed in Books Θ and I, 1155a3–1172a15.

8

1 The term 'contrary' has many meanings (1018a25–38). One major meaning is this: contraries are things which differ most within a genus or kind. In this sense, then, the vice in excess would be contrary to the corresponding vice in deficiency with respect to their natures or definitions; and both vices would be contrary to the corresponding virtue with respect to goodness or final cause, for virtue is the best and the vices are the worst (1107a6–8). With respect to definition, however, the mean is contrary to each of the vices in a qualified manner, i.e., relatively; for the mean exceeds one vice but is exceeded by the other.

2 Such terms are 'small', 'great', 'few', and 'many' may be taken with or without qualification. For example, since by definition a number is a plurality of units, two is few without qualification, for no lesser number exists; but if some qualification is made, such as the number of sides (i.e., straight lines) of a polygon, three is few and the least, for no polygon can have less than three sides. Similarly with the others.

[3] According to nature and definition, then, cowardice is further away from rashness than from bravery; hence it is more contrary to rashness than to bravery.

[4] Perhaps 'propriety' is a synonym of 'temperance'.

9

[1] Perhaps the pleasures of the senses are meant, especially those of touch and taste.

[2] Since virtue is concerned with individual and sensible objects which admit variation of degree as well as of quantity, and since some error of judgment concerning such sensible objects is highly probable, it is not easy to make definite specifications. 428b18–25.

BOOK Γ

1

1 This is ethical virtue.

2 Since 'intention' is a part of the definition of virtue and hence of the definition of happiness (1106b36–7a2, 1102a5–6), and since things done by intention are done voluntarily, a discussion of what is voluntary and what is involuntary is necessary if we are to know what happiness is (for 'voluntary' and 'involuntary' are contraries and hence in the same genus, and contraries are studied by the same science, e.g., oddness and evenness come under arithmetic, and vice and virtue under ethics). Thus, in considering a voluntary *action*, one considers the moving cause of that *action* and hence the moving cause of ethical virtue.

3 In other words, no sane man would throw goods away just for the sake of throwing them away.

4 In such *actions* there are two moving causes, one in the person who *acts* and one external to him; so such *actions* are partly voluntary and partly involuntary.

5 During a storm, a captain may throw goods overboard to safeguard the passengers or he may not do so. Whether he should or not depends on his knowledge of the seriousness of the storm and his sense of values, but in either case the choice lies in him. Each alternative is a mixture. In throwing goods overboard, he increases the chances of saving the passengers, and if he keeps the goods, he decreases the chance of saving the passengers. Moreover, he may place a greater or less value on the goods or on the passengers than he should. The captain's sense of values and his knowledge of a particular situation, then, depends on many particulars of that situation, but the ultimate decision rests on him.

6 What is involuntary to the agent who *acts* is the external cause which imposes a qualification on the *action*, but after the qualification is imposed, the agent *acts* voluntarily. If there were no such qualification, the *action* would be involuntary, for a man would not knowingly choose such *action*.

7 This statement contradicts the opinion that the end never justifies the

means. What is disgraceful in itself is bad, but when one is forced to consider it as a means to a great or noble end, he has to make a choice between two alternatives, each of which is a mixture of bad and good, as in the example previously mentioned (1110a4–8).

8 The fact that (a) a mixed *action* admits of two alternatives (it may or may not be chosen) and that (b) some men are blamed for choosing one alternative while others are blamed for choosing the contrary alternative indicates that mixed *actions* are voluntary rather than involuntary.

9 *Alcmaeon*, Fragment 69, Nauck. Alcmaeon killed his mother Eriphyle to escape the curse of his father Amphiaraos.

10 All things would be done by force; for both noble and pleasant things would be compelling according to the hypothesis, and those which are forced on us by agents, as indicated earlier (1110a1–8), and which are painful, are compelling. This sounds like a stimulus-response situation, in which the stimulus, which is always outside, is the sole agent which decides the man's *action*.

11 If we are compelled by external agents to do whatever we do, it would appear that we are pained when we *act* by force or unwillingly but pleased when we *act* because of pleasure or what is noble (even if the pleasant and the noble are external agents by the hypothesis of these thinkers). We might, then, posit two kinds of agents, those who compel us to do what pleases us and those who compel us to *act* painfully. But this leads to another difficulty. The agent who compels me to do something painfully is not an agent but, like me, is himself compelled to force me to do something; and this leads to an infinite regress without a first mover, a hypothesis rejected by Aristotle (994a5–7). Now there is a difference between being forced by someone outside to perform an *action* and initiating that *action* without being so forced. So why not recognize this difference and accept the common language which indicates this difference? If further differences arise when the *action* is initiated by the agent himself (for the agent may be mad or sane), this is another matter.

12 The term 'external' here is not used in the sense of the pleasant or the noble, as some thinkers think (1110b9–11), but in the sense indicated in 1110a1–8.

2

1 An *action* is done through ignorance if the agent is ignorant of some

phase of that *action*. If the agent regrets that *action*, he is said to have done it involuntarily; but if he does not regret it (for he might do it even if he knew that phase of the *action*), he is said to have done it nonvoluntarily. Evidently, an involuntary *action* is not contradictory but contrary to a voluntary *action*, and what is not voluntary may be involuntary or nonvoluntary, just as what is not equal may be unequal or neither equal nor unequal. For example, green is neither equal nor unequal to five; it is simply nonequal or not equal to five, for only quantities can be equal to each other or unequal to each other, but green is not a quantity. 1055b9–11.

2 The drunkard or angry man *acts* in a certain way because of his drunkenness or anger, even if he is not aware of what he is doing. He is then said to be *acting* in ignorance, not through ignorance; for *acting* through ignorance is not *acting* through any vice but simply because of ignorance, while *acting* in ignorance is *acting* because of some vice.

3 Universal ignorance in ethical matters is ignorance with respect to things of a certain kind and not ignorance of a particular, e.g., of the fact that the person at a distance is one's father. A man who is universally ignorant, then, is one who is disposed to *act* badly with respect to things of a certain kind and so to be bad with respect to the corresponding *actions*. For example, a man who habitually steals *acts* in universal ignorance of what is good or expedient for himself; so he steals not because of his ignorance of the particulars of his *action*, but because of his bad habit.

4 According to one story, Aeschylus was initiated into the Eleusinian Mysteries, according to another, he was not; but he defended himself by claiming that what he said was accidental, not realizing that the Mysteries were not to be revealed. He was acquitted.

5 In the *Cresphontes* of Euripides, the wife of Cresphontes was at the point of murdering her son by mistake but recognized him before *acting*. 1454a5–7.

6 For example, one might strike to kill a snake which is near a man but aim badly.

7 In all these cases the *action* is done through ignorance of a particular.

3

1 Perhaps the reference is to Plato's *Laws*, 863.

2 If things done by force or through ignorance are involuntary and if

that which is voluntary is contrary to that which is involuntary, then things done knowingly and by the agent without external force would be voluntary. If one denies that an *action* performed through *desire* or temper is voluntary, then the distinction between being forced by an external agent (1110a1–4) and not being forced by such agent is lost, and no animal (including men and children) would do anything voluntarily in this manner.

3 If no *action* through *desire* or temper is assumed to be voluntary, no such *action* should be at one time praised and at another time blamed, for praise or blame is thought to belong to what is voluntary. And if praise belongs to noble *actions* and blame to disgraceful *actions*, this too would be ridiculous; for by hypothesis both *actions* are involuntary and both belong to the same man, in fact, to all men.

4 To say that a man should *desire A* but should avoid its opposite *B* is to allow him to choose *A* and reject *B*. Such a choice is impossible if whatever he does is involuntary, for then he would have no choice. But we do say that we should be angry with certain people and that we should *desire* certain things. If so, we admit that there is choice and that we do certain things voluntarily but are forced to do their opposites involuntarily. Perhaps the word 'desire' is better than '*desire*' here.

5 If involuntary *actions* are thought to be painful but those according to *desire* are thought to be pleasant, *actions* according to *desire* cannot be thought to be involuntary, and so they must be voluntary. This is a dialectical argument.

6 What is involuntary applies to error proceeding from thought as well as to error proceeding from *desire* or temper. So if error should be avoided but rightness pursued in matters of thought, such should be the case in matters of passion also, for both feelings and thoughts are human.

4

1 A man may help another in distress and so appear generous; yet his *action* may not be an end in itself but a means to an evil end, and so his intention may not be good. Thus *actions* which appear virtuous may not proceed from virtue.

2 Volition is a genus of intention.

3 As we shall see, intention presupposes deliberation; but children and

brutes act without deliberation, and a thing done on the spur of the moment may be done voluntarily but without deliberation.

4 *Desire*, temper, and wish come under the genus of 'desire'. 700b22. *Desire* is desire of the pleasurable through the senses, wish is desire of the good and requires intellect. Temper is shown in courage, anger, etc., e.g., anger is desire to pain someone for wrongdoing.

5 For example, dogs and horses do not deliberate.

6 Both the continent man and the incontinent man *desire* what is not good for themselves, like drinking to excess, but *desire* conquers knowledge in the latter while knowledge overrules *desire* in the former. 1145b12–4.

7 The same thing cannot be both *desired* and not *desired* at the same time; but it may be *desired* and still not be deliberately chosen at the same time; e.g., intimate relations with another man's wife.

8 Perhaps by 'painful' Aristotle means painful to the senses, and likewise for 'pleasant'.

9 Things done through temper are often done on the spur of the moment, but things done by *desire* may be done in accordance with deliberation; and things done by intention require deliberation, and deliberation takes time.

10 Apparently 'opinion' here is used in a wide sense and applies to any belief. One of its narrow meanings applies to what may or may not be and not to what is necessary or impossible. 88b30–9a3.

11 What we intend is to *act* in some way or other, but opinions are of what is or was or will be the case and *action* is not included and need not follow.

12 In its generic sense, 'right' applies to truth as well as to *action* (427b8–11, 433a26–7, 1142b10–1), but here it is used in its specific sense and applies to certain *actions* or to the desire of such *actions*.

13 That is, they are not necessarily the same, although they may coincide; and, of course, the definitions of intention and of opinion differ.

14 The term 'what' refers to the genus of intention, whether this be the proximate or ultimate or intermediate genus, while 'what kind' refers to the differentia. For example, 'animal', 'substance', and 'living thing' are such genera of a man.

15 In other words, 'volition' is a genus of intention. What follows suggests the differentia.

16 Reasoning or *thought* and choice are elements in the differentia of intention.

5

¹ Some men would deny the principle of contradiction or of the excluded middle or the existence of motion or of knowledge, others would hold that everything is determined or everything is a matter of chance. Similarly, some would think that all things are matters of deliberation, and this would imply that nothing is of necessity true or of necessity false. Aristotle would consider such men uneducated in the principles of analytics, and if their doctrine is superficial, he would not waste much time arguing with them. 77b11–3, 986b25–7, 1005b2–5, 1006a6–8, 1217a8–10.

² The universe for Aristotle exists of necessity and eternally, and there is no point of deliberating about this. Similarly, there are other necessary facts about the universe as a whole, not about some of its parts.

³ For example, Aristotle believed that (a) the outer sphere of the universe is always moved by the prime mover (i.e., God) in the same way, circularly and evenly, and that (b) earth by its nature moves downwards (towards the center of the Earth) if not prevented. Perhaps intellect or art as a moving cause would come under what he calls 'some other cause'. This is mentioned in what follows.

⁴ Another example would be the Sun's position, whose distance from the Earth every year increases and decreases regularly.

⁵ There is no point of deliberating about things happening by luck or chance, for chance is by definition a variable and indeterminate cause and cannot be discovered or brought about by deliberation.

⁶ The phrase 'not always in the same manner' suggests that we deliberate about things which may be brought about in alternative ways. For example, one may make money in a number of ways.

⁷ In deliberating about means to an end, one may find himself limited to just one alternative or be faced with a number of alternatives.

Perhaps an example will illustrate the case of a number of alternatives. Let the end be the purchase of a house. The money required may be obtained by (1) selling some of one's own stocks, or by (2) borrowing from another source, or by (3) a mixture of the two. Thus the end may be brought about by three different means. If one wishes to (2) borrow from another source, he may borrow (a) from a friend or (b) from a bank. If he chooses (b), he has to make sure that he can get the loan from the bank; and if he can, then the possibility of borrowing the money from the bank is the last element in the order of discovery. He then proceeds to go to the bank.

8 In mathematics, one inquires whether A has the property B or not, and it is assumed that A of necessity has the property B, or of necessity does not have the property B; and the same A cannot have B sometimes and not have B at other times.

9 In Commentary 7, the last step in the analysis is the thought that the man can borrow the money from the bank. When this step is put into effect, i.e., when the man proceeds to borrow the money, then this procedure is the first step in the coming to be of the end, i.e., of the purchase of the house.

10 In other words, if A's friend can supply the money, it is A who asks his friend to supply the money and hence it is A who initiates the first step in the coming to be of the end.

11 The end is not an existing particular but a particular to be realized. For example, if A wishes to buy a house, the end is not the house but A's possession of the house.

12 If the steps were infinite, whether in the direction of the end to be realized or in the direction of the first step in the analysis, a man would never attain that end and his thinking and his efforts would be empty or in vain.

13 Both are objects of what may or may not come to be by the man who inquires, but intention is a species of deliberation.

14 The ruling part of a man is his intellect.

15 This appears to be the definition of intention, but some problems appear to arise. A wish is of the end but an intention is concerned with the means to an end (1111b26–30, 1112b11–2, 1113b3–4), and perhaps 'things' here signifies the means. Logically, if an intention is defined as a deliberate desire of a certain kind, it should be a wish (for it is neither a *desire* nor temper since it involves the intellect) and so should be concerned with an end of a certain kind; but it is posited as being concerned with the means relative to an end. Further, lines 1112a1–8 state that men intend what is good or the best, and if intention is concerned with the means, then the words 'good' and 'best' as used here would have to apply to means relative to good ends and not to the ends themselves. Again, why should desires be limited to ends only, if means too may be objects of desire? Since means are relative to ends, it would appear that there are

two kinds of desires, unqualified and qualified, desires of ends being unqualified while desires of means being qualified by being relative to ends.
Finally, even if 'deliberate desire' applies not just to an end but to an end
along with the means relative to that end, as Professor H. H. Joachim
thinks (*Aristotle, The Nicomachean Ethics*, Oxford U. Press, 1955, p. 102),
the distinctions and difficulties we have indicated still appear to stand. Is
there a fourth species of desire? Other problems may be raised.

6

1 Perhaps some Platonists are among them.

2 Perhaps these are the thinkers who hold that man is the measure of
things or that reality is what appears to be the case.

3 If a wish is only of a good, then no one chooses what is bad or no one
chooses wrongly, for one chooses what he wishes. But men do choose
wrongly and admit and speak of having done so. Hence a man may
choose what is bad as well as what is good.

4 If an object of wish exists and if it is always the apparent good, then
since it may appear good to one man but bad to another, it would have
contrary attributes, which is impossible, or else, it would have no definite
nature which limits it to one contrary only. Thus sugar would be both bitter and sweet, or else neither. The difficulties of this position are discussed
in detail in the *Metaphysics*, 1005b11–1011b22.

5 If the good differs from the apparent good in the manner stated here, the
apparent good may still be subdivided into that which is good and that
which is bad. Who decides whether a given apparent good is good or bad?
But this is a different problem.

6 Not every kind of pleasure but certain kinds and in excess. Usually,
these are pleasures of the senses, as in intemperate men. Other pleasures
may be included, such as the inordinate pleasure of having power over
other men.

7 The question concerning who should be the judge of what is good and
what is bad amounts to the question concerning who is really a happy
man. If all men desire happiness but not all attain it, then some men
think and *act* rightly but others do not, and the judge of what is good
and what is bad is the man who thinks and *acts* rightly, i.e., the virtuous
man.

7

[1] 1112a1–2.

[2] Fr. adesp. (? Solon), Berg K³, p. 1356f.

[3] Perhaps these are the statements in lines 1113b3–14.

[4] If a man is not the cause of his *actions*, then the cause is outside of him, and let us say that it is the environment. But what is the environment? If one says that it is another man or other men or society, then the cause would be a man or many men, and this is denied. If one says that it is an animal or a plant, this would be less likely, for then that which cannot think rationally or not think at all would be more of a cause of initiating an *action* regarding what may or may not be than a man who can think rationally and is seen to initiate *action*. If one says that it is an inanimate object, this would be even more absurd. Finally, to say that there is a series of previous causes is to assign an infinity of causes without a first cause; and Aristotle denies the possibility of this. 994a1–b31.

[5] A law of Pittacus. 1274b18–23.

[6] Can an unjust or intemperate man ever become just or temperate? It happens occasionally; but it takes time, since habits are difficult to displace. 8b27–35, 13a18–31.

[7] If, according to these thinkers, all men aim at the apparent good, then they desire the apparent good and so the apparent good is voluntary; and if so, then both virtues and vices would be voluntary, for both what is really good and what is really bad are also apparent goods.

[8] Even if the same end appears by nature good to some but bad to others, still it is by *actions* which we choose to perform that we acquire our habits, whether these be virtues or vices. So since those *actions* by being chosen are voluntary, we are partly responsible for our habits. Consequently, virtues and vices are alike voluntary.

8

[1] In the case of ethical virtues, which are habits, we know that we can acquire them by starting to *act* in a certain manner, and we know that they are strengthened as we continue *acting* in that manner. Hence it is up to us to acquire them or not.

9

¹ 1107a33–b4.

² Fearful things are those which cause fear.

³ There is nothing noble in dying at sea or by disease, unless one endangers his life or dies for the safety of others. It is the safety of others or a similar cause, then, that gives nobility to a brave *action*.

10

¹ The reference is to terrible things which are not beyond the endurance of man.

² Habit or character is like nature (452a27–8), or as we would say, like second nature. Thus just as a thing usually acts according to its nature (e.g., a stone moves downward when released), so when the occasion arises a man *acts* according to the corresponding habit.

³ What is noble in the primary sense here is the noble deed of a brave man. Now we also speak of bravery, which is a habit, as being noble, but in a secondary sense; for bravery disposes one to do brave deeds, which are noble in the primary sense. It is for this reason that bravery is defined in terms of brave deeds; for all virtues are means to happiness, and means are relative to ends and are defined in terms of ends.

⁴ 1107b2, 30, 1108a5.

⁵ 1229b28–30.

⁶ They are all concerned with fear and courage.

11

¹ 1115a4–b6.

² A brave man in the proper sense chooses to face danger because it is noble to do so, regardless of whether honor goes along with it or not. A politically brave man, on the other hand, faces danger not because it is noble to do so but to avoid penalty or reproach and for the sake of honor. Outwardly, the *actions* of both are similar, but the *reasons* for those *actions* differ. The two kinds of bravery are most similar because (a) the effects of the corresponding *actions* are most similar, and (b) both are for the sake of virtue, though in a different way. A brave man in the proper

sense *acts* according to virtue as defined, but a politically brave man *acts* neither for the sake of what is noble nor virtuously (for he is pained by so *acting*) but for the sake of avoiding reproach or penalty and for the sake of gaining honor; for if there were no reproach nor penalty nor honor, he would not be facing danger.

3 *Iliad*, xxii, 100.

4 *Iliad*, viii, 148–9.

5 They are inferior because they go to battle not willingly but by force, and, unlike politically brave men, they have no sense of shame.

6 *Iliad*, ii, 391–3; 1285a10–4.

7 In Plato's *Laches* (199) and *Protagoras* (350, 360), Socrates defines bravery as *knowledge* of fearful and courageous things.

8 In the Sacred War at Coronea, 353 B.C., the Phocians defeated the citizens of Coronea and some Boetians professional soldiers in the battle at the temple of Hermes.

9 *Iliad*, xi. 11, xiv. 151, xvi. 529.

10 *Iliad*, v. 470, xv. 232, 594.

11 *Odyssey*, xxiv. 318.

12 Theocritus, xx. 15.

13 Homer compares Ajax to a stubborn ass. *Iliad*, xi. 558–62.

14 The *reasons* are a noble purpose and *action* dictated by right reason.

15 At the Long Walls of Corinth, 392 B.C. The story is told in Xen. *Hell.* iv. 4, 10.

12

1 Is the pleasant end according to bravery the honor which comes after the brave *action* or the *action* itself, regarded as pleasurable?

2 If a brave man survives and is not wounded, then the memory of his *action* and the honor which follows bring him what he most deserves.

3 Men of little virtue regard the risk of being brave as worth the good they will earn if they survive. Men of great virtue, on the other hand, regard the gain by surviving as little in comparison to what they would lose by death.

13

1 Bravery is a mean with respect to fear and courage, and it is the spirited part of the soul (i.e., temper) which displays fear or courage. Temperance

is a mean with regard to certain bodily pleasures and pains, and these are displayed by the appetitive part of the soul, i.e., the part which *desires*.

2 Odors of perfumes remind them of intimate relations, while odors of dainty dishes remind them of tasty food; and excessive pleasures of such odors indicate indirectly excessive *desires* of touch and taste.

3 By 'others' Aristotle means men who are not intemperate, e.g., those who are simply hungry.

4 Philoxenus, son of Eryxis, 950a2–4, 1231a15–7.

5 *Iliad*, xxiv. 130.

6 The Greek term for 'glutton' is a composite of two terms whose English translations are 'belly' and 'mad'.

14

1 A natural desire, such as hunger, is not a vice, and it is necessary for life. It is accompanied with pain, and the pain of a hungry man goes away when he eats, whether with or without pleasure. What removes this pain, then, is not the pleasure of eating but just the replenishment; so pleasure is not the cause of the removal of the pain. The *desire* of an intemperate man, on the other hand, is acquired, and its pain, unlike that of a natural *desire*, is removed when the corresponding pleasure is fulfilled; hence the presence of its pain is caused by the absence of that pleasure. For, if B is the cause of A, the absence of B is the cause of the absence of A. 78b15–21.

Perhaps by 'because of pleasure' Aristotle means to say 'because of the absence of pleasure'.

2 If the other animals distinguish kinds of food, then a man should do so, for he is more complete. But this argument is dialectical; for, although men appear to show greater discrimination in taste and sight and touch and perhaps even in hearing, their smell is not as discriminating as that of some animals, e.g., dogs.

15

1 Both intemperance and cowardice are vices but in different ways. An intemperate man simply chooses pleasure, whereas a coward accepts the pain of disgrace in order to avoid the pain from danger or to save his life, which is certainly a great good. The choice of a coward, then, is qualified

since he faces a mixture of good and bad, while that of an intemperate man is unqualified. Hence the *actions* of an intemperate man are more voluntary than those of a coward.

2 It is the *act* of cowardice that is not painful and not cowardice itself; for cowardice is a disposition, and it exists in a man even when there is no danger.

3 They are thought to be done under compulsion, but actually they are not done so. The danger facing us is thought to be compelling, but still we choose between alternatives, each of which is a mixture of good and bad, as indicated in Comm. 1.

4 Logically, one does not *desire* a habit but certain kinds of pleasurable things or pleasure; hence no one *desires* to be intemperate. But the intemperate man wishes to be intemperate, whereas the incontinent man does not wish to be intemperate or incontinent but performs an intemperate *act* anyway because his *desire* overpowers his wish or his reason.

5 Since virtues and vices in the proper sense of these terms belong to men who have reached the age of reason, so to speak, and who have chosen to acquire their habits voluntarily, intemperance and temperance can belong only to such men. So just as children (babies or boys and girls)are either devoid of reason or incompletely rational, so they are either devoid of temperance or intemperance or they are temperate or intemperate in a qualified way or incompletely. If we call a child 'intemperate', then, we use the term not in the proper sense but in a qualified sense. What is common to a man and a child who are called 'intemperate' is just the act, without reference to intention; but the man acts through intention, which requires deliberation and choice, while such intention does not yet exist in a child.

As usual, Aristotle discusses a subject, especially when it does not admit of much precision, in terms of its contraries and assumes the reader can fill in the details, Thus in this discussion a man is assumed to have reason but a child not to have reason. But are there not degrees of reason? Certainly. Aristotle would say, in my opinion, that since an intermediate lies between contraries (1057a18–b34), the properties of each contrary belong to the intermediate to the extent or degree that the intermediate possesses that contrary. Intention, vice or virtue, and happiness or unhappiness would then belong to a boy who is sixteen years old to the extent or degree that he possesses reason.

BOOK Δ

1

[1] Perhaps 'judgments' here applies to what may be just or unjust (1134a31–2), for justice is a virtue, or else to other occasions also where a virtue or a vice is involved.

[2] One gives either without being asked or when asked or when he spends, and he takes either when he asks or when he is offered without asking. 1121a12.

[3] An alternative to 'money' is 'unit of measuring wealth'. The Greek term is used in both senses.

[4] Even if all wasteful men wasted their property by being intemperate, the distinction between wastefulness and intemperance would still stand; otherwise confusion might arise. So the manner in which a man wastes his property should not be a part of the definition of wastefulness.

[5] It is not clear whether 'wealth' and 'property' are synonymous or just close in meaning. Property has been defined above (1119b26–7), and the kinds of wealth are listed in 1361a12–25.

[6] If a motion or an *action* is good, that which causes motion or *acts* is better than that which is moved or *acted* upon; and when one treats another, he *acts* on him in a certain way. 430a18–9.

[7] For example, the pain of giving five dollars is greater than the pain of not taking six dollars for most people.

2

[1] It is the least painful of all because any deviation from virtue would be to him more painful. For example, if a poor but virtuous man gives $10, which is the proper amount, and is slightly pained, then by giving less or even none at all he would be more pained.

[2] For example, he may give in order to take or keep more, as in bribery.

[3] A tyrant takes as much as he pleases; so what he gives is not really his own, and he gives not because he is generous but for some other *reason*.

⁴ A man who takes too much will not be the one to give too much; and if he takes not from the right sources, i.e. not from his possessions, he will not be generous even if he gives profusely. Further, if *A* gives to *B* wrongly, *B* takes from *A* wrongly also.

⁵ He may do this through ignorance or by chance or by miscalculation.

⁶ Simonides was quoted as having valued wealth more than wisdom. 1391a8–12.

3

¹ 1119b27–1120a4.

² A private individual here is opposed to, say, a tyrant, for the latter uses property which is public or belongs to others.

³ The discussion here is limited to a wasteful man without an additional vice, say, of taking recklessly from others so as to continue being wasteful.

⁴ Older men tend to be less generous and are inclined to what is useful more than to what is noble. 1156a24–6, 1389b27–9.

⁵ A wasteful man of this sort, to continue being wasteful, combines the element of stinginess which has to do with taking more than one should and from the wrong sources.

⁶ If wasteful men take recklessly to continue being wasteful, they also commit disgraceful acts to get property. We see here an instance of a man with a strong vice (wastefulness) who, in order to perpetuate that vice, finds that he has to resort to other vices, i.e., stinginess and disgraceful conduct to get the means needed; and we may also add intemperance, for wasteful men very often spend money for bodily pleasures. It is like the man who tells a lie but finds that he has to protect it by telling another lie.

⁷ Potentialities or powers are defined and known in terms of the corresponding activities or objects to which they are related (1049b4–17). So the kinds of stinginess, which are similarly related to the corresponding *actions* or objects (deficiency in giving, no giving at all, excess in taking, *reasons* for each, etc.), are shown to exist and are made known through those *actions* or objects.

⁸ An alternative to '*goodness*' is 'equity', for equitable men are fair, and a miser is fair when he neither gives nor takes.

⁹ The term 'both' applies to dice-players as one group and to thieves and robbers as the other group.

¹⁰ Of course, stinginess and wastefulness as extremes are the most contrary with respect to giving and taking. But with respect to goodness and badness, to generosity we should oppose stinginess rather than wastefulness because it is worse than wastefulness and further from the mean. 1107a6–8, 1108b11–9a11.

4

¹ The term μεγαλοπρέπεια comes from μέγας, meaning great, and πρέπον, meaning that which is fitting. For the difference between munificence and generosity, see Comm. 7 of this Section.

² The expense of equipping a trireme (a warship), usually in times of war, was far greater than that of heading a sacred legation.

³ *Odyssey* XVII, 420.

⁴ 1123a19–33.

⁵ Just as a theoretical scientist has the power to discover or view the truth, so a munificent man has the power of viewing what is fitting in matters requiring great expenditure; for this power, as indicated from what follows, is more difficult than that concerned with matters requiring small expenditure.

⁶ 1103b21–3, 1105b25–8.

⁷ 'Generosity' is related to 'munificence' as a genus to a species; for a generous man is concerned with small as well as with great expenditure. Since names are often lacking, Aristotle often uses the same term as a genus as well as the species of it which has no name. 'Generosity', then, will also mean generosity concerning small matters. Aristotle does this for 'chance' and for 'disposition'. 8b35–9a13, 197a36–b37, 1122a20–1, b10–11.

5

¹ Such expenditures, though made for the sake of individuals, are of interest to all citizens or to those in high position. For example, one may spend magnificently to honor in some way a beloved president or some other such great figure.

7

¹ Literally, the term means greatness of soul.

² Any virtue requires a certain amount of knowledge of the things with

which that virtue is concerned. Hence if a man requires of himself that he be worthy or more worthy of great things without being so worthy, and if high-mindedness requires true thoughts of one's worthiness concerning great things, one who is mistaken concerning such things cannot be virtuous.

3 One who is worthy of only small things and requires of himself that he be worthy of them, though he is not high-minded, at least thinks truly. The disposition of being unassuming, then, though not high-mindedness, is one of the lesser virtues.

4 One who requires of himself that he be worthy of greater things than he is worthy of need not think himself worthy of great things; for he may be worthy of only small things and think himself worthy of moderate things, which are neither great nor small.

5 By analogy or proportion, if he were not worthy of great things, he would think himself as not being worthy at all.

6 After the definition of high-mindedness is laid down, this sentence confirms the definition by indicating the existence of that virtue and the appropriateness of the term used for that virtue.

7 If a high-minded man is worthy of the greatest things, then the greatest thing for a man to have would be complete virtue, i.e., all the virtues. But a man having all the virtues would be a good (i.e., virtuous) man without qualification. Hence complete virtue is a mark of a high-minded man without qualification.

8 High-mindedness cannot be the *substance* or the most important part of a virtuous man; for a virtuous man performs an *action* for its own sake and his pleasure in it does not depend on others, whereas high-mindedness is concerned with honors, and honors bestowed upon a man are external. So high-mindedness as a virtue can only be a sort of ornament to the other virtues and depends for its existence partly on those virtues and on those who bestow honors.

9 If happiness depends very little on honor, and if wealth and political power are only instrumental to honor, then happiness depends even less on wealth and political power. 1095b22–6.

8

1 Perhaps 'make men feel more high-minded' is meant. The argument is

dialectical, and Aristotle rejects it by distinguishing between virtue, which is the main good, and good luck and the others, which are instrumental goods.

2 Such men go through the motions of appearing high-minded, and this is easy, but they do not possess virtue and so they are not truly high-minded. For example, a high-minded man may leave the meeting when insulted by the chairman, but not by a worthless member of the club, while an ordinary man may leave the meeting when insulted by anyone, even by a worthless member. Thus the latter only imitates a high-minded man by leaving the meeting, for he shows no discrimination as to when he should leave.

3 When Thetis spoke to Zeus to help her son Achilles, she did not take her son's advice to remind Zeus of her services she had done him. *Iliad* I, 394, 503.

4 The Aldine scholiast quotes Callisthenes as stating that the Spartans behaved in this way towards the Athenians when they were invaded by the Thebans and needed help.

5 Literally, it should be 'because of insult' and not 'when insulted'; but a high-minded man is not disposed to insult others, so the insult here is directed towards him.

6 Things which bear fruit and are beneficial to something else are means or instrumental and not ends, but good ends are better than the good means to them.

9

1 In other words, such a man will not try to develop his good powers; and this point is brought out in what follows.

10

1 1107b24–31.

2 1107b32–8a1.

3 How can it be somehow both? Being at the middle, it is a sort of average of both, as if having some part of each. Orange, for example, lies between red and yellow and seems to be a mixture of both.

4 Even if the mean had a name, the opposition of the extremes (excess and deficiency) as contraries still stands. But when no name exists and the

corresponding virtue is not considered, then the opposition appears to be between one extreme as a virtue and the other as a vice, although both are vices.

11

[1] In other words, since the man who is moderate with respect to anger has no name, he will take on a name which is derived from 'good temper'; he will be called 'good-tempered'. Aristotle prefers not to coin a new term but to use an existing term and change its meaning slightly for theoretical purposes.

[2] For lack of an English term, we are introducing 'inirascibility' as the contrary of 'irascibility'. The term 'inirritability' is not appropriate, for one does not blame an inirritable man.

[3] The term comes from ἄκρος, which means an extreme, and χολή, which means bile.

12

[1] By 'in a similar way' he means in the right manner, etc.

[2] *Good* friends, of course, are virtuous. In English, perhaps 'friendliness' is a proper term for the moderate habit.

[3] For example, such a man will show respect for others and will yield his seat to an old man, and such *actions* issue from his character and not from any feeling of affection.

[4] Such a man will act alike in the sense that his *actions* will issue from his character in general; but what befits a stranger is not what befits a man whom he knows well but is not a friend. For example, a grocer may cash a $500-check for a client he knows, but not for a man who is a stranger in the town.

[5] Such a man would rather cause his neighbor some pain than please him for the moment but expose him to greater harm or disgrace later.

[6] Such a man would choose to give pleasure for its own sake or guard against causing pain for its own sake, that is, if nothing bad were to follow from such choice; but if the pleasure caused or the pain avoided is also attended by other consequences leading to harm or injury or disgrace, then he would consider the whole situation before making his choice.

[7] Apparently, a flatterer is worse than a complaisant man since his primary aim is not to please others but to benefit himself at the expense of others.

8 The extremes would be opposed to each other even if the mean had a name; but in the absence of a name, the opposition with respect to what is good and what is bad escapes notice, for, if a name existed, the mean would be regarded as good but the extremes bad. 1108b11–19.

13

1 By 'things' he means human relations, whether by discourse or *actions*. 1126b11–2.

2 1126b11–7a12.

3 By 'not' Aristotle means not for its own sake. If a man belittles himself not for its own sake but for some other *reason*, he need not be self-depreciatory, for that *reason* may be strong enough even for a truthful or a boastful man to *act* in this manner.

4 An alternative to 'in itself' is 'for its own sake' or 'by itself'.

5 Usually, he who lies for the sake of lying would lie for other bad reasons also. A man who dislikes lying for its own sake, however, may occasionally lie for a good reason. For the most part, then, Aristotle's statement is true. Ethics is not a precise science.

6 Understating the truth is not belittling the truth, for the difference in the first case is small but that in the second is great.

14

1 If a man who uses mockery well is defined by (b), then such a man may have to make jokes of all kinds, for some men are pleased by bad jokes; and if he makes bad jokes, he would listen to them too. But a good man should neither use bad jokes nor listen to them. Hence definition (a) is the proper one.

2 Perhaps he is referring to friendship.

15

1 Shame is felt for a voluntary *action* which is bad; but no man who feels ashamed by such *action* is *good*, for his *action* is voluntary and is therefore bad. A *good* man will perform only *good actions*.

2 In other words, when one *acts* according to virtue, he does nothing to

feel ashamed of; but to feel ashamed after a disgraceful *act* is better than not to feel ashamed, so such shame is *good* hypothetically or relatively.
[3] There is nothing hypothetical about a virtuous *action*, for such *action* is *good* without qualification. But if a *good* man *acts* disgracefully, although he would feel ashamed as a *good* man, his *action* itself is not *good*. So we have a bad *action* followed by the right feeling towards it, not a *good action* with the right feeling or followed by the right feeling. The hypothesis, then, is a bad *action* by a virtuous man but not insofar as he is virtuous, for there is no bad *action* or bad feeling in a virtuous *action*. We have, then, a mixture of two things; a bad *action* followed by the right feeling towards it.
[4] In continence, too, we have a mixture, but of the reverse kind. A continent man performs a good *action* but has the wrong feeling about it, for he is pained.
[5] 1145a15–1152a36.

BOOK E

1

[1] To avoid confusion, we shall posit the meanings of 'justice', 'injustice', 'just', and other allied expressions. We shall first start with the things which may be just or unjust, then proceed to justice and injustice, which exist in men as dispositions and qualities, and to the *actions* which result in what is just or unjust as well as to statements and thoughts concerning them.

The nouns 'the just', 'that which is just', 'a just thing', and 'what is just' will be used synonymously to apply to distributions or exchanges or their parts which are made by men. For example, in a democracy citizens should have or be given the same freedom to vote or equal rights, profits to business partners should be divided in proportion to their investment, unless otherwise specified, and in buying an article each man should pay according to the marked price, unless agreed upon otherwise; and what each should get in each case is the just, or what is just, or a just thing, or that which is just. Similar remarks apply to 'the unjust' or 'that which is unjust' or 'an unjust thing' or 'what is unjust'. Thus if a business partner takes more than he should, or is given less than he should, then he has what is unjust. Further specifications of what is just or unjust are made in the text. The adjectives 'just' and 'unjust' are similarly applied to exchanges, distributions, and their parts. Thus if a business partner receives a proportional part of the profits, that part is just, and so is the distribution, but if he is given less, the part he receives is unjust, and so is the distribution.

Justice is a disposition, acquired by habit, by means of which a man is disposed to do what is just; injustice is the corresponding disposition by means of which a man is disposed to do what is unjust, provided that he gains by his *action*, for when he takes less than he should, he is not unjust but rather generous. Evidently, both justice and injustice are in men and not in other things, and justice is a virtue but injustice is a vice. These restricted meanings of 'justice' and 'injustice' are not entirely in accord with those in the English language, but the distinctions exist and no new terms will be introduced. Perhaps 'disposition of justice' or 'just disposition' would be more proper than 'justice', and we shall use these sometimes.

The adjectives 'just' and 'unjust' are predicated also of statements, whether written or spoken, and of thoughts, and of *actions*, but in a relational and not in a univocal manner. Thus the statement 'a man should get what is just' is related to what is just by signifying what a man should get, and we may speak of it as being a just statement. In an analogous manner, 'a just man' will mean a man who has justice (i.e., a just disposition), which is a virtue, and 'an unjust man' will mean a man who has injustice (i.e., an unjust disposition), which is a vice. If that which is just, or unjust, is done willingly by the agent, it is said to be a just effect, or an unjust effect, respectively. Evidently, that which is just or unjust may be done not willingly but in some other way, e.g., by accident or by force. If a just effect is a correction of what is unjust, it is said to be a restitution. A just *action* is an *action* whose outcome is that which is just, and an unjust *action* is an *action* whose outcome is that which is unjust. Evidently, a just or unjust *action* may be voluntary or not voluntary; and if it is voluntary, the agent of a just *action* may or may not be just or unjust, respectively, for a just *action* is sometimes done by an unjust man for some reason or other, and the same applies to an unjust *action* which is voluntary.

To do what is just is to bring about, voluntarily or not, what is just; and similarly with doing what is unjust. To *act* justly or treat someone justly is to do willingly what is just, and to *act* unjustly or treat someone unjustly is to do willingly what is unjust. Evidently, a man who *acts* justly may not be just, for unjust men sometimes *act* justly; and the same applies to the man who *acts* unjustly. But a man may *act* justly or unjustly by deliberate choice, i.e., from justice or injustice, respectively, and then he is said to be a just or an unjust man, respectively. To be treated or suffer unjustly is to suffer unwillingly what is unjust by another who *acts* unjustly. A verdict is a judgement of that which may be just or unjust.

2 The dialectical method is meant, and Aristotle will start from premises generally accepted as true. The sentence which follows is such a premise. We should add, however, that the method starts first from the things which

are just (i.e., distributions, parts distributed, etc.) and those which are unjust and then proceeds to just and unjust *actions* and to the corresponding dispositions, justice and injustice. This method is suggested in *On the Soul*, 402b10–6, and is often used.

3 Since it is easier for us to observe just *actions* or just distributions or whatever is just than to understand justice as it exists in the soul, justice is formulated in terms of what is just. Besides, justice is acquired from just *actions* and is referred to them, but the converse is not necessarily true.

4 In general, contraries come under the same genus, and a science, which is about one genus of things, will include both contraries under it. Thus philosophy is concerned both with being and with nonbeing, arithmetic both with odd and with even numbers, medicine both with health and with disease; and a doctor should be able to bring about or prevent each of the contraries, e.g., health or disease. Ethical habits, on the other hand, are limited to one contrary, e.g., a temperate man is disposed to do temperate but not intemperate things, and a just man is disposed to do just but not unjust things, for ethical habits include intention. 1127b14.

5 For example, temperance exists in a temperate man and is exemplified in a temperate *action*, and dispositions are usually known or inferred from the corresponding *actions*. Certain activities require external objects also, and in such cases the activities themselves are known by reference to those objects. Seeing, for example, cannot be known or defined without the corresponding objects, i.e., colors (including white and black).

6 The object may be food, or an activity of some kind.

2

1 Why not consider the meanings of 'the just man' first? Perhaps those of 'the unjust man' are more familiar.

2 Evidently, the first sense of 'unjust' is wider than the second, for the grasping man is a lawbreaker, but the lawbreaker is not necessarily grasping.

3 The shift from 'the just man' to 'the just' is an induction or a generalization, for 'the just' is applicable to men, to *actions*, to distributions, etc. Similarly, the terms 'lawful' and 'unlawful' are more general, respectively, than the terms 'lawbreaker' and 'law-abiding'.

4 Such goods would be money, power, honor, etc.

5 The meaning of this statement is not spelled out. We may try an interpretation. Honor is good for all those who deserve it, property is good for necessities and for certain noble things; and, in general, things generally regarded as good are good for those who are virtuous. But those who lack virtue may long for or seek some of these goods but be harmed by them. To seek undeserved honor is bad, to seek property for its own sake or unjustly is also bad; so those who lack certain virtues should not seek the goods which are the rewards of those virtues. What they should seek are the virtues, for, when they possess these virtues, the unqualified goods become goods for them also.

6 The lesser of two evils is better than the greater, what is better is a qualified good; hence the lesser of two evils is a qualified good or a good in some sense.

7 He who is unfair would choose more of a good than he should and also less of what is bad than he should. For example, he would give less money for a common cause than he should.

3

1 Are there unjust laws? If we logically lay down that in one sense 'the lawful' and 'the just' are the same, then if some laws are bad, some just things are bad also. This apparent difficulty, however, is verbal and not real. So the real question is: What laws are rightly framed?

2 If this kind of justice is complete virtue towards another, then it appears that the corresponding laws are rightly framed.

Certain virtues or vices, of course, are not a part of justice or of injustice in this sense. It is a vice to waste one's property, but this is not injustice since generally there are no laws concerning it and no outsider is harmed.

3 Euripides, fragment from *Melanippe* (Nauck, fr. 486).

4 Theognis 147.

5 There seem to be some logical difficulties. Justice here is taken as complete virtue for oneself as well as towards another, whereas justice has already been stated to be complete virtue towards another and not in an unqualified way. Of course, by using justice towards another, one *acts* virtuously, and this contributes to his happiness; so perhaps by implication he uses it for himself. Again, if justice is complete virtue towards

another, how can it be virtue in the most complete sense? Is it by implication? Or is it because, as stated later (1130a7–8), the best man is the one who uses complete virtue towards another and not for himself, something which is more difficult? There are other difficulties.

6 For example, a man may be an inventor and succeed financially, and he may be financially prudent in handling his family obligations; but he may be neither generous towards others nor pleasant in the company of others.

7 Bias was one of the seven sages of ancient Greece.

8 The ruler as a ruler uses those virtues or vices which affect others. So it is possible for a man, who is virtuous with respect to those habits which affect only him (and his family and friends), not to be virtuous or not so virtuous when given the task of ruling others.

9 In Plato's *Republic*, 243c, Thrasymachus defines justice as 'another's good'.

10 Why only his friends and not all others? If one is wicked towards his friends, he is no less wicked towards the others; so by implication it appears that he is wicked towards all others.

11 Such a man, by neglecting what is useful (not what is noble) to himself, has nobility in the highest sense.

12 Two things have the same essence if their definitions, in terms of their indefinables, are the same. Two things are numerically the same if, though they may be called by different names differing in their definitions, they are identical. For example, 'three' and 'less than five by two' are predicated of the same things, but the definitions of the two expressions differ; for 'five' does not appear in the definition of 'three', but it appears in that of 'less than five by two'. The expressions 'justice' and 'virtue' (or perhaps 'complete virtue') are like 'three' and 'less than five by two'.

13 The term 'such-and-such' indicates a quality or a differentia and not a relation.

4

1 Wickedness and villainy appear to exclude each other. Perhaps wickedness applies to the ethical vices in which not much thinking is required, whereas a certain amount of planning or scheming is required in villainy. 1130a16–22, 1135b8–27, 1374b6–10.

2 For example, a man who commits adultery with a woman may pay her

or even be framed; so the man commits adultery through *desire* but the woman for the sake of gain.

³ Any genus and a species of it, of course, come under the same ultimate genus or category; so the definition of a genus is a part of the definition of the corresponding species. Aristotle uses 'justice' in two senses, as a genus and also as a species; and similarly for 'injustice' and the derivative terms. See Comm.⁷ of Section 4 in Book Δ.

⁴ To indicate the two kinds of justice, only examples of injustice are taken. Why? It is easier to notice grasping than the absence of grasping; for when one witnesses a just *act* in the narrow sense, he may not even think of the absence of grasping, but when he witnesses an unjust act in the narrow sense, grasping becomes evident. The absence of grasping, then, becomes better known to us through grasping; and similarly, justice in the narrow sense becomes better known to us through injustice in the narrow sense.

5

¹ We added 'which exist or are done', for the just or the unjust may be a man, or an *action*, or something else.

² An alternative to 'done' is 'which are ordered to be done'. The corresponding Greek terms differ slightly, and manuscripts disagree. The expression 'since the law orders' which follows suggests the second alternative. In either case, the meaning intended is clear.

³ A good man without qualification is one who has the virtues as given in the *Ethics*, and such a man can best exercise those virtues in the best state.

⁴ It belongs to *Politics*. 1276b16–7b32, 1288a32–b2, 1337a11–4.

⁵ To be a good citizen in a dictatorship, such as Nazi Germany, is to abide by its laws, some of which are bad; but such a citizen cannot exercise all the virtues, for the laws prevent it.

⁶ These are the citizens who come under a given constitution.

6

¹ Whatever can be greater or less than another thing can also be equal to some thing. For example, 5 is greater than 3 but less than 8, and it is also equal to the sum of 3 and 2. Now in transactions, what is given may be of greater value or of less value than what is received. Hence it is possible

for what is given to be equal in value to what is received. Fairness may be defined as an equality of what is given to what is received, and so fairness is a species or an application of equality. Evidently, just as the equal lies between the greater and the less, so the fair lies between what is unfair in excess and what is unfair in deficiency.

2 An alternative to 'depends on' is 'exists in'.

3 Perhaps by 'two things' he means (a) the things to be distributed or exchanged and (b) those who are to receive the things to be distributed or exchanged.

4 Perhaps by 'something' he means the things to be distributed.

5 One gets the greater part when he gets more than he merits; and similarly when one gets the smaller part.

6 These are the amounts distributed.

7 If there are three persons who are to share the goods, there will be three parts, and so six things in all; and similarly if there are more than three persons. Thus there are at least four things, two persons and two parts.

8 Perhaps he means equal in merit or value.

9 The equality indicated here is an equality of ratios. If the merits of two persons A and B are m_1 and m_2, respectively, and the amounts they receive are p_1 and p_2, respectively, then the form of the equality or proportion is $m_1:m_2::p_1:p_2$.

10 Of course, those who are unequal may receive unequal parts unfairly, and this happens when the ratio $m_1:m_2$ is not the same as $p_1:p_2$. See previous Comm.

11 From such an assertion it would follow that all free men should receive equal amounts or parts in any distribution, regardless of any other inequality, such as wealth, competency, effort, etc.

12 The literal meaning of the Greek term for 'aristocracy' is the rule by the best, i.e., by the most virtuous.

13 In arithmetic, all units are indivisible and without any difference in quantity or quality (1082b1–7). But in geometry and other fields one may choose a unit by convention, such as a length of one foot or a weight of one pound, but that unit is divisible as a nature because it is a magnitude (1052b20–3a7). Now proportion is applicable to both kinds of units, and even to irrational magnitudes (74a17–25); so it is applicable to all kinds of things which enter into the definition of justice.

14 A discrete proportion is one in which all four terms are different, like the proportion 2:3::10:15.

15 A continuous proportion is one in which the means are the same, like the proportion 2:6::6:18.

16 The things are the goods which the persons possess or receive.

17 Here, A and B are two citizens, C and D are the portions of good they receive or possess. The ratio $A:B$, then, will be the ratio of their corresponding merits; otherwise, the expression '$A:B$' would be meaningless or inapplicable to the proportion which will become a part of the definition of justice.

18 This proportion states that the ratio of what one person merits to the good he receives or is to receive is the same as the ratio of what another person merits is to the good he receives or is to receive.

19 In a proportion, if $A:B::C:D$, then $A:C::B:D$, and also $A+C:C::B+D:D$ and $A+C:A::B+D:B$. For example, 1:3::4:12; hence 1:4::3:12, $(1+4):4::(3+12):12$, and $(1+4):1::(3+12):3$. Similarly, let us assume that A merits three times as much as B and receives C or 30 units of a good while B receives D or 10 such units. Then $A+C$ seems to stand for the conjunction of what A merits and what he has received.

7

1 The term 'person' here means the person with his corresponding merit.

2 A continuous proportion has the form $A:B::B:C$. But justice is so defined that the two means of the proportion cannot both be persons or both be the portions distributed.

3 Let A receive C, and B receive D. If $C:D$ is greater than $A:B$, then A receives more than he merits. For example, if A merits twice as much as B but receives three times as much as B, then $C:D$ is equal to 3:1, and this ratio is greater than the ratio 2:1.

4 The definition of this good includes qualified as well as unqualified goods. The lesser of two evils is a qualified good, for it is not chosen for its own sake but is related to the greater evil; but a noble *action* is a good without qualification, for it is an end in itself and there is nothing evil in it.

5 If the amounts put into the business by two men are in the ratio 2:1, then the earnings should be distributed in the same ratio, other things

being equal. If more than two men are involved, then the earnings should be similarly distributed. For example, if three men contribute amounts in the ratio of 4:3:2, then the earnings should be distributed in the same ratio.

6 If, in a just exchange, A should possess C and B should possess D, but if A *acts* unjustly and possesses $(C + x)$ while B possesses $(D - x)$ after the exchange, then the law takes x from A and gives it to B, thus restoring justice. Both A and B are treated as equals, regardless of their status or other merits as citizens. Of course, there may be added costs or penalties in both civil and criminal suits, such as legal fees, punitive charges, imprisonment, and the like, but whether these should be included when $(C + x)$ and $(D - x)$ are corrected or not, or how they should be considered, is of secondary importance and need not be discussed here.

7 Honor, dishonor, injury, and other such qualities or *actions* or sufferings are not quantities and hence are not measurable. For practical purposes, however, the judge imposes on the guilty measurable penalties within the limits of the law. Such penalties may be payments to the victims or penalties to the state (such as cost to the state or imprisonment), or some other form of punishment if the victim is dead.

8 The Greek terms for 'divided into halves' and 'divider into halves' differ from the Greek terms for 'the just' and 'judge', respectively, by one letter only.

9 The gain and loss in the illustration are equal. But in voluntary and involuntary exchanges which are unjust, the gain and loss may be unequal. Further, in assigning a measured value to the gain and loss, one may have to consider also intention, or accident, or some other cause; for a man who kills another by accident is not so guilty as one who commits murder. These problems, however, are secondary in the present discussion of corrective justice.

10 We omit the sentence in lines 1132b9–11. It appears also in lines 1133a14–6, where it belongs.

8

1 It is assumed that by 'reciprocity' the Pythagoreans meant that what A does to B, whether good or bad, is exactly what B does to A. For example, if A gives to B or steals from B two dollars, then justice requires that B give to A or steal from A two dollars, respectively.

2 Hesiod, Fragment 174 Rzach.

3 In defining justice without qualifying the two kinds, the Pythagoreans failed to make the distinction between distributive and corrective justice. Moreover, the definition given does not fit either kind of justice, as commonly held. It does not fit distributive justice at all; besides, goods should be distributed according to merit and not equally.

4 The two examples indicate that reciprocity of the same thing is not always a good thing; and it is assumed that what is done with justice is a good thing.

5 If an *action* is performed voluntarily, the penalty or the reward should not be the same as that when the *action* is performed involuntarily. Hence the just as a reciprocity cannot be always good.

6 In buying, for example, one exchanges money for shoes, or shoes for flour, not shoes for shoes; and the way in which the exchange is done is indicated in the next paragraph. Again, if one voluntarily steals, the one who suffers should not steal in return; and the thief should not only return the money but also be punished for his *action*. Moreover, if A slanders B, and slandering is bad, B need not and should not slander A in return but may sue for damages, which is money, and so a good.

7 Perhaps 'this' means a reciprocity which is good.

8 To merely return the equivalent of a service is not sufficient; one must take the initiative later to show grace.

9 In other words, to combine A and D and also B and C in the Figure which follows is to say that A receives D from B, and B receives C from A.

10 If C is equal to D in worth, what is given is equal to what is received, and what is done is just. But if C is not equal to D in worth, what is done is not just. For example, if C is worth 1000 times more than D, what is done is not just, but if A receives one thousand D's instead of one D, what is done is just.

In general, let A's unit of product be P and B's unit of product be Q, and let m and n be such numbers that mP is worth nQ. In value, then, mP $= nQ$, and so $P:Q = n:m$; and the latter proportion is said to be equal. So if A receives nQ and B receives mP, what is done is just.

11 In the previous Commentary, what A gives to B is mP, and m is the quantity or number of units of his product while P is the quality or worth of each of those units.

12 In Commentary 9, if C and D were of the same nature, e.g., if both

were shoes, there would be no need for the exchange. The latter part of the sentence is abbreviated; it means: the artists who make the exchange are different in kind, and the worth of each unit of what one artist produces is for the most part not the same as the worth of each unit of what another artist produces.

13 P and Q are said to be comparable if there is some unit which can measure both. For example, if an apple costs five cents and a pear costs seven cents, then their worth can be compared, for they are measurable by the unit of one cent.

14 The measure posited arises from need; the need does not arise from the measure posited. So it is the need that causes the measure, not conversely.

15 Explicitly stated, perhaps the proportion is this: the worth per unit of the farmer's product is to the worth per unit of the shoemaker's product as the number of units received by the farmer is to the number of units received by the shoemaker in the exchange.

16 Perhaps the meaning of this abbreviated expression is as follows. To use an example, let A be a shoemaker, B be a shirtmaker, C be a pair of shoes, D be one shirt, and let C be worth four D's. If A were to give B four C's and to receive one D, B would receive sixteen times the worth of what he gave because of a double advantage: each unit of B's work is worth less than each unit of A's work and so, unit for unit, B would have the advantage; B would receive four units while A would receive one unit and so, in number of units received, B would have a second advantage. If equality is to be achieved, then, the second advantage should go to A, and he should give one unit but receive four units. Universally, then, the proportion should be, to use Comm. 10, $P:Q=n:m$ and not $P:Q=m:n$.

17 A mina was worth 100 drachmae, and a drachma was a monetary unit, like a penny or a dollar in the U.S.A.

9

1 Generosity is a mean between wastefulness and stinginess, bravery is a mean between rashness and cowardice; and in these habits and others like them there are two vices, excess and deficiency, and a virtue between them, and the habits belong to the man who *acts* according to them. This is not the case with justice, for it does not lie between two vices since there is only one vice, injustice, which may be regarded as an excess. The habit

corresponding to deficiency would be that through which the agent gives
more of a good to another and takes less of it for himself, or gives less of
what is harmful to another and takes more of it for himself; but in so
doing he *acts* not unjustly but, if anything, generously or something of
this sort. Moreover, unlike wastefulness and rashness, which harm the
agent but not necessarily others (1106b36–7a2), injustice of necessity
causes harm to someone other than the agent, for the agent gets more
good than he deserves but gives to another less than the latter deserves.
2 The two extremes are not two vices but parts of a single *act* of injustice.
By the same *act* one takes more and another is given less, and taking more
and giving less are extremes, or else the parts given to the patient and taken
by the agent are extremes, the one being less but the other more than
each deserves.
3 In other words, if one *acts* according to injustice, the parts distributed
are unjust in the manner indicated by the last Commentary.
4 In his usual manner, Aristotle starts from what is familiar or what is said
about a thing (1129a3–11) and proceeds to the nature of that thing. In his
work *On the Soul*, for example, he begins with the things, such as colors
and sounds, then proceeds to the activities or sensations of them, which
are seeing and hearing, and finally ends with the powers of sensation,
which are vision and power of hearing. Here, too, he starts with what is
just and what is unjust, then proceeds to the activities, which are *acting*
justly and *acting* unjustly, and finally to the dispositions, which are justice
and injustice.

10

1 To be unjust (for a man) is to have the disposition of injustice, which is
a vice. But one may perform an unjust *action* not from habit but through
the passion of the moment or from ignorance or from some other cause.
Hence one may *act* unjustly and still not be unjust.
2 The phrase 'what kind of unjust effects' in the initial question seeks a
distinction in the *actions* themselves and not in the agent's disposition. The
second question raises a doubt as to the propriety of the initial question.
The two different *reasons* for the *actions* of adultery which do not differ
as *actions* shows by example that, to call a man 'unjust', one should look for
something beyond the *action* itself. A more complete discussion starts with
1135a15, after some preliminary points are made with regard to justice.

³ 1132b21–3b28.

⁴ What is just without qualification as well as politically is what is just among citizens of a state as citizens, who are free men.

⁵ What is just in a limited or qualified sense or by likeness exists, for example, between husband and wife, father and son, and master and slave, but these are household relations and not political relations, i.e., not relations between free men in a state. 1253b1–8.

⁶ A man may *act* unjustly through injustice or not through injustice, but in both cases reason or the law should correct the unjust *act*.

Alternatives to 'written document' for the word λόγος are 'reason' and 'law'. A man may rule according to passion as well as according to reason, for his soul possesses both the rational and the nonrational parts. But if he rules according to reason or law, the nonrational part does not participate. Evidently, laws tend to exclude the nonrational part; hence rule by law is better than rule without law.

⁷ Perhaps these are the goods with which justice, whether distributive or corrective, is concerned and which are listed in 1130b1–4.

⁸ 1130a3–5.

⁹ Strictly, a slave is not a part of a master, for both are separate; but he is like a part in the sense that he belongs to the master just as money, though separate, belongs to the possessor of it. Free men, on the other hand, do not belong to each other, and unqualified justice, which is political, exists only among free men. And since no sensible man intends to harm himself as a whole or in part, whether the part be his money or his slave or his child, no sensible man can do what is politically unjust to himself.

¹⁰ 1134a30.

¹¹ 1134a26–8. They are equal in the sense that they are entitled either to rule or to be ruled politically. The problem as to who should rule is another matter and belongs to politics; but evidently to be free is a necessary but not a sufficient condition for being a ruler, and free men should have equal opportunities.

¹² Though a wife is (for the most part) inferior in intelligence to the husband, still she is regarded as free or almost so. Hence of the kinds of justice in a household, the one between a husband and a wife is closest to being political. Next comes that between father and child, since the child is potentially though not actually free, then that between master and

slave, and finally that between a man and his inanimate possessions. 1259a39–b4, 1260b18–9.

13 For example, it is naturally just in every kind of state not to kill or steal or commit adultery for its own sake or for selfish reasons. 1373b4–20.

14 This is a dialectical argument. The gods are eternal and changeless in character; hence they cannot change in their relations to each other and consequently with respect to justice, for such a change would make them better or worse and so subject to change.

15 That which exists by nature exists either always or for the most part, but that which exists by convention does not exist for the most part except in a qualified way. Men are born with five fingers by nature, and this is so for the most part; but men use a penny (or a dollar) as a unit of exchange not by nature, for the unit of exchange is different in different nations and is the same only in a qualified way, e.g., in the same nation and not universally.

16 Other examples which exist by nature for the most part are: *men* are physically stronger than women, men's hair is not gray when 25 years old; men like to have friends.

17 What is just according to men in a state is what is according to law, and a law may regard as just that prisoners of war become slaves. But this is slavery by convention and not by nature, for some prisoners are intelligent and such men should be free (1254a13–5b15). Existing laws, then, may deviate from what is naturally just. 1288a32–b6.

18 Perhaps such a universal takes the form of a statement or a law, which is universally applicable to many instances. The statement 'If X does Y, then he pays a penalty of Z dollars' may be an example, which is applicable to many individuals.

19 Perhaps what is unjust by nature or enactment is taken without reference to the presence or absence of intention or willingness on the part of the agent. If so, one would first attend to an *action* or distribution or whatever the thing may be and specify it as being just or unjust, and when the specification has been made, one may then proceed to inquire whether the cause was intention or passion or ignorance or something else.

20 It is assumed here that the thing is performed willingly, as indicated later in lines 1135a19–23.

21 How can the thing be unjust prior to its existence? One possibility is that the thing is potentially unjust, and this potentiality may also exist as a

universal statement of what is unjust. If so, then one who knows the statement would have no difficulty in specifying that an instance under that statement is unjust; but whether the cause of that instance is intention or passion or something else is another matter, and that which is unjust becomes an unjust effect when it is performed willingly.

[22] In other words, a restitution is a just effect which corrects an unjust effect or any outcome of an unjust *action*, but a just effect need not be a restitution; for a just effect may not be a correction, like a legal transaction or the outcome of distributive justice.

[23] Perhaps this refers to an intended or lost work on laws or in *Politics*.

[24] Perhaps 'by accident or by force' would be better, as stated later in lines 26–27. In either case, it is only by accident that one does something by force.

[25] 1109b35–1111b3.

[26] The term 'involuntary' is the contrary of 'voluntary', and so it is predicated of *actions* which may be also voluntary. But the pressure of our weight on the floor and getting old and dying cannot be voluntary; so neither are they involuntary. Thus the pressure of our weight and dying and getting old are things which occur but which are not in our power to do or not to do; so they are instances of a part of (a).

[27] The examples of what is done by accident come under (b), that is, they are things done under compulsion; and they are contrasted with the same things when they are done willingly and not under compulsion.

[28] For example, one of the parties may have forgotten that he was notified and claim that he was never notified; and in this case the dispute arises because of forgetfulness and not because of wickedness of anyone of the parties.

[29] More than that, he *acts* from injustice.

[30] Perhaps 'such unjust effects' means unjust effects caused by an *action* which is not only voluntary but also done by intention.

[31] The word 'only' is intended to exclude involuntary *actions*. Of course, the just *action* of a just man is not only voluntary, but also intentional.

[32] If *A* does *B* because of ignorance and *B* is a mistake, then it is only ignorance that caused *A* to do *B*, and *A* would not do *B* if he were not just ignorant. For example, if a hunter who is also a good man shoots at a quail but kills a man who is behind the bushes, he kills because of ignorance. But if a drunken driver runs over a man in ignorance (i.e., not

knowing he is doing so), then this drunkenness caused his ignorance and hence the accident, and so just his ignorance was not the only cause of the accident. Evidently, if A does B because of ignorance, he does B in ignorance, but if he does B in ignorance, he does not necessarily do it because of ignorance.

33 Perhaps by 'a physical passion' Aristotle means a passion which is inherited at birth or arises because of some sickness or mishap and which the possessor cannot control. Neither blame nor pardon applies to the possessor of such a passion, but he is usually confined and so prevented from doing harm. 1148b15–9a20.

11

1 It will be shown later that these have not been adequately specified.

2 Fragment 68 (perhaps from the Alcmaeon), Nauck[2].

3 Contraries are furthest apart, and since '*acting* unjustly' and 'being treated unjustly' are contraries, the expression 'always voluntarily', which qualifies '*acting* unjustly', should either remain the same or change to 'always involuntarily' when it qualifies 'being treated unjustly'; for the contrary of 'always A' is 'always non-A' and not 'sometimes non-A'. The argument is dialectical.

4 Generous people often prefer to take or accept less of a good than they deserve, for, by so doing, they *act* generously.

5 Just as a man who does what is unjust may do so by accident, e.g., under compulsion and not willingly, so a man who suffers what is unjust is not unjustly treated when the agent *acts* unwillingly.

6 Perhaps it is suggested here that, just as *acting* unjustly is voluntary, so being treated unjustly should be involuntary, if the two expressions '*acting* unjustly' and 'being treated unjustly' are to be the two relative or contrary parts of the same *action*. If so, then he who *acts* unjustly does so willingly but against the wishes of the other person, as will be indicated later.

7 The argument which gives rise to the problem is as follows. Since the incontinent man *acts* voluntarily and harms himself, and since it is he who is harmed and also he who *acts* voluntarily, it follows that he is harmed voluntarily or that he is voluntarily treated unjustly. This problem will be considered in Section 15.

8 This is stated as a problem, not a fact.

9 Although an incontinent man *acts* against his wish, it is he himself who *acts*; so he *acts* voluntarily and not under compulsion. How he can *act* voluntarily and yet against his own wish is still a problem at this point. Evidently, what he wishes is not what he *desires*; for he may know that drink harms him, but his *desire* may overrule his wish.

10 *Iliad*, vi. 236.

11 A generous man who gives *acts* voluntarily and not against his own wish. Further, he does something noble in exchange for something useful; and he is better off after the exchange, for what is noble is superior to what is useful.

12

1 Problem (4) was expressly raised in the preceding Section, 1136a33–4. Problem (3) has not been expressly raised; but since he who has more in an unjust distribution either takes more or is given more, one may raise the problem whether the man who is given more is unjust.

2 But can one *act* unjustly towards himself? If not, then the first alternative in problem (3) leads to a difficulty.

3 The Greek term for 'moderate' means also virtuous; and a virtuous man, being generous, will knowingly and voluntarily give more.

4 Since a *good* man gets what is noble, which for him is better than what he gives (what he gives is money or something useful), the difficulty indicated in Commentary 2 disappears.

5 For example, if he gives money, he is harmed financially but he is benefited ethically by his act of generosity.

6 If it is a judge who *acts* unjustly, the party receiving more than he deserves is not the one who *acts* unjustly.

7 The term 'unjust' applies to the part which is more than the receiver deserves.

8 A judge may pronounce the right judgement according to the evidence at hand, but the judgement might be different if all the relevant facts were known; so the judgement is legally right according to the evidence but actually wrong because not all the relevant facts are known. Perhaps the expression 'first kind of what is just' means what is equitable without qualification, and in this case all the relevant evidence would be in, the judgement would be right and equitable, and the laws would be good.

Again, the judgement may be right according to law, but the law may be bad, and so what is just may not be equitable.

13

1 One usually *acts* justly or unjustly by having the disposition of justice or of injustice, respectively. But it takes time and effort to acquire dispositions, and knowledge alone of what is just or unjust is not sufficient. Hence it is not easy to *act* justly or unjustly, unless one is just or unjust, respectively.

2 We speak of just laws, which are statements, as being just, but this is not literally true because no statement as such is either just or unjust. In the main sense, the term 'just' applies to the things which are distributed and to the manner of distribution and to those who are disposed to distribute things in a certain way; but laws are called 'just' in a secondary sense, that is, if they state that distributions should be just in the main sense.

3 Just as one must not only know what produces health but also have the art of bringing about health, so one must not only know what just things are but also acquire the disposition to *act* justly or to distribute things justly.

4 Occasionally a man might do what is unjust, not because he is unjust or *acts* unjustly, but for some other reason, e.g., under compulsion, even if he is just.

5 Men who think that it is in the power of the just man to *act* unjustly confuse the power of doing what is unjust with the disposition to do what is unjust. Although a just man can do what is unjust, the fact is that he will not do it.

6 The unqualified goods are mentioned in 1129b1–6.

7 In fact, gods can have neither excess nor deficiency in them, for gods are not affected by honors or money or property or any unqualified good with which justice is concerned.

14

1 Perhaps 'the same in an unqualified way' means the same in definition but different in name, or else, the same numerically.

2 Under extenuating circumstances a judge may be praised for bending the law somewhat, and though his *action* is on the whole better, he still

violates justice according to the law. In such a case, what is equitable is not what is just; and so one may argue that, since what is equitable is good, what is just is not good.

3 Since 'justice' has two meanings (1) one of which is equity but (2) the other which we shall call '*justice*', and since *justice* falls short of equity because it is written universally and so cannot be rightly applied to certain particular cases, then, though equity is not *justice*, both come under 'justice', and equity is better than *justice*. Furthermore, instead of saying that what is just is not good, we should say that both kinds of what is just are good but what is equitable is better than what is *just*. These distinctions will take care of arguments (a) and (b), which are raised in the text.

4 The term 'just' here means what we called '*just*' in the preceding Commentary, and this is what is just but not equitable; and the *just* and the equitable are the same generically, though not in species.

5 About some things in which there is much variation there can be no single universal statement which is always or perfectly right; and to take care of that variation would either be impossible or require volumes of law, which would make the administration of justice difficult and impracticable.

6 In other words, there are two *reasons* for which a universal statement falls short of what is right; and so there are two ways of making the correction: (a) the subject is variable, and in such a case the presence of an equitable person is always required; and (b) the legislator made only one universal statement for all cases, but he could have made two or three or a small number of less universal but more qualified statements to cover almost all those cases, and this would have been an improvement and closer to equity.

7 The unqualified just is the generically just, and it includes both the equitable and what we called '*just*' in Commentary 3.

8 The terms ἐπανόρθωμα and διόρθωμα are translated as 'correction' and they are close in meaning. Their difference in meaning, if any, is not clear from the context.

9 In equitable administration of the law by more than one person, the decree may take the form of a vote.

10 It is said that polygonal stones were used in such constructions, like the one in Tiryns, and leaden rules, by bending, were useful in measuring such stones.

15

¹ Since *A acts* unjustly towards *B* if and only if *B* is treated unjustly by *A*, and since by definition no one is treated unjustly against his own will (1136b3–9), if *A* commits suicide he is not treated unjustly because he suffers voluntarily. But since *A* does harm as a citizen and in violation of the law, he *acts* unjustly, and as a citizen he *acts* unjustly towards the state. So it is the state that is treated unjustly.

² In Athens the suicide's hand was cut off and buried apart from the rest of the body.

³ Since the phrase '*acting* unjustly' here applies only to the *action* done for the sake of gain, usually material gain, the fact that the *action* as a vice is bad for the agent should be distinguished from the gain which comes from that *action*. Perhaps 'wholly bad' refers to the *action* which as a whole affects the agent adversely in every respect.

⁴ Which other? If *A acts* unjustly, he takes more of a good and he gives less of it to *B*. So *B* is harmed. Now *A* himself is worse off by being unjust, but this relates his vice (injustice) to himself and not the unfair parts of the distribution because of his injustice. So perhaps 'this' refers to the unfair distribution which benefits *A* but harms *B* (usually in material goods), whereas 'the other' refers to the unjust *act* which harms *A* ethically though not materially.

⁵ Just as a coward is wicked because of cowardice and no other wickedness, so he who *acts* unjustly in a limited sense (i.e., only for the sake of gain, as stated in the previous Commentary) is bad because his *action* is unjust in that sense and for no other *reason*.

⁶ To *act* unjustly for gain is to take more for oneself and give less to another. But the same person cannot take more of a thing for himself and give less of that thing to himself at the same time; hence he cannot *act* unjustly towards himself, though by *acting* unjustly he is worse off ethically.

⁷ In committing suicide, *A acts* unjustly willingly or by intention; but he is not treated unjustly, as indicated in Comm. 1, and so he does not *act* unjustly toward himself. Further, he who *acts* unjustly may suffer the same harm later, but not at the same time; and in suffering the same harm he is not being treated unjustly. But this cannot take place in the case of a man who commits suicide, and so such a man does not *act* unjustly towards himself.

[8] As already stated, he who is treated unjustly suffers against his wish and not voluntarily.

[9] Whether for the sake of gain or for the sake of pleasure because of some ethical vice, one *acts* unjustly when he sleeps with another's wife or breaks into another's house or steals another's property. But it is false to say that he *acts* unjustly when he sleeps with his own wife or enters his own house or takes his own property.

[10] The specification was made in 1136b3–9.

[11] Vice is complete or unqualified if it is vice by intention, like intemperance; but it is close to it if it is not by intention, like the vice of a man who willingly does something bad because of passion or who knifes the one who angered him, for there is no deliberation here.

[12] He who is treated unjustly is not, because of this, bad or unjust.

[13] Art is concerned with what happens always or most of the time. It is not concerned with what happens by accident, for this happens occasionally and its nature is indefinite. A house may collapse because of defective materials or negligent workers or an earthquake or a bomb or termites, but this is not the architect's fault.

[14] The greater evil here is not the effect of the stumbling but the death that followed; but this happens infrequently.

[15] Perhaps 'metaphorically' applies to what we call 'just' between the rational and the nonrational parts of a man, as in the case of an incontinent man who wishes one thing but *desires* the contrary, while 'by similarity' applies to certain household relations. 1134a24–30.

[16] If 'in such discussions' is the correct translation, perhaps the reference is to Plato's *Republic*, 351E–352A, 430E–431B, 441D–442D, 443C–444A, where justice is discussed metaphorically or by similarity.

[17] The parts indicated are the rational and the nonrational, and the nonrational may be the part which *desires* or temper (the spirited part). If the rational part directs and guides the nonrational, then there is justice and harmony in the soul, but if the nonrational overpowers the rational, there is injustice and discord. In these cases, Aristotle thinks that 'justice' and 'injustice' are metaphorically used, and that when people speak of a man as being unjust to himself, they have in mind the metaphorical injustice of one part of the soul towards another part. Likewise, injustice by similarity may exist between a master and a slave or between a father and his child, or between a husband and his wife.

BOOK Z

1

[1] 1104a11–27, 1106a26–1107a27.

[2] The expression 'right reason' amounts to 'reason as a prudent man would define it', which is a part of the definition of ethical virtue (1106b36–7a2); for what is right as a mean in ethical virtue is something to be determined by a prudent man. Book Z is concerned with the intellectual virtues; and right reason and prudence, being intellectual virtues, are discussed in this Book.

[3] These are the ethical habits already discussed.

[4] 1094a1–2.

[5] In other words, such a statement is rather empty or too general, and further specifications are needed if one is to *act* in accordance with the mean.

2

[1] 1103a3–7.

[2] The nonrational part, as used here, includes the part which desires and which can listen to reason. 1102a27–3a7.

[3] The phrase 'the kinds of things whose principles' indicates that the investigation is not of the principles but of what follows from the principles, and so reasoning is required. Scientific knowledge, of course, is reasoned knowledge from principles which are invariable or necessarily true; and knowledge of things which may or may not be would be reasoned knowledge from principles which, or some of which, are true but not of necessity. We say 'some of which' in the latter case, for conclusions from premises which are not necessarily true require also principles of reasoning which are necessarily true, e.g., principles of logic.

[4] Just as colors, which are distinct in nature from sounds, can be sensed by vision alone, while sounds can be sensed by hearing alone, so Aristotle postulates two parts of the intellectual soul to correspond to two different kinds of things which can be known, those which vary and those which

are invariant or eternal. Each of these two parts is defined by means of its own objects, and so their definitions will differ; but no assumption is made here as to whether these parts of the soul, besides being distinguishable in definition, are separate in any manner or not. Again, any further subdivision to be made with respect to each of these two parts will not assume any separation.

5 The verb 'to estimate' is used as a genus of 'to deliberate', for we can make an estimate without deliberating; so deliberation is limited to only some of the things coming under estimation.

Since opinion is knowledge but not of that which is necessarily true, is every reasoned opinion an object of the estimative part of the soul? It depends on the meaning of the term 'estimative'. The term applies to the objects of deliberation, but the other objects to which it applies are not specified at present.

6 Perhaps a moving principle is meant. From the power of sensation alone no *action* can result, for such *action* requires or presupposes thought, and this is absent in brutes.

7 To acquire ethical virtue, the ethical good must be known and desired, deliberation must seek the means for it through reason, and desire must pursue it, and this pursuit must be repeated to produce the habit, which is the ethical virtue. Perhaps both knowledge of the good and knowledge of the right means of attaining it are instances of true reason.

8 The term 'goodness' here (and likewise for 'badness') is a genus for things which are ends in themselves, and its species are (a) intellectual truth, which is pursued as an end in itself, and (b) right *action*, which requires truth about what is good and the pursuit of it through right desire. Practical thought which is true, then, leads to right *action*, which is an end in itself.

9 In 1113a10–1 it is stated that intention is deliberate desire, and this brings out the fact that both desire and *thought* are principles of intention since deliberation requires *thought*. If desire is a cause as a mover and is itself moved by the object of desire (whether this be good or apparent good), which is a final cause and is regarded as unmoved, there seems to be a difficulty how the object of desire can move desire in the usual sense in which, for example, a man moves a chair, unless it is both a final cause and a mover. And if it is taken as a mover, it must exist in order to cause motion; but does an object of desire exist if it has not yet been produced?

For example, being a musician may be one's object of desire, if he is not yet a musician, and he may say "this moves me to do certain things"; but this expression seems metaphorical. On the other hand, if the object of desire does not move desire, what is it that moves it?

[10] Intuition is needed for the true principles, and *thought* for whatever follows from true or false principles.

[11] Apparently, intention is taken as a mover after the habit is acquired; for the term 'intention' may be given another meaning also, namely, a preliminary choice after deliberation but prior to the acquisition of the habit.

[12] Apparently, intention is posited as a moving cause, but it has an end in view as a principle, a final cause, good or bad. An intention is said to be good if its final cause is good, but bad if its final cause is bad.

[13] Productive *thought* is to practical *thought* as a product is to an *action*. But although a product, e.g., a knife, is not an end in itself but only an instrument, still it is an instrument for the sake of some end. So if that end is good, the product is good also, but it is relative to that end and is therefore a qualified good. Productive *thought*, then, has a qualified good as its end, for a product is a qualified end (the purpose of an architect is to build a house, which is a qualified end) but this good is instrumental to an unqualified good.

[14] Though both intellect and desire are principles of intention, Aristotle does not seem to take a stand as to whether the genus of intention is 'desire' or 'intellect'. There are dialectical arguments for both positions. (1) Since most men avoid the contemplative life, 'desire' should be the genus, and desire exists in all men. Moreover, when one desires what is bad, he does this in ignorance of what is good and not through his intellect, so while desire is present, there is failure of intellect to some extent. (2) Since man is distinguished from other animals by rationality, his intellect should be in the nature of intention. Moreover, each man is his his intellect, or his intellect most of all (1166a22-3,1168b34-5,1178a2-8).

[15] Fragment 5, Nauck.

3

[1] Since the object of opinion does not exist of necessity, opinion may be true or may be false. For example, if Socrates is sick at time T, this is not a necessary fact, for Socrates could have been well at T; hence 'Socrates is

sick at time T' is an opinion, even if true. As for belief, since 'belief' is a genus of both *knowledge* and opinion (427b24–7), some beliefs are false, and hence a belief may be false.

2 One attribute of *knowledge*, then, is that *knowledge* is true belief and that its object of necessity exists, e.g., it is necessary that the vertical angles be equal and that the three angle bisectors of a triangle meet at a point.

3 These are the things which may or may not be (or come to be). We shall also use the expression 'may vary' synonymously.

4 For example, when we see and talk to Socrates, we can truly say that Socrates exists; but when we neither see nor talk to him but are away from him, we cannot truly say that he necessarily exists, for he may be dead.

5 Things may exist of necessity but in a qualified way; but they need not be thus eternal. If a man exists, a human heart exists of necessity, but this necessity is qualified by the fact that a man exists; and since it is not necessary for a man to exist, it is not necessary for a human heart to exist of necessity or eternally.

6 71a1–17.

7 Induction is a starting point in time, for if a universal principle (e.g., an axiom) is to be learned from preexisting knowledge, it is so learned by induction or dialectically from premises which are more known to us. For example, by giving examples of the fact that equals result if equals are added to equals, that fact is induced to serve as an axiom or principle. Similarly, from the fact that Socrates remains Socrates when he gets sick or turns pale and from other similar facts one may induce the definition of alteration as a change of a substance with respect to quality.

8 By 'syllogism' here Aristotle means a demonstration, i.e., a syllogism whose ultimate premises cannot be demonstrated though they may be induced. Such premises may be axioms or definitions or hypotheses or whatever is immediately evident from them. For example, if a triangle be defined as a three-sided plane figure, it is immediately evident that a triangle is a figure.

9 This is another attribute of scientific knowledge, namely, it is knowledge demonstrated from principles.

10 71b20–72a5.

11 If one is not convinced that the principles which serve as premises are true, how can he be convinced that the conclusion is true? And if he is convinced that the conclusion is a true statement regardless of the princi-

ples, then he does not know the conclusion as a statement which has been demonstrated from principles; for he may know that conclusion as a mere statement, whether by hearsay or by strong belief from examples, or else from premises which are not causes of that conclusion. For example, a man may be convinced of the truth of 'a man can laugh' from the premises 'a man is an animal' and 'all animals can laugh', but the second premise is false and cannot be a cause of the conclusion; and then his *knowledge* of the conclusion is by accident, or better, he has no *knowledge* as '*knowledge*' is properly defined but only knowledge of the fact without the causes, or knowledge from premises not all of which are true. The nature of *knowledge* is fully considered in *Posterior Analytics*, 71a1–100b17.

4

¹ A man who has decided to build a house at a certain place may or may not build it; similarly, a man may or may not perform a noble *action*, such as a large donation for a good cause.

² In producing, one produces something, a product, e.g., a chair or a house, and this is for the sake of something else, e.g., sitting or living comfortably; but in *acting*, like behaving properly at a party, there is no product but only the *action* itself which is performed for its own sake.

³ Why the addition of the word 'true'? One may get the habit of producing things badly, like a bad architect, so we may use 'art' for the good habit and 'bad art' for the bad habit; and in the latter expression, the term 'art' is not used with its first meaning but the whole expression 'bad art' is taken as a single term which is contrary to 'art' as used in the former case. Instead of "bad art", some single term may be used, as in the case of 'cowardice', which is the contrary of 'bravery'. Evidently, bad art is not the same as lack of art, for a man who lacks art has not acquired either the habit of art or that of bad art. Perhaps Aristotle uses 'art' in two senses, for art with true reason and for bad art, the first sense being primary but the second secondary.

⁴ A seed has the moving principle within itself, and after being planted it grows into a tree by itself and into the kind of tree from which it came. A man cannot by any art make an elm seed grow into an oak tree. Likewise, by throwing a rock upward many times a man cannot by any art give the

rock the habit of moving upwards, for it always tends to move down-wards by its nature.

5 If one finds or inherits a fortune, he does so by luck and not by his art of making a fortune. So one may acquire a fortune by art or by luck; and he acquires it by art through one cause, his art, but by luck through any one of many causes which are accidental, for he himself may find it or his uncle may will it to him or someone else may make this possible. So luck is a cause which may involve *thought* or intention, but it is an indefinite or indeterminate cause, for it is variable. The moving cause of a house by its nature is an architect or his art, for architecture, which exists in the archi-tect as a disposition, by its nature causes that house; but the moving cause by luck may be a shoemaker or a musician or a baseball player, if the architect happens to be one of these. But neither does a musician build the house through his musical art nor do any of the others do so through their own art. It is by luck that the house is built by a man who is a musi-cian or a shoemaker, then, for it is not often that a builder is also a musi-cian or also a shoemaker. 195b31–8a13.

6 Fragment 6, Nauck².

5

1 In other words, a prudent man is able to deliberate well about whatever leads to one's happiness as a whole, and happiness as such requires things which are good as well as useful.

2 If there were an art which could be used for some good end, a man who could reason well towards that good would be called 'an artist' and not 'prudent'.

3 This inductive argument is dialectical. From the narrow meaning of 'prudent' Aristotle proceeds to the wide meaning of it.

4 A prudent man posits an end, e.g., happiness for himself. Now this end does not exist of necessity, nor will it exist of necessity, and the means to its attainment may also vary. So deliberation is of something which may or may not be. The principles of scientific knowledge, on the other hand, are necessarily true and do not vary; for the whole is of necessity greater than the part, the addition of equals to equals always yields equal results, and every motion requires a physical body or an underlying subject which remains unchanged. 1112a18–3a2.

5 Financial administrators are prudent in a narrower sense than states-

men, for they are prudent concerning only certain goods which contribute to the happiness of the citizens.

6 A man has become temperate through knowledge that it is good to *act* temperately and through habituating himself to *act* temperately in order to acquire the habit. In so doing, then, he has *acted* prudently.

7 Prudence, of course, extends to all the ethical virtues.

8 Perhaps it is assumed that the starting-point is happiness or a virtue or something which is good for a man, though a man may posit as a starting-point a bad end to be attained.

9 In other words, while there may be a good or a bad artist, both of whom require habituation to become artists, prudence in a man does not admit of these distinctions, for a prudent man always *succeeds* and prudence is always a virtue. The contrary of prudence, which is analogous to bad art, would be imprudence.

10 A good artist has the knowledge of both contraries and the skill of producing both of them; so if he errs in producing a work of art, he does so willingly. A prudent man, on the other hand, has good intentions by definition, so he cannot err as such.

11 Geometry is a disposition with reason, and one may forget it if he is not using it. But one does not forget prudence; either he is prudent or he is not.

6

1 There are principles which are necessarily true even of certain things which vary, but such principles are stated in a somewhat different form. For example, 'There is no science of accidents' and 'In a thing in motion there is a subject which remains the same' are such principles. In the first statement, accidents are variable, and the negative form of the statement makes the principle necessarily true. In the second, the principle indicates the existence of a necessary element (a constant subject) in a thing which moves, but it does not state that the whole thing itself remains the same.

7

1 Translated by John Crossett.

2 In order to define wisdom in the highest sense, Aristotle proceeds inductively from the limited usage of the term 'wisdom' in the arts and

takes the phrase 'most accurate' as the key to the definition. According to 87a31–7, a science is most accurate (1) if it investigates both the fact and the *reason* for it, (2) if it proceeds from fewer principles, (3) if it is prior and so leaves out the specific attributes of a subject and generalizes. Evidently, then, wisdom in the highest sense would be concerned with (a) both principles and what follows from them, with (b) fewer principles which are more universal and philosophical, and with (c) a good which is more general and better than that of an artist (i.e., with happiness which is an end in itself, and in the highest sense). In (a), a wise man must be convinced of the truth of the principles as well as be able to reason from them.

3 Intuition is the faculty which grasps true principles.

4 The term 'leader' seems to refer to intuition, from which scientific knowledge is demonstrated.

5 Divine beings are better than men; hence the science of divine beings is better than politics, which is concerned with men.

6 If wisdom is concerned with the most honorable objects, and if these are invariable and definite and eternal, then it cannot be prudence; for prudence in animals varies from species to species and is concerned with what may or may not be.

7 These are the stars, the Sun, and the Moon, for Aristotle regards these as indestructible, ungenerable, and eternal. 1071b3–6a4.

8 The understanding of divine beings is not useful for other things but is an end in itself and is the most divine activity for man.

If wisdom is such as defined here, how does it differ from metaphysics, which Aristotle calls 'first philosophy'? Perhaps they are the same, for in the *Metaphysics* 'wisdom' and 'wise' are used instead of 'philosophy' and 'philosopher' when the attributes of first philosophy are considered (982a4–3a23).

8

1 In the preceding paragraph, prudence was shown to differ from wisdom with respect to the variability or invariability of their objects, for prudence is concerned with certain things which may or may not be. In this paragraph, the knowledge of a prudent man is subdivided into universal and particular, and so it appears to differ from wisdom, whose objects are only universal; for a prudent man must perform an *action*, and this

necessitates universal knowledge to guide good *actions* and also knowledge of the particulars with which *action* terminates. Thus, to be generous is noble, but if *X*'s *action* towards *Y* is to be generous, *X* must have some knowledge of *Y*, and this is particular knowledge.

There appears to be some difficulty with respect to the objects of wisdom. If wisdom is both scientific knowledge and the intuition of the principles required for that knowledge, and if its corresponding objects are most honorable, then both its intuition and the knowledge which follows from that intuition are universal. But the Sun and the Moon and the prime mover of the universe are most honorable and are individuals, and wisdom concerning them is not universal since they are studied as individuals. To call the prime mover or the Sun 'a species' is to alter the meaning of this term; for a species is by nature predicable of many, but 'the prime mover' or 'the Sun' is not. Is wisdom concerned with some individuals, then, and can there be an intuition of them?

2 Let *A* mean chicken, *B* mean light, *C* mean healthy, and let *AB* mean that chicken is light, and similarly for *BC* and *AC*. Now *A* is taken as a particular and not as a universal term, and both *AB* and *AC* are taken as particular truths known by men of experience who have no knowledge of the universal cause. Such a cause here would be *BC*, and *AC* would be true because of *B*; that is, *AC* would follow from *AB* and *BC*, and this is the kind of knowledge possessed by the scientist but not by the man of experience, for the latter has no knowledge of *BC*. Now if the scientist does not know *AB*, he cannot know *AC* even if he knows *BC*, and so he cannot make a man healthy. A man of experience but without science, on the other hand, knows *AB* and *AC* but not *BC*, and all he needs to make a man healthy is *AC*, even if he does not know that *B* is the cause of *AC*.

Why is it necessary to know the cause at all, one may ask, if *AC* and *AB* are sufficient to make a man healthy. The problem is considered by Aristotle in the *Posterior Analytics*, but we may give a brief answer. He who knows that *B* is the cause of *AC* will know that *B* is the cause also of *PC*, where *P* means any other kind of meat, if he finds that *PB* is true. For example, if he finds that beef is light but pork is heavy, then knowing *BC*, he will conclude that beef is healthy but that pork is not, for lightness of meat is co-extensive with making a man healthy since the cause is co-extensive with the effect. 73a28–4b4, 99a1–b8.

There is another problem. The term 'chicken' is not a particular but a universal, unless it is applied to a particular chicken. If so applied, it is hardly useful; for once a particular chicken has disappeared, *AB* is no longer true, and a particular chicken is not enough to make many sick men healthy. It appears that 'particular' here refers to the ultimate or last species, or else to lower species, but 'universal' refers to something wider than such species and to a premise whose subject is the cause of the attribute; for even if an *action* performed or a thing produced is an individual, our knowledge of its nature and its main attributes arises by virtue of its form or species.

³ The knowledge meant is that of causes. Such is the knowledge of mathematics relative to the mathematical theory of light, for the truths in the latter science depend on those of the former, but not conversely. For example, the angle of incidence is equal to the angle of reflection for light rays falling on a mirror, i.e., $\angle 1 = \angle 2$ in that mirror. Why? Because $\angle a = \angle b$, angles *AMC* and *BMC* are right, $\angle 1$ and $\angle 2$ are compliments of $\angle a$ and $\angle b$, respectively, and all right angles are equal; and all these belong to mathematics.

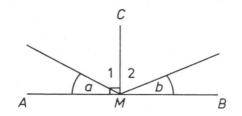

⁴ In other words, they come under the same genus, for both are concerned with things which may or may not be and can be performed by the agent who has prudence or knowledge of politics. But 'prudence' is a wider term, for prudence may be political or personal, and it may be comprehensive or in part; and the term is also analogously applied to some animals other than men. Moreover, their definitions differ; and they differ even if the term 'prudence' were limited to or were coextensive with political matters, for prudence and politics would be defined in different ways, though they would be applicable to the same subjects. 'Prudence' in this sense and 'politics' are like 'equilateral triangle' and 'equiangular triangle', which apply to the same objects; but to be equilateral is to have equal sides whereas to be equiangular is to have equal angles.

5 Legislative prudence is stated in universal terms. Perhaps within this prudence, too, there is a hierarchy. The lawgiver who establishes a good constitution is politically prudent in the highest sense. Then follow various legislative measures which differ in kind and in universality. Finally there are individual acts or measures to be voted on or to be carried out, such as a particular war, a national highway from *A* to *B*, the amount of money for the construction of a public building, and appointing someone to office.

9

1 A variant of 'prudence' is 'knowledge', which is a wider predicate.

2 Prologue to *Philoctetes* (Fr. 787, 78.2, Nauck[2]).

3 Perhaps 'these' refers to public servants.

4 Aristotle rejects the belief that only public servants are prudent. He admits, however, that for personal prudence and self-sufficiency a man must manage a household and do certain things as a citizen (1253a18–30), and these activities involve *actions* with or towards other men; but such *actions* are not those of a public servant.

5 Perhaps 'What has been said' refers to the fact that prudence, unlike science or wisdom, requires experience of many particulars.

6 There is a difference between a man who is just a mathematician and a man who is wise in mathematics. A mathematician takes the principles for granted, without reference to their truth or falsity, and has the ability to proceed to theorems. A man who is wise in mathematics, on the other hand, besides having ability to proceed to theorems, intuits the principles or has truth concerning them, and he is more convinced of them than of the theorems which follow.

Most modern mathematicians tend to say that the truth or falsity of the principles is irrelevant to mathematics and does not concern them, and that their interest lies in what is implied by a set of principles. If they mean what they say, then by definition they cannot be wise in mathematics, and it appears that they are not. For they say, for example, that the sum of the angles of a triangle may be more, or less, or equal to two right angles, depending on the set of postulates concerning a straight line, and their statement indicates that they are not intuiting or are not interested in intuiting a straight line as an ultimate species or in any other way. But a property of a triangle which varies in such a manner necessitates principles which vary, and in such a triangle one such principle is 'straight line', which becomes a genus having differentiae and is not an ultimate species. Euclid uses it as an ultimate species.

7 Aristotle is speaking in a condensed manner. What he means is that a prudent man requires more experience than a scientist or a wise scientist, for some experience is needed in any science.

8 A mathematician abstracts, that is, he selects certain attributes of bodies, such as continuous quantities and indivisible units, and leaves out the rest. But a physicist cannot do this, and so he requires more experience to arrive at the principles of physics.

9 When applied, mathematics too is subject to error. For example, the object drawn by an engineer is usually not an exact triangle, and so the area is usually not exactly half the base times the altitude. The error here lies in the particular and not in the universal.

The term 'heavy water' should not be confused with the modern term with its technical meaning; perhaps it means a solution, mainly of water and some ingredients, with specific gravity greater than that of water or with certain attributes which ordinary or pure water does not possess.

10 Intuition is of what may be definable or indefinable. For example, the straightness of a straight line as a quality appears to be indefinable and must be intuited directly without further analysis. The straight line segment, on the other hand, though definable, is a composite unity having straightness and continuity and end-points, and it must be intuited as such. The Greek text may also be translated as 'for intuition is of indefinable terms, of which there can be no definition', and perhaps the term 'intuition' is used in a generic sense to include both meanings. It is also used for axioms and other kinds of principles.

11 Does the term 'mathematics' mean applied mathematics or pure mathematics? If it means applied mathematics, then in 'X is a triangle' X is an individual whose nature can be judged with the aid of sensation; but if it means pure mathematics, X in that expression is an ultimate species without further differences and must be understood as such. I am not sure which alternative is correct, but I am inclined to take the first; and in this case, the kind of sensation (the term 'sensation' for Aristotle has many senses) is not that of the proper sensibles, i.e., of color or odor or sound or the like, but of an individual quantity or any mathematical object by means of the proper sensibles. 418a7–25, 425a13–b11, 428b22–5.

By 'in the direction of the particular' we mean the direction from the more universal to the less universal till the particular is reached.

¹² The Greek text is condensed and has a variant also. The translation given is my own interpretation. Another alternative to 'than to prudence' is 'than prudence is'. In either case, sensation of a particular mathematical object is closer to sensation of a proper sensible than prudence is; for prudence requires virtue and knowledge of the good besides the sensation that a given particular is of a certain kind.

10

¹ In other words, 'inquiry' is a genus of 'deliberation'.

² For lack of a better term, we use the two words 'good deliberation' as a translation of εὐβουλία. It means a deliberation which is successful and also has a good end. We may also use 'goodness of deliberation'.

³ Rightness and wrongness are contraries in a subject, such as an *action* in war, which can be right or wrong, or an opinion, which can be true or false. Scientific knowledge, on the other hand, is true by definition, and rightness or wrongness as applied to *actions* does not apply to it.

⁴ 'Rightness' is a genus of 'truth', and 'wrongness' or 'error' is a genus of 'falsity'. 'Rightness' applies to *actions* as well as to statements; when applied to statements, it is called 'truth'; when applied to *actions*, the *actions* are good.

⁵ The implication here is that the object of good deliberation is yet to be determined.

⁶ Rightness of deliberation, of course, need not be good deliberation (or goodness of deliberation), for he who deliberates rightly need not have a good end in view. This is brought out in the next paragraph. An example of this would be the use of successful means through deliberation to attain a bad end.

⁷ Just as a true conclusion may follow from premises which are false, whether some or all, so in order to attain a good end a man may reason through false premises or use evil means, such as stealing in order to help a friend in need.

⁸ In other words, one may take so long to deliberate well that it is too late for *action*.

⁹ Happiness is an unqualified end, but part of happiness is a qualified end

relative to happiness as a whole. For example, an *action*, which is an end in itself, may require good deliberation to be virtuous, but since it is not the whole happiness of a man it is a qualified end.

10 The term 'an end' is left unspecified; for that end may be qualified or unqualified. Thus the definition of a good deliberation is wide enough to apply to qualified as well as to unqualified ends. The end, of course, is good, and so are the means, for the true belief of a prudent man includes both.

11

1 Intuition and scientific knowledge are concerned with such objects.

2 These are things which a man who is said to be intelligent may or may not do something about, but they are not objects of art.

3 Since intelligence is concerned with objects of prudence and is true judgement, it cannot be bad but only good, for the end of prudence is good. Thus the adjective 'good' does not add anything when applied to 'intelligence'.

4 To use an analogy, an intelligent man is like a good judge in court who, having heard both sides, uses the law well in pronouncing judgment.

5 It is not clear in what sense the two terms are the same. Are they the same in meaning, the same in genus, the same numerically, or the same in some other way?

6 165b30–4.

7 For example, the law is stated in general terms and cannot take into account the various details that may be involved in a particular *act*, but a judge who has *judgment* is able to judge well by taking into account what the law cannot do because of its universal nature. The Greek word for 'forgiveness' comes from the Greek word for '*judgment*'.

8 The term 'forgiveness' does not quite bring out the proper meaning of συγγνώμη. Perhaps the phrase '*judgment* which, being similar to that of another person, is disposed to forgive that person' would be better.

12

1 All four faculties have particulars as their objects, and in this respect they do not differ; but they differ by being related to those objects in a different way, and this is indicated by the definitions of those faculties.

For example, intuition of a particular is just the knowledge of it, e.g., knowledge that this particular is a loaf or that this loaf is well baked (1112b34–3a2), and this knowledge is immediate and incapable of being demonstrated or proved from immediate premises, or, if it is proved, at least one of its premises is a particular; prudence, on the other hand, is concerned with the use of this knowledge for a good end.

2 An alternative to 'terms' is 'definitions'. For one thing, we know the indefinables through intuition; and likewise for the axioms, for these are indemonstrable. As for definitions, these too are indemonstrable and hence intuited, though some of them admit of demonstration but in a qualified way (90a35–4a19).

But do we use any of these intuitions in intuiting that A is B, where A is a particular? If A is a loaf, we should somehow know what a loaf is, whether analytically through a definition or in a less defined manner. Should we then say that some intuitions of particulars are complete but others are incomplete?

Indefinable terms are ultimates in the sense that they cannot be further analyzed, and, unlike sensible particulars, they are ultimate in the direction of universality. For example, 'quantity' is an ultimate genus and is more universal than its species, e.g., more universal than 'number' or 'magnitude' or 'triangle'. The same applies to differentiae, although ultimate differentiae are not as universal as ultimate genera. For example, 'continuous' is not as universal as 'quantity'.

3 Demonstrations are of necessary facts, as in mathematics, and what results is *knowledge*. Hence the principles of demonstrations, whether terms or definitions or axioms or hypotheses, are immovable or invariable, for if variable, the conclusions could not be necessary truths. Again, only bodies are movable, but terms and definitions are not bodies.

4 If A desires B, then A's final cause is to attain B; and since A may or may not attain B, his final cause may or may not come to be. And if A is to attain B, he must do certain things, and these too may or may not take place. Hence at least one particular and unproved premise must be used to prove a particular conclusion.

5 I am not sure what this part of the sentence refers to.

6 This sensation is not of the proper sensibles (i.e., of color and sound and the rest) but of the unproved particular facts requiring sensation of proper sensibles, as mentioned earlier and in 1142a25–30.

7 In scientific demonstrations, we begin with intuitions or what is in-demonstrable and invariable, and these intuitions are principles; so in this case intuitions are beginnings. In what sense, then, is intuition an end, and what does 'these' refer to? As an end, perhaps 'intuition' refers to the principles which are reached inductively, or to the things to be done in practical matters. In the latter case, if A is to do B, what is A's intuition? Is it of the fact that A should do B or of the fact that doing (or his doing) B is a good, or of something else?

8 Perhaps 'demonstration' here is used in a wide sense to include things which may or may not be. Whether the assertions or opinions of experi-enced and older and prudent men are undemonstrated or indemonstrable, it is true to say that, other things being equal, such assertions have greater probability of truth than assertions of younger men. For any demonstra-tion requires premises, and any indemonstrable or undemonstrated premise requires induction from experience, and older men have more experiences of similar particulars than younger men have. In general, then, while both older and younger men may know all the alternatives in a given case, older men would be better judges of the probability of each alternative.

13

1 The problems raised, of course, are based on misconceptions.

2 Wisdom is concerned with eternal objects and not with changing ob-jects; so it is not concerned with how we may become happy, for becoming happy is an example of a change or a becoming.

3 If a man is good (i.e., virtuous), he will do just and noble things, and so he does not need prudence according to this argument.

4 Merely to know what is just and noble does not make us *act* nobly and justly, for ethical *action* proceeds through ethical habit, and prudence is knowledge but not an ethical habit.

5 An ethical virtue is analogous to health or good physical condition; and just as mere knowledge of health does not make us healthy and so does not make us *act* in a healthy manner, so mere knowledge of an ethical virtue does not make us virtuous and *act* according to that virtue.

6 The object of prudence here would be wisdom, and prudence would have the function of ruling and ordering whatever is connected with wisdom. It would be strange, then, if wisdom, which is superior to pru-

dence by being concerned with eternal and more honorable objects, should turn out to be ruled by prudence.

7 The point made seems to be that the mere possession of wisdom and prudence, the first being knowledge of eternal things but the second of things which become and so may or may not be, is a thing worthy of choice by a man even if nothing else results from them.

8 What wisdom as a possession produces is not an object outside of it, like a chair produced by carpentry or health by the medical art, but its proper activity, which is pleasant and an end in itself and so a part of happiness. The same applies to prudence, though in an inferior manner.

9 Even the mere possession of a virtue, when a man is not exercising it, contributes to happiness; for even if he is not exercizing the virtue, he is more pleased by knowing that he possesses it than he would be if he did not possess it.

10 Which are the other three parts? Perhaps (a) the power of sensation, the power of desiring, and the power of thought generically, the last of which includes intuition and *thought* of what is necessary and of what may or may not be, or (b) the power of desiring, the power concerned with necessary things, and the power concerned with what may or may not be.

11 Clearly, the nutritive part cannot *act* because by its nature it cannot participate in thinking; and it cannot refrain from *acting* for the same reason, for refraining from *acting* is the contrary and not the contradictory of *acting*. That which refrains from *acting* does so after thinking, but that which does not *act* may not have any power of thinking, like a tree or the nutritive part.

12 1135a15–b6.

13 Perhaps this is the disposition to desire the good, not the apparent good; it is called 'natural virtue'. 1144b3–4.

14 This power is shrewdness, and its discussion follows.

15 In other words, when we speak of others as being shrewd or unscrupulous, what we mean is that they have shrewdness, which is common to both unscrupulous and prudent men.

16 The phrase 'eye of the soul' seems to mean shrewdness.

17 Perhaps this is the disposition to desire the good. Prudence, then, would be shrewdness in the use of successful means to bring about an end which is good.

18 The starting point of *action* is the end desired or the final cause,

whether good or bad, for this is the first thing one assumes or posits before proceeding to *act*. For a bad man, the starting-point is bad.

19 The relation is not stated in the proper order; for prudence is to shrewdness as virtue in the main sense is to natural virtue. Prudence requires shrewdness, and virtue in the main sense is best acquired if one has the corresponding natural virtue and so is predisposed to virtue in the main sense. A courageous boy is more likely to become brave when his thought develops than a boy who is afraid. Courage is like matter, the kind of matter which tends to become bravery or rashness (but not cowardice), and shrewdness is similarly related to prudence and unscrupulousness.

20 For example, we say that a boy who has courage and does not use it indiscriminately is brave, but he is only potentially brave; for bravery requires something else, the use of courage at the right time, place, circumstances, etc., and these require right reason, which is acquired at a later age.

21 Perhaps 'intellect' here includes right reason.

22 This is the intellectual part of the soul which is concerned with things which may or may not be, and both shrewdness and prudence are concerned with such things.

23 According to Aristotle, Socrates was right in thinking that virtue cannot exist without prudence, but he was wrong in thinking that virtue is prudence, for wisdom is a virtue but is not prudence, and an ethical virtue (in the main sense) requires prudence but is not prudence.

24 The phrase 'according to right reason' differs from the phrase 'with right reason'. Perhaps the difference is as follows. A man who *acts* according to right reason may do so without having deliberated about it at all or by being told to *act* in this manner, whereas a man who *acts* with right reason has reasoned out or knows his *act* by prudence. Thus the latter man has reasoned knowledge of his *act* but the former may not.

25 It is not clear whether 'ethical virtue' here means natural virtue, which prudence posits, or virtue in the main sense, which is the habit attained. Perhaps it is the former.

26 For example, a child may by nature be inclined to be fair and also be afraid, and his first inclination disposes him to become just while the second disposes him to become a coward.

27 A man who is good without qualification has all the virtues.

[28] Prudence without qualification is meant and not prudence only with respect to some virtues.

[29] Perhaps this is natural virtue.

[30] Wisdom is intuition and demonstrated knowledge concerning eternal and most noble things. Thus it is intuition and reasoning ability that come to know such things and not prudence. Prudence may do what is required for a man to have the opportunity to exercise his powers and become wise, but it does not itself intuit or reason out the objects of wisdom. For example, if a man has the potentiality for wisdom and desires it but cannot exercise that potentiality without a certain minimum of material means, it is prudence that will enable him to acquire those means. In this sense, prudence is like the medical art; for the medical art itself is not health as it exists in the body and does not make one act in a healthy manner but is the kind of knowledge which serves as a means to bringing about health.

BOOK H

1

¹ Up to this point, the ethical and the intellectual virtues and vices have been discussed. In an ethical virtue, reason is true and desire is right, but in an ethical vice, reason is false and desire is wrong; so an ethical virtue is the contrary of an ethical vice. In an intellectual virtue, intuition and reason are true; but in an intellectual vice, there is no truth. In the case of intuition, there is falsity if the opposites of the axioms are posited, e.g., if one thinks that sums of equals may not be equal, and there is absence of intuition if the thing is not intuited at all, e.g., if one has no intuition of redness or of straightness or of what is indefinable, like quality or relation. Further, the absence of true reason is contradictory to true reason, and it may be false reason or no reason at all, as in the case of brutes, which have no reason at all.

Now continence, incontinence, brutality, and what Aristotle calls 'divine virtue' (if this be the right term) are neither virtues nor vices. Continence is a mixture of virtue and vice, and so is incontinence; for a continent man has the right reason concerning a thing but the wrong desire for it, and so does the incontinent man. Brutality, on the other hand, goes beyond the limits of vice and may be regarded as not human. Divine virtue, too, goes beyond the limits of virtue and may be regarded as a perfection which is unattainable or hardly attainable by man but is possessed by the gods. Evidently, then, only virtue and vice have been treated, but the others are yet to be discussed.

² *Iliad*, xxiv, 258–9.

³ Virtues and vices are dispositions acquired by those who have reason. Since brutes have no reason, their dispositions cannot be virtues or vices but are of a different genus.

⁴ 1148b15–9a20.

⁵ In continence, for example, the intellectual part is true, and so it comes under the intellectual virtue, but desire is wrong, and so it comes under

ethical vice. So continence is a mixture of virtue and vice, and hence it belongs to the genus which includes both intellectual and ethical virtue and vice.

6 The facts as they appear are listed in Section 2 which follows; the difficulties are raised in Section 3.

2

1 Evidently, not all the opinions listed are true, for some of them contradict others.

3

1 Right belief, which is true belief, may be either *knowledge* or true opinion or prudence (427b24–7); and each of these will be considered with respect to an incontinent man.

2 Plato's *Protagoras*, 352b. By '*Socrates*' we mean the Platonic Socrates, who speaks for Plato.

3 The argument of *Socrates* denies the existence of incontinence, and this denial goes against the accepted and true opinion under (1) in the previous Section, namely, that a man sometimes does what he believes he should not do.

4 What obviously appears to be the case is that some men know that they should not do something, but sometimes they do it anyway. If so, and if it is true that a man always does what he knows to be best, then some men somehow change from knowing what they should do to not knowing what they should do; and one may inquire how this change takes place.

5 To have *knowledge* is to have strong conviction of certain things which are of necessity true. Whether the term '*knowledge*' as used here includes also axioms and other necessary principles does not affect the argument.

6 Since opinion is of that which may or may not be, Aristotle assumes here for the sake of argument that opinions, or at least some of them, are weak beliefs and do not possess the strength which belongs to *knowledge*.

7 To pardon such men is to go against an accepted opinion under (1) in the preceding Section.

8 If it is prudence which resists *desire*, in a continent man prudence will overcome *desire*, but in an incontinent man it will be overcome by *desire*.

But a prudent man always *acts* in accordance with right *desire* and is never overcome by wrong *desire*.

[9] 1140b4–7, 1141b14–6, 1142a23–9, 1144a30–5a2.

[10] A temperate man is virtuous, and by definition a virtuous man does not have strong or bad *desires*; so a temperate man is not continent, and this goes against an accepted opinion under (3) in the preceding Section.

[11] If not all continence is good, a temperate man is not necessarily continent, and this goes against an accepted opinion under (1) of the preceding Section. Perhaps the continent man is assumed to have strong *desires* in this argument.

[12] If the *desires* of a continent man are weak, whether good or bad, continence will not amount to much.

[13] If continence is disposed to abide by every opinion, it may be bad, and if incontinence is disposed to abandon every opinion, it may be good. But these consequences go against (1) in the preceding Section. Sophocles' *Philoctetes*, lines 895–916.

[14] Both imprudence and incontinence are vices, and to regard the combination of the two as a virtue is absurd, in view of the preceding Section. The reasoning gives the appearance that the combination is a virtue, and he who rejects this reasoning but follows the contrary of the conclusion because he likes that contrary better appears to be like the incontinent man who rejects what his reason tells him because he likes its contrary better.

[15] It is not clear whether this is another example of a paradox or a separate argument. An intemperate man is thought to be worse than an incontinent man, but the argument appears to conclude the opposite.

[16] If incontinence is concerned with all kinds of objects, then the same man will be both continent and incontinent, which seems paradoxical; for he may be continent with respect to honor but incontinent with respect to anger. Is there an incontinent man in an unqualified sense, then, just as there is a being in an unqualified sense? A substance is a being in an unqualified sense, but an attribute is not; so perhaps incontinence in an unqualified sense is limited to certain things only.

4

[1] Perhaps this part of the sentence means that if a difficulty is solved,

then the truths required for the solution of that difficulty have been discovered. For example, is intemperance the same as incontinence? If we know that an intemperate man deliberately chooses to pursue the excesses of bodily pleasures but the incontinent man yields to such pleasures but not deliberately, then we have answered the question.

2 If we attend to the objects with which a continent or an incontinent man is concerned, we leave out the manner in which he is disposed, i.e., we are not concerned with whether he is pained or pleased; and in this respect, perhaps there is no difference between a continent and a temperate man, or between an incontinent and an intemperate man. But the continent man is pained by not following his *desires* while the temperate man is pleased, and in this respect they differ in the manner in which they are disposed; and similarly for the incontinent and the intemperate man.

3 One may still define incontinence so as to include all kinds of objects, but then at least three difficulties arise: (a) the term 'incontinence' may not have been used at that time in that sense; (b) the inclusion of all kinds of objects may make the term defined equivocal or analogous, and not a unique species; and (c) some of the objects defined may already have terms for them.

4 If an incontinent man were disposed in any manner whatsoever towards the objects, some incontinent men would be intemperate (those who deliberately choose to pursue excesses of bodily pleasures) but others would not be intemperate (those who do not so choose deliberately). But then this distinction would still have to be made, and we will be back to incontinence in the limited sense, which is more elementary and so more of a principle.

5 The problem of whether it is possible for a man to be incontinent in this limited sense still remains.

5

1 This view is raised in lines starting with 1145b29.
2 Perhaps the reference is to the firm but false opinion of Heraclitus that all things are in a state of flux, or to Heraclitus' statement that although true reason is common, most men live as if they had a private wisdom (Fragment 2 in Diels-Kranz). Some opinionated but mistaken men, we may add, are more convinced of their opinions than some scientists of

their *knowledge*. Many, if not most, modern mathematicians are hardly convinced of the truth of mathematical axioms and the theorems which follow from them, for they appear to avoid the problem of whether axioms are or should be true.

3 A man may *know* what he should do under certain circumstances (and this is universal knowledge) but fail to apply his *knowledge* at a particular time because of a previous habit or momentary forgetfulness or some other reason. Thus he may possess *knowledge* of what he should do but not use it in a particular case.

4 Perhaps the reference is to premises which are universal and those which are particular. But how can one *act* contrary to *knowledge* if he is using the universal but not the particular?

Now *knowledge* is universal; so since it is demonstrable, a man may be using one of its premises (whether itself demonstrable or not), which is universal, but the opposite or contrary of the other universal premise, thus obtaining a conclusion which is contrary to *knowledge* and is so used. Perhaps there is another alternative. One may be using but mis-applying his *knowledge* because he is mistaken about the particular. He may *know* that it is generous to give to the poor under the proper circum-stances but be mistaken when he gives to X; for X may not be poor or the circumstances may not be proper, and his *action* in this case violates his *knowledge* through misapplication.

5 Perhaps there is some corruption in lines 1147a4–7, and our trans-lation is based on our interpretation. The premise 'dry food benefits every man' is universal and 'X is a man' is particular, and the universal term 'man' is predicated of X, who is the agent. The premise 'such-and-such food is dry' is universal and 'Y is such-and-such' is particular, and the universal 'such-and-such' is predicated of Y, which is a particular thing but not an agent. The agent may be using the universal premise in each case, but he may not, for some *reason*, be using the corresponding particular premise, whether he possesses it as knowledge or not. If so, then he may *act* in violation of the corresponding conclusion in each case, i.e., in violation of 'dry food benefits X' or of 'Y is dry food', or ultimately of the conclusion 'Y benefits X', for his *action* must be directed at Y.

Another problem seems to arise. The agent may be aware of all the premises as statements, but fail to use them as premises for the conclusion according to which he is to *act*. He may then fail to *act* according to the conclusion because of inability to reason. Thus one may know a statement in two ways: (a) as a statement which is true (if true), and (b) as a premise of a conclusion, i.e., both as a true statement and as a part of a syllogism which results in a conclusion. Perhaps Aristotle assumes that a statement, when in use for the sake of *action*, is taken in sense (b), unless it is a conclusion.

6 There is nothing absurd in *acting* against one's *knowledge* if the agent is not using all the knowledge required for his *action*; but it would seem strange if he were using all that knowledge but *acted* in violation of it. Perhaps it is assumed here that only knowledge determines an *action*; for *desire* too may determine an *action*, and if both *knowledge* and *desire* are present, then the stronger of the two prevails.

7 Some beginners in geometry, for example, can state theorems accurately from memory but are unable to apply them to original problems. Their usual statement "I understand the theorem but I cannot apply it" indicates weak understanding or no understanding of the theorem.

8 The analysis of the premises needed to form a conclusion and to act according to it is a matter of logic, and so the corresponding argument is logical. Now the argument here will use premises from physics, in particular, from psychology or the nature of man.

9 The phrase 'a unity is formed' appears to refer to the formation of the syllogism, whose conclusion here is about a particular.

10 The aim is knowledge in this case, and one does not go beyond the conclusion.

11 In a productive science, one produces something according to the conclusion, but in a practical science, one *acts* according to the conclusion. It is only in a theoretical science that one stops at the conclusion as an end in itself.

12 If our wish has its way, then from 'X is sweet' and 'we should not taste sweets' there follows 'we should not taste X', and we avoid tasting X; but if our *desire* has its way, then from 'X is sweet', 'whatever is sweet is pleasant', and 'whatever is pleasant we should taste' there follows 'we should taste X', and we proceed to taste X.

13 It is evident from the preceding Commentary that the incontinent man proceeds somehow syllogistically. Moreover, the premises on which he *acts* are not contradictory; for he is not using but only possessing poten-

tially the premise 'we should not taste sweets', which is contradictory to the conclusion which follows from 'whatever is sweet is pleasant' and 'whatever is pleasant should be tasted'. Thus the beliefs 'sweets should be tasted' and 'sweets should not be tasted' are used by different parts of the soul, and not simultaneously; they are like the power to walk and the power not to walk, which exist in the same man but only potentially and cannot be used simultaneously.

14 By definition, an incontinent being wishes one thing but *desires* the contradictory. Hence brutes cannot be incontinent, for they have *desires* but no wishes.

15 It is an admitted fact that *knowledge* is either dormant or overruled by *desire* during the *action* of an incontinent man; but the *reason* for the change from dormancy to awareness of that *knowledge* belongs to physiology and not to ethics. So Aristotle limits himself to the fact here and does not concern himself with the *reason* for that fact.

16 Perhaps there is some corruption in lines 1147b9–17, and our translation depends on our understanding of the thought. What the incontinent man senses is that *X* is sweet; but he is not using his *knowledge* of the fact that sweets under certain circumstances should not be tasted, either because that *knowledge* is dormant or faint or because it is overruled by his *desire*. Instead, he is using '*X* is sweet' and 'what is sweet is pleasant', perhaps with the added opinion that whatever is pleasant is good; and since his *desire* is of the pleasant, he proceeds to taste *X*. Now what Socrates ought to show is that the incontinent man has no *knowledge*, for, just before *acting*, he is using not *knowledge* but opinions, namely, he is using '*X* is sweet', and 'whatever is sweet is pleasant and good'. Aristotle grants that the premises used are opinions but maintains that it is possible for *knowledge* to be possessed but violated because it is dormant or overruled; and because of this possibility, a distinction arises between an incontinent and an intemperate man.

6

1 Why are pleasures divided into those which are necessary and those which are not necessary, and what is a necessary pleasure?

According to 1015a20–6, that is necessary to a man without which he cannot live or cannot live well. Without the necessary pleasures of food and water, of course, a man cannot live; and without sexual relations, the race cannot survive. But a man can live or live well without victory or honor or riches or other such things; for although these are pursued for their own sake, they are not the chief goods in one's happiness but add only little to it.

Evidently, the terms 'continence' and 'incontinence' are limited to the necessary pleasures, and probably they were so used for the most part in the Greek language, but sometimes also for pleasures which are not necessary. When used in the latter sense, then, they were not used in the main sense but secondarily or in a qualified sense and in virtue of a similarity, for in both senses the similarity is the fact that in incontinence there is excess contrary to reason but in continence there is moderation.

2 According to some commentators, the reference is to the victor of the Olympian games in 456 B.C., whose name was Ἄνθρωπος (='Man'). If the definition of a man be 'rational animal', that of Man would also contain some accidental qualification, for Man is a man with certain particulars or accidents peculiar to him.

3 Intemperance errs both in *desire* and in intention, for it is deliberately pursued; and as such it is a vice without qualification. But incontinence errs only in *desire* and by the fact that *desire* overpowers one's reason. Incontinence, then, is not so bad as intemperance, and one may regard it as a qualified vice or as partly a vice.

4 The four habits mentioned are grouped together because of a single thing, namely, they are all concerned with the same objects, the necessary pleasures and pains.

5 Perhaps 'man' here refers to an incontinent but not intemperate man (with weak or no *desires*), for it is he, rather than an incontinent man with strong *desires,* who is closer to an intemperate man.

6 An alternative translation of the sentence up to here is: "Hence we should call 'more intemperate' ...pains rather than".

7 Perhaps the word 'generically' in 'generically noble' indicates that the *desires* are noble and good not specifically or without qualification but when directed or pursued moderately and not in excess.

8 Perhaps the reference is to lines 1147b23–31, where the intermediates are things which produce the necessary pleasures. The contraries of things which are by nature choiceworthy are not specified but are implied; and

such are things which are by nature disgraceful, like procuring, adultery, and the like.

9 According to the story, Niobe had many sons and many daughters, six of each or seven of each, and boasted of being at least equal to Leto, who had born only two children, Apollo and Artemis. Thereupon Apollo and Artemis killed all the children of Niobe.

10 According to one source, Satyrus, a king of Bosporus, loved his father so excessively that he deified him.

11 A bad actor is not bad as a man, i.e., bad in an unqualified way, but only bad in a qualified way, i.e., bad in acting.

12 The definition of incontinence is such as to include the bodily pleasures, for incontinence is a disposition to *act* according to one's *desire* but in violation of one's reason concerning the bodily pleasures.

A logical problem seems to arise. Aside from linguistic convention, is there any objection against defining incontinence as a disposition to *act* according to one's *desire* but against one's reason? This would be a general definition, and each species of incontinence would contain its own qualification, i.e., 'with respect to bodily pleasures', 'with respect to honor', 'with respect to anger', etc.

Now incontinence with respect to bodily pleasures should be not only avoided but also blamed (1148b5–6); and if this is not the case with the other species of incontinence (1148b2–4), perhaps the qualifications used as differentiae of incontinence will not be coordinate by nature (14b33–5a7). Moreover, incontinence with respect to pleasures always goes against reason, and doing so amounts to going against reason without qualification. But incontinence with respect to temper acts partly against reason and partly with reason and is thus qualified; for the man who is incontinent with respect to anger feels wronged in some way or other, and so he regards it as just to be angered and reciprocates, but he is angered without considering fully the causes and the consequences, like a dog which barks when it hears someone coming without knowing that it is his master. 949b13–9.

13 Lines 1149a12–5 seem to suggest that Phalaris was using a boy's flesh for food and was an unusual sex pervert.

14 According to Aristotle, women are by nature inferior to men, so their disposition to be passive is not the result of any vice but follows from their nature.

¹⁵ An excessive disposition is one which goes beyond the limits of vice, and so it cannot even be a vice. Thus neither snakes nor tigers are vicious, for they do not choose to do things by deliberation, so 'vicious' is applied to them by similarity. But the terms 'dangerous' or 'harmful' would be proper predicates of them.

7

¹ The term 'temper' is used not in a personified manner but to signify a formal cause or part of such a cause; and similarly for *'desire'* which follows.

² Temper, by concluding that it must fight insult or slight because it is right to do so, partakes of reason but, by concluding hastily without full knowledge of the situation, leaves out part of the reason.

³ *Desire* rushes to enjoy a pleasurable thing without the thought of whether this would be right or not.

⁴ One may eat or drink to excess because of excessive *desires*, or he may eat or drink, whether in excess or not, things which are even harmful to himself. *Desires* which are excessive or not necessary are not common, or they are not too common but are peculiar to certain individuals or are acquired. 1118b8–27.

⁵ Author unknown.

⁶ *Iliad*, xiv. 214, 217.

⁷ The reference seems to be to the incontinence through *desires* which are excessive or are of things which are not necessary.

⁸ He who *acts* with anger has been provoked; so he *acts* justly, or partly so because he has been provoked. But he who insults another *acts* unjustly without qualification, and he *acts* with pleasure and not from pain. Thus bad *actions* which give the agent pleasure are more unjust and worse than bad *actions* which are accompanied by pain, and so incontinence through *desire* is worse than incontinence through temper. Incontinence through *desire*, then, is more likely to be incontinence without qualification.

⁹ 1148b15–9a1.

¹⁰ These are virtues and vices, and also continence and incontinence.

¹¹ Perhaps 'in magnitude' means within the limits of opposite vices, but not outside those limits like brutality.

¹² Brutality in certain animals exists by their nature, so such disposition

is not a departure from their nature; but vice exists in men not by nature, for man by nature has reason and vice is a corruption of reason, since it violates reason. Hence vice is worse than brutality. On the other hand, an animal with brutality (e.g., a snake or a tiger) is ordinarily more dangerous than an evil man.

[13] Cyanide is lifeless, but it can be more deadly than most evil men. On the other hand, an evil man can initiate *action* and cause harm, whereas cyanide cannot do so as a mover but causes harm when taken by force or willingly or without knowledge.

[14] Injustice is a quality, and by itself it does not initiate *action*; it is the unjust man who does this, and he does it deliberately and through injustice.

[15] An evil man has more power for harm because of his intellect; e.g., a madman in power may start an atomic war. A tiger or snake, on the other hand, though ordinarily more dangerous than an evil man, is limited to one way of causing harm.

8

[1] Perhaps 'as excesses' refers to the necessary pleasures, like food and drink, which are necessary but are pursued excessively, while 'through intention' refers to those which are not necessary or which are necessary up to an extent, but are deliberately chosen.

[2] The term 'incurable' here means difficult to cure but not impossible to cure.

[3] Such a man was called 'insensible' in 1107b7–8.

[4] The incontinent man pursues pleasures in order to avoid the pain of his strong *desire*, even if he thinks he should not pursue those pleasures; the intemperate man, on the other hand, thinks he should pursue excessive pleasure, regardless of whether he is or is not pained by his *desire*.

[5] This is incontinence.

[6] In both cases, the opposition arises not from thought but from the strength of *desire* relative to that of thought. In the incontinent man, *desire* masters thought, whereas in the continent it is thought which masters *desire*. Analogous remarks apply to the soft man and to the enduring man.

[7] Mastering the pain of a strong *desire* for pleasure, which is what the

continent man does, is more difficult than withstanding the pain of the enduring man; and what is more difficult is generally better.

⁸ Just as continence has been compared to endurance, so incontinence may be compared to softness. Accordingly, the man who is soft is worse than the incontinent man; for the incontinent man is overcome by the pain which accompanies a strong *desire* for pleasure, whereas the man who is soft is overcome by a weak *desire* to avoid pain.

⁹ According to the Aldine scholiast, Philoctetes broke down and cried 'cut off my hand'. Cf. Nauck², p. 803.

¹⁰ Nauck², p. 797.

¹¹ Perhaps a musician at Alexander's Court.

¹² By nature women are not as physically strong as men; and it is by nature that they cannot endure the same physical hardships as men can.

¹³ 1127b33.

¹⁴ It appears that the incontinence here may be unqualified or qualified; for, from what follows, those who do not abide by what they have deliberated upon may be incontinent with respect to bodily pleasures and so are incontinent without qualification, whereas the sharp-tempered are incontinent with respect to temper and so are incontinent in a qualified way.

9

¹ 1150a21.

² 1146a31–b2.

³ Intemperance is a vice, for the possessor of it deliberately chooses it.

⁴ Why is incontinence not continuous? Since reason and passion conflict in the incontinent man, perhaps his passion does not always master his reason; besides, he is curable, and so he is not like the intemperate.

⁵ Why is the genus of incontinence different from that of intemperance? Intemperance is a vice, and 'vice' is a genus. Now a man with a vice thinks that a bad *action* is good, whereas an incontinent man thinks that such *action* is bad. Since the two kinds of thinking are generically different, incontinence differs generically from intemperance.

⁶ Those who lose control of themselves are the impetuous, whether sharp-tempered or irritable, and they yield to a strong passion, whereas those who are weak yield to a weak passion. But those who yield to a stronger passion are more pardonable than those who yield to a weaker

passion; hence those who lose control of themselves are better than those who are weak.

⁷ Though overcome by passion, which should be weaker than reason, the incontinent man will still regain right reason, e.g., after drinking, and will again think rightly after his drunkenness.

⁸ Perhaps 'virtue' here means qualified or natural virtue, or else right thought of what is good, but not virtue in the main sense, for the incontinent man does not possess the habit of *acting* in accordance with his right thought.

⁹ In mathematics, the principles of demonstration are axioms, hypotheses, and definitions, and, as principles, they are indemonstrable and must be intuited as true. Similarly, virtue posits as an indemonstrable principle that certain *actions* are good (and good *actions* lead to happiness), while vice posits an opposite principle; and an incontinent man posits the same principle as a virtuous man does, although he goes contrary to it because of passion. Thus an incontinent man posits a principle which is true and good, while an intemperate man rejects that principle.

¹⁰ To teach is to proceed to impart knowledge by starting with premises and leading to a conclusion. A principle, of course, cannot be a conclusion of a demonstration, so it cannot be taught demonstratively. It might, however, be taught dialectically, but in such a case the premises would be dialectical and not scientific.

¹¹ This principle in a man is virtue, whether natural or acquired by habit, which is disposed to and posits right *action*; and the principle as final cause which virtue posits is the goodness in such *action*.

¹² This is his thought of what is right to do.

¹³ This is the continent man, who, though urged by his passion, restrains himself because his right reason overrules his passion. The contrariety in the continent and incontinent man lies not in their thoughts but in their *actions*. Similarly, the goodness and badness in the two men lie only in their *action*, for both men have the right thought as to what they should do.

¹⁴ Continence is good in a qualified way, for *desire* in a continent man is bad; and incontinence is bad in a qualified way, for thought of what is right to do is good.

10

¹ 1146a16–31.

² Reason may be either true or false; but intention may be either right (in which case what one deliberately chooses is good) or wrong (in which case what one deliberately chooses is bad).

³ Here, what the man desires essentially (i.e., for its own sake) is *B*. But since *A* helps in attaining *B*, *A* is chosen or pursued by being so related to *B* and not for its own sake. *A*, then, is an attribute (here it is a relation) or an accident of *B*. If *A* is a false reason but is thought to be true, it is an accident.

⁴ Just to depart from any opinion does not make one incontinent; for it is when in his *actions* he departs from certain true opinions that he is incontinent without qualification. So if he departs from any opinion, he may be said to be incontinent in a qualified way or by accident.

⁵ The continent man clings to an opinion which is true whereas the obstinate man clings to his opinions regardless of their truth; so the latter is like the former just in clinging to opinion.

⁶ The incontinent man yields to pleasures which are not good. Similarly, the opinionated man yields to the pleasures of adhering to his own opinions, although such pleasures are not good because of the falsity of those opinions. So both yield to bad pleasures rather than to what is good or true.

⁷ See Comm. 13 of Section 3.

11

¹ Right reason states that one should be pleased by bodily things in moderation, but neither in excess nor in deficiency. 1119a5–11.

² Incontinence, continence, and the third habit just indicated have one thing in common, namely, right reason and wrong *desires*; but they differ in their *desires*. So none of them is simply a virtue or simply a vice, though continence is perhaps better than the other two. For virtue has right reason and right *desire*, and vice has wrong reason and wrong *desire*.

³ The kinds of contrarieties between a virtue and the two corresponding vices (excess and deficiency) and the reasons for them are discussed in 1108b11–9a19.

⁴ The incontinent man has right reason but the intemperate man has wrong reason.

⁵ 1144a11–5a11.

⁶ 1144a23–b4.

7 He who understands knows the causes and can apply his knowledge to corresponding situations or use it for further knowledge; but if he is asleep or drunk he cannot do so, and he is like the man who knows what he should do but forgets to do it.

8 He knows that he does what he should not do; and he knows that he does it because of his strong *desire*.

9 Perhaps potential intention is meant, for when the man *acts*, this intention is not actualized.

10 After deliberation, he wishes to be just, but because of his strong *desire* he does what is unjust, although he is not unjust.

11 This is the incontinent man because of *desire*.

12 Burnett: Fr. incert 16; Ross: Fr. 67 Kock. The state sets down its own laws, but it also chooses to disregard them.

13 The wicked man, unlike the half-wicked, resembles a state which deliberately chooses to posit wicked laws and then uses these laws.

14 Since character is a second nature, so to say, by imitating or by being like nature (for nature always acts in the same way while character acts for the most part), and since character exists because of a nature or only in that which has a nature, and nature is prior in existence to character, it is easier to change character than to change nature. 1370a6–9.

15 Fr. 9, Diehl. Translated by John Crossett.

12

1 Since the political philosopher directs man's end, which is the good, and since pleasures and pains are either good or bad, the political philosopher should study pleasures and pains.

Primarily, man's end or good without qualification is happiness. There are also qualified goods. Thus a medical instrument is good for surgery, and a knife is good to cut bread with; and these are goods relative to certain ends, and they may also be used badly, e.g., to injure someone. Is virtue a qualified or an unqualified good? It seems to lie between; for (a) it is relative to happiness since it is not itself but the use of it or the activity according to it which leads to happiness, but (b) neither itself nor the use of it can ever be bad, and the possession of it seems to be good.

2 Since the political philosopher directs man's end, i.e., happiness, which is activity according to virtue, and since virtue is concerned with pleasures

and pains, the political philosopher should examine pleasures and pains.

³ This statement is a dialectical argument.

⁴ Usage, too, confirms the necessity of examining pleasure and pain. According to Aristotle, the word μακάριος (= 'blessed') is an abbreviation of μάλλιστα χαίρειν, whose translation is 'most joyful' and it is a generally accepted opinion that a blessed man is one whose enjoyment is the greatest, as in the case of the gods.

⁵ If (a) pleasure in itself is partly or wholly good, then either pleasure and goodness are identical, or one of them is like a genus of the other, as 'animal' is the genus of 'man'; and if (b) pleasure is an attribute of goodness, it would be similar to such attributes of a man as sickness, whiteness, and being in Athens. These thinkers deny both (a) and (b). An alternative of 'in itself' is 'for its own sake'.

⁶ The building of a house is a process (or generation) but the house is a substance. But no process is a substance, and no substance is a process. Similarly, no pleasure is a good, for a good is never a process but an end of some sort.

⁷ According to these thinkers a temperate man is good, and so is a prudent man, and each of them avoids pleasures; so, they conclude, pleasure excludes goodness.

⁸ Thinking, too, is assumed to be good by these thinkers.

⁹ Children are assumed to be incomplete and inferior, and hence not good or not as good as adults.

¹⁰ A process is for the sake of an end, and a good end is better than the process to it. One enjoys a house more than the building of it, and he enjoys a game more than going to see a game. Since pleasure is a process according to these thinkers, then, it cannot be the highest good.

13

¹ Perhaps 'someone' signifies a person who deviates somehow from what is normal, either mentally or physically. Thus exercises which are good for crippled men may not be good for those who are not crippled, and what is a good education for the mentally weak may not be good for the mentally normal.

² Those who say that pleasure is not a good or not the highest good are in error in using the term 'good' in one sense only; for pleasure, whether a

nature or a disposition or a motion or a generation, may be good in one sense but bad in another. This answers 1 (a) of the preceeding Section and is not inconsistent with (3) of that Section.

3 A sick man, for example, lacks something, and his desire to regain what he lacks is accompanied by pain. The pleasure which he gets in the process of regaining what he lacks in health is the pleasure of that healthy part of him which has not been adversely affected, and, in being a pleasure of a part rather than of the whole, it is a qualified pleasure, and so it is a pleasure which is inferior to the corresponding unqualified pleasure of a completely healthy man.

4 Pain accompanies the feeling of hunger or of disease, and the pleasure which accompanies the process of eating or of being cured (physically or mentally) is not the same as, and not so good as, that of one who is healthy and not hungry or who pursues pleasurable activities, such as research or athletics or other similar forms of enjoyment. The pleasures of a virtuous man in a settled (i.e., normal) state, then, are pleasures without qualification, but those of any other are inferior or harmful to a normal man.

5 The activity of listening to music is not a process but an end in itself. Even in processes, like that of getting well, one must distinguish the pleasure (if one is pleased when getting well) from the process in which it exists. For a process may be pleasant or painful, and pleasure or pain is like an attribute of that process and is not itself a process; for pain as a process would of necessity be changing, but pain may remain in a similar state for some time, and in such a case it would not be a process. This answers (3) of the preceding Section.

6 The pleasure of a normal man is not that of one who is in the process of becoming something; and even the pleasure of a sick man, who is becoming well, is that of the healthy part of him which is not in the process. In both cases, then, we are pleased by using something normal which we already have.

7 The pleasure in a recovery from sickness is followed by an end, which is health; but the pleasure of listening to music or watching a game is not followed by an end, for it is itself the end of that activity.

8 Pleasure is neither a process nor something which is sensed. It is not a color or a sound or something tangible, for proper sensations are of their corresponding proper sensibles and common sensations are of the cor-

responding common sensibles. If a sensation is pleasant, one must distinguish the pleasure in it from the sensation itself, and the same sensible object may be pleasurable to some but painful to others; and there is pleasure is non-sensible activities also, e.g., in thinking. 418a7–25.

9 An actuality is complete, a process is incomplete; hence the two exclude each other. 1048b18–36.

10 Activities which are good for money-making may be strenuous or risky or disgraceful and unhealthy. Hence the contraries of such activities would be healthy though bad for money-making.

11 There is some physical effort in learning, and one's health may be harmed if he does not rest sufficiently. Thus such harm results not from the pleasure of learning, but from physical strain. This answers 1 (d) of the preceding Section.

12 When we acquire an art, we acquire a power or faculty of producing a work of art and not pleasure. If the work of art causes pleasure, it is not itself pleasure. The cook produces pleasurable food, but the latter causes pleasure and is not itself a pleasure. This answers 1(e) of the preceding Section.

13 1152b26–3a7.

14 This answers 1 (b), 1 (c), and 1 (f) of the preceding Section.

14

1 When one is hurt, he is pained without qualification, for to be just hurt is in itself bad; but when the sick man is pained by surgery, he is pained in a qualified way, for although he is impeded from functioning healthily during surgery, he is on his way to recovery. In the latter case he suffers pain not for the sake of pain but for the sake of recovery, which is good, so he suffers pain in a qualified way.

2 The argument may be as follows. If, for Speusippus, pleasure is contrary to pain and to painlessness as the greater is contrary to the less and the equal or as one vice is contrary to the other vice and the mean (1108b11-23), then pleasure would have to be always bad or a species of badness; but Speusippus would not say that pleasure is always bad. Moreover, if what is bad is to be avoided, and if the two contraries of a virtue (e.g., cowardice and rashness) which are bad are to be avoided, both pleasure and pain as such contraries would have to be avoided. Yet men avoid pain but pursue pleasure.

3 The science of robbery or of destroying buildings is bad, but philosophy is good and is the best of all sciences.

4 The unimpeded activity of all the dispositions would be the unimpeded activity of all the virtues; the unimpeded activity of one of those dispositions would be that of the highest virtue, perhaps the activity of the philosopher.

5 Health, wealth, and good luck are goods as means to unimpeded activity or happiness, e.g., to the activity of a philosopher.

6 Virtue is a good but it is for the sake of virtuous activity. So if a virtuous man is prevented from such activity, e.g., by being forced into slavery or by suffering many and great misfortunes, how can he be happy? 1098b31–9a10.

7 Good luck is a means to happiness and is not happiness itself; for one may inherit a fortune and still be miserable. Again, luck is a means to an end; and a man who inherits a billion dollars is no more lucky than a man who inherits a million, if the latter sum is sufficient for virtuous activity.

8 The fact that all pursue pleasure of some kind, whether they attain it or not, is not an accident but a sign that it is a good or the highest good.

9 Hesiod, *Works and Days*, 763.

10 The highest pleasure is divine pleasure, i.e., the activity of God (1072b14–30); and perhaps brutes and men partake of the divine to the extent that they approach such activity.

11 If pleasure is not good or bad for a happy man, neither should pain be good or bad for him. So it should make no difference to him whether he has or he has not the one or the other. But he avoids pain and pursues pleasure. Hence pleasure for a happy man is good and pain is bad.

12 A solution to (2) of Section 12 will now be given.

13 Since bodily pain is bad, and since the contrary of what is bad is good and the contrary of bodily pain is bodily pleasure, bodily pleasure should be good. The conclusion, of course, is not altogether valid, for if bodily pain is bad, some bodily pleasures may be bad and some may be good; and this will be Aristotle's position.

14 To say that what is not bad is good is like saying that what is not unequal is equal, thus using 'equal' in two senses; for unequal things must be quantities, and a man is not unequal to a line since he is not a quantity, so to say that he is therefore equal to a line is to use 'equal' in

another sense. Similarly, 'good' will have two meanings, one of which will be the contrary of bad and the other will be the contradictory but not the contrary of bad. It is with good reason, then, that Aristotle dismisses the discussion of this alternative.

15 Perhaps 'better' signifies the better of two contrary dispositions (or motions), one of which is good and the other bad. Thus within courage, bravery is good and rashness (or cowardice) is bad; and there is no such thing as excess of bravery, just as there is no such thing as excess of truth, for rashness is the excess of courage and not of bravery. On the other hand, where there is an excess, as in courage or the use of property, such excess is bad. So it is the excessive pursuit of bodily goods that is bad and not the moderate pursuit of them, as in the case of drink and sexual relations. What is good in the case of sexual pleasures, then, is the moderate pursuit of them, and what is bad is both the excessive pursuit of them and the pain when one is deprived of them. That the excessive pursuit is bad is evident from the fact that it leads to other pains and makes one more unhappy or less happy.

16 The virtuous man should face certain pains, like the pain in exercise or of bitter medicine for the sake of health. The bad man who avoids such pains is faced with greater pains.

15

1 Perhaps the falsity here is the belief that all bodily pleasures are more worthy of choice than any other selection of pleasures or pains or intermediate feelings. But it is also false that all bodily pleasures are bad. What is true, then, is the fact that some bodily pleasures are good, namely, those which are moderate.

2 For example, the pain of being thirsty is driven out by the pleasure which follows when one is drinking; and the more one is thirsty, the more he is pleased when he drinks.

3 The pleasure of drinking appears in contrast not to the neutral state (i.e., when one is not thirsty) but to the painful state of being thirsty.

4 Pleasures which are remedies are pleasures of a man who is in an imperfect and not a perfect state, and so they cannot be as good as his pleasures when he is in a perfect state. Such pleasures, then, are good not without qualification (for pleasures which are good without qualification

are those of a man in a perfect state) but accidentally or in virtue of a relation, namely, by being pleasures of an imperfect man in the process of becoming perfect.

5 Examples of such thirsts are eating peanuts or pretzels or potato chips excessively in order to enjoy more drinking, and going to burlesque or looking at pornographic material to arouse one's sexual desires.

6 An old man who eats excessively does not harm others, although by accident he may do so, but if he spends excessively, he may have to steal.

7 If a man cannot enjoy the fine arts, intellectual pursuits, and other activities but is limited to bodily pleasures, any choice or comparison of pleasures he makes is limited to the bodily pleasures; and he must pursue these, since to have no pleasure at all is painful. Furthermore, such a man is not likely to pursue bodily pleasures in a moderate manner; for even ethical virtue requires some intellectual ability.

8 According to Theophrastus and Aspasius, Anaxagoras held such a view.

9 In other words, youth is given to remedial pleasures.

10 Examples of activities which are pleasant by nature are: creating a work of art, research, and listening to music; and these activities are ends in themselves. Such activities are not remedies of existing pains but fulfillments.

A difficulty may arise, for it seems that a man who is prevented from pursuing such activities is in pain. But there is a difference; for the thirsty man who is taking a drink is already in pain, whereas he who is about to create a work of art is not yet in pain but will be only when prevented.

11 When we create a work of art, for example, the effort we are putting in is making us tired, and other physical changes occur within our body and mind, some favorable but others unfavorable.

12 When there is an equilibrium, the pains and pleasures of a man neutralize each other and so he appears to be neither in pain nor in a pleasant state.

13 If one's nature were simple, there would be no two elements or parts in him with contrary attributes, e.g., with pain and pleasure, and he would be always *acting* in the same way and experiencing the same thing in accordance with his simple nature; and since his nature would not be subject to destruction or deterioration or imperfection (for a thing which

is imperfect lacks something, and, when this is supplied, the thing is a composite and not simple), it is eternal and perfect and its unimpeded activity is most pleasant. 1072b8–30, 1074b15–5a10.

[14] Euripides, *Orestes* 234.

BOOK Θ

1

¹ Whether friendship is a virtue or something which requires virtue is left open here. Perhaps this is because the term 'friendship' has many meanings. Those who are friends in the highest sense are virtuous, but those who are friends in a limited sense, e.g., for the sake of pleasure or usefulness, may be partly virtuous or even vicious. Again, since virtue is a disposition which is difficult to displace, and since friendship for the sake of usefulness is usually not enduring, it follows that some friendships are not virtues.

² This does not mean, for example, that a man needs friends more than he needs food to live. One of the meanings of 'necessary' is: that without which the good cannot come to be (1015a22–3); so if a man wishes to live well, he needs friends most of all. In one sense, then, friends are means or instruments to what is good, whether good for its own sake or for something else.

³ Friends of the young need not be young, for there are many kinds of friendships, as will be shown later; e.g., there is a friendship between a father and a son. Hence advice can be given to the young from friends; and the old can be helped in other ways.

⁴ *Iliad*, X. 224.

⁵ This is true of friends in the highest sense, for such friends have all the virtues and so are just to each other; and if all the citizens were friends in this sense, they would need no justice because they would be already just.

⁶ A friend, being virtuous, will do justice for its own sake, and most so to a friend, who is like another self.

⁷ Friendship in a limited sense, e.g., for the sake of usefulness or for the sake of being pleased, is instrumental and not noble; but friendship in the highest sense, i.e., when one likes his friend for the latter's own good, is noble.

[8] As we shall see later, friendship in the highest sense exists only among good (i.e., virtuous) men; so good men and friends are the same if 'friends' is taken in the highest sense, assuming that good men have friends. The definition of such a friend, of course, is not the same as the definition of a good man just as the definitions of an equilateral and of an equiangular triangle are not the same, even if these two can be deduced from each other; and two good men need not be friends, for they may not know each other. The argument is dialectical.

The arguments for the goodness of friendship are to some extent dialectical. But this is to be expected at the start, for many distinctions have yet to be made and many difficulties have to be resolved.

2

[1] *Odyssey* XVII, 218.

[2] Literally, it is 'jackdaw to jackdaw'.

[3] See Hesiod, *Works and Days*, 25; 'potter is angry with potter'.

[4] By 'higher' Aristotle means more universal, and physical causes would be more universal than human causes, for physics is more universal than psychology or the study of man. 1005a33–b2.

[5] Fragment 898, 7–10, Nauck[2].

[6] Fragment 8, Diels.

[7] Fragment 22.5, 62.6, 90.1–2, Diels.

[8] Problems in physics would be problems concerning bodies in motion in general. Thus whether it is like or unlike bodies that attract each other would be such a problem. But to call such attraction 'friendship' would be to use the term in a wide sense. Here, the term is limited to men, and so the problem becomes one of ethics and not of physics.

[9] There may be many kinds of friendship, each of them admitting of degree. Again, there is a continuum of colors from black to white, but white and black are different species of color. But can one truly say that, for example, an isosceles triangle is more of an equilateral triangle than a scalene triangle is? Here the species themselves are compared. Whether Aristotle had one of these arguments in mind or some other is not clear.

[10] Perhaps in a lost work. See also 10b26–11a14.

[11] The term 'likeable' ($=\phi\iota\lambda\eta\tau\acute{o}\nu$) is derived from the term 'friendship'

($= \phi\iota\lambda\iota\alpha$). Now we know more about the things we like than about friendship and its kinds. So dialectically we should first proceed by examining the things we like. 106b29–7a2, 1129a5–11.

12 The term 'likeable' here is used as if it were a genus of the good, the pleasurable, and the useful. The pleasurable, then, is only one kind of thing we like, and 'likeable' and 'pleasurable' should not be identified. We like the pleasurable for the pleasure it gives us, not for its own sake, and similarly for the useful, but liking some one for his own sake differs from liking him just for the pleasure he gives us or for his usefulness; and for Aristotle, liking someone for his own sake is more inclusive than liking him for the pleasure he gives or for his usefulness and contributes more to our happiness.

13 The term 'good' here is used in a limited sense; it means something which is an end in itself (or the unqualified good), like a man or happiness. A wider sense of the term includes the useful and the pleasant (1096a19–29, 1362a21–3b4). Anyway, the useful is less important than pleasure or the unqualified good, for we choose it for the sake of pleasure or for the unqualified good.

14 Perhaps if we say that each man likes what appears to be good for himself, still what he likes may be good or may be bad for himself, and so the distinction between what is good and what is bad for himself still stands, regardless of how it appears to himself, and so does the distinction between what appears to himself to be good and is good and what appears to himself to be good but is bad.

15 The reasons are three: the unqualified good, the pleasant, and the useful.

3

1 The attributes he is referring to are: giving pleasure and being useful. An alternative to 'attribute' is 'accident', for giving pleasure and being useful are not enduring or not so enduring as the virtues of a man. Thus if you like a man for what he is you do so for what is permanent about his virtues or his nature (which is a *substance*), and for his own sake, but if you like him in virtue of an attribute you do so for what you get from him because of that attribute, and this is not something that endures. An alternative to 'in virtue of an attribute' is 'indirectly'.

2 What is useful or pleasant to a man changes from time to time. A man

needs money one day, political influence another day, some service another day, etc.

3 What exists at the moment, of course, is mostly limited to what is sensed; so the pleasures of the young are mostly those of the senses. Concerning the character of the young, see 1389a2–b12.

4

1 Perhaps 'alike with respect to virtue' refers to those virtues which are common to the two friends; for it is unlikely that both friends have all the virtues. Perhaps such friends have most of the virtues, especially the ethical.

2 The attribute may be pleasure or usefulness. A bad man may be well disposed to someone for some reason, but this is by accident; and a man who strongly likes pleasure and not much else may be well disposed towards another who provides pleasure, but this is only one of the goods. But he who wishes the good of his friend for the latter's sake is virtuous, and so he is good in the fullest sense.

3 The friendship of good men tends to be lasting, for since such men have all or most of the virtues, which are difficult to displace (8b27–35), they tend to remain good all their lives and hence to be similarly disposed to their friends.

4 Friends who are good without qualification also like what is good without qualification, and so they like each other. But he who is good to another in this manner is also good to him with respect to any part of his goodness, and each such part may be unqualified pleasure or unqualified usefulness (for qualified pleasure may be pleasure for the moment but lead to harm in the long run, or it may be pleasure to a bad man but the contrary to a good man, and similarly for unqualified usefulness).

5 If both friends are good, their *actions* will be the same or similar, for they are virtuous; hence those *actions* will be pleasant to both.

6 By 'in virtue of each' perhaps he means in virtue of the fact that each friend is good without qualification.

7 The term 'these' applies to the unqualified good and the unqualified pleasure, for the useful is liked for the sake of these and is secondary.

8 Complete virtue is a rare thing in a man, and even more rare in two men who are to be friends.

5

¹ Such friendship contains all the kinds of goods, whether pleasure or usefulness or goodness for its own sake; and these are the goods in the highest degree, for they are such goods without qualification. What is a good to a virtuous man, for example, is not as much of a good to a bad man, for it is a virtuous man who enjoys most or makes the best use of a good.
² The problem raised in 1155b12–3 is now answered. There are three kinds of friendship: the perfect, the one for the sake of pleasure, and the one for the sake of usefulness. The first is related to each of the other two as a whole to a part; for it contains all the goods, while each of the others is limited to only one good. The term 'friendship', then, in a way, is like the term 'being'; for 'being' is primarily predicated of a substance (e.g., a man) and secondarily of an attribute (e.g., of sickness), and a substance is related to an attribute of it as a whole to a part or as the complete to the incomplete.
³ One may either restrict the term 'friendship' to the close association between good men or extend it to other kinds of close associations also. Since Aristotle intends to discuss many kinds of close associations, he chooses the second alternative and at the same time retains the popular usage of the term. This alternative gives rise to certain problems. Is the term 'friendship' a genus or is it used like the term 'being'? How are the kinds of friendship related?
⁴ Perhaps 'primary' refers to the fact that this friendship is the best with respect to final cause and hence first, while 'principal' refers to the fact that it is a whole and perfect and inclusive, and hence it has dominance over any of its parts.

6

¹ In a primary friendship, a man likes his friend for the latter's sake and as a substance or a whole; but in a qualified friendship, a man likes not his friend as a whole but only the usefulness or the pleasure he receives, and usefulness or pleasure is only an attribute. In both cases a man likes something, so there is a resemblance; but they differ in that the first man likes a whole or that which is good without qualification, while the second likes a part or what appears to be a good (whether without qualification or not).

² Author unknown.

³ More freely, the phrase 'man's nature' or 'the nature of an animal' would be better than 'nature'. Perhaps it was popular to use just 'nature'.

⁴ The needy desire company mostly for usefulness, while virtuous men desire company as an end in itself and for the sake of what is noble.

7

¹ One should like and choose what is good or pleasant, not what appears to be so but is not. But if A, or B, or both are not virtuous, some things which appear good to one or to both of them are not good without qualification; hence the same things cannot all appear to be good to both of them, and their friendship cannot be entirely harmonious. If both A and B are virtuous, on the other hand, the same things both appear and are actually good to them; hence no disagreement can arise.

² It would appear that as a disposition becomes stronger, intention becomes weaker, and that intention is practically absent when friendship is very strong. On the other hand, a disposition in ethics is formed after deliberation and choice, and so intention is required in the formation of such a disposition. The problem that one might raise, then, is how intention enters in the formation of a disposition; for once friendship as a disposition is stabilized, a friend does not again go through the steps of deliberating and choosing in order to like his friend.

³ If A and B are virtuous, then A likes B for B's sake and treats B likewise. So A's *actions* and feelings towards B are good to A and please him; but they are also good to B and please B, for by being virtuous and good, respectively, they are good for A as well as for B.

If A and B are friends only for the sake of usefulness, then what B receives from A does not by itself please A; for A is pleased only in what he receives and not in what he gives, and giving to B is for the sake of what he receives from him. A would be more pleased if he gave less or nothing to B. Thieves, for example, cooperate for the sake of usefulness; and each would be more pleased if he worked less and received more of the stolen goods, but this would please the other less.

⁴ Manuscripts differ, and the alternative to 'in pleasure' is 'in kind'; and this has some plausibility, for pleasure is not the only thing a friend returns.

⁵ The requirements in love or in a perfect friendship are many and noble,

and with respect to goodness they exceed those of other human associations.

6 And, we may add, it is not easy for one person to attend in excess to many friends at the same time.

7 As already indicated elsewhere, it is difficult for a man to be completely virtuous, intellectually as well as ethically, and hence even more difficult for many men to be so and get to know each other.

8 An alternative to 'by means of' is 'for the sake of'. The word διά has both meanings.

9 Perhaps this is the case because the useful is instrumental to what is an end in itself, while pleasure is an end in itself. This is also evident from experience.

10 He is referring to Plato's universal good, for this is an Idea or a Form and not something that one can possess.

11 If A surpasses B in all respects, then there can be no equality in give and take, and perfect friendship becomes difficult. But if A surpasses B in one respect while B surpasses A in another, then there can be a give and take, not of the same kind of things but analogously. Thus A may be useful to B, and B pleasant to A.

12 By definition, if both A and B are good, then their friendship will be perfect, and such is the friendship they seek. But if A is good and B is rich, then B must be sufficiently good, though not perfectly good, to be a friend of A, otherwise A, being virtuous, will not welcome him as a friend. B's usefulness, then, may make up for what he lacks in virtue. Some of Socrates' friends, as dramatized by Plato, illustrate this point.

8

1 Perhaps he is referring to the incomplete friendships, e.g., for the sake of pleasure or usefulness, already considered.

2 Children are like parts of a whole and are neither complete nor citizens, but both rulers and subjects are citizens; hence the potentialities and relations in the two cases differ, and so do the kinds of friendship.

3 If friendship is thought to be an equality of a certain kind, each of two friends should receive the same as he gives, or else something analogous to it. Now if A is superior to B, and both are friends, since A cannot receive from B the same thing as he gives to him, then he must receive

from *B* something which is analogous. For example, a father gives birth to his son, brings him up, and gives him an education, and these cannot be repaid in kind; hence the son should love his father more than he is loved by him, and he should obey or yield to him, if an analogous equality is to characterize their kind of friendship.

9

1 Equality in what is primarily just is equality of ratios, i.e., if *M* and *N* are the merits of *A* and *B*, respectively, and if *X* and *Y* are what they receive, then the ratio $M:N$ is equal to the ratio $X:Y$. For example, if in business *A* contributes $2X$ but *B* contributes *X*, then *A* should receive twice the profits that *B* does. Equality in what is secondarily just belongs to corrective justice, as discussed in Book E.

2 If, as it is said, a friend is another self, and, so to speak, a man is equal to himself, and if a good man likes himself most of all and friendship is best among good men, then friendship is best between equals, especially when these are good, and a man would choose an equal for a friend. Friendship according to merit would be friendship among unequals in virtue; but such friendship is incomplete and hence secondary.

3 This is another dialectical argument. Since men are less likely to be friends if they differ more, they are more likely to be friends if they differ less; hence they are most likely to be friends if they do not differ at all but are equal.

4 Can a man, especially when good, wish the goods for himself most of all and still wish good for his friend? The difficulty is only apparent. A virtuous activity involving another person is pleasant, and since it is virtuous, it does good to that other person also, including a friend. However, if a man wishes the goods for himself most of all, his primary wish will be primarily for himself and secondarily for his friend. It appears, however, that the difference between the primary and the secondary wishes becomes greater as the two friends become less virtuous, for the more virtuous the friends, the more their wishes and goods coincide. The definition of primary friendship, too, indicates this; for a virtuous friend wishes the other friend's good for the latter's sake. But if *A* wishes *B* to be a god, *B* as a god will no longer be a good to *A*, for *A* will not receive from *B* what he receives from a good friend.

⁵ Perhaps by 'this' he means being honored, not being liked.

⁶ See also 1095b22–31.

10

¹ See Comm. 3 of Section 8.

² If *B* is inferior to *A* and both are friends, like the friendship of a son and his father, their likes and dislikes are not quite the same because of their difference; and their friendship tends to change because *B* is changing but not *A*, for *A*'s habits are assumed to be stabilized. But if *A* and *B* are equal and good and friends, since virtues are difficult to change, their likes and dislikes and dispositions tend to remain the same, and so does their friendship.

³ Virtue is a mean and is unique; but vice may be an excess or deficiency, and vicious men may vary with respect to the kinds of vices or with respect to each vice. Generous men are not likely to be friends with the stingy. Further, there is no harmony among the habits of a bad man, and he tends to change along with varying circumstances and what results from them. Thieves may cooperate to rob a bank but quarrel over the distribution of the loot.

⁴ Perhaps he is referring to the difference in the needs of such friends.

⁵ The Greek lends itself to alternative interpretations, and hence to alternative translations; and ours is just one. For one thing, that which desires is not the contrary as an attribute but the subject which has that contrary, and naming the subject by an attribute of it is only an accident (192a9–25) and is indirect naming. For example, if a poor man wishes to become rich, it is not his poverty that wishes it nor he along with his poverty but he apart from his poverty. Again, what is often desired is the intermediate or the mean, for in such cases it is this that is good; so what the subject desires is to acquire part of the other contrary and retain part of the contrary it has in order to arrive at the mean.

11

¹ 1155a22–8.

² He is using 'friendship' in the wide sense: any association so formed that each party gets some good from the other; but 'friendship' in this wide sense and 'association' are not synonymous, for two citizens of a state, which is an association, may not know each other at all, and knowledge of each other appears to be a requirement in a friendship.

Of course, the term 'friendship' may be extended to include any association.

12

[1] The difference meant is with respect to the end or the final cause of a state.

[2] A man elected or appointed by ballot to be a king is not necessarily superior in all good things (virtue, wealth, etc.), and so he may be a king in name only and not by definition.

[3] Again, the contrariety here is one with respect to end or final cause.

[4] A bad king, of course, is not a king in the main sense of the term but is equivocally called 'a king'.

[5] Contraries in the proper sense are furthest apart (1018a25–31, 1055a3–5). Tyranny and kingdom are such contraries, for kingdom is the best and tyranny is the worst. Of good states, the least good is democracy, and opposed to this is mob rule, which is therefore the least bad. From good to bad, then, the order is: kingdom, aristocracy, democracy (timocracy), mob rule, oligarchy, and tyranny, and the oppositions are kingship – tyranny, aristocracy – oligarchy, and democracy – mob rule.

[6] The transitions are smallest, for a monarchy remains a monarchy, a rule by the few remains a rule by the few, etc; and they are easiest, for if a king becomes bad or is replaced by a bad man, it is not difficult for him or for the man who replaces him to make the transition; similarly if the change is from aristocracy or from timocracy.

[7] The word 'appears' here is appropriate, for the functions of a master and a tyrant are not quite the same, and Aristotle's distinction between natural and conventional slavery requires discussion, given in *Politics* (1253b14–5b15).

[8] Unlike a democracy, whose elected rulers rule over free men according to law or reason, the rule in a mob rule government is subject to chance or emotion rather than to law or reason. In a dwelling without a master or with a weak master, though there is an association of individuals and hence the possibility of some common good, such good is hardly realized because there is hardly a rule or reason to bring it about.

13

[1] Children can hardly repay their parents for the goods they receive, but

they can go as far as they can; and honoring their parents is one way of repaying, loving them more is another, helping them in a variety of ways is another.

2 Aristotle believes that, on the whole, a man is superior to a woman in the virtues (intellectual as well as ethical); hence he should be directing the more important issues of a household.

3 Even friendship for the sake of usefulness, which is the weakest friendship of the three, cannot exist here; for give and take is not reciprocal.

4 Insofar as a slave is a man, he should be allowed a certain amount of happiness (if 'happiness' be the right term), as much as his limited virtues and his status allow. Perhaps it is for this reason that, in the *Politics* (1254b39–5a2), Aristotle says that it is both just and to the slave's interest that he should be ruled and work for his master. But the implication here is that the master is virtuous; for the less the master is virtuous, the less he is just towards the slave, and under a bad master perhaps a natural slave is worse off than if he were free. So while one might see the point of allowing natural slavery (not slavery by convention) in a state in which most citizens are virtuous, one might also be skeptical as to whether such a state is probable. Was Aristotle, then, advocating natural slavery for any state or just for a state in which most citizens are virtuous?

5 Perhaps such friendships are not the best, since it is friendship in the primary sense that is the best, and the best friendship is more possible between virtuous persons who are more likely to be in good states.

14

1 Any two citizens or neighbors would be friends of this kind; for a man does not choose those who are to be his fellow-citizens, but he agrees to abide by the same laws, nor does he usually choose his next-door neighbor, but he tends to accept him whoever he may be.

2 A person is related to a part of himself as a whole to a part; and the whole rules the part or owns the part or is superior to the part. The part, then, is related to the whole not in the same but, if at all, in the converse manner.

3 Perhaps by 'these' he means (a) the same parents and (b) the relation of a brother to a brother.

4 Perhaps 'ancestor' is in the singular because Aristotle believed that it is the father who supplies the form in the offspring.

5 The formation of couples (of the relationship between husband and wife in the case of men) occurs even among other animals, and the more so for the higher animals (1252a26–30); but the formation of a state (a political association) is limited to men, for here reason is required (1253a10–8). Thus the formation of couples is prior in existence and necessary to the formation of the state. Further, couples are formed for the sake of reproduction, so life may continue, while a state is formed for the sake of a good life (1252b27–30); but life is prior in existence to good life, for if one lives well, he lives, but if he lives, he does not necessarily live well. Thus men tend by nature to form couples more than to be political.

6 Men live together not only for the sake of living, which includes the necessary pleasures or pleasures of the senses, but also for the sake of living well, which includes the pleasures of the intellect also.

7 Since the functions are by nature divided, each should perform his or her proper function so that both may gain as a whole.

8 Two things are included: (a) the useful and the pleasant, and (b) enjoyment through virtue. The first appears to afford usefulness and the necessary pleasures, while the second adds the higher pleasures, those that come through ethical and intellectual virtues. It appears, then, that Aristotle does not limit the friendship of a husband and a wife to just the necessities of living but extends it also to living well, although only to the extent that this is possible; for the difference between a man and a woman does not make them altogether similar, and similarity is necessary for a friendship in the highest or most complete sense.

9 The term 'friend' here seems to be used in a narrow sense, and it excludes the relation to a stranger or to a comrade or to a classmate. The point made is that since there are differences in the kinds of friendships, what is just in them is not altogether the same but differs in certain respects from one kind of friendship to another.

15

1 1156a7–b12.

2 In other words, since a man who is superior gives more, his friend should somehow make up by paying honor or loving more or making up in some other way.

³ The receiver, though he expected no complaint, should be willing to return the equivalent to the giver if the latter has complained.

⁴ Even men who are not friends give for the sake of giving.

⁵ The attitude of a good man who receives should be that, in the event of a mistake, he should be willing to give the equivalent, even if he did not expect the mistake to happen.

⁶ If the service rendered is of the same kind as the good returned, the problem raised seems easier to solve. For example, if the service rendered is an amount of money, the return should be an equal amount, other things being equal. A difficulty arises, however, if other things are not equal. The benefactor may himself need the money very badly, and so may the beneficiary; and in such a case, the benefactor's service is worth more to the benefactor than that amount, and the benefit to the beneficiary is likewise worth more than that amount. If the service rendered is not of the same kind as the good returned, we have the added difficulty of finding a common measure.

⁷ Since virtue is a habit acquired through good intention, and since intention is deliberative desire or desiring intellect (1113a9–12, 1139b4–5), the main principle in virtue is its intention, for this initiates and determines the kind of habit which is to be acquired.

16

¹ The benefits conferred by the two parties in such a case appear to each recipient of less worth than expected; and so their friendship is dissolved.

² Disagreements arise because the measure of value or what is good differs for each kind of man. Ultimately, of course, the measure depends on what each of these men considers happiness to be, and happiness is the first principle of ethics.

BOOK I

1

1 In such a friendship, what is given and what is received are not the same in kind but different or analogous; and the desire by both parties to make the exchange may lead to an equality, in a sense, which preserves the friendship. As already stated, 'friendship' here is used in a wide sense; two men enter into a friendship if each receives some good from the other. Thus a political friendship is an association between citizens who exchange goods, such as shoes for dresses. 1158b23–8, 1162a34–b4, 1163b1–12.

2 Shoes and dresses are not of the same kind, but the desire to make an exchange led men to make a comparison and later to introduce a common measure by convention. Thus, if the shoemaker and the dressmaker are willing to exchange two pairs of shoes for one dress, a sort of equality arises because of desire, and a common measure of such desire further facilitates exchanges for all kinds of goods.

3 The usefulness of a person is not permanent, or not so permanent as his habits; and the same applies to the pleasure which a person may give. Thus a young man in love with a young lady soon changes his mind and falls in love with another young lady.

4 What makes a man's character are his habits, and these are by nature hard to change. 8b27–35.

5 The expectation of getting what was promised was pleasant; so he was getting pleasure for singing.

6 Hesiod, *Works and Days*, 368.

7 By definition, sophistry appears to be wisdom but is not. So many or most sophists, to make sure of being rewarded, fixed the price before undertaking to teach wisdom. As the text suggests, complaints arose because students discovered that they did not receive what was promised them.

8 1162b6–13.

9 An equivalent return is meant.

2

1 Since his very existence is caused by his father and his debt to his father is the greatest and can never be repaid (1162a4–7, 1163b18–21), this debt has first priority. So if he should ransom his father rather than even himself, certainly he should ransom his father rather than someone else to whom he owes less than he owes his father.

2 In other words, if what is owed is of considerably more worth for a noble or urgent cause than it is to the creditor, then it should be used for such a cause.

3 For example, a corrupt politician may help a good man and later request a return but for an evil cause. Should the good man return such a favor?

4 1094b11–27, 1098a26–9, 1104a1–10.

3

1 1162b23–5.

2 Here it appears that his friend made no pretense of loving him for his character.

3 An alternative to 'more honorable' is 'more valuable'.

4 1156b19–23.

5 1157b22–4, 1158b33–5.

4

1 Perhaps he is referring to those quarrels in which a man tries to correct his friend for the latter's good.

2 Friendship is a two-way relation, and those related are called 'friends'.

3 1113a22–33.

4 1098b11–2.

5 1099a11–5, 1102b27–8. Not only is there no contradiction in the intellectual virtues and no strife in the ethical virtues, but there is also harmony between the two, since the nonrational part of the soul obeys the rational part. 1098a4–5.

6 If a man be defined as a rational animal, then 'rationality' is the differentia; and rationality (or the thinking part of the soul), as stated in the *Metaphysics* (1038a19), seems to be the *substance* of a man, for this directs and pervades all of man's activities. Something to this effect is indicated in 1166a22–3, 1168b34–5, and 1177b30–8a7 also.

⁷ If we choose to change with respect to quality or quantity or relation or some other attribute, we still keep our identity or *substance*; but if we choose to change with respect to *substance*, this would be our destruction. Any choice, then, is for the good of the man who makes the choice and does not necessitate his destruction. So to say that a man wishes to be God, in view of the fact that God is perfectly good, is to say either that he wishes to be like God and thus keep his own identity but acquire perfect virtue, or that he wishes to be God himself, which is impossible, since God already exists.

⁸ In this paragraph Aristotle shows dialectically how the four definitions of a friend given by others in lines 1166a2–8 fit in with man's relation to himself.

⁹ The term 'excess' here should not be taken in a bad sense, like an excess of drinking. It indicates great intensity of feeling or attitude, or a friendship which resembles most one's relation or love towards himself.

¹⁰ Manuscripts differ; and an alternative translation is: "still others, who have committed terrible deeds because of their evil habits, hate or shun life or even commit suicide."

¹¹ Whether the thing done by an evil man is good or bad, what follows still stands; for if it is good, the appetitive part of the soul is distressed while the thinking part is pleased, but if it is bad, the reverse is the case.

5

¹ 1155b32–6a5.

² Both these men are friends only in a qualified way, for the sake of usefulness or pleasure, not according to virtue or complete friendship.

³ By 'friend' here he means friend according to virtue.

⁴ The phrase 'of some kind' indicates qualified virtue or some part of virtue, but not total virtue. For example, a brave man is virtuous with respect to bravery, and he is well disposed to another brave man just because of this quality, not because of complete virtue. The examples which follow indicate this point.

⁵ An alternative to 'beautiful' is 'noble'; but it makes no difference here which is meant, for in either case one is well disposed because of some virtue and not because of complete virtue.

6

¹ Concord, then, may be defined as sameness of opinion and intention about practical matters of considerable importance and of common interest to most or all.

² 1285a29–b1.

³ Eteocles and Polynices, in the *Phoenissae* of Euripides.

⁴ If each of *A* and *B* wants to be the leader, then each will say 'I want to be the leader'; thus in a sense each will have the same thought. But the pronoun 'I' signifies *A* for *A* and *B* for *B*, and so the two statements signify different subjects. But if all the citizens of a state say 'the best should rule', this statement will have the same meaning for all, for 'the best' has the same meaning for all citizens.

⁵ *Good* men have the same thoughts in themselves, for, unlike a bad man, a *good* man is consistent in thoughts and there is harmony in his soul (1166a10–b29); and *good* men have the same thoughts in relation to one another, for the subject of a *good* man's thought is the same as that of another *good* man's corresponding thought. In short, *good* men do not differ with respect to truth and goodness or virtue, especially virtue towards another.

⁶ The current in the channel between the island of Euboea and the mainland of Greece changes directions many times a day.

7

¹ Epicharmus, Fragment 146, Kaibel.

² The argument, somewhat expanded, is as follows. We choose and love existence, which for us is living and *acting*. But living and *acting* for an artist is producing a work of art, and a work of art is part of that production (for one does not just produce but produces something). Hence, in his love of producing a work of art, the artist somehow loves the work which is being produced; and he loves it when it has been produced, for then it is complete, it exists actually and not potentially (a good work is better if it exists actually than if it exists potentially), and it is his own.

³ Just as the result of the artist's production is the work of art, so the result of the benefactor's *action* is the service which is in the person who has received it by that *action*. Hence just as the artist loves his work of art,

so the benefactor loves his service which exists in the receiver.

4 In other words, it is noble to give but not noble to receive, for the service, which is a good, is the work of the giver (or the result of his *action*) and not that of the receiver.

5 A virtuous man is more pleased by *acting* nobly than by receiving a benefit; for though both the noble *action* and the benefit are goods, the former is his own while the latter is another's and is given to him. If the receiver loves his benefactor as a benefactor, it is for the sake of the usefulness received and not for the benefactor's own sake. Hence the giver, being the better man as a giver, is considered more worthy of being loved than the receiver as a receiver.

6 Remembering and expecting, too, are activities, but they are different from the activities which are directed to the present. For example, listening to music differs from and is better than remembering that one listened to music. Further, of pleasurable objects of the same kind, that which exists at present is more pleasurable than that which existed in the past or that which is expected in the future, e.g., the performance of a symphony is more pleasurable when listened to than when remembered.

7 One might argue that a good conferred, though noble, lasts as long as the usefulness of it to the receiver. Perhaps the pleasure of the benefactor for having done something noble lasts longer than the pleasure which the receiver gets from the usefulness of the benefit received. The argument may be dialectical.

8 Just as a noble *action* is more pleasant to the benefactor than the usefulness resulting from that *action* is to the receiver, so the memory of that *action* is more pleasant to the benefactor than the corresponding memory of the usefulness resulting from that *action* is to the receiver.

9 Perhaps the argument is as follows. He who is to be benefited takes pleasure in anticipating a good he will receive. But he who is to benefit another cannot be pleased by something he has not done yet, or is less pleased than when he does it; and besides, in conferring a benefit in the future, some effort may be required, and this effort, apart from its effect, may not be pleasant.

10 Acting, if good, is more honorable or more noble than being acted upon (430a18–9), and loving is to being loved as acting well is to be acted upon well. Hence the man who performed a good *action* is more honorable

or more noble and hence more worthy of love than the man who is benefited by that *action*.

11 Those who have made money regard it as their own work, and so they value it more and love it more than if they had inherited it; for to inherit money is to be benefited by what belongs to another and is received.

12 Perhaps by 'this' Aristotle is referring to the effort made and the fact that one knows more that what he gives is his own than the receiver does who receives it.

8

1 1166a1–b29.

2 Literally, it is 'the knee is very close to the shin', but if the expression is truncated, it may mean that friends are closer than the knee is to the shin.

3 The proverbs given indicate singleness, community, equality, and closeness, respectively, and these are instances of unity. But unity in the highest sense is attributed to that which is indivisible or undivided, and a man is more indivisible from himself than even from his friend. Hence if one should love his friend more than a stranger and, in general, one who is nearer more than one who is farther, then he should love himself most of all since he is nearest to himself.

4 The expression 'pleasures of the body' may be misleading, for it may mean that what is pleased is the body; but what is pleased is the soul and not the body (1099a7–8). The expression 'bodily pleasures', on the other hand, suggests pleasures through the body, with the understanding that it is the soul which is so pleased.

5 The truth of this statement appears to assume a more literal meaning of 'self-lover'. If one loves more that which is better for himself, then a successful self-lover in the highest sense would be virtuous, for it is through virtue that he would attain happiness, which is the highest good for himself. Accordingly, a man who is ruled by his intellect is more of a self-lover in this sense than one who is ruled by his passions.

6 This is the rational part of the soul.

7 This would be, in a state, the government which legislates, executes, and judges; and in a man, this would be the rational part of his soul. But is not a man as a whole, which includes the rational part, better than that part of his soul? A qualification is added later in line 1169a2.

⁸ In a continent man, the rational part rules over the passions, even if the man is pained; but in an incontinent man, the passions overrule the rational part.

⁹ If a man is defined as a rational animal, then 'rationality' as the differentia would be the most essential predicate of the man and his *substance*, so to say. 1038a18–20.

¹⁰ What is thought to be expedient is what most men usually desire, namely, property, honor, and bodily pleasures.

¹¹ Virtue, of course, is not an end in itself but a means to happiness as an end; but it is the best means to that end, if external impediments are not taken into account.

¹² What an evil man does is not the best for himself, even if he thinks so.

¹³ Can intellect choose what is not best for itself? No, for then it would be not through intellect but through ignorance that a man makes the choice. It is assumed, then, that the intellect is true, and so is knowledge in general; and whether a man made a choice through the intellect or through ignorance is another problem. 100b5–14.

¹⁴ Achilles, for example, chose a short and glorious life rather than a long but inglorious life.

¹⁵ In taking for himself a greater good he does not become grasping, for this is not the kind of good which is subject to distribution. Thus if a good man does not help another, neither of the two benefits by such inaction, but if he helps another, both benefit; for the benefactor earns nobility, which for him is better than what he gave, and the beneficiary earns something useful. It appears, then, that the *action* of the benefactor produces a good which did not exist before that *action*.

9

¹ Euripides, *Orestes* 667. The first argument is as follows. A self-sufficient man is regarded as one who by himself has no other need; so if a man, when by himself, feels the need of something else, he cannot be self-sufficient. Evidently, the word 'self-sufficient' here is used in a narrow sense, but the solution to the problem raised requires a wider sense of the word, or else, the use of an additional word. Aristotle uses the word to mean that a man is self-sufficient if, when he possesses certain goods (including friends), he has no need of any other goods.

2 As a man, a happy man by nature must be political and so live with others, and as a happy man, he must by nature live with others and *act* towards others in a certain way, i.e., virtuously, if he is to live pleasantly. This is the opposite argument.

3 The pleasures of amusement and relaxation are also needed, but they are less important than those of serious work. 1176b12–30.

4 It is true that a happy man does not need friends for the sake of usefulness or of pleasure (in the narrow sense), but it does not follow that he does not need friends in the main sense of the term, i.e., friends with complete virtue.

5 1098a15–7.

6 1099a21.

7 *Actions* of virtuous men are pleasant by nature because they are virtuous, and they are pleasant to the friends of virtuous men because they are close to them and because such friends are virtuous.

8 A happy man is complete if he exercises both his intellectual and his ethical virtues. To exercise his ethical virtues (some of them, anyway) he needs other men, and friends most of all. And he needs others even in the exercise of some of his intellectual virtues, for philosophizing and other scientific investigations are not solitary activities but depend to some extent on communication. Plato's Academy and other schools were set up for this reason. 1177a32–b1.

9 Theognis, 35. In exercising virtue with others, one is both pleased by the exercise and makes his virtue more stable and hence more perfect.

10 Both dialectical and logical inquiries use premises which are not limited to a subject but have wider application. An inquiry which is more physical into a subject would use more premises which are proper to the subject or more premises which are less wide in application or closer to the subject. Premises which follow from the definition of a man as a man, for example, would be proper to a man and hence to whatever may belong only to a man, such as happiness or friendship.

11 413b1–2, 418b18–9.

12 In general, any potency is defined in terms of the corresponding activity; and in all animals a natural potency exists for the sake of the corresponding activity. For example, vision is defined as the power to see; and it exists for the sake of seeing. Evidently, seeing is better than

vision, and, in general, a good activity is better than the corresponding potency. 1049b4–1051a33.

13 1172a19–1176a29. Are all definite things good? Perhaps the term 'definite' is used in a narrow sense. The definite is to the indefinite as the perfect is to the imperfect; and just as a thing is perfect in one way only but imperfect in many ways, so is definiteness related to indefiniteness. For example, happiness is unique, for there is only one way (a definite way) of having all the virtues; but one may be unhappy in many ways (an indefinite number of ways), for he may lack a number of virtues in many ways.

Dialectically, perfection is to discord as truth is to contradiction; and truth is to contradiction as existence is to nonexistence; for truth signifies existence, and contradiction signifies non-existence. Hence perfection is to discord as existence is to non-existence. Thus God, who is perfect, is a being who exists in the fullest sense eternally. Conversely, the more a thing is imperfect, the more it tends to non-existence; for sickness and pain and discord in the soul make life miserable and even lead to death. But perfection is by nature good and pleasant; hence sensing and thinking, which constitute existence or living for a man, when free from evil and corruption and pain, which tend to lessen it, are good and pleasant by nature.

14 The term αἰσθάνεσθαι has more than one meaning (425a27–30, b12–25, 455a12–20). In its proper sense it means to sense, like seeing a color or hearing a sound or tasting a flavor. In another sense it means to be aware or to be conscious, and we are using 'to be aware' here. There are other senses.

15 Two important premises here are 'what is choiceworthy to a good man is needed by him' and 'a good friend is choiceworthy to a good man'. The latter premise is more convincing than the former. The former implies that a man cannot be completely happy if an object which is choiceworthy to him is lacking.

Logically, since a good man is a man and a man is by nature political (1097b11), a good man can best fulfill his political nature by having virtuous friends; for he can best share his *actions* and thoughts with those whose *actions* and thoughts are like his own, and it is such men who are best suited to be his friends. To be self-sufficient and happy, then, a virtuous man needs virtuous friends.

10

1 Hesiod, *Op*. 715 Rzach.

2 Examples of such friendships are Theseus and Perithous, Achilles and Patroclus, Orestes and Pylades, Phintias and Damon, and Epaminondas and Pelopidas.

11

1 The distinction is between necessity and self-sufficiency, between living and living well. When the necessities are supplied, the right use of them and the right activities lead to noble *actions* and hence to living well. But how can two virtuous friends *act* nobly in times of prosperity if, in a generous *act*, one gives while the other receives? Perhaps at such times generosity is of little importance to them, for what is useful would be of little importance; besides, virtuous men would tend to be equally reciprocal in giving and taking.

2 Who is the better man? Since a virtuous man is disposed to be pleasant to his friend, he would not allow him to share his grief. Besides, it is virtuous *action* that plays the dominant role in happiness, not matters of fortune; and, according to 1100b30–5, a virtuous man 'will bear misfortunes with calm ... through nobility of character and greatness of soul'. The next paragraph adds some qualifications.

3 Fr. adesp. 76 Nauck[2].

12

1 Lines 1245b23–4 (*Eudemian Ethics*) suggest that 'this' refers to awareness. An alternative would be that it refers to friendship, for the activity of friendship, too, would be living together.

2 Manuscripts differ. An alternative to 'in which they think they can live together' is 'in the best way possible', and this is somewhat suggested by lines 1245a18–21 (*Eudemian Ethics*).

3 Theognis 35.

BOOK K

1

¹ The word 'these' refers to pleasures and pains which, if rightly pursued, contribute greatly to our happiness.
² Eudoxus is one among these thinkers. 1172b9.
³ Speusippus is one among these thinkers.
⁴ The mean state would be virtue, which chooses certain pleasures and certain pains and avoids the others.
⁵ Those who fail to make distinctions may be misled in thinking that the contradictory of 'all pleasures are bad' is 'all pleasures are good'; for the contradictory of 'all pleasures are bad' is 'some pleasures are not bad'.

2

¹ Eudoxus was an eminent mathematician, astronomer, and philosopher, and had belonged to Plato's Academy. Evidently, the highest good for him was pleasure, and this was like the *Good* for Plato or like happiness for Aristotle.
² 115a25–31.
³ An alternative to 'the good itself' is 'Goodness Itself', and this is Plato's first principle or Idea and the cause as form of all other good things; and as such a cause, like God, it cannot be bettered by the things it causes.

According to one of the variants, the translation would be 'for the good cannot become more choiceworthy by the addition to it of anything'. For Plato, of course, the good is Goodness Itself.
⁴ Plato's refutation of pleasure as the good (*Philebus* 20E–22E, 60B–61B) rests on the further assumption that the good is complete and self-sufficient and so cannot become more choiceworthy by the addition of another good; and Aristotle agrees with this (117a16–21, 1097b6–21).
⁵ One might wonder how both good and bad creatures (e.g., men) could

desire generically the same things, let us say pleasure. The answer is that even bad creatures have some goodness in them and are not totally bad, and that their desire of generically the same things arises from the good part in them. What is totally bad, like impossible things, cannot exist but destroys itself (1126a8–13).

6 Speusippus is foremost among these thinkers 1153b1–7.

7 Cowardice is opposed to rashness, and both are opposed to bravery; and wastefulness is opposed to stinginess, and both are opposed to generosity. But double oppositions such as these do not apply to pleasure and pain; for pain and pleasure are not both avoided as vices nor both pursued as virtues.

8 For Speusippus, the good is happiness; but happiness is a perfect habit or disposition, and so it is a certain kind of quality. For Aristotle, on the other hand, happiness is not a quality but an activity according to a certain quality, i.e., according to virtue; for a man may have the virtues and not be using them, and, if so, he may not be happy, e.g., when many and great misfortunes befall him. 1098b31–9a7, 1100a5–9.

9 Perhaps the reference is to Speusippus and Xenocrates, and also to Plato (*Philebus* 24E–25A, 31A). The argument is that the indefinite, like the infinite or the unlimited, partakes of badness and not of goodness, for what is good has definiteness or measure or proportion and does not vary. For Plato, the material principle is the *Dyad*, and this is infinite or unlimited, and it is nonbeing or hardly a being; and it is the cause of plurality and variation and is bad. For Speusippus, the material principle analogous to the *Dyad* is *Plurality*; and for Xenocrates, it is the *Indefinite Dyad*.

10 If pleasure is not a good because variation of degree is attributed to the man who may be pleased more or less and not to pleasure itself, then the virtues too cannot be good; for men may be virtuous or *act* virtuously more or less. But the virtues are obviously good.

11 Even a proportion may be definitely stated within certain limits. For example, one may say that a certain attribute is present in a substance if that substance is a mixture of three parts of A and from nine to ten parts of B, and that attribute would then admit of variation of degree within these ratios.

12 According to these thinkers, the good is perfect and has everything and needs nothing which pertains to its nature as good. Accordingly, to exist

in perfection is to exist without changing; for, in changing, a thing is either in the process of being perfected or in the contrary process, and in neither process does it remain in a state of perfection. But pleasure according to them is a motion or a generation, and each of them is a change; hence pleasure is not perfect and consequently is not the good.

13 Some motions admit of being slower or faster, others do not. One may walk or grow or recover from sickness sometimes fast and sometimes slow; but the motion of the outer sphere of the universe is constant (288a13–5), yet it may be compared with other motions with respect to being slower or faster.

14 We may change slowly or quickly from a painful or neutral state to a state of pleasure, but during the state of pleasure we are being pleased not quickly or slowly but more or less; for the state of being pleased is at every moment complete, whereas quickness or slowness applies to a motion which reaches its completion precisely at the last moment.

15 As the argument is perhaps too condensed, we offer an interpretation. In a generation, there is a subject which remains the same and which loses one form (or privation) and gains another. For example, if water becomes air, the subject in that generation is, let us say, the molecules, and one form is that of water but the other is that of air. If pleasure is a generation – let us assume the subject to be an animal or a body – what would be the two corresponding forms? No new form is gained by the animal or the body, but only an attribute if anything, and no form is destroyed since the animal or the body still has the form of an animal. Further, since pain would be a destruction, either the body or the animal would necessarily be destroyed at the end of pain; and this is false, for an animal may remain an animal at the end of pain.

16 Replenishment is the taking in of food, and this is an increase with respect to the quantity of matter. But such increase is a change of the body and not of the soul, while pleasure, if a change at all, would be a change with respect to the soul, for only the soul can be pleased. It is true, of course, that while there is a bodily increase (the taking in of food), there is also pleasure in the soul (perhaps not always), but pleasure is distinct from such increase; for the increase is an attribute of the body, while pleasure is an attribute of the soul. The same applies to pain when one has an operation.

17 Since there are pleasures while there is no replenishment, pleasure

cannot be replenishment; and since such pleasures are not preceded by pain, pleasure cannot be a generation from a contrary, whether this be pain or need. If pleasure is a generation (whether of the body or of the soul) from a neutral state as the starting contrary, what will the final contrary be? If it is again a neutral state, both contraries would be identical, and this is both impossible and also contradicts the definition of generation; and if it is pain, the final contrary would be a destruction and not a form, for pain as the contrary of pleasure would have to be a destruction. But the starting-point and final end of a generation are forms and not changes, e.g., if a body changes from being white to being black, whiteness and blackness are forms and not changes.

[18] One may hold that what is pleasant to those who are badly disposed is better than what is painful to them and that, as long as they are pleased, the source of pleasure should make no difference. One argument against this view is that given later in lines 1173b28–4a4. Another is that pleasures from vices run up against pleasures from other habits, for harmonious pleasures arise only from the virtues. Thus the pleasure of stealing faces such painful feelings as that of being caught, etc. There are other arguments.

[19] The pleasure of listening to symphonies and concertos by one who has taste and understanding in music is superior to the pleasure of listening to a popular tune by an ordinary man. Evidence of this is the fact that many of us, as we grow, tend to appreciate more the music of the masters and less that of popular composers, but the reverse appreciation hardly occurs. Again, we prefer being with close friends to being with business friends, and this indicates that the pleasure of being with close friends is better than that of being with business friends.

[20] There seems to be some difficulty with the argument, and this may arise from understanding the term 'pleasure' as used by Aristotle. If seeing and knowing and being aware of having virtues are not accompanied by pleasure, why do we pursue such activities? Is it because they contribute to happiness in other ways while their avoidance does not? Is it because in the long run disgraceful pleasures harm us whereas such activities make us happier?

[21] Since pleasures differ in kind and so in goodness, and since the good for man is happiness, which does not include all kinds of pleasure, the good cannot be only pleasure.

3

¹ Perhaps the principle here is the fact that pleasure is a complete activity; and this distinguishes it from motions and generations, which are incomplete activities. A complete activity is one in which every part of that activity is perfect in itself and lacks nothing. In contrast, a motion is in the process of becoming something, and it is complete only when its end is reached. If I enjoy walking for its own sake, I enjoy every part of that walk, even if walking is a motion; but if I walk for the sake of meeting a friend, every part of that walk is for the sake of the last moment, at which I meet my friend. The discussion of complete and incomplete activities belongs to *Metaphysics*, and the definitions of motion and of generation are given in the *Physics*. 1048b18–35, 200b12–2b29.

² 200b12–2b29.

³ Why the term 'most'? A motion is complete only if the end is reached or only at the last moment. There is also the circular motion of the universe, and this has no final end, or else it is itself an end; so either every part of it is complete or there is no completeness in it at all. Perhaps this motion is complete, for it is eternal and a necessary attribute of the universe and has no potentiality of being otherwise; and a necessary and unchanging attribute of a thing is not incomplete. 1050b22–8.

⁴ The starting and end points of the foundation of a house differ from those of the roof, and so do the corresponding motions.

⁵ For example, motion is divisible, and the term 'motion' is predicated both of a whole motion and of part of that motion, and a part of a motion is not a whole. But 'pleasure' is predicated only of that which is a whole; for if one is pleased during time T, his pleasure during any part of T is a whole.

⁶ Seeing is not in the process of becoming, for a man starts seeing immediately when he opens his eyes. The same applies to a point or a unit, for it is a whole, so to say; and there is no such thing as half a unit which might be generated since a unit is indivisible, but generation takes time and no part of such a unit (for a unit has not parts) can be generated in a part of that time. 1002a30–4.

4

¹ The doctor is a cause as a mover, for he is not health but only generates

health. Similarly, the sensible object causes sensation as a mover, i.e., it only stirs or activates the faculty or the corresponding organ, whether through a medium or not. For example, the sound of an object activates the air, and then the activated air reaches the ear. Again, we are healthy or act healthily through health, which is a cause as form, and we sense through the faculty of sensation, and that faculty is a cause as form. If the doctor is perfect and if perfect health is restored, then the healthy activity which follows is at its best. Similarly, if the sensible object is noblest and if the corresponding faculty of sensation is excellently disposed, the activity of that faculty is perfect; and the perfection of this activity is pleasure. Thus the sensible object is perfect as a mover, the faculty is perfect as form, and pleasure is perfect as final cause.

2 That which is acted upon is the organ or the faculty of sensation.

3 The disposition which resides in the agent is the faculty of sensation in the case of sensing. Now even if the faculty of sensation is perfect, pleasure may still not be present, as when one is asleep.

4 As we get increasingly tired, pain increases, and so the faculty or the organ becomes less perfect in fuctioning; or else, pain increases and the mixture of pain and pleasure loses perfection. Of course, if the activity of the faculty loses intensity because of tiredness, the corresponding pleasure is diminished.

5 Perhaps 'this' refers to perfect living.

5

1 If a house and a chair are imperfect, what is needed to perfect the house is not the same as what is needed to perfect the chair; and similarly with animals and activities and other things.

2 For example, seeing is not hearing, and thinking mathematically is not composing a poem.

3 Since the differentiae of distinct genera or species are different, the corresponding properties or attributes must be different also (1b16–24). But pleasures of different activities are proper to the corresponding activities; hence they are different.

4 The expression 'almost' indicates that there is some difference. Proper pains tend to destroy an activity and have a harmful effect on a man, but alien pleasures have the effect not of harming the man but of merely

destroying the activity by replacement, i.e., by substituting another activity which is pleasant.

5 Evidently activities are related to the pleasures in them or to the desires for them as subjects to attributes. Thus the goodness or badness of a pleasure or of the desire for it depends directly, respectively, on the goodness or badness of the corresponding activity. Those who assert that all pleasures are bad, then, will have to assert also that all the corresponding human activities are bad.

That pleasure is related to the corresponding activity as an attribute to a subject is evident from the fact that the same activity can be sometimes pleasant and sometimes painful. As for the desire of a pleasure, such desire is related to that pleasure and hence to the corresponding activity; for it makes no difference whether we speak of the desire of drinking or of the desire of the pleasure of drinking.

6 The desire of an activity precedes that activity, and the activity may not even come to be; but the pleasure of an activity exists in that activity or is simultaneously with it. Further, pleasures are perfections of activities while desires appear to be rather potencies for them; and pleasures are not painful while desires, such as of drink, are painful.

Since the same kind of activity may be painful to one man but pleasant to another, it follows that an activity and its corresponding pleasure (when one is pleased by that activity) are not the same in definition but are related as already stated in the last Commentary.

7 Separation is different from distinction. Just as the sickness of Socrates cannot be separated but can be distinguished from Socrates, for sickness is an attribute but Socrates is a substance, so the pleasure of an activity cannot be separated but can be distinguished from that activity.

8 Of the five kinds of sensations, seeing is the most accurate. 437a3–9, 980a22–7.

9 Since pleasures as perfections differ and exist in different activities, and since questions may be raised concerning the relative goodness of different activities, similar questions may be raised concerning different pleasures.

10 Fragment 9, Diels.

11 Who decides as to which of the so-called 'pleasures' are really or by nature pleasures, or, if we put it in another way, which of all the pleasures are good? A standard is sought, and this standard is virtue, or the man who has virtue. A virtuous man is like the straight line, which measures

all other lines, or like a healthy man when compared to the sick man. The curved line is measured by taking the limit of the sum $\sum\sqrt{\varDelta x^2+\varDelta y^2}$, where each $\sqrt{\varDelta x^2+\varDelta y^2}$ is a straight line, and the curve $y=x^2$ is defined in terms of a set of straight lines (x, y) called 'abscissas' and 'ordinates'; and taking a curved line to measure any other line leads to difficulties. Similarly, taking as standard pleasures those of a bad man would lead to suffering and ruin, for many disharmonies would arise within the soul and from the outside.

12 The problem raised now is whether there is one kind or many kinds of pleasures which are good; and, if many, whether there is such an order among them that some are better than others, and whether there is one of them which is the best. If there is an ordering, then happiness must take it into account and be defined in terms of it.

6

1 1095b22–6a2, 1098b29–9a7.

2 1098a5–7.

3 What is stated here is that some men choose amusement for its own sake and not for the sake of something else; and a sign of this is that they do so even if the consequences may be harmful, and evidently they do not choose amusements for the sake of harmful consequences. Whether they should choose amusements for their own sake or for the sake of something else is another matter, to be discussed later.

4 1062b35–3a10, 1113a22–33.

5 A Scythian sage; travelled through Asia Minor and Greece.

6 1098a15–8, 1176a35–b9.

7

1 1095b14–6a10, 1141a18–b3, 1143b33–4a6, 1145a6–11.

2 1097a25–b21, 1175b36–6a29.

3 *Actions* require greater physical effort than speculation and are therefore more tiring and more painful.

4 In speculation, inquiry is for the sake of knowledge.

5 Since a man, unlike God, is not perfect but can learn from others as well as by himself, he will be happier with colleagues than without them.

6 We toil for the sake of something else, e.g., a laborer goes to work

not for the sake of working but to make gain so he may be engaged in pleasurable activities which are ends in themselves.

[7] The contrast is between the intellect, which is solely concerned with eternal truths, and ethical virtue, which is concerned with particulars; and from this contrast follows the contrast between the corresponding activities.

Perhaps the word 'composite' refers to that part of the soul which requires or is defined in terms of the body also. The faculty of sensation, for example, is such a part, and activities according to ethical virtues and vices, though requiring thought, are concerned with particulars which require matter and with what may or may not be. But the intellect, when concerned with eternal truths, depends on the body very little and indirectly. For example, contemplation in the highest sense is concerned with what is eternal, but he who contemplates has also human needs and requires financial means in order to contemplate.

[8] Perhaps 'a man' and 'human life' pertain to that part of a man and the corresponding life which are concerned with all matters except eternal truths. This seems to be indicated by what follows.

[9] 1169b33, 1176b26–7.

[10] If a man be defined as a rational animal, then rationality is his differentia; and the differentia is proper to a thing and distinguishes it from other things. So since the best and most pleasant activity of a man is that which is according to what is proper to him, and since rationality in its highest form is concerned with the highest objects, which are eternal and most honorable, man's most pleasant activity, which is happiness at its best, would be concerned with such objects.

8

[1] This is ethical virtue.

[2] See Commentary 7 of the previous Section.

[3] 430a10–25.

[4] The statesman must live according to his rank, and this requires additional expense, though not much more as far as necessities go; but taken as a whole, the external goods needed to fulfill ethical virtue exceed those needed for contemplation. Nowadays, of course, this is not quite true; for some elaborate experiments require much expense.

[5] Ethical virtue is meant.

[6] Men of material means tend to avoid theoretical activity.

[7] By 'a man' Aristotle means a man faced with ethical problems and decisions.

[8] This argument rests on popular opinion and is therefore dialectical; but it is quite in agreement with Aristotle's position.

[9] 1072b7–28.

[10] Happiness in the highest sense belongs to a being because of contemplation, for only contemplation can cause it. Thus ethical and other *actions* cannot add to such happiness; and they contribute to the happiness which is inferior in kind.

9

[1] Herodotus, i. 30.

[2] 1215b6–14; Diels, *Vorsokratiker* 46a30.

[3] The phrase 'as they are thought to have' indicates that the argument is dialectical; for, from what Aristotle said about the prime mover in Book Lambda of the *Metaphysics*, I do not think that he would assent to the premise that the gods are concerned with human matters.

10

[1] In what other way? One may try by himself to acquire and then to use virtue, after learning what virtue is and how it can be acquired. Now this assumes that he will learn it, that he will be convinced that virtue is good, and that he will proceed to acquire it in order to use it. But the situation is not so simple. Children hardly form good habits by conviction, and as they grow, it is difficult to change their habits if these are bad, in spite of instruction. So another way is external guidance, and force if necessary, for most people are led by their passions. Thus we are faced with the necessity of a principle which would direct the formation of virtue as far as possible, and this principle is the state, both its laws and the administration of them. Parents can direct the formation of virtue, too, but partly; besides, they are parts of the state. What remains, then, is to discuss the nature of a state, the kinds of states, and other related problems. Politics is concerned with such problems, and Aristotle takes this up in his next book, *Politics*.

2 Theognis, 432–4.

3 Nature's part is what we nowadays call 'inherited characteristics', physical and intellectual.

4 1369b16–8.

5 These are men who inherited inferior characteristics, physical or intellectual, especially the latter; and such men are more likely to follow the passions than right reason. To assume that all men or the great majority of them can lead a life of virtue would be, for Aristotle, something highly improbable. If so, then, in framing laws and constitutions, the lawgiver should keep in mind the nature of the subject-matter, i.e., the kinds of men who are to be citizens of the state.

6 Laws tend to be impersonal and not subject to passions, for they are framed after long deliberation and are intended to be equally applicable to all.

7 *Odyssey*, ix, 114.

8 Perhaps 'so' refers to what has just preceded, namely, a deliberate choice on the part of a citizen to correct the state's neglect of the education of its citizens. A citizen may help his children and friends toward virtue, or he may help his fellow-citizens indirectly and in a universal way, e.g., by becoming himself a lawgiver.

9 If individual is better than group instruction or treatment, is universal knowledge of any help to individual instruction or treatment? Universal knowledge is not only helpful, but also necessary. If one out of twenty patients suffering from a certain disease requires a different treatment, this is so because he differs by having certain attributes, let us say X, not possessed by the other patients. Now the doctor must know that patients who have the disease but also have X require such-and-such treatment, for how else can he treat the patient? This knowledge is less universal than that for the other nineteen patients and all others like them, but it is still universal. What we have stated here is indicated in the text by the phrase 'for all men or for all men of a certain kind'.

10 In the preceding Commentary, if the man who has also an attribute X, whether he knows it or not, observes that he gets well by doing a certain thing, he knows the fact that he gets well but not the *reason*, and he is his own best doctor if the doctor fails to diagnose that, besides having the disease, he has also X. 981a12–24.

11 Perhaps 'faculties' refers to the arts, or mainly to them, for by defini-

tion a faculty is an ability to act in a certain way, and it is acquired abilities that are considered here. 1094a9–16.

[12] What is suggested here is that a man who has long experience of a certain subject can act rightly with respect to that subject and still not know the subject scientifically nor have the ability to teach it. Politics seems to come close to being such a subject.

[13] The aim of rhetoric is persuasion, which is effected by logic or by arousing the emotions of the audience or by prestige, whereas the aim of politics is to frame good laws for the sake of the happiness of the citizens of a state.

GLOSSARY

In the English-Greek Glossary, if an English term is used in many senses or has one or more synonyms, this is indicated. When convenient, we often give the definition of a term, e.g., of the term 'happiness'; when not convenient, we often give the reference to page and lines according to the Bekker text, as in the case of the terms 'similar' and 'complete'. Some terms, especially those which are elementary, are not defined.

In the Greek-English Glossary, English synonyms used for the same Greek term are separated by a comma; for example, the translation of τέλειοs is 'complete' or 'perfect', and the latter two terms are separated by a comma in the Glossary and have the same meaning. But if separated by a semicolon, the English terms are not synonymously used. For example, the translations of πολιτεία are 'government' and 'democracy', and these are not synonyms.

I. ENGLISH–GREEK

abashed man   καταπλήξ   A man who is ashamed of everything. 1108a34.

abuse   ὕβρις   See 'insult'.

accident   συμβεβηκός   B is an accident of A if 'A is B' is true sometimes, but neither always nor for the most part. For example, to be a geometrician is an accident of a man, and so is finding a coin when looking for Socrates. 1025a14–30.

acting justly   δικαιοπραγεῖν   See 'justly, *acting*'.

acting unjustly   ἀδικεῖν   See 'unjustly, *acting*'.

action   πρᾶξις   An action chosen by man, usually ethical, for its own sake, with understanding and certainty and without hesitation. 1048b18–36, 1105a28–33, 1140b6–7, 1154b18–28, 1197a3–16, 1325b14–23. Synonym: 'doing'.

activity   ἐνέργεια   A term with a wide meaning, having as species such things as action, thinking, sensing, awareness, and so on. 1045b27–52a11. Synonyms: 'exercise' (sometimes).

acuteness   ἀγχίνοια   Discernment which grasps the cause or middle term. For example, on seeing that the lighted part of the Moon faces the Sun, an acute man grasps the *reason* for it. 89b10–20.

affirmation   κατάφασις   A statement signifying that something belongs to something else, e.g., such forms as 'all A is B', 'some A is B', 'some A is not-B', and so on. 17a25.

alteration   ἀλλοίωσις   Motion with respect to quality; e.g., becoming sick or blushing. 226a26–9, 270a27–30, 319b10–4.

ambition φιλοτιμία Disposition to desire more honor than is right. 1107b27–31.
amusement παιδιά.
analogy ἀναλογία Synonym: 'proportion'.
anger ὀργή, θυμός (sometimes).
appetitive part of the soul ἐπιθυμιτικόν The part of the soul which is concerned
    with *desires*.
architectonic ἀρχιτεκτονικός.
argument λόγος.
aristocracy ἀριστοκρατία A government in which the rulers are few and are the
    best or most virtuous.
arithmetic ἀριθμητική The science of (whole) numbers.
art τέχνη *Knowledge* of how to produce something, e.g., steel or a bridge. 1140a6–23.
as ἦ See 'insofar as'.
assertion φάσις.
association κοινωνία.
attribute συμβεβηκός A thing which cannot exist apart from a substance; e.g.,
    whiteness is in a body, fever exists in an animal, and whiteness and fever are at-
    tributes.

bad φαῦλος; κακός The first term is more general than the second. For linguistic
    propriety, we use 'bad' instead of 'vicious', for a man is not called 'vicious' for every
    kind of vice.
bashful αἰδήμων.
because διά To say that *A* is *C* because of *B* is to say that *B* causes *C* to belong to *A*.
    Synonym: 'through'.
beginning ἀρχή See 'principle'.
blessed μακάριος Continuously happy without impediments, external or internal.
    Thus, the gods are regarded as blessed, and few men come close to blessedness.
boastfulness ἀλαζωνεία 1127a13–22.
boor ἀγροῖκος.
bravery ἀνδρεία A virtue which disposes one to do noble deeds in dangerous situa-
    tions. 1115a5–7b20, 1366b11–2.
brutality θηριότης 1148b15–9a20.
buffoonery βωμολοχία 1128a33–b1.
by its nature καθ' αὐτό 1022a14–36.

category κατηγορία The categories are the highest genera of things. Examples:
    substance, quantity, quality, relation. 1b25–11b7.
cause αἰτία, διότι Synonyms: '*reason*', 'the why'. 1013a24–4a25.
change μεταβολή The species of change are generation, destruction, alteration,
    increase, decrease, and locomotion, and the last four are motions.
character ἦθος.
choose αἱρεῖσθαι.
city πόλις.
complaisant ἄρεσκος One who, for the sake of giving pleasure, is disposed to praise
    everything and to find fault with nothing. 1126b11–4.
complete τέλειος Synonym: 'perfect'. 1021b12–2a3.
conclusion συμπέρασμα.
concord ὁμόνοια Sameness of thought about practical and expedient matters of

considerable importance; e.g., the thought by people that the best should be the rulers. 1167a22–b16.

conspicuous consumption βαναυσία Lavish wastefulness, marked by ostentation and lack of taste.

constitution πολιτεία.

contemplative θεωρητικός See 'theoretical'.

continence ἐγκράτεια A habit which disposes a man to have bad *desires* and to know it, but he does not yield to them because his reason or wish is stronger than his *desires*. 1145b8–52a33.

contrary ἐναντίον The primary meaning is: contraries are the most different in each genus; e.g., whiteness and blackness, justice and injustice, rashness and cowardice. For secondary meanings, see 1018a25–35, 1055a3–b29.

contrary to general opinion παράδοξον.

courage θάρρος A feeling which disposes a man to meet danger.

cowardice δειλία A vice by which one is disposed to avoid meeting dangers.

custom ἔθος, νόμος (sometimes) A habit established by acceptance or acquired by repetition of the same *action*; a repeated *action* leading to a habit in the first sense.

deception ἀπάτη.

definition ὅρος, ὁρισμός, λόγος A statement of the nature or essence of a thing.

deficiency ἔλλειψις The contrary of 'excess'.

deliberate choice See 'intention'.

deliberation βούλευσις, βουλή Inquiry into the means needed to bring about a desired end, usually in practical matters. 1112a18–3a2.

democracy πολιτεία, τιμοκρατία A good rule (according to law) by the many or by those who pay taxes. Synonym: 'timocracy'.

demonstration ἀπόδειξις A syllogism through the cause of that which is necessarily true. 71b9–18.

denial ἀπόφασις A statement signifying that something does not belong to something else; for example, the forms 'no *A* is *B*' and 'some *A* is not *B*'.

desire ὄρεξις The three species of desire are wish, *desire*, and temper, the first being the object of thought, the others being objects of passion or feeling. 1187b37.

desire ἐπιθυμία Desire through sensation of pleasure or of what appears to be pleasure but is not. 146b36–7a4, 414b2–14.

discernment εὐστοχία Ability to grasp quickly what is similar in things which differ considerably. 1412a11–2.

discussion λόγος.

disgraceful αἰσχρόν.

dishonor ἀτιμία The contrary of 'honor'.

disposition ἕξις, διάθεσις A quality in virtue of which one tends to do things of a certain kind in the same way; e.g., through justice we tend to do just things, and through bravery we tend to *act* bravely. Synonym: 'habit'.

doctrine δόξα An opinion concerning important things.

doing πρᾶξις See '*action*'.

effeteness τρυφή A habit which disposes one to avoid all pain, even when pain is for his own good. 1150b1–5, 1221a28–9.

emulation ζῆλος.

end   τέλος   For example, the end of artistic activity is a work of art, and the end of a man's activities is happiness.

endurance   καρτερία   A habit according to which one is disposed to bear as he should physical effort which gives pain. 1150a9–15, 1202b30–3.

envy   φθόνος   Pain when another man, who is good and is of about equal status, appears to be doing well and deservedly so. 109b36–7, 1386b18–20, 1387b21–7.

equal   ἴσον.

equitable   ἐπιεικής   See 'equity'. Synonym: *'good'*.

equity   ἐπιείκεια   A virtue by which one *acts* rightly towards others, either (1) justly (i.e., according to law), or (2) rightly when the law does not specify, whether due to omission or to the fact that laws cannot always include all the circumstances in the various situations. 1137a31–8a3, 1374a26–b1.

essence   τὶ ἦν εἶναι   The nature of a thing, that without which as the minimum a thing cannot exist. The essence of a thing excludes accidents which the thing may have.

estimate   λογισμός   See 'judgment'.

estimative part of the soul   λογιστικόν   That part of the soul which *thinks* and concludes about things that are not necessary but may or may not be or come to be. Such *thinking* is called 'judging'.

ethical   ἠθικός   Pertaining to man's dispositions, either virtues or vices.

ethical habit   ἔθος.

evil habit   μοχθηρία   This habit is less general than vice but more general than wickedness. Perhaps it is a habit which harms or injures another. So wastefulness would not be evil. 1121a26-7.

example   παράδειγμα.

excellently   εὖ   Synonym: 'well'.

excess   ὑπερβολή.

exchange   συνάλλαγμα   An *action* involving two persons. It need not be by mutual agreement, as in the case of stealing, in which one gains and the other loses. 1131a2–9.

expectation   ἐλπίς.

expedient   συμφέρον   Good for something else. 1160b2–3, 1362a17–21, 1390a1.

experience   ἐμπειρία   Knowledge produced from many memories of the same thing; for example, knowledge that Socrates, suffering from disease X, recovered every time he took medicine Y. 980b28–1a12.

extravagance   ἀπειροκαλία   Wastefulness on a large scale. 1107b16–20.

fact   ὅτι.

faculty   δύναμις   Natural or acquired ability by a man to do something or do it well; e.g., medical art or running ability or vision. Synonym: 'power'.

fair   ἴσον   That which is equal or proportional in distributions or transactions and is just.

falsity   ψεῦδος   A statement or belief signifying that something is the case, when it is not, or that something is not the case, when it is; also, the object signified. 1011b25–7, 1051b3–5, 33–5.

familiar   γνώριμος.

fear   φόβος.

feeling   πάθος   Synonym: 'passion'.

flatterer   κόλαξ   1108a26–9.

for the sake of   οὗ ἕνεκα, καθ' αὐτό, δι' αὐτό   Synonym: 'purpose', sometimes 'end'.

form   εἶδος, ἰδέα (sometimes).

Form εἶδος For Plato, a Form is a pattern or model, changeless and eternal, and
it is posited as the cause of the existence and the nature of sensible and destructible
things of one kind, as of horses. Synonym: 'Idea'. 987a29–b22.

friendliness φιλία

friendship φιλία There is friendship without qualification (in its perfect form),
and also in a qualified sense (as between business friends for the sake of material
gain).

function ἔργον.

generosity ἐλευθεριότης A virtue by which one is disposed to give or take property
as he should.

genus γένος.

geometry γεωμετρία The science of magnitudes.

God θεός For Aristotle, the prime mover, who is immaterial and eternal and the
best being in the universe.

good ἀγαθόν That which is aimed at or chosen as an end or means to an end; in a
limited sense, 'the good' signifies the highest or ultimate good for man, but it is left
open as to what it is, whether pleasure or honor or something else; sometimes,
'good' and 'virtuous' have the same meaning when predicated of a man.

good ἐπιεικής See 'equitable'.

Good ἀγαθόν For Plato, this is God, who is the first cause, or it is an Idea according
to which all good things among the sensibles are modelled.

good intelligence εὐσυνεσία See 'intelligence'.

good temper πραότης A virtue with respect to anger or temper. 1125b26–6b9.

good will εὔνοια.

government πολιτεία.

grasping man πλεονέκτης One who is disposed to take more of material goods
than he should or to give less than he should. 1129b1–10.

habit ἕξις, διάθεσις A disposition acquired by repetition, e.g., a vice or virtue.

happiness εὐδαιμονία Virtuous activity of the soul throughout life. There are two
kinds of virtues, ethical and intellectual. 1102a5–6.

harm βλάβη.

harsh χαλεπός.

hatred μῖσος.

high lineage εὐγένεια direct descent from ancestors many of whom were eminent in
virtue or riches or some other thing worthy of honor, as in the case of a man whose
ancestors were great rulers. 1360b31–8.

high-mindedness μεγαλοψυχία A virtue according to which a man rightly regards
himself as worthy of high honor and *acts* rightly according to such belief. 1123a34–
5a35.

honor τιμή 1101b10–2a4, 1361a27–b2.

hot-tempered ἀκρόχολος.

humor γελοῖον.

idea ἰδέα.

Idea ἰδέα Same as 'Form' for Plato.

ignorance ἄγνοια One is ignorant of something either if he has no thought about
it or if he is mistaken about it. 79b23–4. Error or right *action* through (or because of)
ignorance is error or right *action* in which ignorance alone is the cause of the out-

come, and the agent may or may not have wished the outcome. He who *acts* in ignorance does not *act* through ignorance; e.g., in the case of a drunkard, drunkenness is part of the cause of his *action* when he kills someone accidentally. 1110b24–30.

imprudence ἀφροσύνη The contrary of 'prudence'.

incontinent ἀκρατής A man who has bad *desires* and knows that they are bad, but he yields to them because his *desires* overpower his wishes or his reason. 1145b8–52a33.

indignation, righteous νέμεσις.

indirectly κατὰ συμβεβηκός.

induction ἐπαγωγή

inirascibility ἀοργησία The contrary of 'irascibility'.

injustice ἀδικία A habit by which one is disposed to do what is unjust. 1134a1–7.

inquiry μέθοδος Systematic inquiry.

insensible ἀναίσθητος The contrary of 'intemperate'.

insofar as ᾗ *A* is *C* insofar as it is *B* if *B* is the cause of *C*'s belonging to *A*. For example, a straight line is infinitely divisible insofar as it is continuous because just continuity is the cause of the infinite divisibility; but it is not infinitely divisible insofar as it is a straight line or a line or a one-dimensional magnitude. Synonym: 'as'.

instrumental χρήσιμος See 'useful'.

insult ὕβρις To cause harm or pain by an action (speech, violence, etc.) calculated to shame the patient and only please the agent. Synonym: 'abuse'.

intellect νοῦς The faculty which grasps principles, e.g., axioms and definitions and essences; God. 84b35–5a1, 100b5–17, 1140b31–1a8, 1143a25–b17. Synonym: 'intuition', in the first sense.

intellectual διανοητικός Virtues may be ethical or intellectual, and the latter are possessed or are acquired by learning while the former rather by habit. 1103a14–8.

intelligence σύνεσις Ability to use opinions in judging well objects of prudence, when someone else speaks about them. 1142b34–3a18. Synonym: 'good intelligence'.

intemperance ἀκολασία A vice with regard to bodily pleasures. 1117b23–9b18.

intention προαίρεσις A choice of the apparently best of the alternatives deliberated upon. Synonym: 'deliberate choice'. 1113a2–7.

intermediate μέσον See 'mean'.

intuition νοῦς See 'intellect'.

involuntary ἀκούσιον The contrary of 'voluntary'.

irascibility ὀργιλότης A vice which disposes a man to excessive anger. 1108a4–8.

irony εἰρωνία See 'self-depreciation'.

irrational ἀλόγιστος The contrary of 'rational'.

irritable μελαγχολικός.

judgment λογισμός; κρίσις The activity of the estimative part of the soul, which deals with things which may or may not be or come to be; the activity of a faculty of sensation, which discriminates objects within its own province, e.g., vision discriminates colors only.

judgment γνώμη Right judgment by an equitable man as such concerning particulars. 1143a19–35.

just *action* δικαιοπραγία An *action* whose outcome is something which is just. 1133b30–2.

just, doing what is δίκαιον πράττειν Such *acting* need not be voluntary. 1135a15–9.

just effect δικαιοπράγημα A just thing done willingly. 1135a8–13, 19–23.
just thing δίκαιον Synonym: 'the just', 'what is just'. 1131a9–2b20.
justice δικαιοσύνη A virtue by which one is disposed to do what is just. 1134a1–6. Sometimes used generically to include also equity. 1137b24–5.
justly, *acting* δικαιοπραγεῖν Doing willingly what is just. 1135a15–9.
justly, treated δικαιοῦσθαι 1136a10–b14.

kind εἶδος.
kingdom βασιλεία A government ruled by a king, i.e., by a man who is the most virtuous or the best and hence who rules for the good of the governed. 1160b2–3.
knowledge γνῶσις It is a genus having as species sensation, opinion, scientific knowledge, etc.
knowledge εἰδέναι See 'understand'.
knowledge ἐπιστήμη Knowledge of the causes of a thing which exist of necessity, e.g., demonstrative knowledge of the fact that vertical angles are equal. Synonyms: 'scientific knowledge', 'science'. 71b7–16.

law νόμος The term is used in a legalistic sense, and not as in 'the laws of nature'.
life, way of life βίος.
like ὅμοιος Usually, things are said to be like whose quality is one. 1018a15–9, 1021a11–2, 1054b3–14. Synonym: 'similar'.
low lineage δυσγένεια The contrary of 'high lineage'.
lowly ἀγεννής.
low-mindedness μικροψυχία A vice according to which a man regards himself as worthy of less honor than he is worthy and *acts* according to that belief. 1123b9–13.
malevolent κακοῦργος.
mean, adj., n. μέσον, μεσότης Of habits, those which are neither in excess nor in deficiency but are just right and dispose a man to lead a happy life. Synonym: 'moderation'.
meanness μικροπρέπεια Stinginess when great sums are involved. Its contrary is 'munificence'. 1122a28–30.
method μέθοδος.
mob rule δημοκρατία Rule by the many or a majority, but by vote rather than by law. It is a deviation or perversion of democracy, and demagogues flourish in it.
model παράδειγμα.
moderation See 'mean'.
monarchy μοναρχία A state ruled by one man.
motion κίνησις Change with respect to quality or quantity or place, but not with respect to substance.
munificence μεγαλοπρέπεια Generosity in which great sums are involved. 1122a18–22.

natural gift εὐφυία.
nature φύσις 192b8–3b21, 1014b16–5a19.
nature, by its φύσει, καθ' αὐτό.
noble καλόν Pertaining to worthy ends. It is a species of the good. 1364b27–8, 1366a33–7b20.
nonrational ἄλογος What is nonrational need not be unreasonable, e.g., the falling of a stone is nonrational, for a stone has no ability to reason.
nonvoluntary οὐχ ἑκών.

number ἀριθμός The term is limited to whole numbers without direction, and the least number is 2.

oligarchy ὀλιγαρχία Rule by the few who are interested only for their own good. It is a perversion of aristocracy.

opinion δόξα A belief of that which may or may not be. 89a2–3, 100b5–7, 1039b31–40a1, 1051b5–10.

opposition ἀντίθεσις Things may be opposed to each other as contradictories, or as contraries, or as a relative to its correlative, or as a possession to its privation. 11b16–9, 1018a20–b8.

ordinary people οἱ πολλοί Such people have little education and not much virtue, and they are inclined to follow the pleasures of the senses rather than those of thought. Synonym: 'most people'.

pain λύπη.

paradox θέσις A belief which is contrary to what is accepted by known philosophers, e.g., the belief that contradiction is impossible. 104b19–24.

passion πάθος Synonym: 'feeling'.

penalty τιμωρία.

perfect τέλειος Synonym: 'complete'. 1021b12–2a3.

philosophy φιλοσοφία The science dealing with the most general principles and causes of things. 1003a21–32, 1026a10–32, 1060b31–1b17, 1064a28–b14.

pleasure ἡδονή In general, it may be of thought or of action or of the senses; in a limited sense, it is of the senses. 1095b16–7, 1152a36–4b31, 1369b33–5.

politics πολιτική The science of government.

power δύναμις.

practical πρακτικός Pertaining to *action*.

praise ἔπαινος 1101b12–31, 1367b26–7.

predicate, v. κατηγορεῖσθαι.

principle ἀρχή The first thing from which something either is or is generated or is known. 1012b34–3a23. Synonyms: 'beginning', 'starting-point'.

product ἔργον.

proportion ἀναλογία Synonym: 'analogy'.

prudence φρόνησις (a) Generically (for all animals), the ability to look after one's own good, 1141a20–8; (b) specifically (for men), a disposition by means of which one can deliberate truly concerning one's conduct for a good life, 1140a24–b30.

public writings ἐξωτερικοὶ λόγοι.

punishment κόλασις.

purpose οὗ ἕνεκα Synonyms: 'final cause', 'end' (sometimes).

quality ποιόν This is one of the categories or highest genera. 8b25–11a38.

quantity ποσόν This is one of the categories or highest genera. 4b20–6a35.

rashness θρασύτης A vice which disposes a man excessively to meet dangers. 1104a21–2.

reason λόγος.

reason διότι, αἴτιον Synonyms: 'cause', 'the why'.

reciprocity ἀντιπεπονθός Giving and taking in return. In the Pythagorean sense, what is returned is the same as what is given; in a wider sense, what is returned need not be the same as what is given.

relation πρός τι This is one of the categories or highest genera. Synonym: 'relative'. 6a36–8b24.

reputation δόξα.

reputation, bad ἀδοξία.

restitution δικαίωμα Correction of an unjust effect. 1135a13.

ridiculous γελοῖος.

righteous indignation νέμεσις.

rightness ὀρθότης In a limited sense, it applies to *action*; in a general sense, it applies also to truth.

sane νοῦν ἔχων.

science ἐπιστήμη See '*knowledge*'.

scientific knowledge See '*knowledge*'.

self-depreciation εἰρωνία A disposition to think or speak of oneself as being less worthy than one actually is and to *act* accordingly. 1127a22–3, b22–3. Synonym: 'irony'.

self-sufficiency αὐτάρκεια A situation in which nothing more is needed for, say, happiness or any other state.

sensation αἴσθησις It also means the power of sensation.

senseless ἀνόητος.

shame αἰσχύνη.

shame, sense of αἰδώς.

shrewdness δεινότης Ability to act successfully upon the means leading to a practical end, whether good or bad. 1144a23–8.

similar ὅμοιος See 'like'.

simply ἁπλῶς See 'without qualification'.

softness μαλακία A habit according to which one is disposed to avoid physical effort which gives pain when one should bear it. 1116a14–5, 1150a14–5, 32–b5.

soul ψυχή The form of a man or any animal or even a plant. In the case of a man, it includes such powers as sensation, thinking, growing, and self-motion.

species εἶδος.

spirit θυμός See 'temper'.

starting-point ἀρχή See 'principle'.

state πόλις.

statement λόγος.

stinginess ἀνελευθερία A vice by which one is disposed to give less and take more than he should in matters of property.

substance οὐσία One of the categories. A substance exists as something separate, like a man or a tree, unlike attributes (e.g., whiteness, sickness, and hardness) which exist in substances. 1a1–4b19. Sometimes, a man's property.

substance οὐσία The essence or form or nature of a thing, that without which as a minimum a thing cannot exist, like the soul of a man, and it excludes accidents and also matter. It extends to all categories.

succeed κατορθοῦν Succeed in doing what is right.

temper θυμός That quality by which one shows courage or anger or their contraries.

temperance σωφροσύνη A virtue with regard to bodily pleasures, especially those of touch and taste. 1117b23–9b18.

theoretical θεωρητικός The term is applied to an activity or a possession which is concerned with truth for its own sake, especially necessary truth. Synonym: 'contemplative'.

think διανοεῖν   To combine concepts, thus forming true or false beliefs or arguments and the like. The power which does this is the *thinking* part of the soul.

thoughtless   ἀνόητος.

through   διά   See 'because'.

timocracy   τιμοκρατία   Synonym: 'democracy'. The term suggests a government in which its citizens pay taxes.

truth   ἀλήθεια   A statement or *thought* of that which is, that it is, or of that which is not, that it is not; what is signified by a statement or *thought* as just indicated. 1011b25–7, 1051b3–5, 33–4.

truthful   ἀληθής   One who is disposed to speak truly.

tyranny   τυραννίς   A government by one man who rules not for the good of the governed but for what appears to be good for himself. 1060b2–3.

unambition   ἀφιλοτιμία   A vice by means of which one is disposed to desire honor less than he should. 1107b27–9.

understand   εἰδέναι   To know, usually through the causes, but not through sensation. 184a10–4, 194b17–20, 981a21–30, 983a25–6. Synonym: 'know'.

unequal   ἄνισον.

unfair   ἄνισος   Disposed to take more or give less than one should in transactions or distributions of goods.

universal   καθόλου   That which by nature is predicable of or belongs to many. For Plato, universals are Forms or Ideas (see 'Form'). 17a39–40, 1038b11–2.

unjust thing   ἄδικον   1131a9–2b20.

unjust, doing what is   ἄδικον πράττειν   1135a15–9, 1136a27–8.

unjust effect   ἀδίκημα   An unjust thing done willingly by the agent. 1134a12–3, 1135a8–13, 19–23, b16–24.

unjust, suffering what is   ἄδικον πάσχειν   1136a27–8.

unjustly, *acting*   ἀδικεῖν   Doing willingly what is unjust. 1135a16–7, 1136a16–7.

unjustly, be treated   ἀδικεῖσθαι   Suffer unwillingly what is unjust. 1136b1–13.

unqualified   ἁπλῶς   See 'without qualification'.

unreasonable   ἄλογος.

unscrupulous   πανοῦργος   One who is shrewd and is disposed to be grasping in every way and from all sources. 1144a23–8.

unwilling   ἄκων.

useful   χρήσιμον   That which exists or becomes for the sake of something else and not for its own sake, like a spoon or money. Thus the enjoyment of music, being an end in itself, is good but not useful. Synonym: 'instrumental'. 101a25–8, 742a32, 1096a7.

vanity   χαυνότης   A vice which disposes a man to regard himself as worthy of high honor when he is not so worthy and to speak or *act* according to that opinion. A vain man is one who has that vice.

vengeance   τιμωρία.

verdict   δίκη   Judgment of what is just or unjust. 1134a31–2.

vice   κακία   A habit which is contrary to virtue (usually ethical virtue).

virtue   ἀρετή   Ethical or intellectual habit by the use of which, barring accidents, one leads a happy life. 1106b36–7a7. Occasionally, any excellence, even of a thing which is not a man, e.g., of a good horse or a violin.

virtuous   σπουδαῖος   Having virtue. Synonym: 'good'.

vision ὄψις Power to see.
voluntary ἑκούσιον.

wastefulness ἀσωτία A vice which disposes a man to use more property than he should.
well εὖ Synonym: 'excellently'. Also used as a noun.
well-disposed εὔνους Having good will towards others.
whatness τὸ τί ἔστι The nature of a thing, as signified by its definition.
why, n. διότι Synonyms: 'cause', '*reason*'.
wicked πονηρός Usually, a man who is able and disposed to be grasping, especially with respect to material goods.
willing ἑκών.
wisdom σοφία Intuition and *knowledge* of the most honorable things. 1141a9–20.
wish βούλησις Desire of the good or what appears to be good, but it is neither *desire*, which is limited to the pleasure of the senses, nor temper. 1113a14–b2.
without qualification ἁπλῶς Without any limitations or restrictions. Synonyms: 'simply', 'unqualified'.
witty εὐτράπελος.
work ἔργον.

II. GREEK-ENGLISH

ἀγαθόν good; the good; *Good, God* (for Plato)
ἀγεννής lowly
ἄγνοια ignorance
ἀγνοῶν be in ignorance of, be ignorant of
 δι' ἄγνοιαν because of ignorance, through ignorance
 μετ' ἀγνοίας with ignorance
ἀγροῖκος boor
ἀγχίνοια acuteness
ἀδικεῖν *acting* unjustly
ἀδικεῖσθαι be treated unjustly
ἀδίκημα unjust effect
ἀδικία injustice
ἄδικον unjust thing, the unjust
ἄδικον πάσχειν suffer what is unjust
ἄδικον πράττειν do what is unjust
ἀδοξία bad reputation
αἰδήμων having a sense of shame
αἰδώς shame
αἱρεῖσθαι choose
αἴσθησις sensation; power of sensation
αἰσχρόν disgraceful
αἴτιον cause, *reason*
ἀκολασία intemperance
ἀκούσιον involuntary
ἀκρασία incontinence
ἀκρόχολος hot-tempered

ἄκων unwilling
ἀλαζωνεία boastfulness
ἀλήθεια truth
ἀληθής truthful
ἀλλοίωσις alteration, change in quality
ἀλόγιστος irrational
ἄλογος nonrational; unreasonable
ἀναίσθητος insensible
ἀναλογία analogy, proportion
ἀνδρεία bravery
ἀνελευθερία stinginess
ἄνισον unequal; unfair
ἀνόητος senseless
ἀντίθεσις opposition
ἀντιπεπονθός reciprocity
ἀοργησία inirascibility
ἀπάτη deception
ἀπειροκαλία extravagance
ἁπλῶς unqualified, without qualification
ἀπόδειξις demonstration
ἀπόφασις denial
ἄρεσκος complaisant
ἀρετή virtue
ἀριθμητική arithmetic
ἀριθμός number
ἀριστοκρατία aristocracy
ἀρχή principle, beginning, starting-point
ἀρχιτεκτονική architectonic
ἀσωτία wastefulness
ἀτιμία dishonor
αὐτάρκεια self-sufficiency
ἀφιλοτιμία unambition
ἀφροσύνη imprudence

βαναυσία conspicuous consumption
βασιλεία kingdom
βίος life, way of life
βλάβη harm
βούλευσις, βουλή deliberation
βούλησις wish
βωμολοχία buffoonery

γελοῖον humor
γελοῖος ridiculous
γένος genus
γεωμετρία geometry
γνώμη *judgment*
γνώριμος familiar
γνῶσις knowledge

δειλία cowardice
δεινότης shrewdness
δημοκρατία mob rule
διά because, through
διάθεσις disposition, habit
διανοητικόν *thinking* part of the soul
διανοητικός intellectual
διανοεῖν *think*
δι᾽ αὐτό because of itself, for its own sake
δίκαιον just thing, what is just
δίκαιον πράττειν do what is just
δικαιοπραγεῖν *act* justly
δικαιοπράγημα just effect
δικαιοπραγία just *action*
δικαιοσύνη justice
δικαιοῦσθαι be treated justly
δικαίωμα restitution
δίκη verdict
διότι cause, *reason*, the why
δόξα opinion; doctrine; reputation
δύναμις power; faculty
δυσγένεια low lineage

ἐγκράτεια continence
ἔθος ethical habit; custom
εἰδέναι know; understand
εἶδος species; kind; form; Form (for Plato)
εἰρωνία irony, self-depreciation
ἑκούσιον voluntary
ἑκών willing
ἑκών, οὐχ nonvoluntary
ἐλευθεριότης generosity
ἔλλειψις deficiency
ἐλπίς expectation
ἐμπειρία experience
ἐναντίον contrary
ἐνέργεια activity, exercize (sometimes)
ἕξις habit, disposition
ἐξωτερικοὶ λόγοι public writings
ἐπαγωγή induction
ἔπαινος praise
ἐπιείκεια equity
ἐπιεικής equitable, *good*
ἐπιθυμία *desire*
ἐπιθυμιτικόν appetitive part of the soul
ἐπιστήμη science, *knowledge*, scientific knowledge
ἔργον function; product; work; difficult task
εὖ well, excellently
εὐγένεια high lineage

εὐδαιμονία   happiness
εὔνοια   good will
εὔνους   well-disposed
εὐστοχία   discernment
εὐσυνεσία   good intelligence
εὐτράπελος   witty
εὐφυΐα   natural gift

ζῆλος   emulation

ᾗ   insofar as, as
ἡδονή   pleasure
ἠθικός   ethical
ἦθος   character

θάρρος   courage
θεός   God
θέσις   paradox
θεωρητικός   theoretical, contemplative
θηριότης   brutality
θρασύτης   rashness
θυμός   temper, spirit; anger (sometimes)

ἰδέα   idea; form; Idea (for Plato)
ἴσον   equal; fair

καθ' αὐτό   by its nature; for the sake of
καθόλου   universal
κακία   vice
κακός   bad
κακοῦργος   malevolent
καλόν   noble
καρτερία   endurance
καταπλήξ   abashed man
κατάφασις   affirmation
κατηγορεῖσθαι   predicate, v.
κατηγορία   category
κατορθοῦν   *succeed*
κίνησις   motion
κοινωνία   association
κόλαξ   flatterer
κόλασις   punishment
κρίσις   judgement

λογισμός   judgment, estimate
λογιστικόν   estimative part of the soul
λόγος   reason; definition; statement; argument; discussion; written document
λύπη   pain

μακάριος blessed
μαλακία softness
μεγαλοπρέπεια munificence
μεγαλοψυχία high-mindedness
μέθοδος method; *inquiry*
μελαγχολικός irritable
μέσον intermediate; mean; middle class
μεσότης moderation, mean
μεταβολή change
μικροπρέπεια meanness
μικροψυχία low-mindedness
μῖσος hatred
μοναρχία monarchy
μοχθηρία evil habit

νέμεσις righteous indignation
νόμος law; custom (sometimes)
νοῦν ἔχων sane
νοῦς intuition, intellect

ξυνιέναι understand

ὀλιγαρχία oligarchy
ὅμοιος like, similar
ὁμόνοια concord
ὀργή anger
ὀργιλότης irascibility
ὄρεξις desire
ὀρθότης rightness
ὁρισμός, ὅρος definition
ὅτι fact
οὗ ἕνεκα purpose, for the sake of, final cause
οὐσία substance; *substance*; substance (i.e., one's property)
ὄψις vision

πάθος passion, feeling
παιδιά amusement
πανοῦργος unscrupulous
παράδειγμα model; example
παράδοξον contrary to general opinion
πλεονέκτης grasping man
ποιόν quality
πόλις state; city
πολιτεία government; constitution; democracy
πολιτική politics
πολλοί, οἱ ordinary people, most people
πονηρός wicked
ποσόν quantity
πρακτικός practical

πρᾶξις *action*, doing
πραότης good temper
προαίρεσις intention, deliberate choice
πρός τι relation

σοφία wisdom
σπουδαῖος virtuous, good
συμβεβηκός accident; attribute
συμπέρασμα conclusion
συμφέρον expedient
συνάλλαγμα exchange
σύνεσις intelligence, good intelligence
σωφροσύνη temperance

τέλειος complete, perfect
τέλος end
τέχνη art
τὶ ἔστι, τὸ whatness
τὶ ἦν εἶναι essence
τιμή honor
τιμοκρατία timocracy, democracy
τιμωρία penalty; vengeance
τρυφή effeteness
τυραννίς tyranny

ὕβρις insult, abuse
ὑπερβολή excess

φάσις assertion
φαῦλος bad
φθόνος envy
φιλία friendship; friendliness
φιλοσοφία philosophy
φιλοτιμία ambition
φόβος fear
φρονεῖν think wisely
φρόνησις prudence
φύσις nature
χαλεπός harsh
χαυνότης vanity
χρήσιμον useful, instrumental

ψεῦδος falsity
ψυχή soul

INDEX

Abashed man 31
acting unjustly: impossible towards
    oneself 99
action, virtuous 25
    little knowledge required 25
    requirements 25
actions: some imply vice or virtue 29
Aeschylus 37
ambition 30, 70
amusement: necessary to life 76
Anacharsis 192
Anaxagoras 107, 197
Argives 51
art: definition 104
art, bad: definition 104

Bias 80
bitterness 71
boastfulness 31, 74
boorishness 31, 75
bravery
    nature of 29, 46
    qualified, kinds 49
brutality 124
buffoonery 31, 75

Carcinus 128
cause: honorable if good 18
child: not partaking of happiness 14
coin:
    its cause is need 87–8
    measure of exchange 87
complaisance 31, 72
concord 170
conspicuous consumption 30, 62
continence 39, 117, 131
cowardice 30, 48
Crete: lawgivers of 18

deliberation:
    definition 42

discussion 40
genus of intention 42
good, nature of 110
not of eternal things 40
not of things by chance 40
of means, not of ends 41
species of inquiry 41
Demodocus 129

Empedocles 141
ends, kinds 1
endurance 127
envy 32
Epicharmus 171
equity, nature of 97
error, indefinite 28
ethics:
    aim of 22
    part of politics 2
    subject of, inaccurate 2, 10, 22
Eudoxus, on pleasure 182
Euripides 141
excess, no excess or deficiency of 29
extravagance 30, 62

falsity, not harmonious 11
feeling, synonym 'passion'
flattery 31, 73
force, by: definition 35
friendliness 31, 72–3
friends: few are better 177
friendship:
    among unequals 148
    origin of 166
    three kinds 142

generosity 30
gift, natural 45
good:
    as an end 6–7
    as an instrument 6